LYSIAS

THE ORATORY OF CLASSICAL GREECE

Translated with Notes • Michael Gagarin, Series Editor

VOLUME 2

LYSIAS

Translated by S. C. Todd

UNIVERSITY OF TEXAS PRESS, AUSTIN

Publication of this book has been generously assisted by grants from the National Endowment for the Humanities and the Gladys Krieble Foundation.

Printed in the United States of America

First edition, 2000

∞ The paper used in this book meets the minimum requirements of ANSI/NISO Z39.48-1992 (R1997) (Permanence of Paper).

Library of Congress Cataloging-in-Publication Data

Lysias.
[Speeches. English. Selections]
Lysias / translated by S. C. Todd. — 1st ed.
p. cm. — (The oratory of Classical Greece ; v. 2)

Includes index.
ISBN 0-292-78165-2 (alk. paper)
ISBN 0-292-78166-0 (pbk. : alk. paper)
1. Lysias Translations into English. 2. Speeches, addresses, etc., Greek Translations into English. 3. Athens (Greece)—Politics and government Sources. I. Todd, S. C. (Stephen Charles), 1958– . II. Title III. Series.
PA4242.E5 T64 2000
885'.01—dc21

99-6344

CONTENTS

SERIES EDITOR'S PREFACE

This is the second volume in a series of translations of *The Oratory of Classical Greece.* The aim of the series is to make available primarily for those who do not read Greek up-to-date, accurate, and readable translations with introductions and explanatory notes of all the surviving works and major fragments of the Attic orators of the classical period (ca. 420–320 BC): Aeschines, Andocides, Antiphon, Demosthenes, Dinarchus, Hyperides, Isaeus, Isocrates, Lycurgus, and Lysias.

—M.G.

TRANSLATOR'S PREFACE

A first draft of this translation was completed in 1995–1996, which I spent on research leave as Junior Fellow at the Hellenic Center in Washington D.C., as a by-product of a project to produce a historical commentary on the speeches and fragments of Lysias.

I would like to express my thanks to the following: the Directors and Senior Fellows of the Center, for electing me and supporting my project; Stephen Lambert and Kathryn Morgan (my colleagues as Junior Fellows), for reading various bits of the manuscript, as did also Chris Carey; Alan Boegehold, who read the finished manuscript for the Press and drew my attention to some last-minute inaccuracies; and the staff at the University of Texas Press (particularly Jim Burr, Carolyn Cates Wylie, and Nancy Moore) for their support, encouragement, and efficiency in turning my typescript into a finished book. My greatest debt, however, is to Michael Gagarin, who read the entire manuscript several times as series editor, with a level of detailed attention for which I shall eventually forgive him.

—S. C. TODD
September 1998

SERIES INTRODUCTION

Greek Oratory

By Michael Gagarin

ORATORY IN CLASSICAL ATHENS

From as early as Homer (and undoubtedly much earlier) the Greeks placed a high value on effective speaking. Even Achilles, whose greatness was primarily established on the battlefield, was brought up to be "a speaker of words and a doer of deeds" (*Iliad* 9.443); and Athenian leaders of the sixth and fifth centuries,[1] such as Solon, Themistocles, and Pericles, were all accomplished orators. Most Greek literary genres—notably epic, tragedy, and history—underscore the importance of oratory by their inclusion of set speeches. The formal pleadings of the envoys to Achilles in the *Iliad*, the messenger speeches in tragedy reporting events like the battle of Salamis in Aeschylus' *Persians* or the gruesome death of Pentheus in Euripides' *Bacchae*, and the powerful political oratory of Pericles' funeral oration in Thucydides are but a few of the most notable examples of the Greeks' never-ending fascination with formal public speaking, which was to reach its height in the public oratory of the fourth century.

In early times, oratory was not a specialized subject of study but was learned by practice and example. The formal study of rhetoric as an "art" (*technē*) began, we are told, in the middle of the fifth century in Sicily with the work of Corax and his pupil Tisias.[2] These two are

---

[1] All dates in this volume are BC unless the contrary is either indicated or obvious.

[2] See Kennedy 1963: 26–51. Cole 1991 has challenged this traditional picture, arguing that the term "rhetoric" was coined by Plato to designate and denigrate an activity he strongly opposed. Cole's own reconstruction is not without prob-

scarcely more than names to us, but another famous Sicilian, Gorgias of Leontini (ca. 490–390), developed a new style of argument and is reported to have dazzled the Athenians with a speech delivered when he visited Athens in 427. Gorgias initiated the practice, which continued into the early fourth century, of composing speeches for mythical or imaginary occasions. The surviving examples reveal a lively intellectual climate in the late fifth and early fourth centuries, in which oratory served to display new ideas, new forms of expression, and new methods of argument.[3] This tradition of "intellectual" oratory was continued by the fourth-century educator Isocrates and played a large role in later Greek and Roman education.

In addition to this intellectual oratory, at about the same time the practice also began of writing speeches for real occasions in public life, which we may designate "practical" oratory. For centuries Athenians had been delivering speeches in public settings (primarily the courts and the Assembly), but these had always been composed and delivered impromptu, without being written down and thus without being preserved. The practice of writing speeches began in the courts and then expanded to include the Assembly and other settings. Athens was one of the leading cities of Greece in the fifth and fourth centuries, and its political and legal systems depended on direct participation by a large number of citizens; all important decisions were made by these large bodies, and the primary means of influencing these decisions was oratory.[4] Thus, it is not surprising that oratory flourished in Athens,[5] but it may not be immediately obvious why it should be written down.

The pivotal figure in this development was Antiphon, one of the fifth-century intellectuals who are often grouped together under the

---

lems, but he does well to remind us how thoroughly the traditional view of rhetoric depends on one of its most ardent opponents.

[3] Of these only Antiphon's Tetralogies are included in this series. Gorgias' *Helen* and *Palamedes*, Alcidamas' *Odysseus*, and Antisthenes' *Ajax* and *Odysseus* are translated in Gagarin and Woodruff 1995.

[4] Yunis 1996 has a good treatment of political oratory from Pericles to Demosthenes.

[5] All our evidence for practical oratory comes from Athens, with the exception of Isocrates 19, written for a trial in Aegina. Many speeches were undoubtedly delivered in courts and political forums in other Greek cities, but it may be that such speeches were written down only in Athens.

name "Sophists."[6] Like some of the other sophists he contributed to the intellectual oratory of the period, but he also had a strong practical interest in law. At the same time, Antiphon had an aversion to public speaking and did not directly involve himself in legal or political affairs (Thucydides 8.68). However, he began giving general advice to other citizens who were engaged in litigation and were thus expected to address the court themselves. As this practice grew, Antiphon went further, and around 430 he began writing out whole speeches for others to memorize and deliver. Thus began the practice of "logography," which continued through the next century and beyond.[7] Logography particularly appealed to men like Lysias, who were metics, or noncitizen residents of Athens. Since they were not Athenian citizens, they were barred from direct participation in public life, but they could contribute by writing speeches for others.

Antiphon was also the first (to our knowledge) to write down a speech he would himself deliver, writing the speech for his own defense at his trial for treason in 411. His motive was probably to publicize and preserve his views, and others continued this practice of writing down speeches they would themselves deliver in the courts and (more rarely) the Assembly.[8] Finally, one other type of practical oratory was the special tribute delivered on certain important public occasions, the best known of which is the funeral oration. It is convenient to designate these three types of oratory by the terms Aristotle later uses: forensic (for the courts), deliberative (for the Assembly), and epideictic (for display).[9]

---

[6] The term "sophist" was loosely used through the fifth and fourth centuries to designate various intellectuals and orators, but under the influence of Plato, who attacked certain figures under this name, the term is now used of a specific group of thinkers; see Kerferd 1981.

[7] For Antiphon as the first to write speeches, see Photius, *Bibliotheca* 486a7–11 and [Plut.], *Moralia* 832c–d. The latest extant speech can be dated to 320, but we know that at least one orator, Dinarchus, continued the practice after that date.

[8] Unlike forensic speeches, speeches for delivery in the Assembly were usually not composed beforehand in writing, since the speaker could not know exactly when or in what context he would be speaking; see further Trevett 1996.

[9] *Rhetoric* 1.3. Intellectual orations, like Gorgias' *Helen*, do not easily fit into Aristotle's classification. For a fuller (but still brief) introduction to Attic oratory and the orators, see Edwards 1994.

THE ORATORS

In the century from about 420 to 320, dozens—perhaps even hundreds—of now unknown orators and logographers must have composed speeches that are now lost, but only ten of these men were selected for preservation and study by ancient scholars, and only works collected under the names of these ten have been preserved. Some of these works are undoubtedly spurious, though in most cases they are fourth-century works by a different author rather than later "forgeries." Indeed, modern scholars suspect that as many as seven of the speeches attributed to Demosthenes may have been written by Apollodorus, son of Pasion, who is sometimes called "the eleventh orator."[10] Including these speeches among the works of Demosthenes may have been an honest mistake, or perhaps a bookseller felt he could sell more copies of these speeches if they were attributed to a more famous orator.

In alphabetical order the Ten Orators are as follows:[11]

- AESCHINES (ca. 395–ca. 322) rose from obscure origins to become an important Athenian political figure, first an ally, then a bitter enemy of Demosthenes. His three speeches all concern major public issues. The best known of these (Aes. 3) was delivered at the trial in 330, when Demosthenes responded with *On the Crown* (Dem. 18). Aeschines lost the case and was forced to leave Athens and live the rest of his life in exile.

- ANDOCIDES (ca. 440–ca. 390) is best known for his role in the scandal of 415, when just before the departure of the fateful Athenian expedition to Sicily during the Peloponnesian War (431–404), a band of young men mutilated statues of Hermes, and at the same time information was revealed about the secret rites of Demeter.

[10] See Trevett 1992.

[11] The Loeb volumes of *Minor Attic Orators* also include the prominent Athenian political figure Demades (ca. 385–319), who was not one of the Ten; but the only speech that has come down to us under his name is a later forgery. It is possible that Demades and other fourth-century politicians who had a high reputation for public speaking did not put any speeches in writing, especially if they rarely spoke in the courts (see above n. 8).

Andocides was exiled but later returned. Two of the four speeches in his name give us a contemporary view of the scandal: one pleads for his return, the other argues against a second period of exile.

- ANTIPHON (ca. 480–411), as already noted, wrote forensic speeches for others and only once spoke himself. In 411 he participated in an oligarchic coup by a group of 400, and when the democrats regained power he was tried for treason and executed. His six surviving speeches include three for delivery in court and the three Tetralogies—imaginary intellectual exercises for display or teaching that consist of four speeches each, two on each side. All six of Antiphon's speeches concern homicide, probably because these stood at the beginning of the collection of his works. Fragments of some thirty other speeches cover many different topics.

- DEMOSTHENES (384–322) is generally considered the best of the Attic orators. Although his nationalistic message is less highly regarded today, his powerful mastery of and ability to combine many different rhetorical styles continues to impress readers. Demosthenes was still a child when his wealthy father died. The trustees of the estate apparently misappropriated much of it, and when he came of age, he sued them in a series of cases (27–31), regaining some of his fortune and making a name as a powerful speaker. He then wrote speeches for others in a variety of cases, public and private, and for his own use in court (where many cases involved major public issues), and in the Assembly, where he opposed the growing power of Philip of Macedon. The triumph of Philip and his son Alexander the Great eventually put an end to Demosthenes' career. Some sixty speeches have come down under his name, about a third of them of questionable authenticity.

- DINARCHUS (ca. 360–ca. 290) was born in Corinth but spent much of his life in Athens as a metic (a noncitizen resident). His public fame came primarily from writing speeches for the prosecutions surrounding the Harpalus affair in 324, when several prominent figures (including Demosthenes) were accused of bribery. After 322 he had a profitable career as a logographer.

- HYPERIDES (390–322) was a political leader and logographer of so many different talents that he was called the pentathlete of orators.

He was a leader of the Athenian resistance to Philip and Alexander and (like Demosthenes) was condemned to death after Athens' final surrender. One speech and substantial fragments of five others have been recovered from papyrus remains; otherwise, only fragments survive.

- ISAEUS (ca. 415–ca. 340) wrote speeches on a wide range of topics, but the eleven complete speeches that survive, dating from ca. 390 to ca. 344, all concern inheritance. As with Antiphon, the survival of these particular speeches may have been the result of the later ordering of his speeches by subject; we have part of a twelfth speech and fragments and titles of some forty other works. Isaeus is said to have been a pupil of Isocrates and the teacher of Demosthenes.

- ISOCRATES (436–338) considered himself a philosopher and educator, not an orator or rhetorician. He came from a wealthy Athenian family but lost most of his property in the Peloponnesian War, and in 403 he took up logography. About 390 he abandoned this practice and turned to writing and teaching, setting forth his educational, philosophical, and political views in essays that took the form of speeches but were not meant for oral delivery. He favored accommodation with the growing power of Philip of Macedon and panhellenic unity. His school was based on a broad concept of rhetoric and applied philosophy; it attracted pupils from the entire Greek world (including Isaeus, Lycurgus, and Hyperides) and became the main rival of Plato's Academy. Isocrates greatly influenced education and rhetoric in the Hellenistic, Roman, and modern periods until the eighteenth century.

- LYCURGUS (ca. 390–ca. 324) was a leading public official who restored the financial condition of Athens after 338 and played a large role in the city for the next dozen years. He brought charges of corruption or treason against many other officials, usually with success. Only one speech survives.

- LYSIAS (ca. 445–ca. 380) was a metic—an official resident of Athens but not a citizen. Much of his property was seized by the Thirty during their short-lived oligarchic coup in 404–403. Perhaps as a result he turned to logography. More than thirty speeches survive in whole or in part, though the authenticity of some is doubted.

We also have fragments or know the titles of more than a hundred others. The speeches cover a wide range of cases, and he may have delivered one himself (Lys. 12), on the death of his brother at the hands of the Thirty. Lysias is particularly known for his vivid narratives, his *ēthopoiïa*, or "creation of character," and his prose style, which became a model of clarity and vividness.

THE WORKS OF THE ORATORS

As soon as speeches began to be written down, they could be preserved. We know little about the conditions of book "publication" (i.e., making copies for distribution) in the fourth century, but there was an active market for books in Athens, and some of the speeches may have achieved wide circulation.[12] An orator (or his family) may have preserved his own speeches, perhaps to advertise his ability or demonstrate his success, or booksellers may have collected and copied them in order to make money.

We do not know how closely the preserved text of these speeches corresponded to the version actually delivered in court or in the Assembly. Speakers undoubtedly extemporized or varied from their text on occasion, but there is no good evidence that deliberative speeches were substantially revised for publication.[13] In forensic oratory a logographer's reputation would derive first and foremost from his success with jurors. If a forensic speech was victorious, there would be no reason to alter it for publication, and if it lost, alteration would probably not deceive potential clients. Thus, the published texts of forensic speeches were probably quite faithful to the texts that were provided to clients, and we have little reason to suspect substantial alteration in the century or so before they were collected by scholars in Alexandria (see below).

In addition to the speaker's text, most forensic speeches have breaks for the inclusion of documents. The logographer inserted a notation

---

[12] Dover's discussion (1968) of the preservation and transmission of the works of Lysias (and perhaps others under his name) is useful not just for Lysias but for the other orators too. His theory of shared authorship between logographer and litigant, however, is unconvincing (see Usher 1976).

[13] See further Trevett 1996: 437–439.

in his text—such as *nomos* ("law") or *martyria* ("testimony")—and the speaker would pause while the clerk read out the text of a law or the testimony of witnesses. Many speeches survive with only a notation that a *nomos* or *martyria* was read at that point, but in some cases the text of the document is included. It used to be thought that these documents were all creations of later scholars, but many (though not all) are now accepted as genuine.[14]

With the foundation of the famous library in Alexandria early in the third century, scholars began to collect and catalogue texts of the orators, along with many other classical authors. Only the best orators were preserved in the library, many of them represented by over 100 speeches each (some undoubtedly spurious). Only some of these works survived in manuscript form to the modern era; more recently a few others have been discovered on ancient sheets of papyrus, so that today the corpus of Attic Oratory consists of about 150 speeches, together with a few letters and other works. The subject matter ranges from important public issues and serious crimes to business affairs, lovers' quarrels, inheritance disputes, and other personal or family matters.

In the centuries after these works were collected, ancient scholars gathered biographical facts about their authors, produced grammatical and lexicographic notes, and used some of the speeches as evidence for Athenian political history. But the ancient scholars who were most interested in the orators were those who studied prose style, the most notable of these being Dionysius of Halicarnassus (first century BC), who wrote treatises on several of the orators,[15] and Hermogenes of Tarsus (second century AD), who wrote several literary studies, including *On Types of Style*.[16] But relative to epic or tragedy, oratory was little studied; and even scholars of rhetoric whose interests were broader than style, like Cicero and Quintilian, paid little attention to the orators, except for the acknowledged master, Demosthenes.

Most modern scholars until the second half of the twentieth century continued to treat the orators primarily as prose stylists.[17] The

---

[14] See MacDowell 1990: 43–47; Todd 1993: 44–45.

[15] Dionysius' literary studies are collected and translated in Usher 1974–1985.

[16] Wooten 1987. Stylistic considerations probably also influenced the selection of the "canon" of ten orators; see Worthington 1994.

[17] For example, the most popular and influential book ever written on the orators, Jebb's *The Attic Orators* (1875) was presented as an "attempt to aid in giving

reevaluation of Athenian democracy by George Grote and others in the nineteenth century stimulated renewed interest in Greek oratory among historians; and increasing interest in Athenian law during that century led a few legal scholars to read the orators. But in comparison with the interest shown in the other literary genres—epic, lyric, tragedy, comedy, and even history—Attic oratory has been relatively neglected until the last third of the twentieth century. More recently, however, scholars have discovered the value of the orators for the broader study of Athenian culture and society. Since Dover's groundbreaking works on popular morality and homosexuality,[18] interest in the orators has been increasing rapidly, and they are now seen as primary representatives of Athenian moral and social values, and as evidence for social and economic conditions, political and social ideology, and in general those aspects of Athenian culture that in the past were commonly ignored by historians of ancient Greece but are of increasing interest and importance today, including women and the family, slavery, and the economy.

GOVERNMENT AND LAW IN CLASSICAL ATHENS

The hallmark of the Athenian political and legal systems was its amateurism. Most public officials, including those who supervised the courts, were selected by lot and held office for a limited period, typically a year. Thus a great many citizens held public office at some point in their lives, but almost none served for an extended period of time or developed the experience or expertise that would make them professionals. All significant policy decisions were debated and voted on in the Assembly, where the quorum was 6,000 citizens, and all significant legal cases were judged by bodies of 200 to 500 jurors or more. Public prominence was not achieved by election (or selection) to public office but depended rather on a man's ability to sway the

---

Attic Oratory its due place in the history of Attic Prose" (I.xiii). This modern focus on prose style can plausibly be connected to the large role played by prose composition (the translation of English prose into Greek, usually in imitation of specific authors or styles) in the Classics curriculum, especially in Britain.

[18] Dover (1974, 1978). Dover recently commented (1994: 157), "When I began to mine the riches of Attic forensic oratory I was astonished to discover that the mine had never been exploited."

majority of citizens in the Assembly or jurors in court to vote in favor of a proposed course of action or for one of the litigants in a trial. Success was never permanent, and a victory on one policy issue or a verdict in one case could be quickly reversed in another.[19] In such a system the value of public oratory is obvious, and in the fourth century, oratory became the most important cultural institution in Athens, replacing drama as the forum where major ideological concerns were displayed and debated.

Several recent books give good detailed accounts of Athenian government and law,[20] and so a brief sketch can suffice here. The main policy-making body was the Assembly, open to all adult male citizens; a small payment for attendance enabled at least some of the poor to attend along with the leisured rich. In addition, a Council of 500 citizens, selected each year by lot with no one allowed to serve more than two years, prepared material for and made recommendations to the Assembly; a rotating subgroup of this Council served as an executive committee, the Prytany. Finally, numerous officials, most of them selected by lot for one-year terms, supervised different areas of administration and finance. The most important of these were the nine Archons (lit. "rulers"): the eponymous Archon after whom the year was named, the Basileus ("king"),[21] the Polemarch, and the six Thesmothetae. Councilors and almost all these officials underwent a preliminary examination (*dokimasia*) before taking office, and officials submitted to a final accounting (*euthynai*) upon leaving; at these times any citi-

---

[19] In the Assembly this could be accomplished by a reconsideration of the question, as in the famous Mytilenean debate (Thuc. 3.36–50); in court a verdict was final, but its practical effects could be thwarted or reversed by later litigation on a related issue.

[20] For government, see Sinclair 1988, Hansen 1991; for law, MacDowell 1978, Todd 1993, and Boegehold 1995 (Bonner 1927 is still helpful). Much of our information about the legal and political systems comes from a work attributed to Aristotle but perhaps written by a pupil of his, *The Athenian Constitution* (*Ath. Pol.*—conveniently translated with notes by Rhodes 1984). The discovery of this work on a papyrus in Egypt in 1890 caused a major resurgence of interest in Athenian government.

[21] Modern scholars often use the term *archōn basileus* or "king archon," but Athenian sources (e.g., *Ath. Pol.* 57) simply call him the *basileus*.

zen who wished could challenge a person's fitness for his new position or his performance in his recent position.

There was no general taxation of Athenian citizens. Sources of public funding included the annual tax levied on metics, various fees and import duties, and (in the fifth century) tribute from allied cities; but the source that figures most prominently in the orators is the Athenian system of liturgies (*leitourgiai*), by which in a regular rotation the rich provided funding for certain special public needs. The main liturgies were the *chorēgia*, in which a sponsor (*chorēgos*) supervised and paid for the training and performance of a chorus which sang and danced at a public festival,[22] and the trierarchy, in which a sponsor (trierarch) paid to equip and usually commanded a trireme, or warship, for a year. Some of these liturgies required substantial expenditures, but even so, some men spent far more than required in order to promote themselves and their public careers, and litigants often try to impress the jurors by referring to liturgies they have undertaken (see, e.g., Lys. 21.1–5). A further twist on this system was that if a man thought he had been assigned a liturgy that should have gone to someone else who was richer than he, he could propose an exchange of property (*antidosis*), giving the other man a choice of either taking over the liturgy or exchanging property with him. Finally, the rich were also subject to special taxes (*eisphorai*) levied as a percentage of their property in times of need.

The Athenian legal system remained similarly resistant to professionalization. Trials and the procedures leading up to them were supervised by officials, primarily the nine Archons, but their role was purely administrative, and they were in no way equivalent to modern judges. All significant questions about what we would call points of law were presented to the jurors, who considered them together with all other issues when they delivered their verdict at the end of the trial.[23] Trials were "contests" (*agōnes*) between two litigants, each of

---

[22] These included the productions of tragedy and comedy, for which the main expense was for the chorus.

[23] Certain religious "interpreters" (*exēgētai*) were occasionally asked to give their opinion on a legal matter that had a religious dimension (such as the prosecution of a homicide), but although these opinions could be reported in court

whom presented his own case to the jurors in a speech, plaintiff first, then defendant; in some cases each party then spoke again, probably in rebuttal. Since a litigant had only one or two speeches in which to present his entire case, and no issue was decided separately by a judge, all the necessary factual information and every important argument on substance or procedure, fact or law, had to be presented together. A single speech might thus combine narrative, argument, emotional appeal, and various digressions, all with the goal of obtaining a favorable verdict. Even more than today, a litigant's primary task was to control the issue—to determine which issues the jurors would consider most important and which questions they would have in their minds as they cast their votes. We only rarely have both speeches from a trial,[24] and we usually have little or no external evidence for the facts of a case or the verdict. We must thus infer both the facts and the opponent's strategy from the speech we have, and any assessment of the overall effectiveness of a speech and of the logographer's strategy is to some extent speculative.

Before a trial there were usually several preliminary hearings for presenting evidence; arbitration, public and private, was available and sometimes required. These hearings and arbitration sessions allowed each side to become familiar with the other side's case, so that discussions of "what my opponent will say" could be included in one's speech. Normally a litigant presented his own case, but he was often assisted by family or friends. If he wished (and could afford it), he could enlist the services of a logographer, who presumably gave strategic advice in addition to writing a speech. The speeches were timed to ensure an equal hearing for both sides,[25] and all trials were completed within a day. Two hundred or more jurors decided each case in the popular courts, which met in the Agora.[26] Homicide cases and

---

(e.g., Dem. 47.68–73), they had no official legal standing. The most significant administrative decision we hear of is the refusal of the Basileus to accept the case in Antiphon 6 (see 6.37–46).

[24] The exceptions are Demosthenes 19 and Aeschines 2, Aeschines 3 and Demosthenes 18, and Lysias 6 (one of several prosecution speeches) and Andocides 1; all were written for major public cases.

[25] Timing was done by means of a water-clock, which in most cases was stopped during the reading of documents.

[26] See Boegehold 1995.

certain other religious trials (e.g., Lys. 7) were heard by the Council of the Areopagus or an associated group of fifty-one Ephetae. The Areopagus was composed of all former Archons—perhaps 150–200 members at most times. It met on a hill called the Areopagus ("rock of Ares") near the Acropolis.

Jurors for the regular courts were selected by lot from those citizens who registered each year and who appeared for duty that day; as with the Assembly, a small payment allowed the poor to serve. After the speakers had finished, the jurors voted immediately without any formal discussion. The side with the majority won; a tie vote decided the case for the defendant. In some cases where the penalty was not fixed, after a conviction the jurors voted again on the penalty, choosing between penalties proposed by each side. Even when we know the verdict, we cannot know which of the speaker's arguments contributed most to his success or failure. However, a logographer could probably learn from jurors which points had or had not been successful, so that arguments that are found repeatedly in speeches probably were known to be effective in most cases.

The first written laws in Athens were enacted by Draco (ca. 620) and Solon (ca. 590), and new laws were regularly added. At the end of the fifth century the existing laws were reorganized, and a new procedure for enacting laws was instituted; thereafter a group of Law-Givers (*nomothetai*) had to certify that a proposed law did not conflict with any existing laws. There was no attempt, however, to organize legislation systematically, and although Plato, Aristotle, and other philosophers wrote various works on law and law-giving, these were either theoretical or descriptive and had no apparent influence on legislation. Written statutes generally used ordinary language rather than precise legal definitions in designating offenses, and questions concerning precisely what constituted a specific offense or what was the correct interpretation of a written statute were decided (together with other issues) by the jurors in each case. A litigant might, of course, assert a certain definition or interpretation as "something you all know" or "what the lawgiver intended," but such remarks are evidently tendentious and cannot be taken as authoritative.

The result of these procedural and substantive features was that the verdict depended largely on each litigant's speech (or speeches). As one speaker puts it (Ant. 6.18), "When there are no witnesses, you (jurors) are forced to reach a verdict about the case on the basis of the prosecutor's and defendant's words alone; you must be suspicious and examine their accounts in detail, and your vote will necessarily be cast on the basis of likelihood rather than clear knowledge." Even the testimony of witnesses (usually on both sides) is rarely decisive. On the other hand, most speakers make a considerable effort to establish facts and provide legitimate arguments in conformity with established law. Plato's view of rhetoric as a clever technique for persuading an ignorant crowd that the false is true is not borne out by the speeches, and the legal system does not appear to have produced many arbitrary or clearly unjust results.

The main form of legal procedure was a *dikē* ("suit") in which the injured party (or his relatives in a case of homicide) brought suit against the offender. Suits for injuries to slaves would be brought by the slave's master, and injuries to women would be prosecuted by a male relative. Strictly speaking, a *dikē* was a private matter between individuals, though like all cases, *dikai* often had public dimensions. The other major form of procedure was a *graphē* ("writing" or "indictment") in which "anyone who wished" (i.e., any citizen) could bring a prosecution for wrongdoing. *Graphai* were instituted by Solon, probably in order to allow prosecution of offenses where the victim was unable or unlikely to bring suit himself, such as selling a dependent into slavery; but the number of areas covered by *graphai* increased to cover many types of public offenses as well as some apparently private crimes, such as *hybris*.

The system of prosecution by "anyone who wished" also extended to several other more specialized forms of prosecution, like *eisangelia* ("impeachment"), used in cases of treason. Another specialized prosecution was *apagōgē* ("summary arrest"), in which someone could arrest a common criminal (*kakourgos*, lit. "evil-doer"), or have him arrested, on the spot. The reliance on private initiative meant that Athenians never developed a system of public prosecution; rather, they presumed that everyone would keep an eye on the behavior of his political enemies and bring suit as soon as he suspected a crime, both to harm his opponents and to advance his own career. In this way all public officials would be watched by someone. There was no disgrace in admitting that a prosecution was motivated by private enmity.

By the end of the fifth century the system of prosecution by "any one who wished" was apparently being abused by so-called sykophants (*sykophantai*), who allegedly brought or threatened to bring false suits against rich men, either to gain part of the fine that would be levied or to induce an out-of-court settlement in which the accused would pay to have the matter dropped. We cannot gauge the true extent of this problem, since speakers usually provide little evidence to support their claims that their opponents are sykophants, but the Athenians did make sykophancy a crime. They also specified that in many public procedures a plaintiff who either dropped the case or failed to obtain one-fifth of the votes would have to pay a heavy fine of 1,000 drachmas. Despite this, it appears that litigation was common in Athens and was seen by some as excessive.

Over the course of time, the Athenian legal and political systems have more often been judged negatively than positively. Philosophers and political theorists have generally followed the lead of Plato (427–347), who lived and worked in Athens his entire life while severely criticizing its system of government as well as many other aspects of its culture. For Plato, democracy amounted to the tyranny of the masses over the educated elite and was destined to collapse from its own instability. The legal system was capricious and depended entirely on the rhetorical ability of litigants with no regard for truth or justice. These criticisms have often been echoed by modern scholars, who particularly complain that law was much too closely interwoven with politics and did not have the autonomous status it achieved in Roman law and continues to have, at least in theory, in modern legal systems.

Plato's judgments are valid if one accepts the underlying presuppositions, that the aim of law is absolute truth and abstract justice and that achieving the highest good of the state requires thorough and systematic organization. Most Athenians do not seem to have subscribed to either the criticisms or the presuppositions, and most scholars now accept the long-ignored fact that despite major external disruptions in the form of wars and two short-lived coups brought about by one of these wars, the Athenian legal and political systems remained remarkably stable for almost two hundred years (508–320). Moreover, like all other Greek cities at the time, whatever their form of government, Athenian democracy was brought to an end not by internal forces but by the external power of Philip of Macedon and his son Alexander. The legal system never became autonomous, and the rich sometimes complained that they were victims of unscrupulous litigants, but there is no indication that the people wanted to yield control of the legal process to a professional class, as Plato recommended. For most Athenians—Plato being an exception in this and many other matters—one purpose of the legal system was to give everyone the opportunity to have his case heard by other citizens and have it heard quickly and cheaply; and in this it clearly succeeded.

Indeed, the Athenian legal system also served the interests of the rich, even the very rich, as well as the common people, in that it provided a forum for the competition that since Homer had been an important part of aristocratic life. In this competition, the rich used the courts as battlegrounds, though their main weapon was the rhetoric of popular ideology, which hailed the rule of law and promoted the ideal of moderation and restraint.[27] But those who aspired to political leadership and the honor and status that accompanied it repeatedly entered the legal arena, bringing suit against their political enemies whenever possible and defending themselves against suits brought by others whenever necessary. The ultimate judges of these public competitions were the common people, who seem to have relished the dramatic clash of individuals and ideologies. In this respect fourth-century oratory was the cultural heir of fifth-century drama and was similarly appreciated by the citizens. Despite the disapproval of intellectuals like Plato, most Athenians legitimately considered their legal system a hallmark of their democracy and a vital presence in their culture.

THE TRANSLATION OF GREEK ORATORY

The purpose of this series is to provide students and scholars in all fields with accurate, readable translations of all surviving classical Attic oratory, including speeches whose authenticity is disputed, as well as the substantial surviving fragments. In keeping with the originals, the language is for the most part nontechnical. Names of persons and places are given in the (generally more familiar) Latinized forms, and names of officials or legal procedures have been translated into English equivalents, where possible. Notes are intended to provide the necessary historical and cultural background; scholarly controversies are

[27] Ober 1989 is fundamental; see also Cohen 1995.

generally not discussed. The notes and introductions refer to scholarly treatments in addition to those listed below, which the reader may consult for further information.

Cross-references to other speeches follow the standard numbering system, which is now well established except in the case of Hyperides (for whom the numbering of the Oxford Classical Text is used).[28] References are by work and section (e.g., Dem. 24.73); spurious works are not specially marked; when no author is named (e.g., 24.73), the reference is to the same author as the annotated passage.

ABBREVIATIONS:

Aes.	=	Aeschines
And.	=	Andocides
Ant.	=	Antiphon
Arist.	=	Aristotle
Aristoph.	=	Aristophanes
Ath. Pol.	=	*The Athenian Constitution*
Dem.	=	Demosthenes
Din.	=	Dinarchus
Herod.	=	Herodotus
Hyp.	=	Hyperides
Is.	=	Isaeus
Isoc.	=	Isocrates
Lyc.	=	Lycurgus
Lys.	=	Lysias
Plut.	=	Plutarch
Thuc.	=	Thucydides
Xen.	=	Xenophon

NOTE: The main unit of Athenian currency was the drachma; this was divided into obols and larger amounts were designated minas and talents.

1 drachma	=	6 obols
1 mina	=	100 drachmas
1 talent	=	60 minas (6,000 drachmas)

[28] For a listing of all the orators and their works, with classifications (forensic, deliberative, epideictic) and rough dates, see Edwards 1994: 74–79.

It is impossible to give an accurate equivalence in terms of modern currency, but it may be helpful to remember that the daily wage of some skilled workers was a drachma in the mid-fifth century and 2–2½ drachmas in the later fourth century. Thus it may not be too misleading to think of a drachma as worth about $50 or £33 and a talent as about $300,000 or £200,000 in 1997 currency.

BIBLIOGRAPHY OF WORKS CITED

Boegehold, Alan L., 1995: *The Lawcourts at Athens: Sites, Buildings, Equipment, Procedure, and Testimonia*. Princeton.

Bonner, Robert J., 1927: *Lawyers and Litigants in Ancient Athens*. Chicago.

Cohen, David, 1995: *Law, Violence and Community in Classical Athens*. Cambridge.

Cole, Thomas, 1991: *The Origins of Rhetoric in Ancient Greece*. Baltimore.

Dover, Kenneth J., 1968: *Lysias and the Corpus Lysiacum*. Berkeley.

———, 1974: *Greek Popular Morality in the Time of Plato and Aristotle*. Oxford.

———, 1978: *Greek Homosexuality*. London.

———, 1994: *Marginal Comment*. London.

Edwards, Michael, 1994: *The Attic Orators*. London.

Gagarin, Michael, and Paul Woodruff, 1995: *Early Greek Political Thought from Homer to the Sophists*. Cambridge.

Hansen, Mogens Herman, 1991: *The Athenian Democracy in the Age of Demosthenes*. Oxford.

Jebb, Richard, 1875: *The Attic Orators*, 2 vols. London.

Kennedy, George A., 1963: *The Art of Persuasion in Greece*. Princeton.

Kerferd, G. B., 1981: *The Sophistic Movement*. Cambridge.

MacDowell, Douglas M., 1978: *The Law in Classical Athens*. London.

———, ed. 1990: *Demosthenes, Against Meidias*. Oxford.

Ober, Josiah, 1989: *Mass and Elite in Democratic Athens*. Princeton.

Rhodes, P. J., trans., 1984: *Aristotle, The Athenian Constitution*. Penguin Books.

Sinclair, R. K., 1988: *Democracy and Participation in Athens*. Cambridge.

Todd, Stephen, 1993: *The Shape of Athenian Law*. Oxford.

Trevett, Jeremy, 1992: *Apollodoros the Son of Pasion*. Oxford.
———, 1996: "Did Demosthenes Publish His Deliberative Speeches?" *Hermes* 124: 425–441.
Usher, Stephen, 1976: "Lysias and His Clients," *Greek, Roman and Byzantine Studies* 17: 31–40.
———, trans., 1974–1985: *Dionysius of Halicarnassus, Critical Essays*. 2 vols. Loeb Classical Library. Cambridge, MA.
Wooten, Cecil W., trans., 1987: *Hermogenes' On Types of Style*. Chapel Hill, NC.
Worthington, Ian, 1994: "The Canon of the Ten Attic Orators," in *Persuasion: Greek Rhetoric in Action*, ed. Ian Worthington. London: 244–263.
Yunis, Harvey, 1996: *Taming Democracy: Models of Political Rhetoric in Classical Athens*. Ithaca, NY.

There is now a collection of speeches with legal interest and a good brief introduction to Athenian law in Christopher Carey, *Trials from Classical Athens* (London, 1997).

SUPPLEMENTARY BIBLIOGRAPHY FOR VOLUME 2

Carey, C., 1989: *Lysias: Selected Speeches.* Cambridge.
Davies, J. K., 1971: *Athenian Propertied Families.* Oxford.
Edwards, M., and S. Usher, 1985: *Greek Orators,* I, *Antiphon and Lysias.* Warminster.
Fornara, C. W., 1983: *Archaic Times to the End of the Peloponnesian War.* Cambridge.
Harding, P., 1985: *From the End of the Peloponnesian War to the Battle of Ipsus.* Cambridge.

MODERN EDITIONS OF LYSIAS (INCLUDING THOSE CITED FOR NUMBERING OF FRAGMENTS)

Albini, U., 1955: *Lisia: i discorsi.* Rome.
Baiter, J. G., and H. Sauppe, 1839: *Oratores Attici,* vol. 1 (of 2). Zurich.
Gernet, L., and M. Bizos, 1955: *Lysias: Discours.* Budé edition, 3d ed., 2 vols. Paris.

Hude, K., 1912: *Lysiae Orationes.* Oxford Classical Text. Oxford.

Lamb, W. R. M., 1930: *Lysias, with an English Translation.* Loeb Classical Library. Cambridge, MA.

Medda, E., 1992–1995: *Lisia, Orazioni: Introduzione, premessa al testo, traduzione e note.* 2 vols. Milan.

Thalheim, Th., 1913: *Lysiae Orationes.* Teubner edition, 2d ed. Leipzig.

LYSIAS

Translated with introduction by S. C. Todd

INTRODUCTION

CHRONOLOGY

Lysias, like other orators, was the subject of a biographical tradition in antiquity.[1] There is a rather muddled account in Pseudo-Plutarch's *Lives of the Ten Orators* and a more cautious one at the beginning of the essay *On Lysias* by the ancient rhetorical theorist Dionysius of Halicarnassus. The two are basically in agreement that Lysias was born in 459/8 BC and died ca. 380 BC. Given that all the surviving speeches that can be dated belong in the period 403–380, the proposed date of death seems plausible, but the date of birth less so, partly because it would entail Lysias having begun his career as speechwriter in his mid-50s, which would be unusual though not impossible, and partly because Dionysius (unlike Pseudo-Plutarch) never states the date of birth as a fact: instead, he presents it as an inference from what seems to be the fact that Lysias went to join the colony at Thurii in Southern Italy at the age of 15, combined with what may be no more than the assumption that he did so at the foundation of the colony in 443/2 BC (Dion. Hal., *On Lysias* §1). Many scholars have suggested that Lysias may have joined the colony around 430, giving a date of birth ca. 445.

The ancient biographers drew mainly on information that Lysias composed for cases in which he was himself involved, one of which survives complete (speech 12), and another in substantial papyrus fragments (Fr. 7 [*Hippotherses*]). Close verbal parallels indicate that both

[1] The best treatment of the life of Lysias is in Dover (1968: 28–46), which takes full account of the evidence that has been discovered since the work of nineteenth-century scholars like Blass.

of these speeches were used by Pseudo-Plutarch or his sources,[2] but it is important to remember that Lysias may have manipulated the facts about his past to suit his own objectives. Apart from the two speeches, the other primary evidence consists of an anecdote in a speech from the 340s[3] and two dialogues of Plato in which Lysias and his family appear.

Plato's *Republic* is set in the house of Lysias' father Cephalus, and Plato's *Phaedrus* focuses on a discussion of a speech about love written allegedly by Lysias.[4] There have been attempts to identify dramatic dates for these dialogues: the discussants in the *Phaedrus,* for instance, are Socrates (who died in 399) and Phaedrus (in exile from 415 to 404), and the discussion presupposes that the poets Sophocles and Euripides are apparently still alive (hence no later than 406), but also that Lysias is active and in Athens, rather than in Thurii (which might tend to undermine Dionysius' statement that he returned in 412/1: *On Lysias* §1). Similarly the *Republic* is located at the time of the introduction to Athens of the festival of the Thracian goddess Bendis (probably but not certainly around 430), at a time when Cephalus is still alive and Lysias and his brothers are still in Athens. If the dialogues have consistent dramatic dates, they raise as many questions as they solve for the biography of Lysias. But the dramatic dates of other Platonic dialogues are equally problematic, and it may be better to use these two dialogues as evidence for Lysias' fame and his family's wealth and social status, despite their being metics (noncitizens resident in Athens), rather than for chronology.

---

[2] E.g., the reference to the house with two doors (Lys. 12.15; cf. [Plutarch], *Lysias* 835f), and the details of material supplied to the democratic counterrevolutionaries in 404/3 (Lys., Fr. 7.e, lines 163–167, and Fr. 7.f, lines 168–170; cf. [Plutarch], *Lysias* 835f).

[3] Dem. 59.21–22 speaks of Lysias maintaining a mistress, at a date that seems to be towards the end of the 380s, and during the lifetime of his mother. The latter piece of information, if not the former, has sometimes been held to imply a later rather than an earlier date of birth.

[4] Some modern scholars regard the speech (which is quoted verbatim in Plato's *Phaedrus* 230e–234c) as genuine, and some editors include it as speech 35 in the corpus of Lysias, but in my view it is probably a parody of Lysias' style written by Plato himself, and so is not included in this volume.

CAREER

Lysias is said to have studied oratory with its Syracusan inventor Corax and with Nicias[5] during his time in Thurii. This may well be true, though Thurii and Syracuse are some 200 miles apart, and ancient biographers are sometimes over-keen to establish connections between teachers and likely pupils. In any event, there seems to be a gap between his return to Athens and the start of his career as a speechwriter. This gap is most easily explained by the events of 404/3, the year of the oligarchic junta traditionally known as the Thirty Tyrants, which was imposed by the Spartans following the surrender of Athens at the end of the Peloponnesian War (431–404). Lysias himself recounts how he and his brother Polemarchus were among a small group of metics arrested by the Thirty, allegedly on suspicion of being hostile towards the regime, but really (according to Lysias) in order to confiscate their considerable wealth (Lys. 12.12–19). Polemarchus' execution forms the subject of speech 12, an accusation of judicial murder against one of the Thirty. Lysias himself escaped to join and assist the democratic counterrevolutionaries, and his later attempts to recover at least part of his confiscated property form the subject of Fragment 7 (*Hippotherses*).

After the regime of the Thirty had collapsed in a reign of terror and a civil war, the Spartan king Pausanias permitted the restoration of democracy in 403, subject to a general amnesty designed to protect from threat of litigation all former supporters of the oligarchy except the Thirty themselves and about thirty others who had held named offices as their immediate subordinates. We are told that Lysias himself was a beneficiary of a decree proposed immediately after the restoration by Thrasybulus, one of the democratic leaders, granting citizenship to those metics who had assisted the democrats, but that this decree was promptly challenged by Archinus, one of the other democratic leaders, and annulled as unconstitutional. Given that a decree would normally be suspended pending the challenge, it is quite likely that Lysias never enjoyed the citizenship, and certainly he reverted

[5] [Plutarch], *Lives of the Ten Orators* 835d. Nicias is otherwise unknown and may be a mistake for Tisias (Corax's fellow Syracusan and fellow inventor of rhetoric).

thereafter to the status of metic or more specifically *isotelēs* (a privileged subgroup of metics with tax privileges).

As a noncitizen, Lysias was unable to vote or to take an active part in politics, and we do not know whether he was able to appear in court to deliver speech 12; nor do we know the result, if it ever came to court (cf. the Introduction to Lys. 12). But he seems to have been sufficiently pleased with it to take up a career as a speechwriter, whether because he had discovered a talent he had not previously recognized, or because the confiscation of his property had encouraged him to find an additional source of income.

Given his own sufferings under the Thirty, we might expect Lysias to take a consistent stand against former supporters of the oligarchy. In the event, however, at least some of his clients were clearly implicated to some degree, including for instance the speakers of Lysias 25 and of Fragment 9 (*Eryximachus*), both of whom had remained in Athens under the Thirty. Some scholars have argued that Lysias was prepared to write speeches only for moderate rather than for extreme former oligarchs,[6] but this may be to take Lysias' rhetoric too much at face value, because it is Lysias, speaking through the mouth of his clients, who distinguishes them from the extremists. If oligarchs are to be divided into "nice" and "nasty" groups, it is striking how often a speaker is to be found among the former and his opponent among the latter.

Other scholars[7] have taken a much more hostile line, regarding Lysias simply as an unscrupulous advocate willing to write for anybody who will pay. There is probably some truth in this, but it is important not to impose our own concepts of political consistency. Political alliances in Athens were much more personal and less permanent than is the case in a modern system of party politics, and Lysias and his contemporaries may have been less concerned than we would about his readiness to support people who had behaved in ways that to us seem indistinguishable from those that elsewhere he is happy to attack.

---

[6] Thus, e.g., D. G. Lateiner, "Lysias and Athenian Politics" (unpublished dissertation, Stanford University, 1971).

[7] See the discussion of, e.g., F. Ferckel, *Lysias und Athen* (Würzburg, 1937) in Todd (1990: 163).

STYLE

Lysias was noted in antiquity as master of the language of everyday life. This led to his being regarded by later readers as the preeminent model of "Atticism," as opposed to the more florid "Asiatic" style. His particular skill is in narrative, and it is in this context that Dionysius comments on his ability to "smuggle persuasion past the hearer" (*On Lysias* §18). This is seen particularly in Lysias 1, where the story of the speaker's friend Sostratus appears first as an innocuously incidental detail, of the sort that seems so trivial that it lends veracity to the surrounding narrative (1.22–23), which the hearer then has no reason to doubt when the behavior of Sostratus later forms the basis of the defense against premeditation (1.39–40).

Also famous in antiquity, and still much discussed, was Lysias' skill at *ēthopoiia* (lit. "creation of character"; Dionysius, *On Lysias* §8). Earlier scholars tended to presuppose that this referred to the characterizing of individuals, and they sought for evidence of aristocrats speaking like aristocrats and peasants speaking like peasants. Usher (1965), however, has argued convincingly that *ēthopoiia* is not the creation of individual characteristics (for which Dionysius uses the term *to prepon,* lit. "that which is fitting": *On Lysias* §9), but the portrayal of favorable character, or, as Usher translates it, "moral tone."[8] But Usher himself does find evidence of individual characterization in at least some of the speeches: particularly the defense speeches, including most notably the naiveté of Euphiletus in Lysias 1, the dignified embarrassment of the speaker in Lysias 3, the sparkling confidence of Mantitheus in Lysias 16, and the shameless attempts of the speaker in Lysias 24 to play to the gallery. Usher finds less evidence of individual characterization in the prosecution speeches, but he highlights the heavy sarcasm of Lysias 10, and the detailed and unfavorable portrait not of the defendant Eratosthenes but of his alleged ally Theramenes in Lysias 12.[9]

Lysias' skill in argument was less highly rated by Dionysius, who says that Lysias was better at discovering arguments than at deploying them (*On Lysias* §15), and he complains elsewhere of the lack of

[8] Usher (1965: 99 n. 1).

[9] Thus Usher (1965: 101–105), but see further the Introduction to Lys. 1.

emotional power in the arguments (*On Lysias* §19). This may be to miss the significance of Lysias' admitted mastery in narrative: as we saw in the case of speech 1, for instance, it is the apparently artless construction of the narrative that persuades the hearer to accept the facticity of details which later turn out to be central to the argument of the speech, and in this case at least, emotional power is hardly appropriate. It is interesting to compare Dionysius' verdict on the arguments of Lysias' fellow orator Isaeus, which is that the latter deploys his arguments better (*On Isaeus* §14) but that his rhetorical brilliance is constantly in danger of exciting the suspicions of the hearer (*On Isaeus* §16).

SURVIVAL AND AUTHENTICITY

Pseudo-Plutarch says that 425 speeches attributed to Lysias were current, of which 233 were regarded as genuine by leading ancient critics ([Plutarch], *Lives of the Ten Orators* 836a). Of these 425, only 31 survive in medieval manuscripts of Lysias.[10] Why these particular speeches have survived in this order is a difficult question, but it seems to have been a more random process than is the case with Antiphon and Isaeus (cf. the Series Introduction). The survival of a speech, therefore, cannot be taken as evidence that it was one of Lysias' finest, let alone that it was (or was regarded) as authentic, either in the sense of being genuinely by Lysias or in the sense of being a genuine speech. Indeed, the surviving corpus includes two works that clearly are not genuine speeches in their own right: Lysias 11 is simply an epitome of Lysias 10, and Lysias 8 is not a speech at all but perhaps an open letter.

Authenticity is a complex problem, and it is important to distinguish at least two questions: first, whether and to what extent a speech was written for and delivered at the occasion at which it purports to have been delivered, and secondly, whether and to what extent it was written by Lysias. Scholars have traditionally focused on the second of these questions, but for most historical purposes the first is more im-

[10] Though modern editors usually add three speeches (Lys. 32–34) which are extensively quoted by Dionysius of Halicarnassus in his essay *On Lysias* (cf. below), and occasionally also the "Lover's Speech" placed in the mouth of Lysias in Plato's *Phaedrus* (sometimes numbered as Lys. 35; cf. above, n. 4).

portant, because a genuine document (whatever its authorship) can be used as evidence for attitudes and perceptions at the time of writing. In this regard the situation is relatively uncomplicated, because apart from Lysias 11 (see above), the only serious doubts concern Lysias 6 and Lysias 15, and in both cases the balance of opinion is now in their favor; and although Lysias 2 is clearly not a genuine speech, and Lysias 12 (possibly) and Lysias 34 (probably) may not actually have been delivered, nevertheless even Lysias 2 may well be a genuine and contemporary pamphlet.[11] A related problem, how far a speech may have been revised between trial and "publication," is more difficult to resolve,[12] but this does not generally affect the value of the text as a fourth-century document.

The problem of authenticity in its traditional sense, that of authorship, is one that exercised scholars in antiquity (including Pseudo-Plutarch, above) as well as today. Unattributed works circulating in antiquity tended to be attracted to famous authors, and such attributions could occasionally be challenged on more-or-less objective criteria. For instance, Dionysius of Halicarnassus argued that Lysias could not have written the two speeches written for Iphicrates, because they belonged some years after his presumed death around 378 (Dion. Hal., *On Lysias* §12). It is on the basis of similar considerations that modern scholars agree that Lysias 20, which belongs in 410 or 409, is too early to be by Lysias, whose career makes best sense if it began in 403/2. More commonly, however, surviving ancient judgments of authorship are based on subjective or unstated criteria and may have been contentious even in antiquity. Such unexplained ancient judgments cannot in my opinion be relied on today.

One criterion of authorship that ancient scholars certainly did use was style (Dionysius claims that it was this that first roused his doubts about the speeches for Iphicrates, above). As a native speaker with access to the entire corpus, Dionysius will have been in a better position to make such judgments subjectively than are modern scholars, but there have been attempts by modern scholars to use the statistical

[11] The arguments are briefly set out in the individual introductions to the various speeches.

[12] On this issue I take a more pessimistic view than Gagarin (in the Series Introduction), for reasons well set out by Dover (1968: 167–170).

analysis of stylistic traits as the basis of a more objective verdict. Such analysis, however, has led to very different conclusions,[13] and to my mind, the question of authenticity in the sense of authorship is ultimately unresolvable. Fortunately, however, it rarely matters for the interpretation of the speech, though there are a few occasions when it would give an added piquancy if we could be sure that the speech was written by Lysias, as for instance in the comments on metics in Lysias 22.

FRAGMENTS

In addition to the speeches preserved as works of Lysias among medieval manuscripts, we also possess over 300 quotations in later authors, from over 100 lost speeches; these vary from single words or short phrases to several paragraphs. Three of these extended quotations are indeed conventionally treated in modern editions as part of the corpus,[14] but also included in this volume are the six further fragmentary speeches from which we have the longest quotations in later authors. They have been selected because they are sufficiently substantial to give a clear idea of what was happening in the speech and are therefore likely to be of most interest to readers of this series. Four of them[15] are quoted by Dionysius of Halicarnassus in his essays *On Isaeus* and *On Demosthenes,* in each case as the basis of a comparison between different orators writing on similar subjects. The other two[16] are quoted by Athenaeus in the *Deipnosophistae* ("Scholars at Dinner"), a compendious account of a fictitious banquet that provides Athenaeus with an opportunity for those present to cap each others' quotations on abstruse subjects (e.g., fish in books 7–8, drinking cups in book 11, courtesans in book 13). Such extended quotations, how-

[13] Cf. the stylometric analysis by Dover (1968), with rebuttal by Usher (1976). Usher followed this with a more sophisticated analysis by computer (S. Usher and D. Najock, "A Statistical Study of Authorship in the Corpus Lysiacum," *Computers and the Humanities* 16 [1982]: 85–105), but I am not convinced that this technique sufficiently acknowledges the extent to which different speeches may be striving for different types of effect.

[14] Lys. 32–34; cf. above, n. 10.

[15] Frs. 2 (*Teisis*), 3 (*Pherenicus*), 5 (*Archebiades*), and 6 (*Sons of Hippocrates*).

[16] Frs. 1 (*Aeschines*) and 4 (*Cinesias*).

ever, are rare. More typical as sources of fragments are advice on speechwriting in ancient rhetorical handbooks (e.g., Fr. 2.a), and articles in ancient lexica, or dictionaries-cum-encyclopedias (e.g., Frs. 3.b and 5.b).[17]

One of the areas in which our knowledge of Lysias has been increased since 1900 has been by the discovery and decipherment of papyri. Papyrus was a form of paper that was used throughout the ancient world, but because the dry climate encouraged preservation the vast majority of surviving papyri come from Egypt. It is characteristic of literary papyri that they are significantly older than the medieval manuscripts and that they reflect a period when a much greater range of literature was extant. However, it is also characteristic of surviving papyri that they are "fragments" in the literal sense of being damaged scraps of material. Works of Lysias have at present been securely identified on five papyri, two of them containing portions of speeches that we already possessed, but at least three of them containing portions of more than one speech. Five of these fragmentary speeches on papyri seem sufficiently substantial to be worth including in this volume.

For want of any better arrangement, the eleven fragmentary speeches are arranged in the following order: first the speeches preserved as quoted fragments (Frs. 1–6) and then those preserved on papyrus (Frs. 7–11), with each group being arranged in descending order of the scale of what remains. There is no single reliable and comprehensive edition of the papyrus fragments, though they are to be included in the new edition of the Oxford Classical Text that is being prepared by Chris Carey, who has kindly allowed me to make use of some of his readings. For the speeches, I have used the existing Oxford Classical Text, edited by Karl Hude (Oxford, 1912).

FURTHER READING

The political history of the period is discussed in J. K. Davies, *Democracy and Classical Greece* (London, 2d ed., 1993), 134–150, and in more detail in B. S. Strauss, *Athens after the Peloponnesian War*

[17] Other lexicographical entries are mentioned as appropriate in the introductions to the various fragmentary speeches.

(London and New York, 1987). There are useful and up-to-date commentaries on selected speeches by Carey 1989[18] and by Edwards and Usher 1985.[19] K. J. Dover, *Lysias and the Corpus Lysiacum* (Berkeley and Los Angeles, 1968), contains an excellent survey of the evidence for the life of Lysias and is an important study of the question of authorship: on this, however, see also S. Usher, "Lysias and His Clients," *Greek, Roman, and Byzantine Studies* 17 (1976): 31–40. Other important papers on Lysias include J. J. Bateman, "Some Aspects of Lysias' Argumentation," *Phoenix* 16 (1962): 157–177; and S. Usher, "Individual Characterisation in Lysias," *Eranos* 63 (1965): 99–119. The history of scholarship on Lysias is discussed in some detail, if in passing, by S. C. Todd, "The Use and Abuse of the Attic Orators," *Greece & Rome* 37 (1990): 159–178.

[18] The speeches covered are Lys. 1, 3, 7, 14, 31, and 32.

[19] The commentary on Lysias is by Usher and covers Lys. 1, 10, 12, 16, 22, 24, and 25.

1. ON THE DEATH OF ERATOSTHENES

INTRODUCTION

At first sight, this appears to be a speech about adultery,[1] but in fact the case concerns homicide. Euphiletus, the speaker, has caught a man called Eratosthenes committing adultery with his wife and pleads justification for having killed him. Trials for justifiable homicide at Athens came before the court of the Delphinium, and it is possible (though not certain) that they were heard by a specialist panel of Ephetae, rather than by a regular dikastic court consisting of ordinary citizens selected by lot.[2] As usual, we do not know the result of the case, but the speaker will be declared guiltless if the court decides in his favor. If they decide for his opponents (who are presumably the dead man's relatives, as was normal in homicide cases), he will be convicted of deliberate homicide and punished accordingly.

Euphiletus cites three laws in his support (at 1.28, 1.30, and 1.31).

---

[1] There has been considerable dispute in recent scholarship (based partly on this speech) over the meaning of the Greek word *moichos.* The most detailed treatment of the subject is by D. Cohen (*Law, Sexuality and Society* [Cambridge 1991], 98–132), who argues that a *moichos* was strictly an "adulterer" (i.e., somebody who has sex with a married woman), and this view has won some support. Other scholars, however, have continued to believe that what mattered was the civic status of the woman (rather than whether she was married), and possibly whether the action was committed indoors.

[2] The speech does not make any obvious concessions to the legal sophistication of its hearers (there seems to be no expectation that they will see through the use of selective quotation at 1.32–33; cf. below, n. 5), but this might mean that an ephetic as well as a dikastic court was liable to be taken in by this sort of argument.

The manuscripts of our speeches do not normally preserve the texts of documents read out in court, but scholars have plausibly identified one of these with a law on justifiable homicide quoted at Demosthenes 23.53: "If somebody kills a man after finding him next to his wife or mother or sister or daughter or concubine kept for producing free children, he shall not be exiled as a killer on account of this." In law, therefore, Euphiletus' action in killing the adulterer would seem justifiable. Lysias' problem, however, is that for a husband to kill an adulterer at Athens appears to have been unusual—and this creates suspicion. We know nothing about the opponents' arguments except what we can infer from Euphiletus' speech. It does seem, however, that they are taking the case seriously. They have evidently claimed that Euphiletus had enticed his victim into the house with the intention of killing him (cf. 1.37), and that the adulterer had not finally been captured in bed but had succeeded in escaping to the hearth of the house (1.27), thereby throwing on Euphiletus the sacrilege of removing him by force. It is not clear that either of these claims would undermine the legal basis of Euphiletus' case, but the prosecution presumably expect the court to regard his action in such circumstances as an improper (and therefore unlawful) exercise of his statutory rights.

We have already noted that the speaker's name is Euphiletus: this information arises from a chance remark he reports in 1.15. Otherwise, nothing more is known about him than can be inferred from his speech, and one of the main attractions of the speech is the extraordinarily vivid picture of Euphiletus' domestic circumstances. He is evidently a farmer, living either in the city or in one of the surrounding villages (his neighbors are mentioned at 1.14, but cf. also 1.10n and 1.23n) and walking out to his fields (1.11, 1.20). The unexpectedness of his return from the countryside in 1.11 suggests that he has been spending some days there. Presumably this is what he does at peak agricultural seasons, and he will have a hut or a shed where he can sleep. It is unlikely that he has a second house: we hear of only one domestic slave, who helps Euphiletus (not his wife) with the shopping, takes her turn minding the baby, and is (as usual) sexually available to her master. Euphiletus' wife at first sight appears dominated by her husband—it is the women's former rooms upstairs that are capable of being locked—but she is nowhere blamed for the affair, and she is quite capable (at least, as Lysias represents her) of outwitting her husband in private conversation (1.12–13).

Euphiletus' victim Eratosthenes is named several times.[3] He cannot be firmly identified, but the name is very rare in Athens. The only other classical Athenian known to us with the same name is the member of the Thirty Tyrants who is accused by Lysias in speech 12 of having killed Lysias' brother Polemarchus. It has been suggested that the two are either the same Eratosthenes (in which case, of course, the dead man in Lysias 1 must previously have been acquitted of killing Polemarchus) or that they are closely related (Greek names tend to run in families). There are considerable problems with such an identification (most notably, why the connection with the Thirty is never mentioned[4]), but lingering hatred of the Thirty would provide a motive for Euphiletus' unparalleled action and would also suggest an attractive answer to one of the most puzzling problems behind this speech: how could a man like Euphiletus, from a one-slave family, afford to commission a speech from a (presumably expensive) orator like Lysias, unless Lysias had particular reasons for waiving his fees?

One of the most striking features of this speech is the absence of reference to events outside the domestic sphere. For this reason it cannot be dated more narrowly than the broad confines of Lysias' career. However, the world that Lysias creates for us here, in what is perhaps his finest short speech, is extraordinarily vivid. There is some use of detailed legal argument, in particular that adultery is a more serious offense than rape (1.32–33).[5] For the most part, however, it is the narrative that dominates the speech, creating a version of the story

[3] After naming Eratosthenes in the introduction, Lysias takes considerable care throughout the preliminary narrative to refer to him as "this man," etc., rather than by name. This may be designed to support the claim that Euphiletus knew nothing of the affair until the news was broken to him in 1.16.

[4] A possible explanation might be that to attack the Thirty would be to admit a motive, and that Lysias is leaving the opposition with the opprobrium of bringing up this subject if they dare.

[5] The argument relies on selective quotation, because Lysias fails to mention that there were certainly other laws available which allowed for less severe penalties against adulterers, and that the law of *hubris* (which could result in a death sentence) may have been available against rape. (Both E. M. Harris, "Did the Athenians Regard Seduction as a Worse Crime than Rape?," *Classical Quarterly* 40 [1990]: 370–377, and C. Carey, "Rape and Adultery in Athenian Law," *Classical Quarterly* 45 [1995]: 407–417, agree on this point, though differing on much else.)

that makes Euphiletus' behavior appear to be what the laws "order" (whereas in fact they merely "permit"), and indeed turning the case from a prosecution of Euphiletus by Eratosthenes' relatives for homicide into a prosecution of Eratosthenes by "the laws" for adultery.

There are useful commentaries on the speech by Carey 1989 and by Usher in Edwards and Usher 1985. The latter is more accessible to the non-Greek reader, because the notes are keyed to an English translation, but I am not convinced by Usher's insistence that Euphiletus is portrayed as a man whose response to adultery would be anger. A modern pleader would tend to play this case as a crime of passion, but what is striking is the atmosphere of terrible calm in which Euphiletus represents himself not as outraged individual but as quasijudicial representative of the city (this point is well made by Carey, p. 62).

1. ON THE DEATH OF ERATOSTHENES: DEFENSE SPEECH

[1] I should be very glad, gentlemen, if in this case you are the same sort of judges towards me as you would be towards yourselves, if you had suffered what I have. For I know full well that if you held the same opinions about others as you do about yourselves, there would not be a single one of you who would not be angry at what has happened; instead, you would all regard as trivial the penalties for those who do things like this. [2] Indeed, this verdict would be shared not only by you, but throughout Greece: this is the only crime for which both democracy and oligarchy give the same right of revenge to the powerless against the most powerful, so that the lowliest citizen has the same position as the greatest. Clearly therefore, gentlemen, everybody believes this is the most terrible outrage. [3] I am sure you all agree about the level of the penalty. Nobody rates the matter so lightly as to think that those responsible for such offenses ought to be pardoned or that they deserve only a trivial punishment. [4] As far as I can see, gentlemen, my job is to demonstrate the following: that Eratosthenes committed adultery with my wife; that he corrupted her, disgraced my children, and humiliated me by entering my house; that there was no prior hostility between us except for this; and that I did not do what I did for the sake of money, to become rich instead of poor, or for any other reward except for the vengeance permitted by law. [5] So I shall tell you everything I did from the beginning, leaving nothing

out, but telling the truth. This in my opinion will be my only refuge, if I can tell you everything that happened.

[6] After I decided to get married, men of Athens, and brought my bride home, for a while my attitude was not to trouble her too much but not to let her do whatever she wanted either. I watched her as best I could and gave her the proper amount of attention. But from the moment my son was born, I began to have full confidence in her and placed everything in her hands, reckoning that this was the best relationship.[1] [7] In those early days, men of Athens, she was the best of women: a good housekeeper, thrifty, with a sharp eye on every detail. But my mother's death was the cause of all my troubles. [8] For it was while attending her funeral that my wife was seen by this fellow and eventually corrupted by him: he kept an eye out for the slave girl who did the shopping, put forward proposals, and seduced her.

[9] Now before continuing, gentlemen, I need to explain something. My house has two stories, and in the part with the women's rooms and the men's rooms, the upper floor is the same size as the floor below.[2] When our baby was born, his mother nursed him. To avoid her risking an accident coming down the stairs whenever he needed washing, I took over the upstairs rooms, and the women moved downstairs. [10] Eventually we became so used to this arrangement that my wife would often leave me to go down and sleep with the baby, so that she could nurse it and stop it crying. Things went on in this way for a long time, and I never had the slightest suspicion; indeed, I was so naive that I thought my wife was the most respectable woman in Athens.[3]

[11] Some time later, gentlemen, I returned unexpectedly from the country. After dinner, the baby began to cry and was restless. (He was being deliberately teased by the slave girl, to make him do this, because the man was inside the house: I later found out everything.) [12] So I

---

[1] Or "reckoning that our relationship was as secure as it could be" (lit. "was the strongest").

[2] Or perhaps, "the upper floor (i.e., the women's rooms) is the same size as the lower floor (i.e., the men's)."

[3] Lit. "in the *polis* (city)," but the word includes the surrounding countryside as well as the urban center and does not necessarily imply that they live in the city itself.

told my wife to go down and feed the baby, to stop it crying. At first she refused, as if glad to see me home after so long. When I became angry and ordered her to go, she said, "You just want to stay here and have a go at the slave girl. You had a grab at her once before when you were drunk." [13] I laughed at this, and she got up and left. She closed the door behind her, pretending to make a joke out of it, and bolted it.[4] I had no suspicions and thought no more of it, but gladly went to bed, since I had just returned from the country. [14] Towards morning, she came and unlocked the door. I asked her why the doors had creaked during the night, and she claimed that the baby's lamp had gone out, so she had to get it relit at our neighbors'. I believed this account and said no more. But I noticed, gentlemen, that she had put on makeup, even though her brother had died less than a month earlier. Even so, I did not say anything about it but left the house without replying.

[15] After this, gentlemen, there was an interval of some time, during which I remained completely unaware of my misfortunes. But then an old woman came up to me. She had been secretly sent, or so I later discovered, by a lady whom this fellow had seduced. This woman was angry and felt cheated, because he no longer visited her as before, so she watched until she found out why. [16] The old woman kept an eye out and approached me near my house. "Euphiletus," she said, "please do not think that I am being a busybody by making contact with you. The man who is humiliating you and your wife is an enemy of ours as well. Get hold of your slave girl, the one who does the shopping and waits on you, and torture her: you will discover everything. It is," she continued, "Eratosthenes of the deme Oe who is doing this. He has seduced not only your wife but many others as well. He makes a hobby[5] of it." [17] She said this, gentlemen, and left. At once I became alarmed. Everything came back into my mind, and I was filled with suspicion. I remembered how I had been locked in my room, and how that night both the door of the house and the

---

[4] It is not linguistically clear whether this is a lock from which she can remove the key, or a bolt which remains on the outside of the door, and both are archaeologically attested. A bolt (unlike a key) would imply that she is concerned simply to prevent her husband getting at the slave girl, rather than the slave girl getting in.

[5] *Technē,* lit. "craft-skill," almost "profession."

courtyard door had creaked (which had never happened before), and how I had noticed that my wife had used makeup. All these things flashed into my mind, and I was full of suspicion. [18] I returned home, and told the slave girl to come shopping with me,[6] but I took her to the house of one of my friends and told her that I had found out everything that was going on in my house. "So it is up to you," I said, "to choose the fate you prefer: either to be flogged and put out to work in the mill, and never have any rest from such sufferings; or else to admit the whole truth and suffer no punishment, but instead to be forgiven for your crimes. No lies now: I want the full truth." [19] At first she denied it and told me to do whatever I pleased, because she knew nothing. But when I mentioned the name Eratosthenes to her and declared that this was the man who was visiting my wife, she was astonished, realizing that I knew everything. She immediately fell at my knees and made me promise she would suffer no harm. [20] She admitted,[7] first, how he had approached her after the funeral, and then how she had eventually acted as his messenger, and how my wife had in the end been won over, and the various ways he had entered the house, and how during the Thesmophoria,[8] when I was in the country, my wife had attended the shrine with his mother. She gave me a full and accurate account of everything else that had happened. [21] When she had finished, I said, "Make sure that nobody at all hears about this, otherwise nothing in our agreement will be binding. I want you to show me them in the act. I don't want words; I want their actions to be clearly proved, if it is really true." She agreed to do this.

[22] After this there was an interval of four or five days, as I shall bring clear evidence to show.[9] But first, I want to tell you what

---

[6] Lit. "to accompany me to the Agora," as in 1.16.

[7] Lit. "accused," which has a slightly stronger flavor and prefigures the way in which Euphiletus constructs himself as the judge of Eratosthenes' case at 1.26.

[8] A women's festival in honor of Demeter, celebrated in the autumn. Men were excluded, and women camped out together for three days (as in Aristophanes' *Women at the Thesmophoria*).

[9] He does not in fact produce such evidence, nor is it obvious why he should wish to do so. Many scholars suspect that some words have dropped out of the text between "days" and "as."

happened on that last day. There is a man called Sostratus, who was a close friend of mine. I happened to meet him, at sunset, on his way back from the country. I knew that if he arrived at that time, he would find none of his friends at home, so I invited him to dine with me. We returned to my house, went upstairs, and had supper. [23] After he had had a good meal, he left, and I went to bed. Eratosthenes entered the house, gentlemen, and the slave girl woke me at once to say he was inside. I told her to take care of the doors, and going downstairs, I went out silently. I called at the houses of various friends: some I discovered were out, and others were not even in town.[10] [24] I gathered as many as I could find at home and came back. We collected torches from the nearest shop and made our way in; the door was open, because it had been kept ready by the slave girl. We burst open the door of the bedroom, and those of us who were first to enter saw him still lying next to my wife. The others, who came later, saw him standing on the bed naked. [25] I struck him, gentlemen, and knocked him down. I twisted his arms behind him and tied them, and asked why he had committed this outrage against my house by entering it. He admitted his guilt, and begged and entreated me not to kill him but to accept compensation. [26] I replied, "It is not I who will kill you, but the law of the city. You have broken that law and have had less regard for it than for your own pleasure. You have preferred to commit this crime against my wife and my children rather than behaving responsibly and obeying the laws."

[27] So it was, gentlemen, that this man met the fate which the laws prescribe for those who behave like that. He was not snatched from the street, nor had he taken refuge at the hearth, as my opponents claim. How could he have done so? It was inside the bedroom that he was struck, and he immediately fell down, and I tied his hands. There were so many men in the house that he could not have escaped, and he did not have a knife or a club or any other weapon with which to repel those coming at him. [28] I am sure you realize, gentlemen, that men who commit crimes never admit that their enemies are tell-

---

[10] The word literally means "in the deme," and could equally well be used whether Euphiletus lives in the city of Athens or in an outlying village.

ing the truth, but instead they themselves tell lies and use tricks to provoke their hearers to anger against the innocent.

So, first of all, please read out the law.

[LAW]

[29] He did not dispute it, gentlemen. He admitted his guilt, he begged and pleaded not to be killed, and he was ready to pay money in compensation. But I did not accept his proposal. I reckoned that the law of the city should have greater authority; and I exacted from him the penalty that you yourselves, believing it to be just, have established for people who behave like that.

Will my witnesses to these facts please come forward.

[WITNESSES]

[30] Read me this law also, the one from the inscribed stone on the Areopagus.[11]

[LAW]

You hear, gentlemen, how the court of the Areopagus (to which the ancestral right of judging homicide cases belongs, as has been reaffirmed in our own days) has expressly decreed that a man is not to be convicted of homicide if he captures an adulterer in bed with his wife and exacts this penalty from him. [31] Indeed, the lawgiver was so convinced that this is appropriate in the case of married women that he has established the same penalty in the case of concubines, who are less valuable. Clearly if he had had a more severe penalty available in the case of married women, he would have imposed it; but in fact he was unable to find a more powerful sanction than death to use in their case, so he decided the penalty should be the same as in the case of concubines.

Read me this law as well.

---

[11] The Areopagus (consisting of former Archons) was the most famous Athenian homicide court. For the identification of the law cited here with the one quoted in Dem. 23.53, see the Introduction.

[LAW]

[32] You hear, gentlemen: if anybody indecently assaults a free man or boy, he shall pay twice the damages; if he assaults a woman (in those categories where the death sentence is applicable), he shall be liable to the same penalty. Clearly therefore, gentlemen, the lawgiver believed that those who commit rape deserve a lighter penalty than those who seduce: he condemned seducers to death, but for rapists he laid down double damages. [33] He believed that those who act by violence are hated by the people they have assaulted, whereas those who seduce corrupt the minds of their victims in such a way that they make other people's wives into members of their own families rather than of their husbands'. The victim's whole household becomes the adulterer's, and as for the children, it is unclear whose they are, the husband's or the seducer's. Because of this the lawgiver laid down the death penalty for them.[12]

[34] In my case, gentlemen, the laws have not only acquitted me of crime but have actually commanded me to exact this penalty. It is for you to decide whether the law is to be powerful or worthless. [35] In my opinion, every city enacts its laws in order that when we are uncertain in a situation, we can go to them to see what to do, and in such cases the law commands the victims to exact this penalty. [36] So I ask you now to reach the same verdict as the law does. If not, you will be giving adulterers such immunity that you will encourage burglars to call themselves adulterers too. They will realize that if they describe adultery as their object and claim that they have entered somebody else's house for this purpose, nobody will dare touch them. Everyone will know that we must say good-bye to the laws on adultery and take notice only of your verdict—which is the sovereign authority over all the city's affairs.

[37] Please consider, gentlemen: my opponents accuse me of having ordered my slave girl on the night in question to fetch the young man. In my view, gentlemen, I should have been acting within my rights in capturing in any way possible the man who had corrupted my wife. [38] Admittedly if I had sent her to fetch him when words

[12] The argument here is discussed in the Introduction at n. 5.

alone had been spoken but no act had been committed, then I would have been acting unlawfully; but if I had captured him, whatever my methods, when he had already done everything and had repeatedly entered my house, then I would regard myself as acting properly. [39] But consider how they are lying about this as well, as you can see easily from the following argument. As I told you before, gentlemen, Sostratus is a close friend of mine. He met me around sunset on his way home from the country, he had dinner with me, and when he had eaten well, he left. [40] But just think for a moment, gentlemen. If I had been laying a trap that night for Eratosthenes, would it not have been better for me to dine somewhere else with Sostratus, instead of bringing him back home for dinner and so making the adulterer less likely to risk entering my house? And secondly, does it seem plausible to you that I would send away the man who had had dinner with me, and remain behind alone and unaccompanied, instead of asking him to stay and help me punish the adulterer? [41] Then again, gentlemen, do you not think I would have sent messages during the day to my acquaintances, asking them to meet at a friend's house—whichever was nearest—rather than running around during the night the moment I heard the news, not knowing who I would find at home and who would be out? In fact I called on Harmodius[13] and on another man, who were out of town (I had no reason to expect this), and I found others not at home; but I went around and gathered everybody I could. [42] And yet if I had planned it all in advance, do you not think I would have gathered some slaves together and warned my friends: then I could have entered the bedroom with complete safety (how was I to know whether he too might be armed?), and could have exacted the penalty with the maximum number of witnesses? But in fact I knew nothing of what was going to happen that night, so I took with me those I could find.

My witnesses to these facts will please come forward.

---

[13] Harmodius cannot be identified, but he has the same name as one of the two tyrannicides (Harmodius and Aristogeiton, who became popular heroes following their assassination of Hipparchus in 514 BC), and since the name is rarely attested outside this family, it is possible that this is a descendant.

[WITNESSES]

[43] You have heard the witnesses, gentlemen. Examine the affair in your own minds as follows. Ask yourselves if there had ever been any enmity between Eratosthenes and myself except for this. You will not find any. [44] He had not maliciously brought a public prosecution against me, he had not tried to expel me from the city, he had not brought a private prosecution, and he did not know of any offense of mine that I would kill him for, out of fear that it would become public knowledge. And if I had succeeded, I had no hope of receiving any money (some people do admittedly plot the deaths of others for this purpose). [45] So far from there being any dispute or drunken brawl or other disagreement between us, I had never even seen the man before that night. What was I hoping for, then, by running so great a risk—if I had not in reality suffered the most terrible of injuries at his hands? [46] And why did I commit this impious act after summoning witnesses, given that if I had wanted to make away with him illegally, I could have prevented them all from knowing about it?

[47] So, gentlemen, I do not accept that this penalty was exacted privately on my own behalf. Instead, it was for the sake of the whole city. If men who commit this sort of offense see the rewards that await such crimes, they will be less eager to commit them against other people—provided they see you holding fast to the same opinion. [48] Otherwise, it would be much better to erase the existing laws and enact others, which would impose penalties on men who guard their own wives, and grant total impunity to those who commit offenses against married women. [49] It would be far more just to do this than to let citizens be trapped by the laws: for the laws instruct the man who catches an adulterer to treat him in any way he pleases, whereas the court turns out to be far more dangerous to the victims than to the men who break the law and dishonor other people's wives. [50] For I am now on trial for my life, my property, and everything else—simply because I obeyed the laws of the city.

2. FUNERAL SPEECH

INTRODUCTION

Thucydides reports the wartime custom of burying publicly at an annual ceremony those Athenians who had died in combat, and of commissioning a leading citizen to deliver a public funeral speech in their honor (Thuc. 2.34), a custom that Thucydides himself made famous through the speech in praise of Athens itself which he puts into the mouth of Pericles at the end of the first year of the Peloponnesian War in 431/0 BC (Thuc. 2.35–46). Lysias 2 purports to be the equivalent speech delivered during one of the years of the Corinthian War. This war had broken out in 395 BC, when Athens joined the former Spartan allies Corinth, Argos, and Thebes in rebellion against Sparta, and was to drag on until 387, when the Spartans gained the support of Persia and settled the stalemate in their favor.

Virtually all of Lysias' speeches are written as if for a trial, though some may not actually have been delivered. Lysias 2 is one of only two fully preserved speeches that has not even a superficial connection with a lawcourt.[1] The style of the speech is like nothing else in the corpus, but this may be partly a question of what was felt appropriate to the genre of funeral speeches. We possess about half a dozen such speeches,[2] and they have attracted considerable interest from recent

[1] Lys. 8 is the other one. Lys. 33 and 34 also have no connections with the lawcourt, but they are preserved only in part, as quoted by Dionysius of Halicarnassus. Dionysius' difficulties in finding an Assembly speech by Lysias are discussed in the Introduction to Lys. 34.

[2] Apart from this speech, the others are the one attributed to Pericles by Thucydides (above); a short fragment of a speech by Gorgias (Fr. 6 D–K, trans. by

scholars. In particular, an important book by Loraux (see below) has drawn attention to the way in which the dead are praised in these speeches in terms of their ancestry, with certain stock episodes being used repeatedly to glorify the heroic past of Athens, as if what is being constructed within the genre is a semiofficial patriotic history of Athens designed for an Athenian audience. Given that few modern readers are able to take this seriously as an account of the Athenian past, one way of reading this speech is to compare it with others within the genre, in order to distinguish the individual slant that is being put on the common themes. Another is to look at the common themes themselves and to consider why this is the version of the past that is becoming semiofficial.

Modern interpreters of Lysias working on this speech have traditionally focused on the question of authenticity, but there has been a tendency to compress the question of whether the speech is by Lysias with the question of whether it was written for the occasion it envisions. It presumably cannot have been written for Lysias to deliver in person, because Lysias was not an Athenian citizen, and only a citizen would be invited to deliver the public funeral speech. Similarly, it seems unlikely that it can have been written by Lysias for somebody else to deliver, because the sort of leading citizen who was commissioned to deliver the speech would presumably have written it himself. One possibility is that the speech was written and delivered by somebody else, and subsequently misattributed to Lysias, but it is hard to see why a speech by a leading politician would have circulated without ever being attributed to the name of its real author. It may therefore be better to see Lysias 2 as a rhetorical exercise or a pamphlet rather than a genuine speech, intended all along to be read rather than spoken. It was quite possibly written around the end of the 390s: there is nothing in it that need have been written later, and ancient writers are not usually good at avoiding anachronism.

M. Gagarin and P. Woodruff, *Early Greek Political Thought from Homer to the Sophists* [Cambridge, 1995], at pp. 202–203); what seems to be a parody of a speech placed by Socrates (in Plato's *Menexenus*) in the mouth of Artemisia; a rather turgid one attributed to Demosthenes (Dem. 60); and some papyrus fragments of a famous speech by Hyperides following the first year of the Lamian War in 322 (the only one that focuses on an individual, the general Leosthenes).

One of the most interesting features of the speech is the treatment of the democratic restoration of 403/2: other speeches in the corpus (e.g., Lys. 13, 26, 31) make clear that the restoration was followed by considerable bitterness against former supporters of the oligarchy, and the picture painted here of magnanimous democrats (Lys. 2.61–65) is something of a whitewash. Particularly striking is the prominent place given to the role played by metics in assisting the democratic restoration (Lys. 2.66). It is dangerous to hang too much on this single passage, but this could be read as an indication that the speech is indeed by Lysias himself, given that it is difficult to see anybody else at this date whose brief was to say nice things about metics.

The best general treatment of funeral speeches, with discussion of many of the historical allusions, is N. Loraux, *The Invention of Athens: The Funeral Oration in the Classical City* (Cambridge, Mass., 1986, Eng. trans. [by A. Sheridan] of 1981 French original). Also useful (especially for its table of parallels between Lys. 2 and other funeral speeches) is J. E. Ziolkowski, "National and Other Contrast in the Athenian Funeral Speeches," in J. E. Ziolkowski and H. A. Khan, eds., *The Birth of the European Identity: The Europe-Asia Contrast in Greek Thought, 490–322 BC* (Bari, 1993), 1–35.

2. FUNERAL SPEECH FOR THOSE WHO ASSISTED THE CORINTHIANS

[1] My fellow-mourners: if I thought it possible to describe in words the merits of the men who are lying here, I would make that a criticism of those who assigned me to speak with only a few days' notice. But in fact the whole of time would not be enough for any man to prepare a speech that equals the achievements of the dead. This, it seems to me, is why the city provides for those who are to speak here by giving them short notice. The idea is that in this way they would most readily gain the sympathy of their hearers. [2] Although my speech is about the dead, nevertheless I am competing not against their achievements but against those who have previously delivered speeches about them. The merits of the dead have created an abundant resource both for those who are able to act and for those who are willing to speak. As a result, many fine things have been said about them by previous speakers, but much has been omitted, and

enough remains for the speeches of their successors. The dead were experienced in every land and sea, and their merits are sung among all men everywhere by those who regret their own weaknesses. [3] I shall first recount the dangers faced by our ancestors long ago, relying on tradition for the memory, for it is right that all men should remember our ancestors as well. We should sing their praises in ceremonial songs; we should speak of them in the memories of good men; we should honor them on occasions like the present; and we should bring up the living to know the achievements of the dead.

[4] The Amazons, daughters of Ares, lived long ago by the river Thermodon.[1] They were the only ones among their neighbors to have iron weapons, and they were the first human beings to ride on horseback. On this basis—by surprise and by the inexperience of their opponents—they captured those who fled, and escaped those who pursued. They were regarded as males by their courage rather than females by their nature; they seemed superior to men in spirit, not inferior to them in body. [5] While they were ruling over many races, and had enslaved those who lived near them, they heard great things about this land of ours. Gathering together the most powerful tribes, thanks to their high reputation and widespread ambition, they attacked our city. But when they encountered brave men, they displayed spirits to match their bodies; and while they gained a reputation opposite to their previous one, they gave the appearance of being women more because of the danger they faced than because of their women's bodies. [6] They alone were given no chance to learn from their errors and make better plans for the future; nor could they return home and tell about their own disasters or about our ancestors' merits. They perished here and paid the penalty for their folly. They made the memory of this city immortal on account of its achievements; they left their own homeland without a name on account of their disaster. They coveted unjustly what was not theirs, so it was only just that they lost what was their own.

[7] When Adrastus and Polynices campaigned against Thebes and

---

[1] The legend of the Amazon invasion of Greece, and their defeat by the Athenian hero Theseus, is frequently mentioned by Isocrates (e.g., Isoc. 4.68–70, 7.75, and 12.193) and is referred to in passing in Aeschylus, *Eumenides* 685–690. For a detailed but much later version of the story, see Plutarch, *Theseus* 26–28. (Thermodon is a river in Pontus, now northeastern Turkey.)

were defeated, the Thebans would not allow the bodies to be buried.[2] The Athenians believed that if these men had done anything wrong, they had paid the ultimate penalty by dying; but that the gods below were not receiving their dues, and the gods above were being treated with impiety because the sacred rites were being polluted. First they sent heralds and asked to take up the bodies, [8] believing that honorable men should punish their enemies while alive, but that to display courage at the expense of dead bodies was the sign of those who lack self-confidence. They could not get what they requested, so they made war against Thebes, even though no previous quarrel existed between the Thebans and themselves. They did not do this to please those Argives who were still alive, [9] but because they believed that those who died in war deserved to receive the customary rites. So they risked danger from one side on behalf of both: on behalf of the Thebans, so that they should no longer display arrogance towards the gods by wronging the dead; on behalf of the Argives, so that they should not return home prematurely without the honor due to their fathers, without proper Greek rites, and without the common hope of burial. [10] This was their intent, and since they reckoned the fortunes of war to be common to all men, they made many enemies, and they defeated them in battle because they had justice as their ally. They were not stirred up by success to desire a greater punishment for the Thebans. Instead, in response to impiety they displayed their own merits. They collected the prize for which they had come, the bodies of the Argives, and they buried them in their own territory at Eleusis. That was how they treated those of the Seven against Thebes who had died.

[11] Some time later, after Heracles had vanished from among men, his children were fleeing from Eurystheus.[3] They were driven away by all the other Greeks, who were ashamed to do this but afraid of Eurystheus' power, and they came to our city and sat down at the altars as suppliants. [12] Despite Eurystheus' demands, the Athenians refused to surrender them. They respected the bravery of Heracles more than they feared the danger to themselves. They believed they should fight for the weaker on the side of justice rather than please

[2] What follows is the story of the Seven against Thebes, which was popular in Greece and is the subject of two surviving tragedies (Aeschylus' *Seven against Thebes* and Euripides' *Phoenician Women*).

[3] The story in this paragraph forms the subject of Euripides' *Children of Heracles*.

those in power by surrendering those they had wronged. [13] Eurystheus, together with those who at that time controlled the Peloponnese, launched a campaign. The Athenians, however, did not waver even when facing danger, but kept to their previous resolve, even though they had received no personal benefits from the children's father and could not know what kind of men they would turn out to be. [14] They had no previous quarrel with Eurystheus and stood to gain no advantage except to their reputation. Nevertheless, they did what they thought just, and risked great dangers on the boys' behalf. They pitied those who were being wronged, in the belief that they deserved help. They hated the oppressors and wanted to hinder them. They believed that free men do not act unwillingly, that just men help those who are wronged, and that courageous men fight and die, if necessary, for both these principles. [15] Such was the state of mind on both sides that Eurystheus and his followers did not look to acquire anything as a gift, whereas the Athenians insisted that Eurystheus, himself a suppliant, had no right to drag away those who were suppliants at Athens. They drew up their forces in battle and defeated his army, which had come from the whole Peloponnese. They gave bodily security to the sons of Heracles and also freed their minds from fear, decorating them for their father's bravery with a garland that consisted of the dangers they themselves had undertaken. [16] Thus the boys had a much happier life than their father. He brought many benefits to humanity in general, and filled his life with toil and victory and honor; but although he punished other wrongdoers, he could not defeat Eurystheus, who was his enemy and had wronged him personally. His sons, on the other hand, on one single day saw themselves rescued and their enemies punished—and all because of our city.

[17] It was fitting for our ancestors to be single-minded in their fight for justice, because the origin of their life was just. The ancestors of other communities came together from all sorts of places, casting out their predecessors and living on land not originally their own. Our ancestors, on the other hand, were born from the soil, so they had the same land of Attica as both mother and fatherland.[4] [18] They were

[4] The idea of autochthony—that is, that Attica belonged to the Athenians not because their ancestors had conquered it (as the Spartans' ancestors had conquered Laconia) but because they had been born from its soil—was an important part of Athenian mythology (cf., e.g., Thuc. 2.36.1 and Dem. 60.4).

the first people, and at that time the only ones, to drive out their autocratic rulers and to establish democracy, in the belief that the greatest harmony is for everybody to be free. They allowed everybody to share in the hopes that result from danger, and governed themselves with freedom of spirit. [19] They honored the good, and punished the bad, according to the law. They thought that to be controlled forcibly by each other was proper for animals, but that humans should determine justice by means of law and persuade by using reason: they should be ruled by law and taught by reason, and their actions should serve both ends.[5]

[20] The ancestors of those who lie here achieved many fine and wonderful things, by the nobility of their nature and their spirit alike. But their descendants, by their own bravery, have left many great and ever-memorable trophies all over the world. They were the only ones to undergo dangers against countless thousands of barbarians, on behalf of the whole of Greece. [21] For the King of Asia[6] was not content with what he already possessed but wanted to enslave Europe as well, and he sent an army five hundred thousand strong. They believed that if they could either make our city a willing ally or force it unwillingly, they would easily gain control of the rest of the Greeks. So they sailed to Marathon, thinking that this would leave our ancestors very short of allies, if they could force the issue while Greece was still divided how best to repel the invaders. [22] In addition, because of previous actions[7] they retained the following opinion of the Athenians: that if they attacked any other city, they would have to fight not just that city but Athens as well, because the Athenians would eagerly come to the rescue of those who were being wronged. On the other hand, they thought that if they came here first, the rest of the Greeks would not

---

[5]The Greek sentence contains complex wordplay between two contrasting pairs of words: *nomos* (here broadly "law," though in other contexts also meaning "custom," as in 2.25) and *logos* ("rationality"); and *logos* (also meaning "word") and *ergon* ("action"). It is impossible to capture the wordplay in English, as a result of which the sentiments may appear even more labored than they are in Greek.

[6]Darius, in 490 BC. For an account of these events, see Herod. 6.42–140.

[7]The Athenians (together with the people of Eretria, who are not mentioned here) had helped in the early stages of the Ionian Revolt against Persia in ca. 498 BC (Herod. 5.97–103).

dare defend another city, if this meant creating open hostilities with Persia. [23] That was their plan, but our ancestors took no account of military danger. They reckoned that among brave men, a glorious death leaves behind an immortal fame. They did not fear the massive number of their opponents but put greater confidence in their own ability. They were ashamed that the barbarians were within their territory, and so did not stay to learn whether any allies would help them. Rather than owe their safety to others, they preferred the rest of the Greeks to be in debt to them. [24] So they marched out, few against many, all in agreement on this point: that death could be shared with everybody but bravery only with a few; because of death, the lives they possessed were not their own, but the fame they would leave behind because of the dangers that they faced was theirs and theirs alone. They believed that those who could not win on their own would not be able to win with the help of allies either. If defeated, they would only die a little earlier than the others; if victorious, they would make the others free. [25] They proved to be brave men, who did not spare their own bodies and were not faint-hearted in the pursuit of excellence. They respected their own laws[8] more than they feared danger at the hands of the enemy. They put up a trophy on behalf of Greece over the barbarians, who had left their own country and invaded another in pursuit of wealth, violating the boundaries of the land. [26] They responded to the danger so quickly that the same messengers announced to the rest of the Greeks both the arrival of the barbarians and the victory of our ancestors. None of the others had time to fear the coming danger, but when they heard about it, they rejoiced in their own freedom. In view of deeds performed long ago, therefore, it is not surprising that even today their merit is praised by all men as if their actions were still new.

[27] Later on,[9] Xerxes King of Asia came to despise Greece. He was cheated of his hope, humiliated by events, oppressed by disaster, and angry at those responsible. He had not previously known a reverse and had not encountered brave men. After considerable preparation, he came here ten years later, leading twelve hundred ships and a land

---

[8] The Greek word *nomos* means "custom" as well as "law."

[9] In 480–479. These events are treated in detail in Herod. 7.4–9.122.

army of such enormous size that it would be a massive task to list even the nations that followed him. [28] The clearest evidence of their number is this: although it would have been possible for his army to cross from Asia to Europe on a thousand ships at the narrowest part of the Hellespont, he refused to do that, because he thought it would waste too much of his time. [29] Instead, he showed contempt for the natural order, for the affairs of the gods, and for human intentions. He constructed a path across the sea, and forced sailing to take place on land, by yoking together the Hellespont and cutting a trench through Athos.[10] This was done without resistance, as some obeyed involuntarily whereas others voluntarily turned traitor. The former were unable to defend themselves, and the latter were won over by bribes: in both cases fear and profit corrupted them. [30] When they saw that this was the condition of Greece, the Athenians embarked on their ships to help the Greeks at Artemisium, while the Spartans and some of their allies marched to Thermopylae, hoping they could block the road because of the narrowness of the pass. [31] The battles took place at the same time, and the Athenians were victorious by sea. As for the Spartans, they did not lack spirit, but were betrayed by their small numbers, and by those who they thought would protect them and for whom they were running the risks. They were not defeated by their opponents but died where they were drawn up in the battle line. [32] In this way the one group suffered misfortune, but the others gained control of the pass, and they marched on Athens. When our ancestors heard about the Spartan disaster, they were in two minds about the situation facing them. They knew that if they met the barbarians on land, their opponents could sail with a thousand ships and capture an empty city. If, however, they embarked on their triremes, the city would be captured by the land army. They could not both defend themselves and provide adequate protection. [33] There were two proposals: either they would have to abandon the fatherland, or they could join the barbarians and enslave the Greeks. They decided that freedom accompanied by bravery and poverty and exile was better

[10] The reference is to two of Xerxes' most celebrated preparations for his invasion: the building of a bridge of boats across the Hellespont (Herod. 7.33–37) and the cutting of a canal across the isthmus of Athos (Herod. 7.22–24).

than the enslavement of their fatherland with wealth and shame. For the sake of Greece they abandoned their city, so that they could confront each of the dangers in turn rather than both at once. [34] They sent their wives and children over to Salamis out of danger, and there they assembled their allies' fleet. Not many days later, the barbarians' land army and fleet arrived. Could anybody have seen it without fear?—so great and terrible a danger was faced by our city for the freedom of the Greeks. [35] What was in the mind of people who looked on the men in those ships, with danger pressing and no assurance of their safety? What was in the minds of those who were about to fight at sea for their friends and for the prize of Salamis? [36] Against them in every direction was drawn up such a mass of the enemy that to contemplate their own death was the least of the evils facing them: but the greatest calamity was what they expected their people to suffer if the barbarians triumphed. [37] Facing such uncertainty, they must have greeted each other frequently, and perhaps they lamented their own fate. They knew their ships were few, they saw the enemy's vast fleet, and they understood that Athens had been abandoned, that Attica was being ravaged and was full of the barbarians, that the sanctuaries were on fire, and that all these terrible things were happening close at hand. [38] Meanwhile, they heard the battle hymns of the Greeks and the barbarians mingled together, the cheering of both sides, and the noise of ships being damaged. They saw the sea full of bodies, with many wrecked ships sinking, both friendly and hostile. For a long time the battle was evenly matched: now they seemed to be victorious and safe, now defeated and destroyed. [39] In their fear, they evidently thought they saw many things they did not see, and heard many things they did not hear.[11] How they prayed to the gods and reminded them of their sacrifices! What cries of pity for children, of longing for women, and of mourning for fathers and mothers![12] What accounts of future evils, if things should turn out badly! [40] Which of the gods would not have pitied them because of the great dangers? Which mortals would not have wept? Who would

---

[11] The reference is presumably to the types of apparitions reported in Herod. 8.84, and Plutarch, *Themistocles* 15.

[12] Or "cries for pity from children, of longing from women, and of mourning from fathers and mothers."

not have admired them for their fortitude? They vastly exceeded all other men in courage, both in their counsels and in the perils of war—for they abandoned their city, embarked on ships, and drew up their spirits (few as they were) against the hosts of Asia. [41] Victorious in the sea battle, they showed everybody that it is better with few men to run risks for the sake of freedom, rather than with many to be ruled for the sake of your own slavery. [42] These men accomplished many glorious deeds for the freedom of Greece. Themistocles, their general, was best prepared in thought and action. Their ships outnumbered those of their allies put together, and their men were the most skilled. Which of the other Greeks could have competed with them in planning, in numbers, or in bravery? [43] It was only fair that they received the prize of victory from the Greeks without dispute; it was only reasonable that they obtained a good fortune to match their dangers, and that they displayed their own bravery—genuine and homebred—to the barbarians of Asia.

[44] This was how they performed in the sea battle. By assuming the largest share of the risk, they obtained freedom for the others everywhere through their own bravery. Later on, the Peloponnesians began to build a wall round the Isthmus of Corinth, because they wanted security for themselves. They thought that they were now safe from danger by sea, and were content to overlook the rest of Greece, which was under barbarian control. [45] The Athenians, however, angrily warned them that if they held to this plan they would have to build a wall round the entire Peloponnese: if they themselves were betrayed by the Greeks and so took the side of the barbarians, the latter would not need a thousand ships, and the wall at the Isthmus would be no help to the Peloponnesians, because control of the sea would belong without risk to the Great King. [46] The Peloponnesians heard this, and realized they were committing an injustice and were in error in their plans, whereas what the Athenians were saying was just, and their advice was good. They therefore sent help to Plataea. The majority of their allies deserted their ranks under cover of night because of the number of the enemy, but the Spartans and the people of Tegea repelled the barbarians, and the Athenians and Plataeans fought and overcame all those Greeks who had despaired of freedom and were content with slavery. [47] On that day they achieved the most wonderful end to their previous perils: they estab-

lished freedom securely for Europe. In all their dangers, they gave proof of their own merits: both alone and with others, fighting on foot and at sea, against barbarians and Greeks, they were honored by all—both those who shared their perils and those they opposed—as the leaders of Greece.[13]

[48] Later on,[14] war arose between Greek cities, because of rivalry and envy stemming from previous events. Everybody thought highly of themselves, and each side needed only small grievances as a pretext. The Athenians fought a sea battle against the Aeginetans and their allies, and captured seventy of their triremes. [49] While they were blockading Egypt and Aegina at the same time, and the best of their young men were away in the ships or the land army, the Corinthians and their allies came out in force and occupied Geranea,[15] believing that they would either have an empty territory to invade or force the expedition to return from Aegina. [50] The Athenians had the courage not to recall any of their soldiers, whether far off or close at hand.[16] The older men, and those who were still under age, confident in their own bravery and scornful of their attackers, decided to face the danger on their own, the older men being courageous from experience, and the younger courageous by nature. [51] The former had often displayed their bravery, and the others were copying them; the older ones knew how to give orders, and the younger ones were skilled at obeying them. [52] Under the command of Myronides as general, they marched out to the Megarid. With those who were already losing their

[13] This account of the battle of Plataea in 479 BC is even more pro-Athenian than that of Herodotus (9.25–85), for whom the failure of some allied contingents to take part in the battle is the result of muddled maneuvering rather than desertion.

[14] What follows is an extremely brief version of some of the events in the period 478–431 (for which see Thuc. 1.89–117, itself a summary account). The events mentioned here (in Egypt, against Aegina, and at Megara) all took place around 458–456 BC. It is striking that no mention is made, e.g., of Cimon's victory over the Persians at Eurymedon (ca. 468 BC) or the growth of Athenian power symbolized by the building of the Long Walls linking Athens to Piraeus (ca. 458).

[15] Near Megara (between Athens and Corinth), which at that time was allied with Athens.

[16] I.e., from Egypt ("far off") or from Aegina ("close at hand").

strength and those who had not yet achieved it, they defeated the full force of their enemies, who had decided to invade Athenian territory. Instead, they met them in a different land, [53] and set up a trophy in memory of their accomplishment, which was glorious for them but shameful for their opponents. Some were strong no longer, the others were not yet strong, but both groups showed themselves superior in courage. They returned home with a fine reputation, and some resumed their education, the others their counsel for the time they had left.

[54] It would be hard for one man to recount individually the dangers faced by so many, or to describe in a single day the things achieved throughout the whole period. What speech, what time span, what orator would be sufficient to reveal the bravery of the men who lie here? [55] With their many labors, their famous struggles, their glorious risks, they set Greece free, they proved their fatherland the best, and they ruled the sea for seventy years.[17] [56] They freed their allies from civil strife, refusing to enslave the masses to the few, but enforcing equal shares for all. They did not render their allies weak, but strengthened them too. They proved their own power to be such that the Great King stopped coveting what did not belong to him, but gave up part of what he owned, and feared for what remained his. [57] During that period no triremes sailed out of Asia, no tyrant was installed among the Greeks, and no Greek city was enslaved by the barbarians. This was the level of respect and fear that their bravery inspired among all mankind. This is why they alone deserve to be champions of Greece and leaders of the cities.

[58] They displayed their merits even in times of misfortune. When the fleet was destroyed in the Hellespont[18] (either through the fault of the generals or else as a result of divine intervention), and the disaster that followed overwhelmed both us who suffered it and the rest of the Greeks too, it soon became clear that the power of our city meant the security of Greece. [59] It was under the leadership of others that

---

[17] "Seventy" is an approximation: from the founding of the Athenian naval confederacy in 478 BC to the end of the Peloponnesian War in 404.

[18] At Aegospotami in 405 BC (for which see Xen., *Hellenica* 2.1). This was the battle that decisively lost the Peloponnesian War for Athens. As often in the speeches of Lysias, it is referred to indirectly rather than by name.

the Greeks were defeated at sea by those who had never previously had a fleet.[19] They sailed to the Hellespont and enslaved the Greek cities. Tyrants were established, some as the result of our misfortune, and others following the victory of the barbarians. [60] So Greece should cut its hair in mourning at this tomb, and weep for those who lie here, because the freedom of the Greeks lies buried with their bravery. Greece suffered disaster when it was bereaved of them, but the King of Asia rejoices, because he can deal with other leaders. Slavery has encircled Greece because it is deprived of them. With others leading us, the Great King is filled with a desire to emulate the ambition of his ancestors.[20]

[61] These events have led me to mourn for the whole of Greece, but we should rightly commemorate in private and in public those men who fled from slavery and struggled for justice.[21] Facing all sorts of enemies, they fought for democracy, returning from exile to Piraeus. They were not compelled by law but persuaded by their own noble nature. In new dangers, they copied the ancient bravery of their ancestors, [62] hoping by their own lives to gain a city they could share with the others. They preferred death with freedom to life with slavery, and were no less ashamed at the disasters they had suffered than angry at their enemies. They preferred to die in their own land rather than live in the land of others. They took as their allies the oaths and the agreements,[22] and as their opponents not simply their traditional enemies but also their own citizens. [63] Nevertheless, they did not fear the number of those against them but put their own bodies in danger. They set up a trophy over their enemies and placed the tombs of the Spartans as witnesses of their bravery near this monu-

---

[19] The reference is probably to the victory of the Persian fleet (with tacit Athenian support not mentioned here) over the Spartans at Cnidus in 394 BC.

[20] I.e., the current Great King Artaxerxes, given that he had already regained control of the Greek cities of Asia Minor, is now keen to copy Xerxes and conquer the rest of the Greeks.

[21] This paragraph deals with the civil war of 404/3 and the democratic restoration ("oaths and agreements" at 2.62 is a standard term for the amnesty of 403/2 BC), for which see generally the Introduction to Lys. 12.

[22] See previous note.

ment.[23] Thus they proved that the city was great, not weak, and that it was united, not crippled by strife; and they put up walls to replace those that had been destroyed. [64] Those who returned from exile showed that their counsels were akin to the deeds of those who lie here, in that they decided not to punish their opponents but to rescue the city. Because they could not be defeated, and did not desire more for themselves, they shared their own freedom with those prepared to endure slavery, while themselves refusing to share the slavery of the others. [65] They defended themselves with great and glorious deeds, showing that the city's previous misfortune was not because of its own fault or the enemy's merits. If they were able to return to their land while fighting against fellow-citizens and in the face of the Peloponnesians and other hostile forces, it is clear that united they would easily have defeated them.

[66] These men are respected by all mankind, because of the dangers they faced at Piraeus. But we should remember also to praise the foreigners buried here,[24] who assisted the democracy and fought for our safety. They regarded bravery as their fatherland and made a noble end to their lives. In return, the city gave them official burial and mourning, and allowed them for all time to have the same honors as citizens.

[67] Those who are buried here brought help to the Corinthians when they were wronged by former friends, and became their new allies. The Athenians did not share the attitude of the Spartans, who envied what belonged to the Corinthians; the Athenians pitied them because of the wrong done to them, and, forgetting previous quarrels, placed a high value on existing friendship. Thus they made their own merits clear to the whole of mankind. [68] They had the courage to make Greece great not only by facing danger for their own safety but by dying for the freedom of their enemies: they were fighting against Sparta's allies for the freedom of those allies. If they had been victorious, they would have regarded their opponents as worthy of the same

---

[23] The amnesty of 403 came after some fighting involving not just Athenian oligarchs and democrats but also Spartan forces. Those Spartans who were killed in battle here received honorific burial at Athens.

[24] See the Introduction.

benefits. As it was, they were unlucky, and made the slavery of the Peloponnesians secure. [69] For the latter, given their situation, life was pitiable and death was desirable. The Athenians, however, were enviable in life and in death. They had been schooled in the bravery of their ancestors, and as adults they preserved the glory of their ancestors and displayed their own merits. [70] They were responsible for many benefits for their fatherland, they remedied much of the misfortune suffered by others, and they banished the fighting far from their own territory.

They ended their lives as good men deserve to die, repaying their fatherland with trophies but leaving their parents to grieve. [71] Those who are left alive have every right to miss them, to be sorry for themselves, and to pity their relatives for the rest of their lives. What pleasure remains for them, when men like these are buried?—men who valued everything else less than bravery, who have themselves been deprived of life, who have made their wives widows, who have turned their children into orphans, and who have left their brothers and mothers and fathers desolate. [72] Despite the many terrible things that have happened, I envy their children, for they are too young to know what fathers they have lost. But I pity those who gave birth to them, for they are too old to forget their misfortune. [73] What could be more dreadful than to give birth to children, to bring them up, and then to bury them? To be weakened by old age, to be without friends, without means of livelihood, and without hope? To have previously been envied and now to be pitied for the same reason, and for death to be preferable to life? The braver the dead, the greater the grief of those bereaved. [74] When should they cease from grieving? At times of disaster for the city? But at such times it is reasonable for others also to remember them. At times of general rejoicing? But surely it is right to grieve, when their own children are dead and the living are benefiting from their bravery. Or should it be at private times of danger, when they see their former friends avoiding them in their troubles, and their enemies boasting about the misfortunes they are suffering? [75] The only reward, it seems to me, that we could give those who lie here, would be to value their parents as much as they themselves did, to welcome the children as if we were their parents, and to offer the same support ourselves to their widows as they did when alive. [76] Who is there who deserves our praise more than those who lie here? Who among the living is more rightly appreciated than their relatives, who rejoice in their bravery just as much as others, but who alone have a legitimate share in the misfortunes of their death.

[77] I do not know why we must lament like this, for we were always aware that we ourselves are mortal. So why should we now mourn something which we have been long expecting to suffer? Why should we grieve so at natural misfortunes, since we know that death is the common fate for the best and the worst of men? It does not overlook the wicked, nor does it respect the good, but presents itself equally to everybody. [78] If those who avoid military danger could be immortal for the rest of time, it would be right for the living to mourn the dead forever. As it is, human nature is subject to disease and old age, and the divine power that controls our fate is inexorable. [79] So we should regard as the most blessed of men those who died after facing dangers for all that is greatest and most glorious. They did not surrender their affairs to chance, or await the whims of death, but chose the best of fates. Their memory will never grow old, and their glory is envied by all men. [80] Those who are mourned as mortal in their bodies are praised as immortals for their bravery. They have a state funeral, and in addition, contests of strength, wisdom, and wealth are celebrated in their honor, because those who have died in war deserve to be granted the same honors as the immortals. [81] So then, I declare them happy in their death, and I envy them. These are the only men who I think are better off to have been born,[25] for although they have mortal bodies, nevertheless they have left behind an undying memory of their bravery. All the same, ancient precedents must be upheld. Let us therefore observe ancestral custom and mourn for those who are buried here.

---

[25] An allusion to a famous saying, "not to be born is best" (e.g., Sophocles, *Oedipus at Colonus* 1224–1225).

3. AGAINST SIMON

INTRODUCTION

Lysias 3 and 4 both concern cases of "wounding with premeditation (*pronoia*)," which apparently meant with the intention of killing, or as we might say, "attempted murder." This offense at Athens was subject to the same special procedural rules as murder itself. It was heard not by an ordinary dikastic court but by the Council of the Areopagus, which is the reason for the address "members of the Council" in both speeches. Not only litigants (as in regular trials) but also witnesses had to swear a special oath, the *diōmosia,* and indeed nobody could be called as a witness who had not previously so sworn.[1] There was in addition at least formally an obligation on litigants not to introduce irrelevant material into their speeches, which is made the excuse for limiting the extent of such material here at 3.46. It is not clear on what substantive basis (if any) premeditated wounding was differentiated from simple assault, but there is a hint at 3.28 that possessing a weapon could be represented as a significant criterion.

At issue in Lysias 3 is a quarrel and a series of fights arising out of disputed possession of a live-in rent boy. The latter's name is Theodotus, and he is described as a young man (*meirakion*) from Plataea.[2] The significance of his status as a Plataean is disputed. Plataea had been an ally of Athens, and had offered unique military assistance at

---

[1] The seriousness of the *diōmosia* is mentioned at 3.1, and the ban on calling witnesses who had not so sworn is used to explain the failure to call them at 4.3.

[2] The word *meirakion* denotes a male in his late teens.

the battle of Marathon in 490 BC. When Plataea was destroyed by Thebes in 427 (it was not rebuilt until 386), the Plataeans were offered the special privilege of Athenian citizenship if they chose to register for it.[3] It seems unlikely, however, that Theodotus' family was registered as Athenian citizens, not least because the speaker envisages the possibility of his having to give evidence under torture (3.33), which was never applied to citizens. It is possible that Theodotus was a Plataean slave, but on the other hand he is assumed to be capable independently of entering into an agreement to provide sexual services (3.22–26). More probable is the suggestion that he was part of an informal underclass of free Plataeans who had not bothered to register and whose civic status was indeterminate.

Nothing is known about the parties to the dispute,[4] apart from what can be gleaned from the speech. The speaker is the defendant. He does not give his name, but the claim that he has performed many liturgies implies that he is wealthy (3.47), and his hints about jealousy (3.9) suggest that he is portraying himself as a politically active member of the elite. This may, however, be an exaggeration, because part of his tactic throughout the speech is to simulate embarrassment by portraying himself as too respectable and too old to have wanted to make the matter public by initiating litigation—despite the fact that (according to his own version of events) injuries had been suffered on all sides, and the real provocation had come from his opponent. We have only the speaker's side of the story, but reading between the lines, we may suspect that there was more provocation from the speaker than he claims—for instance, when he placed Theodotus at the house of Lysimachus (3.10), which, as he promptly admits, was close to the house that Simon had rented (3.11).

Simon, the prosecutor, is represented as a much poorer man, but there are hints that he is lying about his wealth (3.21–26). It is continuously implied that Simon has overstated the seriousness of his

---

[3] The continuing existence of this Plataean émigré community, and the status of its *bona fide* members as Athenian citizens, forms the background to Lys. 23.

[4] Nor indeed about any of the various people named incidentally in the text (with the possible exception of Laches; cf. 3.45n).

injuries, and there is a comic flavor in the speaker's account of the fighting at 3.15–18.[5] Simon is also repeatedly characterized as violent and lawless, notably in the one anecdote in the speech that can be dated (3.45): the expedition to Corinth and the battle of Coronea took place in 394 BC, so the speech must be some time (but we do not know how long) after that date.

Two useful recent books that deal with aspects of violence at Athens are N. R. E. Fisher, *Hybris: A Study in the Values of Honour and Shame in Ancient Greece* (Warminster, 1992), and D. Cohen, *Law, Violence and Community in Classical Athens* (Cambridge, 1995). On the details of the speech, see Carey 1989.

3. AGAINST SIMON: DEFENSE SPEECH

[1] I already knew many disreputable things about Simon, members of the Council,[1] but I did not expect him to reach such a level of audacity that he would bring a prosecution, pretending to be the victim in an affair for which he himself deserves to be punished, and that he would appear before you after swearing such a great and serious oath.[2] [2] If anybody else were going to decide my case, I would be very worried about the danger. I know that carefully prepared tricks or mere chance can sometimes produce wholly unexpected outcomes for those on trial, but because I am appearing before you, I remain confident that I shall receive justice. [3] I am particularly upset, members of the Council, at being forced to speak about matters like this in front of you. I put up with mistreatment, because I was ashamed at the prospect of many people knowing all about me. But Simon has put me under such pressure that I shall tell you the full story without hiding anything. [4] If I have done anything wrong, members

---

[5] Another comic touch may be the speaker's exaggeration of the respectability of his own female relatives at 3.6, though a serious point is being made here. Contrast the care taken by the speaker of Dem. 47.38 in a similar situation to check that his opponent was unmarried, and that therefore it was safe for him to enter the house.

[1] The Council of the Areopagus; cf. the Introduction.

[2] The *diōmosia* (the special oath in homicide cases), for which see the Introduction.

of the Council, I do not expect any mercy, but if I can show that I am not guilty of any of the charges that Simon has stated on oath, even though it is obvious that I have behaved rather foolishly towards the young man, given my age, I shall ask you to think no worse of me. You know that desire affects everybody and that the most honorable and restrained man is the one who can bear his troubles most discreetly. In my case Simon here has prevented all this, as I shall show you.

[5] We were both attracted, members of the Council, to Theodotus, a young man from Plataea. I expected to win him over by treating him well, but Simon thought that by behaving arrogantly and lawlessly he would force him to do what he wanted. It would be a lengthy task to list all the wrongs that Theodotus suffered at his hands, but I think you should hear the offenses he committed against me personally. [6] He found out that the young man was staying with me, and came to my house drunk one night. He knocked down the doors and made his way into the women's rooms, where my sister and my nieces were—women who have been brought up so respectably that they are ashamed to be seen even by relatives. [7] Simon, however, reached such a level of arrogance (*hubris*) that he refused to leave, until the men who were present, together with those who had accompanied him, realized that by entering the rooms of young orphaned girls he was behaving unacceptably, and threw him out by force. Far from apologizing for this outrageous conduct, he found out where I was having dinner and did something that was extraordinary and (unless you know his criminal insanity) unbelievable. [8] He called me out of the house, and as soon as I came out, he immediately tried to hit me. I defended myself, so he moved off and threw stones at me. He missed me but hit his own companion Aristocritus with a stone, injuring his forehead. [9] For my part, members of the Council, I felt this was appalling treatment, but as I said earlier, I was embarrassed by the experience and decided to put up with it. I preferred not to bring legal action over these offenses, rather than appear foolish to my fellow-citizens. I knew that the affair would be seen as typical for a criminal like him but that my misfortunes would be laughed at by many of those who are always jealous of anybody who tries to play a responsible role in the city. [10] I was so unsure how to react to his lawlessness, members of the Council, that I decided it would be best to leave

Athens. So I took the young man—you need to know the whole truth—and left the city. When I thought that enough time had passed for Simon to forget him and to be sorry for his earlier offenses, I returned. [11] I went to live in Piraeus,[3] but my opponent immediately heard that Theodotus had returned and was staying with Lysimachus, who lived close to the house he himself had rented. He called on some of his friends to help him. They began eating and drinking, and set a lookout on the roof, so that they could seize the young man when he came out. [12] It was at this moment that I arrived from Piraeus, and since I was passing, I called at Lysimachus' house. After a little while we came out. These men, who were by now drunk, jumped on us. Some of those present refused to join this attack, but Simon here, together with Theophilus, Protarchus, and Autocles, began dragging the young man off. But he threw off his cloak and ran away. [13] I reckoned he would escape, and they would be embarrassed and give up the chase as soon as they met anybody, so I went away by a different route. You see how carefully I tried to avoid them, since I thought everything they did was trouble for myself. [14] So where Simon claims the battle occurred, nobody on either side had his head broken or suffered any other injury. I will produce those who were present as witnesses for you.

[WITNESSES]

[15] Those who were present, members of the Council, have testified that he was the one who intentionally attacked me, not the other way around. After this, the young man ran into a fuller's shop, but they charged in and started to drag him off by force. He began yelling and shouting and calling out for witnesses. [16] Many people rushed up, angry at what was happening, and said that it was disgraceful behavior. My opponents ignored what they said, but beat up Molon the fuller and several others who tried to protect Theodotus. [17] I was walking along by myself when I happened to meet them in front of

---

[3] The timing and purpose of this visit are left vague, perhaps deliberately. Theodotus remains at the house of Lysimachus, which is evidently in Athens itself, and it is striking that this just happens to be close to where Simon is living (see the Introduction).

Lampon's house. I thought it would be a terrible disgrace just to watch this lawless and violent assault on the young man, so I grabbed him. I asked why they were acting so illegally towards him, and they refused to answer. Instead, they let go of the young man and started hitting me. [18] A fight developed, members of the Council. The young man was throwing things at them and defending himself. They were throwing things at us, and were still hitting him, because they were drunk. I was defending myself, and the passersby were all helping us, because we were the ones being attacked. In the course of this melee, we all got our heads cracked. [19] As soon as they saw me after this episode, the others who had joined Simon in this drunken assault asked my forgiveness—not as victims but as wrongdoers. Since then, four years have passed, and at no time has anybody brought a prosecution against me. [20] My opponent Simon, who was the cause of all the trouble, kept the peace for a while because he was afraid. However, when he heard that I had lost some private cases arising from an *antidosis,*[4] he grew contemptuous of me and recklessly forced this trial on me. To show that here too I am telling the truth, I shall produce those who were present as witnesses.

[WITNESSES]

[21] You have heard what happened, both from me and from the witnesses. For my part, members of the Council, I could wish Simon shared my opinions, so that you could hear both of us tell the truth and then easily make the right decision. But since he pays no attention to the oath he has sworn, I shall also try to explain to you the ways in which he has lied. [22] He had the nerve to claim that he gave Theodotus three hundred drachmas and made an agreement with him, and that I plotted to turn the young man against him. But if this were true, he should have called for support from as many witnesses as possible and dealt with the matter according to the laws. [23] However, it

---

[4] A person liable to a liturgy (see the Series Introduction) could challenge a richer man either to undertake it in his place or else to exchange properties with him: this exchange was called an *antidosis.* Details are unclear, but it seems most likely that the speaker accepted the exchange and that disputes then arose about the content or value of the properties.

is clear that he has never done anything of the sort. Instead, in his insolence[5] he beat up both of us, battered down the doors, and entered by night into the presence of freeborn women. You should regard this, members of the Council, as the strongest evidence that he is lying to you. [24] Look at what he said, which is quite unbelievable: he has valued his entire property at two hundred and fifty drachmas[6]—but it would be incredible if he hired somebody to be his boyfriend for more money than he actually possesses. [25] He has become so reckless that it was not enough for him simply to lie about having paid the money, but he even claims to have recovered it. And yet how can it be plausible that at one moment we should have committed the offense of which he has accused us—the alleged plot to defraud him of three hundred drachmas—but that after winning the fight we should have given him back the money, when we had received no formal release from legal charges and were under no obligation to pay? [26] In fact, members of the Council, he has devised and constructed the whole story. He says he paid the money, so that he would not appear to be treating the young man so outrageously in the absence of an agreement. But he claims to have got it back, because it is evident that he never brought a prosecution to claim the money and in fact made no mention of it.

[27] He alleges that I beat him up in front of his house and left him in a terrible state. But it appears that he pursued the young man for more than four stades[7] from his house without any difficulty. More than two hundred people saw him, but he denies it.

[28] He says we came to his house carrying a piece of broken pottery and threatened to kill him—and that this constitutes "premeditation." In my opinion, however, members of the Council, not only you (who are experienced in examining cases like this) but everybody else can easily see he is lying. [29] Would anybody think it credible that in a premeditated plot I came to Simon's house in daytime with

---

[5] Lit., "he committed *hubris,*" a form of aggravated assault so outrageous that it was the subject of a special public prosecution.

[6] It is difficult to imagine a context for this valuation unless Simon also has been involved in a challenge to undertake a liturgy (cf. 3.20n above). It would be interesting to know more about this than Lysias tells us.

[7] About half a mile. (A stade is the length of a running track, about 200 yards.)

the young man, when so many people were gathered there?—unless of course I had so lost my mind that I was eager to fight alone against so many, particularly when I knew he would be pleased to see me at his door. This is the man who came to my house and entered it by force, who dared to search for me without consideration for my sister or my nieces, and who called me out and attacked me after discovering where I was dining. [30] On that occasion, I kept quiet and tried to avoid notoriety, in the belief that his wickedness was simply my misfortune. Can I really (as he claims) have developed a passion for notoriety later on? [31] If the young man were living with him, there would be a certain logic in his false claim that I was compelled by passion to behave in an improbably stupid way. As it is, however, Theodotus was not even on speaking terms with him, but hated him more than anyone and was living with me instead. [32] So does any of you think it credible that I previously sailed away from the city taking the young man with me to avoid fighting with my opponent, but when I came back I took him to Simon's house, where I was bound to run into trouble? [33] And is it credible that I was plotting against him, given that I arrived at his house so unprepared that I could not call on any friends or slaves or anybody else for help—except this child,[8] who could not give me any assistance, but was capable of denouncing me under torture if I did anything illegal? [34] Was I so stupid that while plotting against Simon not only did I not watch to see where he could be found alone, either by night or by day, but in fact went where I was bound to be seen by lots of people and get beaten up—as if I were premeditating against myself, so that my enemies would be most able to carry out their aggravated assault?[9]

[35] Another point to consider, members of the Council, is that simply from the details of the fight it is easy to recognize he is lying. As soon as the young man realized what was happening, he threw off his cloak and ran off. My opponents pursued him, while I left by

---

[8] Only here is Theodotus described as *paidion* (small child) rather than *meirakion* (teenage boy)—presumably an attempt to minimize his age so as to suggest that he was not strong enough to fight with adults. The significance of this passage (with its implication that Theodotus could have been subjected to torture) for determining his civic status is discussed in the Introduction.

[9] *Hubris:* cf. 3.23n above.

a different route. [36] So who should you consider responsible for what happened: those who ran away or those who tried to catch them? In my view, everybody knows that those who are afraid run away, whereas those who pursue want to do something wrong. [37] If my account sounds reasonable, what actually happened was no different. They seized the young man and began dragging him forcibly off the street. When I happened to meet them, I did not touch them but simply grabbed hold of the young man, whereas they continued dragging him off by force and began beating me up. This has been affirmed by witnesses who were present. So it would be terrible if you decide I premeditated this affair, when they have behaved in such a disgraceful and lawless fashion. [38] What would have been my fate if the opposite of what happened had taken place? What if I, together with many friends, had met Simon, and had fought him, beaten him, chased after him, caught him, and then tried to drag him off by force—given that now, when my opponent has behaved like this, I am the one who is facing this trial, in which I risk losing my fatherland and all my property? [39] And here is the strongest and clearest proof: he claims that I have wronged him and plotted against him, but he did not venture to take any legal action [10] for four years. Other people who are in love, and are deprived of what they desire, and are beaten up, immediately seek revenge while they are angry. This man does it much later.

[40] I think it has been clearly demonstrated, members of the Council, that I am not responsible for any of what has happened. My attitude towards disputes like this is that although I had often been abused and assaulted by Simon, and had even had my head broken, nevertheless I did not venture to take legal action. I thought it dreadful to try to throw people out of their fatherland simply because of a quarrel over a boy. [41] I also thought there could be no premeditation in wounding if somebody wounded without intent to kill: for who is so naive that he premeditates long in advance how one of his enemies will be wounded? [11] [42] Clearly our lawgivers also did not think they

---

[10] Lit. "bring an *episkēpsis*" (preliminary denunciation), similarly in 3.40.

[11] A shameless quibble on the meaning of the term "premeditation" (*pronoia*), which denotes the intent not to wound but to kill.

should prescribe exile from the fatherland for people who happen to crack each other's heads while fighting—or else they would have exiled a considerable number. On the other hand, they did establish such severe penalties for those who plot to kill others, and wound but do not succeed in killing. The lawgivers thought that those who have plotted and premeditated ought to pay the penalty: even if they did not succeed, nevertheless they had done their best.[12] [43] And indeed, on many previous occasions you have given the same verdict about premeditation. So it would be a terrible thing if you were to impose such severe penalties, including expulsion of citizens from their fatherland, when people are wounded while fighting because of drunkenness or quarreling or games or insults or over a *hetaira* (courtesan)—the sorts of things that everybody regrets when they recover their senses.

[44] I am very confused about my opponent's character. Being in love and being a sykophant[13] do not seem to me compatible: the first is characteristic of simple people, the second of those who are particularly unscrupulous. I wish I were allowed to demonstrate his wickedness by referring to other events. That way, you would recognize that it would be far more just for him to be on trial for his life than to put other people in danger of exile. [45] I shall omit everything else, but mention one episode I think you should hear about, as evidence of his outrageous audacity. At Corinth, arriving after the battle against the enemy and the expedition to Coronea,[14] he had a fight with Laches his commander and beat him up. When the army marched out in full force, he was judged an insubordinate criminal and was the only Athenian to be publicly censured by the generals.

[46] I could tell you many other things about him, but since it is

---

[12] I.e., "even if the lawgivers did not succeed in preventing all such cases." Or it may refer to the assailants: "Even if they did not succeed (in killing), nevertheless they had done the best they could (to kill)."

[13] Malicious prosecutor.

[14] In 394 (see the Introduction). Laches is described here specifically as Taxiarch (regimental commander, for which cf. 13.79n). He may be the same person as the Laches, father of Melanopus, who is mentioned at Dem. 24.126–127.

unlawful to mention irrelevant material in your court,[15] please bear this point in mind: my opponents are the ones who enter our houses by force; they are the ones who pursue us; they are the ones who drag us off the street by force. [47] Remember this, and deliver a just verdict. Do not let me be unjustly expelled from my fatherland, for which I have faced many dangers and performed many liturgies. I have never been responsible for any harm to the fatherland, nor have any of my ancestors; instead, we have brought many benefits. [48] So I rightly deserve pity from you and from others, not only if I should suffer the fate that Simon intends but simply because I have been compelled by these events to undergo such a trial.

---

[15] For this rule in homicide cases, which the speaker has of course just violated, see the Introduction.

4. ON A PREMEDITATED WOUNDING

INTRODUCTION

Like Lysias 3, this is a speech about attempted murder (lit. "wounding with premeditation"), the rules for which are discussed in the introduction to that speech. There are some notable resemblances between the two speeches. Not only do they both concern love quarrels, but in both speeches there is mention of an *antidosis* (exchange of property in the context of a challenge to undertake a liturgy: 3.20, 4.2), both defendants are alleged to have fought using a piece of broken pottery (3.28, 4.6), and both speakers envisage the possibility of extracting evidence under torture (3.33, 4.10). On the basis of such parallels, it has been suggested that the present speech is not by Lysias but is instead a later rhetorical exercise based on its predecessor. This is possible, but the parallels are neither so striking nor so close as to be conclusive. Broken pottery, for instance, is readily available as an informal weapon in a world where glass was rare, and it is likely to have played a similar role (and to have raised similar questions about premeditation) as the use of broken glass in modern pub fights. On the other hand, whereas in Lysias 3 torture is merely a hypothetical possibility, in this speech it is proposed by the speaker and is made the subject of a formal and extended challenge.

There are also significant differences between the two speeches. Theodotus was a male Plataean, and probably free; here the object of the dispute is a woman and a slave, and what is in dispute is the question of whether she belongs purely to the opponent or (as the speaker claims) jointly to both parties. Whereas Lysias 3 concentrated on the details of the fight and the quarrel, here the dispute is assumed rather than stated, and the focus is on the challenge to provide the slave to give evidence under torture (a challenge which is common in the orators but which is routinely rejected) and the rhetorical advantages to be extracted from the opponent's expected rejection. The result is (at least to modern readers) a less vivid and less satisfactory speech than Lysias 3: there is far less narrative detail here and no indication of date. Some scholars, indeed, believe that Lysias 4 may be incomplete and that the narrative may have been lost, leaving only the concluding proof section of the original speech.

4. CONCERNING A PREMEDITATED WOUNDING: PROSECUTOR AND CLIENT UNKNOWN

[1] The dispute about whether we were reconciled is a remarkable one, members of the Council.[1] It is also remarkable that although he cannot deny giving back the yoke of oxen, the slaves, and everything he had received under the terms of the *antidosis,*[2] and our reconciliation agreement clearly covered everything, nevertheless he denies the clauses in which we agreed to share the slave girl. [2] Clearly he made the *antidosis* because of her, and the only reason he can give for having returned what he had received—assuming he wishes to tell the truth—is that our friends had reconciled us on all these matters. [3] I wish he had not been excluded by lot from serving as a judge at the Dionysia,[3] which would have shown you that he was reconciled to me,

---

[1] The Council of the Areopagus; cf. the Introduction to Lys. 3.

[2] A person liable to a liturgy (compulsory sponsorship of, e.g., a choral production at a festival) could challenge a richer man either to undertake the liturgy in his place or else to exchange properties with him. This was called an *antidosis* ("exchange").

[3] The Dionysia was an Athenian religious festival at which competitions were staged for tragedy, comedy, and dithyrambic poetry. The reference to tribal competitors implies that what is at issue here is the dithyrambic competition. The system of judging has been variously reconstructed. The most attractive suggestion is by M. Pope ("Athenian Festival Judges—Seven, Five, or However Many," *Classical Quarterly* 36 [1986]: 322–326), who argues that ten judges, one from each tribe, were initially chosen to cast votes, but that their individual voting tablets were then opened in random order until one contestant received an unbeatable majority, at which point the unopened voting tablets were simply discarded (or in Lysias' words, "excluded by lot").

and gave his verdict in favor of my tribe. In fact, after writing this on his voting tablet, he was excluded by lot. [4] Philinus and Diocles know that I am speaking the truth about this, but they are not allowed to testify, because they have not sworn the oath[4] concerning the charge on which I am the defendant. Otherwise you would have known for certain that we were the people who proposed him as judge and that he took his seat because of us.

[5] But let us assume, if he wishes, that he was my enemy. I grant him that, because it makes no difference. So I went out myself to kill him, or so he claims, and entered his house by force. Then why did I not kill him, since I had him in my hands, and had so overpowered him that I had taken the slave girl as well? Let him explain that to you—but he has nothing to say. [6] Moreover, you all realize that he would have died more quickly if struck by a knife than if punched by a fist. But clearly not even he accuses us of going out armed with anything of the sort. Instead, he says he was struck with a piece of broken pottery. And yet it is already clear from what he has said that there was no premeditation. [7] If there had been, we would not have gone out like that, because it was unclear whether at his house we would find a piece of broken pottery or anything else with which to kill him, so we would have taken something with us from home. But we admit we were going after boys and flute girls, and that we had been drinking; so how can this be premeditation? I certainly do not think it can.

[8] My opponent is lovesick in a different way from other people. He wants two things: to retain the slave girl and not to give back the money. He has been aroused by the slave girl, he is prone to drunken violence and too quick with his fists, and one has to defend oneself. As for the slave girl, at one moment she says she prefers me, at another she says she prefers him, because she wants to be loved by both.[5] [9] I have been good-natured right from the beginning, and I still am; but he has become so surly that he is not ashamed to call a black eye a "wound," to be carried around on a litter, and to pretend he is in a

[4] For the special use of this oath (the *diōmosia*) in homicide cases, see the Introduction to Lys. 3. We are not told why Philinus and Diocles have failed to swear it, or whether they could have sworn if they had wanted to.

[5] This is rather different from what is said at 4.17.

terrible condition—all for the sake of a slave prostitute, and he could have undisputed control of her if he simply paid me back the money. [10] He claims he has been the victim of terrible plots, and disagrees with us on every point; but although he could have conducted an examination of the slave girl under torture, he refused to do so. In the first place, she would have made clear whether she belonged jointly to both of us or privately to him, whether I had contributed half the money or he had given it all, and whether we had been reconciled or were still enemies. [11] Moreover, she would have made clear whether we had gone out because we had been sent for or without anybody inviting us, and whether he had begun the fight or I had struck him first. On each of these points, and on others, she would easily have made the truth clear to them and to everybody else.

[12] I have demonstrated to you by many testimonies and pieces of evidence, members of the Council, that there was no premeditation and that I committed no offense against him. If I had refused the challenge to torture, you would have inferred that my opponent seemed to be speaking the truth. I claim that there should be just as strong an inference that I am not lying, since he has refused to put the slave girl to the test. I also claim that his statement that she is free[6] should not carry so much weight. I too am equally concerned in her freedom, because I paid an equal sum of money. [13] He is lying, not telling the truth. It would be extraordinary if I could make whatever use of her I wished in order to ransom my body from the enemy,[7] but when I risk losing my fatherland, I am not even allowed to learn the truth from her about the charges on which I am being tried. It would be far more just to interrogate her about this charge than to sell her in order to ransom me from the enemy. At least it is possible for somebody who is well off to pay the ransom from other assets if the enemy agree to it. But this cannot be done in the case of personal enemies: they do not wish to receive money but make it their task to drive you out of your fatherland. [14] So you should not accept his argument

---

[6] If she was free, she could not be interrogated under torture. Several surviving speeches either allege that the opponent has freed (or claims to have freed) a slave precisely for this reason (Isoc. 17.17), or seek to rebut a similar claim made against the speaker by his opponent (Dem. 29.14).

[7] He means that he could have raised money towards his hypothetical ransom by selling his alleged share in her.

that the slave girl cannot be tortured because he claims she is free. Rather, you should convict him of sykophancy,[8] because he believes that he can easily deceive you despite omitting so conclusive a test. [15] You must not regard his challenge about the points on which he wants his own slaves tortured as more trustworthy than ours. What those slaves knew was that we went to his house—something we too acknowledge. But she would know better whether we were sent for or not, and whether I struck or received the first blow. [16] Moreover, if we had tortured his own personal slaves, they would have acted automatically to please him and would have spoken untruthfully against me. The woman, however, was jointly owned, since both parties had contributed money. And she knew the most, since it was because of her that we did everything we did. [17] Everybody will be aware that I was at a disadvantage if she was tortured, but I was willing to run that risk: it is clear that she thought much more of my opponent than of me, and that she had joined him in injuring me but had never joined me in wronging him. Nevertheless, I wanted to make use of her, whereas my opponent did not trust her.

[18] Since the danger I face is so great, members of the Council, you should not readily accept my opponent's statements. Bear in mind instead that the trial involves my fatherland and my life. Take all these challenges into account. Do not seek proofs that are still stronger than these: I would not be able to produce any others apart from these to show that I did not premeditate anything against him. [19] I am upset, members of the Council, at being placed at risk on such important charges because of a girl who is a prostitute and a slave. What harm have I ever done to the city, or to my opponent himself, or to any other individual citizen? I have never done anything of the sort, but I am in danger—quite unreasonably—of bringing a far greater disaster on myself because of them. [20] I beg and beseech you, by your children, by your wives, and by the gods who control this place, have pity on me. Do not look on while I fall into his power, and do not involve me in such an irremediable disaster. I do not deserve to be exiled from my fatherland, nor does he deserve to exact so great a penalty from me for wrongs he falsely claims to have suffered.

---

[8] Malicious prosecution.

5. FOR CALLIAS

INTRODUCTION

Most of this speech has disappeared, because two pages have dropped out of the Palatinus manuscript. It is possible to calculate the amount that has disappeared (900–1,200 words in the Greek text, or perhaps 1,500–1,800 words of English), but we can only guess how much of this belonged to the end of Lysias 5 and how much to the start of Lysias 6.[1]

All we know about the case is what can be inferred from the remainder of the speech. The speaker is appearing on behalf of a man named Callias, who is evidently a metic[2] (5.2) and is evidently one of a number of defendants (cf. 5.3n). The trial is taking place as a result of a denunciation made by slaves (5.4–5). The manuscript title implies that the charge is temple robbery (*hierosulia,* lit. "theft of sacred things"), but this need not imply burglary, of which there is no hint. The term could for instance be used to cover an accusation of fraud against a sacred treasury. It is notable that the speech is addressed to an ordinary dikastic court (5.1), and not the Areopagus, which heard

[1] Codex Palatinus X, now in Heidelberg, was written in the twelfth century AD and is the source from which all other manuscripts of Lys. 3–31 have been copied. (It also contains Lys. 1 and 2, but there are some independent manuscripts of these speeches.) We know that there was no missing speech between Lys. 5 and Lys. 6 (as there was in the gap between Lys. 25 and Lys. 26), because the Palatinus has a list of its contents on the opening page.

[2] A noncitizen resident in Athens. This means that he cannot be identified with, e.g., Callias the opponent of Andocides (cf. the Introduction to Lys. 6), who was a citizen.

most cases involving religious matters (cf. Lys. 7), but since we do not know what Callias is alleged to have done, it is hard to be sure of the significance of this. Given the paucity of its remains, it is hardly surprising that the speech has attracted little interest from scholars.

5. ON BEHALF OF CALLIAS: DEFENSE SPEECH ON A CHARGE OF TEMPLE ROBBERY

[1] If Callias were on trial on anything except a capital charge, gentlemen of the jury, I would be satisfied by what the other speakers have already said. But since he is urging and begging me, and is my friend, and my father's too during his lifetime, and we have had many dealings with each other, it seems to me shameful not to assist Callias, as far as I can, in the interests of justice.[1] [2] Moreover, it was my opinion that his life as a metic in this city was such that he should sooner receive a reward at your hands than be put in such great danger on charges like this. In fact the plotters are making life just as dangerous for those who commit no crimes as for those who are responsible for many evils. [3] It would be wrong for you to regard the statements of slaves as trustworthy, and these men's[2] statements as untrustworthy. Bear in mind that nobody, whether a private individual or an official, has ever brought a charge against Callias, that while living in this city he has done you much good, and that he has reached this stage in his life without reproach. These men, on the other hand, have committed many crimes throughout their whole life, have experienced many troubles,[3] and are now making speeches about freedom as if they have been responsible for something good. [4] I am not surprised. They know that if they are shown to be lying, they will suffer nothing worse than they do now, whereas if they deceive you, they will be released from their present troubles. You must regard such people as untrustworthy, whether as prosecutors or as witnesses, who make these statements about other people for their own substantial

[1] There are some parallels here with the prologue of Lys. Fr. 3 (*Pherenicus*), also delivered in support of a noncitizen.

[2] In context this must refer to Callias, but the plural here (as at 5.5) suggests that he is one of a number of defendants.

[3] Or "done many wrongs."

profit. Much more trustworthy are those who place themselves in danger while assisting the community. [5] In my view, you should regard this trial not as the private concern of the defendants but as the common concern of everybody in the city. These are not the only people who have slaves; everybody else does as well. Our slaves will observe the plight of the defendants, and will no longer consider how they can become free by serving their masters, but by falsely denouncing them . . . .

6. AGAINST ANDOCIDES

INTRODUCTION

Lysias 6 belongs to a very well known case, the prosecution of Andocides, which took place in the second half of either 399 or more probably 400 BC. The date is important, because this is either shortly after or more likely shortly before the trial of Socrates in the Spring of 399. There are several important parallels between the trials of Andocides and of Socrates. Both concern charges of impiety, and it is possible that Socrates' prosecutor Meletus was the same man as the Meletus who was involved with the prosecution of Andocides. Scholars have frequently suggested that the conviction of Socrates reflects some sort of conservative religious reaction to the defeat of Athens in the Peloponnesian War and to the intellectual rationalism of the late fifth century, and a tone of conservative religious extremism underlies Lysias 6 also.

Although the trial of Andocides took place either in 400 or in 399, the case had its origins in the affairs of the Herms and of the Mysteries fifteen years earlier. A Herm was a stone pillar, dedicated to the god Hermes, with the god's head carved at the top, and with an erect carved phallus protruding from the center of the front of the stone. Shortly before the departure of the military expedition to Sicily in 415, most of the Herms in Athens were defaced in the course of a single night. At about the same time, it became rumored that various leading citizens had been celebrating parodies of the Eleusinian Mysteries in private houses. Both the mutilation and the parodies were major acts of sacrilege, and the two scandals tended to become conflated.

Precisely how far Andocides was implicated is uncertain, because he is himself our main informant and is hardly dispassionate.[1] He denies any part in parodying the Mysteries, but he admits that he had known about the mutilation of the Herms in advance, and that when arrested as a result of a false denunciation in 415, he had secured his freedom (and, he claims, that of a good many innocent people) by denouncing his fellow-conspirators. There is reason to suspect that he also denounced himself, relying on a promise of immunity in return for his information. This immunity, however, was promptly undermined by the passing of a decree proposed by Isotimides, which on pain of death banned from temples and other public places those who had admitted committing impiety. This decree made Andocides' position at Athens untenable, and he withdrew into voluntary exile, from which he did not finally return until the amnesty came into effect in 403. Nevertheless, it was by no means clear what impact if any the amnesty will have had on the decree of Isotimides,[2] and after several years, a group of Andocides' personal and political opponents[3] combined to bring the present case against him by *endeixis* (indict-

[1] Lys. 6 (which is probably, as we shall see, the speech of one of the subsidiary prosecutors) tends to assume rather than to argue Andocides' guilt, so our main evidence is Andocides' defense speech at this trial (And. 1). References to the events of 415 in Thucydides 6.27–28 and in Plutarch, *Alcibiades* 19–23 do not allow us to construct an alternative account, but do serve to question Andocides' veracity at certain points—which is itself further undermined by previous compromising admissions made by Andocides himself (in And. 2, delivered in 410–405; cf. the Introduction to And. 2 in volume 1 of this series, *The Oratory of Classical Greece,* 141–142).

[2] Whereas the prosecutor in our speech appears to assume that Andocides is protected by the amnesty (cf. the specious attempt to argue it away at Lys. 6.37–41), Andocides as defendant takes considerable care to subsume the amnesty within a much wider context of reconciliation, which implies that in his view the amnesty itself is not sufficient protection (And. 1.71–91).

[3] The chief prosecutor Cephisius (otherwise unknown) was assisted by Epichares (also unknown), Meletus (possibly the prosecutor of Socrates; cf. above), and Agyrrhius (a leader of the democratic restoration). A supporting role was apparently played by Andocides' distant relative and personal enemy Callias, the leader of one of the oldest and richest families in Athens, who himself held one of the religious offices at the Mysteries (that of *Dadouchos* or "torchbearer"; cf. further 6.10n).

ment) for exercising rights to which he was not entitled: specifically, for entering temples since 403 in defiance of the decree of Isotimides.[4] In law, the prosecutors' case was arguably valid, because the alleged offense was what Andocides had been doing not before but after the passing of the amnesty. However, the contrary view could be taken, and we may suspect that it had never occurred to anybody to ask whether the decree of Isotimides had been invalidated by the amnesty. In the event, Andocides was acquitted. He had powerful supporters with good democratic credentials,[5] and the jury was evidently happy in this case to accept his generous interpretation of the law.

Lysias 6 is an animated but somewhat inarticulate piece of work, which largely eschews both historical narrative and legal argument, and concentrates instead on the dangers that will result to the community if impiety is left unpunished. Some earlier scholars argued that it was either a late rhetorical exercise or perhaps a political pamphlet produced after Andocides' acquittal by a disappointed religious extremist. The more recent consensus, however, is that this may well be a genuine speech. It cannot be the speech of the main prosecutor Cephisius, because he is named in the third person at 6.42, but it could be the speech of one of his assistants.[6] This hypothesis would account for the speaker's failure to deal with the charges, because these would have been covered by Cephisius himself.

The proposition that this is a genuine speech does not of course entail the proposition that it is by Lysias, and the overwhelming majority of scholars have argued that Lysias cannot have written a speech with such a tortuous style and with such poorly constructed arguments. This is of course a subjective decision, but I certainly find it

---

[4] The case was heard by an ordinary dikastic court. There was also a subsidiary charge of committing impiety by placing a suppliant's branch on the altar during the festival (And. 1.110–116). There is no explicit reference to this charge in our speech, though see Lys. 6.30n.

[5] He calls Anytus and Cephalus, two of the leaders of the democratic restoration, to speak for him (see And. 1.150).

[6] If Meletus is the same man as the prosecutor of Socrates, he might be a plausible candidate for the religious views espoused by the speaker of Lys. 6, but it could be Epichares or even Agyrrhius (though we might have expected a politician of his assumed caliber to have been more articulate).

difficult to envisage how such a sharp operator as Lysias would have committed the fundamental error of allowing one of his clients openly to attack his fellow-prosecutor (6.42). The speaker's function was presumably to strengthen the prosecution by appealing to certain types of religious sensibility—above all, perhaps, by making it seem that the families of both the leading male priesthoods of the Eleusinian Mysteries (not simply Callias the Torchbearer but also the grandson of a Hierophant; cf. 6.54) were united behind the prosecution. In the event, the speaker's incompetence may have made him more of a liability than an asset.

There is no easily accessible specialist work on Lysias 6, but there is a lot of useful material in commentaries on Andocides 1: D. M. MacDowell, *Andokides: On the Mysteries* (Oxford, 1962) is outstanding, but in places it presupposes knowledge of Greek; more accessible for the non-Greek reader are M. Edwards, *Greek Orators,* IV, *Andocides* (Warminster, 1995), and MacDowell's own translation of Andocides in the first volume of *The Oratory of Classical Greece* series (Austin, 1998). For a recent if tendentious interpretation of the affair of the Herms and the Mysteries, see W. D. Furley, *Andokides and the Herms: A Study of Crisis in Fifth-century Athenian Religion* (*Bulletin of the Institute of Classical Studies,* Supplement 65, 1996).

6. PROSECUTION SPEECH AGAINST ANDOCIDES FOR IMPIETY

[1][1] . . . he tied his horse to the doorknob of the sanctuary, as if making a gift of it, but the following night he stole it away. The man who did this perished by hunger, the most terrible death. Even though many good things were laid on his table, a totally disgusting smell seemed to come from the wheat bread and the barley cake, and he could not eat. Many of us have heard the Hierophant[2] telling this

[1] The beginning of this speech has disappeared, because two pages have dropped out of the manuscript, for which see the Introduction to Lys. 5.

[2] The *hierophantēs* (lit. "displayer of sacred things") was one of the religious offices at the Eleusinian Mysteries. The post had formerly been held by the speaker's great-grandfather (6.54), and could only be held by a member of the *genos* Eumolpidae (cf. 6.10n).

story. [2][3] [3] So I think it is right for me now to recall against my opponent what was said at the time, so that not only are his friends destroyed by this man and his words, but also he in his turn will be destroyed by somebody else.

It is impossible for you on your part, as you cast your votes, to show either pity or favor to Andocides, because you know how actively these two goddesses[4] punish wrongdoers. Everybody should expect that the same will happen to himself and to other people. [4] Imagine that today, by your verdict, Andocides departs unscathed from this trial, and goes on to enter the selection as one of the nine Archons, and is chosen by lot as Basileus.[5] What else will he have to do but conduct sacrifices and offer prayers according to ancestral custom, sometimes at the Eleusinium[6] here in Athens, and sometimes at the sanctuary at Eleusis, and he will be in charge of the festival of the Mysteries, responsible for ensuring that nobody commits a crime or acts impiously towards the sacred rites. [5] How do you think the initiates who come to the ceremony will feel, when they see who the Basileus is and remember all his impious actions? How do you think the rest of the Greeks will feel, who come because of the ceremonies, either to sacrifice at the festival or to attend it as spectators?[7] [6] Because of his impious actions, Andocides is hardly unknown to those abroad or those who live here, since people who have committed exceptional deeds, either good or evil, necessarily become well known. In addition, Andocides has annoyed many cities during his travels:

---

[3] Editors agree that 6.2 of the manuscript ("that Andocides destroyed his own blood relatives and his friends by denouncing them") should be omitted. It is evidently a later insertion by a copyist who misunderstood the function of the cautionary tale in 6.1 and thought that the Hierophant's story was about Andocides' impiety.

[4] Demeter and Persephone, the two goddesses of the cult of the Eleusinian Mysteries.

[5] The second of the nine Archons, all of whom were selected by lot. The Basileus (lit. "King Archon") was responsible for homicide trials and other religious matters.

[6] The sanctuary of the Eleusinian goddesses at Athens, on the north slope of the Acropolis, above the Agora.

[7] Or "as sacred envoys."

Sicily, Italy, the Peloponnese, Thessaly, the Hellespont, Ionia, Cyprus. He has been a flatterer to many kings with whom he has had dealings, all except Dionysius of Syracuse.[8] [7] Dionysius was either the luckiest of them all or else was different in character from the rest. Alone of those who had dealings with Andocides, he was not deceived by a man of this type, who had the special talent of doing no harm to his enemies, but whatever harm he could to his friends. So, by Zeus, if you show any unjust favoritism towards Andocides, it will be hard for you to escape the attention of the Greeks.

[8] You need now to make a decision about Andocides. You know full well, men of Athens, that you cannot retain both Andocides and your ancestral laws. One of two things must happen: either you must wipe out the laws or you must get rid of this man. [9] He has reached such a level of audacity that he makes speeches about the law, arguing that the law referring to him has been annulled and that he is already allowed to enter the Agora and the sacred places[9] . . . even today in the Council-chamber of the Athenians.[10] [10] And yet they say Pericles once advised you that in the case of those who committed impiety, you should apply not only the written laws but also the unwritten ones according to which the Eumolpidae[11] expound sacred law—laws that nobody has ever had the authority to abolish or has dared to speak against, and people do not even know who established

---

[8] For Dionysius the tyrant of Syracuse in Sicily, see the Introduction to Lys. 33.

[9] Editors suspect that there is a gap, probably of only a few words (e.g., "and to deliver speeches"), in the manuscript.

[10] The Council of Five Hundred. This passage does not necessarily mean that he was a member of the Council at the time of the trial, though it does imply active participation in public life: Andocides himself mentions an appearance that he made before the Council probably in 401 to bid for a public contract (And. 1.134).

[11] The Eumolpidae were a *genos* (a fictive descent group organized around a cult). They provided one of the religious officials who presided at the Eleusinian Mysteries (the Hierophant; cf. 6.1n), and they also had the exclusive right of expounding the sacred law about the festival. Cf. And. 1.115–116, where Callias attempted to expound it and was prevented from doing so on the grounds that he was not a member of the Eumolpidae but of the *genos* Kerukes (who provided the other religious officials for the Mysteries but did not have the right to expound).

them—for he believed that in this way offenders would pay the penalty not simply to humans but to the gods. [11] Andocides has showed such disregard for the gods, and for those who are responsible for avenging them, that before he had been back in the city for ten days, he brought a prosecution for impiety before the Basileus and had it accepted, even though he himself was Andocides and had behaved in this way towards the gods. Indeed—pay very close attention here—he claimed that Archippus was committing impiety towards his own ancestral Herm.[12] [12] Archippus defended himself, claiming that the Herm was safe and intact, and had not suffered the fate of the other Herms. Nevertheless, to avoid being troubled by a person of this caliber, he paid some money and was released from the charge. But if Andocides thinks it is right to punish somebody else for impiety, then it is legitimate and reverent for others to do the same to him.

[13] He will argue that it is unacceptable for an informer to suffer the extreme penalty, whereas those who were denounced have full citizen rights now and share in the same privileges as you.[13] If so, he will not be delivering a defense speech for himself, but will in fact be accusing other people. Those who decided to receive the others back from exile are of course criminals and are guilty of the same impiety; but if you, who have sovereign power, are the ones who undermine the vengeance of the gods, it will be you not they who are guilty. Do not choose to bring this guilt on yourselves, when you can remove it by punishing the criminal. [14] In addition, those denounced by Andocides denied parodying the Mysteries, whereas he admitted doing so. And yet even in the Areopagus, the most sacred and just of courts, a person who admits his crime is executed, whereas if he denies it, he is put on trial, and many such people are found to have done nothing wrong. So you should not have the same opinion about those who deny and those who confess. [15] It seems to me astonishing that if

---

[12] For Herms, see the Introduction to Lys. 6. It is not clear whether this Herm is Andocides', or Archippus', let alone in what sense a Herm can be said to be "ancestral."

[13] With the exception of a few who were executed, the majority of those denounced in 415 escaped into exile. We know of several who were recalled individually during the next decade (like Alcibiades), but it seems likely that the remainder were allowed to return under the amnesty of 403/2.

somebody wounds a man physically, in his head, his face, his hands, or his feet, then according to the laws of the Areopagus, he will be exiled from the city of his victim, and if he returns there, he will be prosecuted by *endeixis* (indictment) and executed. But if somebody injures the statues of the gods in the same way, will you not even prevent him from entering their sanctuaries or punish him if he does? It is both legitimate and commendable to pay regard to those at whose hands in future you may experience either good or evil. [16] They say that many of the Greeks exclude people from their temples because of impious actions committed here at Athens; but you, who are the victims of the offense, are paying less attention than other people to your own laws. [17] My opponent is far more impious than Diagoras the Melian.[14] Diagoras committed impiety by speaking against holy things and festivals that were foreign to him, but this man has committed impiety by acting against those of his own city. You should be more angry, men of Athens, at citizens who commit offenses than at foreigners who offend against the same holy things, for the latter is a remote crime, as it were, but the former is close to home. [18] You should not set free those criminals you have to hand, while seeking to capture those who are in exile, proclaiming by herald that you will give a talent of silver to anyone who arrests or kills them.[15] Otherwise, it will seem to the Greeks that you are more keen to show off than to punish. [19] Andocides has made it clear to the Greeks that he does not worship the gods.[16] He became involved in ship owning and traveled by sea—not because he was afraid of what he had done but be-

---

[14] Diagoras of Melos, known as "*atheos*" ("the godless one") was outlawed from Athens apparently for mocking the Eleusinian Mysteries. Aristoph., *Birds* 1073–1075 parodies the decree which (probably in 415/14) outlawed him and promised a reward of a talent to anybody who killed him.

[15] As in the case of Diagoras; see preceding note.

[16] The verb *nomizō* (used also in the charge on which Socrates was convicted at around the same time as this trial) can mean either "worship" or "believe in." The argument here is that Andocides' seafaring shows him to be irreligious, because by deciding to travel by sea, a polluted person risks involving his fellow-passengers if the gods decide to punish him by sinking the ship: Andocides demolishes this argument at And. 1.137–139.

cause he was shameless. But god brought him back, so that he could come to the scene of his crimes and pay the penalty at my instigation. [20] I predict that he will indeed pay the penalty, and that would in no way surprise me. God does not punish instantaneously; that sort of justice is characteristic of humans. I find evidence for this in many places: I see others who have committed impiety and have paid the penalty much later, and their children paying the penalty for the crimes of their ancestors. In the meantime god sends much fear and danger to the criminals, so that many of them are keen to die prematurely and be rid of their sufferings. In the end, god imposes an end on their life, after ruining it in this way.[17]

[21] Examine the life of Andocides himself, from the moment he committed his impiety, and see if any other life has been similar. After he committed his crime, he was summarily fined and dragged into court. He locked himself up by proposing imprisonment as the penalty if he failed to hand over his attendant.[18] [22] He knew full well that he would not be able to hand over the attendant, who had been killed because of Andocides' crimes, to prevent him becoming an informer. Surely one of the gods must have destroyed his mind, if he thought it was easier to propose imprisonment rather than money, when his hopes were the same in either case. [23] As a result of this proposal, he was imprisoned for nearly a year. While in prison, he informed against his own relatives and friends, because he had been granted immunity if he were found to be telling the truth. What sort of a character do you think he has, given that he behaved in the most terrible and shameful way by denouncing his own friends, and his own chance of rescue was very unclear? [24] Later on, after he had killed the people he said he most valued, it was decided that his information was true,[19] and he was set free—and you voted specifically that he

---

[17] Cf. Lys. Fr. 4 (*Cinesias*), §3.

[18] Penalties in Athenian courts were often determined by the jury voting between alternative proposals put forward by the two litigants. Andocides' own version of these events is completely different: he claims that he did hand over a slave to confirm his story, and implies that he was immediately released (And. 1.64).

[19] Or possibly "he decided to make a truthful denunciation," implying that he had previously lied.

should be excluded from the Agora and from the sanctuaries, so that even if he were injured by his enemies, he would not be able to punish them.[20] [25] Nobody else has ever suffered *atimia* (deprivation of civic rights) on a charge like this, ever since Athens has been worthy of eternal memory. That is only fair, because nobody else has ever committed similar actions. Should we consider the gods or chance as responsible for these events? [26] After this, he sailed off to the court of the king of Citium,[21] and was imprisoned after being caught by him in an act of treason. He had to fear not simply death but daily torture, because he expected to have his extremities[22] cut off while he was still alive. [27] He ran away from that danger and sailed back to his own city at the time of the Four Hundred.[23] God had granted him such forgetfulness that he chose to return to the very people he had wronged. On arrival, he was imprisoned and tortured, but instead of being executed, he was released. [28] From there he sailed to the court of Euagoras,[24] king of Cyprus, and was imprisoned after committing a crime. He ran away from him as well—fleeing from the gods here, fleeing from his own city, fleeing to the first place he could reach. What pleasure is there in this life—often suffering pain and never having any respite? [29] After sailing from there back here to his own city during the democracy, he bribed the Prytaneis[25] to introduce him here, but you expelled him from the city, thus making secure for the gods the laws that you had voted. [30] Right to the end, neither democracy nor oligarchy nor tyrant nor city was willing to receive this man. For the whole time since his impiety, he has wandered continually, always trusting more in those who do not know him than in those who do, because of the crimes he has committed against those he knows. Now finally he has reached this city, and has suffered *endeixis*

---

[20] Most Athenian courts were in the Agora, so the ban on entering there would make it impossible for him to bring legal action in his own name.

[21] A city in Cyprus.

[22] I.e., fingers, toes, etc.

[23] The first oligarchy, in 411 BC.

[24] Euagoras is discussed in the Introduction to Lys. 19. He had close diplomatic dealings with Athens throughout his reign (ca. 411–374).

[25] The executive committee of the Council of Five Hundred. This was apparently the occasion for which And. 2 was written.

(indictment) on two charges at the same time.[26] [31] His body is always in chains, and his property is being reduced as a result of the dangers he faces. When somebody divides up his own livelihood among enemies and sykophants,[27] such a life is not worth living. God realized this, and gave him his life, not to preserve him but to punish him for past impieties. [32] Now finally Andocides has handed himself over to you to do as you wish: not that he trusts in his innocence, but he is driven by some god-sent compulsion. You see Andocides being saved from perils, and you know that he has committed unholy acts—but there is no need, by Zeus, for any of you, young or old, to lose faith in the gods. Bear in mind that it is better to live half a life free from pain than to live twice as long but suffer like him.

[33] He has reached such a level of shamelessness that he is preparing for a political career. He has already delivered public speeches; he has made accusations; he has challenged some of the public officials at their *dokimasia;*[28] and he enters the Council-chamber and gives advice about sacrifices, processions,[29] prayers, and oracles. But what sort of gods do you think you will please if you follow his advice? If you choose to forget the things that were done by this man, gentlemen of the jury, do not expect the gods to forget as well. [34] He thinks that he has the right to take an active part in the city, and not remain inactive as befits a criminal. Instead, his attitude is as if he himself had exposed those who committed offenses against the city. He is plotting how he can become more powerful than other people, as if the reason why he had not been punished was something other than your gentleness and the lack of time available. Now he has continued to commit

---

[26] On this reading (which is in my view the most likely one), the two charges would be entering sanctuaries in 400 BC in defiance of the decree of Isotimides, and placing a suppliant's branch on the altar (see the Introduction). However, the words "charges" and "time" are implied rather than stated in the Greek text, which could therefore mean "has twice suffered *endeixis* at the same (place)." Some scholars see this as a reference to an otherwise unknown previous trial.

[27] Malicious prosecutors.

[28] Nothing more is known about these activities, though it is clear from And. 3 that he did build a political career during the 390s. For the *dokimasia* or scrutiny of incoming public officials, see the Introduction to Lys. 16.

[29] Or "revenues."

offenses against you, and has not escaped notice, but will be punished as soon as he is put on trial.

[35] He will also rely on the following argument. (I must tell you what defense my opponent will deliver, so that you can make a better decision after hearing from both sides.) He claims that he did much good for the city, by bringing a denunciation and putting an end to the state of fear and disruption that existed at the time. [36] But who was responsible for these great troubles? Was it not Andocides himself, by behaving as he did? Should we feel grateful to him as a benefactor, because he brought a denunciation, for which you rewarded him with immunity?—and are you therefore responsible for the disruption and the troubles, because you were trying to discover those who had committed impiety? Surely not. Indeed, precisely the reverse: he was the one who disrupted the city, and you restored it.

[37] I hear that he intends to defend himself on the grounds that the agreements[30] are valid for him, just as for the rest of the Athenians.[31] He thinks that if he produces this specious argument, many of you will vote to acquit him, because you will be afraid of breaking the agreements. [38] On this point I shall argue that Andocides has nothing to do with the agreements: certainly not, by Zeus, the ones you arranged with the Spartans, nor the ones that those from Piraeus swore towards those in the town (*astu*). Though we were so many, none of us had committed the same crimes as Andocides, or anything like them, such that he too could take advantage of us. [39] We were not fighting for his sake, and did not become reconciled only when we could extend a share in the agreement to him as well. The agree-

---

[30] The reference is to the amnesty of 403/2. As the phrase "(agreements) with the Spartans" implies, this was a settlement imposed by Pausanias of Sparta on the two warring Athenian factions (the former oligarchic supporters in the town and the democratic counterrevolutionaries in Piraeus). However, the text of the amnesty as quoted in *Ath. Pol.* 39.5 shows that it did not simply cover offenses committed by members of one group against members of the other. For similarly restrictive misinterpretations of the amnesty, cf. Lys. 13.88–89 and 26.16–20.

[31] Andocides does not in fact concentrate on the amnesty (which is mentioned only briefly at And. 1.90–91), but instead focuses on a very exaggerated reading of legal reform in the period around 403 BC, to give the impression that the decree of Isotimides has been annulled (And. 1.72–105).

ment and the oaths took place not for the sake of one man, but for the sake of us—those from the town and those from Piraeus. It would be strange if, when we were in a difficult situation, we had taken an interest in Andocides (who was not in Athens) and how his offenses could be wiped out. [40] I suppose somebody may claim that the Spartans, in the agreements made with them, took an interest in Andocides because they had received some benefit from him. But did you take an interest in him? In return for what benefaction? Because he had often faced danger on your account for the sake of the city? [41] This defense of his is not true, men of Athens. Do not be deceived. What would break the settlement is not Andocides now paying the penalty for his own offenses, but if a person is somehow punished as an individual because of public disasters.

[42] Perhaps he will accuse Cephisius[32] as well, instead of himself. And he will have a point—the truth should be told. However, you could not in a single ballot punish both the defendant and the accuser. Now is the time to make a just decision about my opponent. Another opportunity will come for Cephisius, and for all the rest of us whom my opponent will now mention. Do not, just because you are angry with somebody else, acquit this criminal now.

[43] He will argue that he became an informer;[33] and that nobody else, if you punish him, will be willing to bring denunciations before you. But Andocides has his informer's reward from you: he saved his own life when other people died because of his reward. You are responsible for his survival, but he himself is the cause of his own suffering and perils, because he has broken the terms of the immunity decree on the basis of which he became an informer. [44] Do not encourage informers to commit crimes—those they have already committed are quite sufficient—but punish offenders. The other informers, all those who denounced themselves after being convicted on shameful charges, realize one thing at least, that they must not annoy those they have wronged; instead, they accept that they are regarded as Athenians with full citizen rights only when they are away from

---

[32] Cephisius, the chief prosecutor, is discussed in the Introduction.

[33] Andocides does not in fact say this, at least in the version of his speech that we possess as And. 1.

Athens, but that while they are here, they are regarded as impious criminals by the citizens they have injured. [45] The greatest criminal of them all, apart from the defendant, was Batrachus.[34] He became an informer under the Thirty, and even though the agreements and oaths applied to him just as to those from Eleusis,[35] he was afraid of you—whom he had wronged—and went to live in another city. Andocides has wronged the gods themselves as well. By entering their sanctuaries, he has treated the gods worse than Batrachus treated humans. If somebody is a more insane criminal than Batrachus, he should be very glad to be spared by yourselves.

[46] Come now, what grounds have you for acquitting Andocides? Because he is a brave soldier? But he has never gone on campaign away from the city—neither as a cavalryman nor as a hoplite, neither as a trierarch nor as a marine soldier, neither before nor after the disaster,[36] even though he is more than forty years old. [47] Other exiles served as joint trierarchs with you in the Hellespont. Remember the great evils and the war from which you rescued yourselves and the city. You undertook great physical labors, you spent a great deal of private and public money, and because of the war, you buried many good men from among the citizens. [48] Andocides did not experience any of these sufferings[37] . . . to save the city. He claims he should now have

[34] Batrachus is almost certainly the same man as the informer who is mentioned at Lys. 12.48. Since the name is fairly rare, he may also be the subject of one of Lysias' lost speeches, "On the Death of Batrachus": this would be interesting, because it suggests that there may have been people at Athens who felt bitter enough to murder him.

[35] Former supporters of the oligarchy, who had joined the Thirty at Eleusis under the terms of the amnesty of 403/2.

[36] As usual in Lysias, the decisive Athenian defeat at Aegospotami (405 BC) is glossed with a euphemism. The force of the argument here is considerably weakened by Andocides' age: he was apparently in his early forties at the time of the speech and so had lived as an adult at Athens only from the late 420s to 415 and from 403 to the date of the speech probably in 400, during which there had been no campaigns.

[37] There appear to be two short gaps, probably of only a few words, in 6.48. A plausible restoration of the first gap is "and did not contribute anything"; and of the second gap, "or anything else did he contribute, so that."

a share in the life of the city, even though he is committing impiety within it. He is wealthy and powerful, and has become the friend (*xenos*) of kings and tyrants—or so he boasts, because he knows your habits—but what war tax (*eisphora*) . . . they might do good to him. [49] He knew that the city was in great turmoil and danger, but although he was a shipowner, he did not have the courage to rouse himself and help his fatherland by importing grain. Metics from abroad, simply because they were metics,[38] helped the city by importing grain. But as for you, Andocides, what service have you performed? What sort of crimes have you remedied? What sort of upbringing have you repaid . . . [39]

. . . [50] . . . men of Athens, remember what Andocides has done. Bear in mind also the festival for which you have been specially honored by many people. Because you have often seen and heard them, you are by now so numbed by my opponent's offenses that even what is terrible no longer seems terrible to you. But focus your attention, let your minds imagine they are seeing what my opponent has done, and you will come to a better decision. [51] This man put on a ceremonial robe. He mimicked the sacred rites and revealed them to those who were not initiates. He gave voice to words that must not be spoken. He mutilated the gods whom we worship, and to whom we sacrifice and pray, honoring them and purifying ourselves. This was why priestesses and priests stood facing the west and cursed him, shaking out their purple robes according to ancient and ancestral custom.[40] [52] He has admitted his actions, and is still breaking the law you established, that he should be excluded from the sanctuaries as unclean. He has entered our city, breaking all these restraints. He has sacrificed on the altars, where he was not allowed to do so. He has gone to the sanctuaries, which were the subjects of his impiety. He has entered the Eleusinium and washed himself in the holy basin. [53] Who should tolerate such things? What friend or relative or deme

[38] Lit. "metics and foreigners, because of their metic status," but in English (though not in Greek) this makes it sound as if metics were not foreigners.

[39] A page has dropped out of the Palatinus manuscript here, leaving a gap of some 450–600 words.

[40] Cf. Plutarch's account of the curses imposed on Alcibiades (Plut., *Alcibiades* 22 and 33).

member needs to do a favor secretly for my opponent and publicly incur the hatred of the gods? You should realize that by punishing Andocides and getting rid of him, you are purifying the city and freeing it from pollution, driving away the scapegoat, and getting rid of something accursed—because this man falls into that category.

[54] I would like to tell you the advice that our grandfather Diocles,[41] son of the Hierophant Zacoras, gave when you were deciding how to deal with a man from Megara who had committed impiety. Other people recommended executing the Megarian immediately without trial, but Diocles advised putting him on trial for the sake of mankind, so that other people would hear and see and be more law-abiding—and he said that for the sake of the gods, each one of you, on leaving home, should come into the courtroom after deciding individually what someone guilty of impiety ought to suffer. [55] You too, men of Athens, must not be persuaded by this man. You know what you have to do. You have in your hands a man who has clearly committed impiety. You have seen and heard his crimes. He will beg and beseech you, but do not have pity. Those who die unjustly, not justly, are the ones who deserve your pity.

---

[41] The context for this advice may be the Megarian Decree(s) of the 430s. Neither Diocles nor Zacoras is otherwise known, but the significance of Zacoras' having been Hierophant is discussed in the Introduction.

7. CONCERNING THE *SĒKOS* [1]

INTRODUCTION

The olive tree played an important role in Athenian mythology, as a symbol of the prosperity and identity of Athens. The goddess Athena, or so the story went, in her successful contest with Poseidon over which should be patron of the city, staked her claim by planting the first olive on the Acropolis. In the classical period, a proportion (we do not know what proportion) of the olive trees grown in Attica were held to be offshoots of Athene's original olive, and were therefore regarded as sacred.

These sacred olive trees were public property, even though many of them were growing on private land. The Aristotelian treatise on the *Constitution of Athens* (*Ath. Pol.* 60.2) reports two changes between earlier practice and the treatment of these trees at the time of writing (in the 330s or 320s BC). The first of these changes is that whereas previously the olives from such trees had been collected by public officials for use in supplying the oil for the prizes at the Panathenaic festival, they were now granted to the landowner in return for a flat payment of oil. The second change is that although anybody who cut down a sacred olive tree or uprooted its stump could in theory still be tried for impiety before the Areopagus and sentenced to death, nevertheless in practice such trials were no longer held. Lysias 7 (presumably dating from soon after 397/6, which is the latest date mentioned:

[1] A *sēkos* is either the stump of a sacred olive tree or else the fence marking out such a stump; see below.

7.11) is a defense speech by a landowner accused of contravening this law. It corresponds closely to the *Ath. Pol.*'s description of earlier practice, except that the penalty envisaged seems to be not death but exile with confiscation of property (7.3, 7.32).

For a modern reader, it is difficult to make sense of the idea that uprooting a tree can be impiety, because we do not live in a society that regards trees as sacred. It may help to understand the religious sentiments involved if we consider the moral outrage that would be caused if somebody today were to desecrate a crucifix outside a church, or perhaps (to focus on the civic as well as the religious aspects of the symbol) a war memorial or a national flag. Also important in understanding Lysias 7, however, may be the background of political bitterness arising from the oligarchic revolution of 404/3 BC. The speaker is evidently a very rich man: he claims to have undertaken various liturgies (7.31n), and the estate with the disputed olive is only one of his properties (7.24). Like many rich men, however, he is also compromised by his oligarchic sympathies. At the outset (7.4), he describes his purchase of the estate with the bland and ambiguous phrase "when peace had been made," which sounds like the end of the Peloponnesian War in 405/4, but he later (7.9) lets slip that this actually took place during the Archonship of Pythodorus (404/3), by which time the Thirty Tyrants had come to power. Not only does this imply that he remained in Athens under the Thirty,[2] but it also suggests that he may have been one of those who took advantage of the fact or the threat of the Thirty's confiscations in order to acquire property cheaply.

The speaker defends himself by asserting that nobody would call him a fool, and that nobody but a fool would have committed such an offense for which there were substantial risks and no conceivable motives (7.12–19). His discussion of poverty as a motive (7.14) conveniently suppresses the possibility that rich men may want to be richer. He attempts to shift the blame by suggesting that the damage might have been committed by one or other of the competing forces

[2] Cf. the defensive tone of the claim at 7.27 to have done nothing wrong under the Thirty.

during the war (7.6). He draws attention to the series of tenants who have rented the land between 404/3 and 397/6,[3] and who can testify that there was no sacred olive on the property in their time (7.9–10), thus neatly ignoring the possibility that he might have removed it during the five-day period between his initial purchase of the property and the start of the first tenancy. In addition, he seeks to undermine the charge by dismissing his opponent as a sykophant (or in other words a vexatious prosecutor who is unfairly victimizing an inoffensive rich man like himself) and by emphasizing that the prosecutor Nicomachus[4] is too young to be speaking from personal knowledge about the tree in question (7.29). Tied to this is the allegation that the prosecution have shifted the grounds of the accusation (7.2; cf. 7.11). It is difficult to assess this allegation, because the meaning of the terminology is not wholly clear. The general word for an olive tree is *elaa,* which may be private or nonsacred (*idia*), but may also be a *moria* or sacred olive. The traditional interpretation of *sēkos* is that it is the dead stump of a (sacred) olive; outside this speech, however, the normal use of the word is to describe a wooden fence, particularly one marking out a sacred area, and it is therefore possible that *sēkos* here denotes a fence distinguishing a *moria* from a nonsacred olive.[5]

S. Isager and J. E. Skydsgaard, *Ancient Greek Agriculture: An Introduction* (London and New York, 1992) has an appendix on the sacred olives. On the details of the speech, see Carey 1989.

---

[3] The pattern of short-term leasing revealed at 7.10 is fascinating, particularly given the background of recent civil strife. It would be very interesting to know whether the tenants were rich men seeking quick profits, or poor men desperate enough to accept uneconomic leases. Unfortunately, however, there are no parallel sources that would allow us to make comparisons.

[4] About whom we know nothing except his name (7.20, 7.36, 7.39). There is no reason to identify him with anybody else of that name: in particular, he cannot be the defendant in Lys. 30, who must be older.

[5] This reading of *sēkos* as fence is put forward by Lin Foxhall in her forthcoming book, *Seeking the Ancient Economy: Olive Culture in Ancient Greece.* The term *sēkos* has been retained throughout this translation in order not to prejudice the interpretation. *Elaa* has been translated throughout as "olive" or "olive tree," and *moria* as "sacred olive" or "sacred olive tree."

7. SPEECH TO THE AREOPAGUS COUNCIL: DEFENSE SPEECH CONCERNING THE *SĒKOS* [1]

[1] In the past, members of the Council, I used to believe that by living a quiet life, anybody who so desired could avoid becoming involved in legal proceedings or public affairs. Now, however, I have landed so unexpectedly in the middle of accusations brought by wicked sykophants [2] that, were such a thing possible, even those not yet born should in my view already be afraid about the future. Because of people like my opponent, the same dangers face both the innocent and those who have committed many offenses. [2] What makes the trial particularly awkward is that initially they accused me of removing an olive tree from the ground, and in the course of their investigations, they questioned the people who had purchased the right to collect the crop of the sacred olives.[3] But since they could not by this means discover anything I had done wrong, they are now claiming that I removed a *sēkos;* they think that this accusation will be the most difficult for me to refute and that they will be more able to say whatever they please. [3] My opponent has come here after careful planning, but I have to defend myself on a charge that concerns both my fatherland and my property, after hearing it at the same time as you who are going to decide the case. Nevertheless, I shall try to make things clear to you from the beginning.

[4] The estate in question used to belong to Peisander, but when his property was confiscated, Apollodorus of Megara received it as a gift from the People (*dēmos*).[4] He farmed it for a while, but shortly

---

[1] The meaning of this term is discussed in the final paragraph of the Introduction.

[2] Malicious prosecutors.

[3] Athens did not have a civil service to collect taxes, and so each indirect tax was normally collected by those private individuals who had offered the highest bid at a public auction for the right to collect it (for an example of such an auction, see And. 1.133–136).

[4] Apollodorus was rewarded for his involvement in the assassination of Phrynichus, one of the leaders of the Four Hundred, in 411 BC. Peisander was one of the other leaders: his property was evidently confiscated after he fled to join the Spartans on the collapse of the oligarchy. The date at which the speaker acquired the property is discussed in the Introduction.

before the Thirty, Anticles purchased it from him and rented it out. I bought it from Anticles when peace had been made. [5] In my view, members of the Council, my task is to show that when I acquired the estate there was neither an olive tree nor a *sēkos* on it. I do not see that I can legitimately be punished for the period before this, even if there had been many sacred olive trees on it: If they did not disappear because of us, then it is not right that we should be on trial as criminals for other people's offenses.

[6] You are all aware that the war caused a great many evils. Distant estates were cut down by the Spartans, and those nearby were plundered by our friends. How could it be right for me to be punished now for the disasters which befell the city during that period? What is more, this estate was confiscated in wartime and remained unsold for more than three years.[5] [7] So it is not beyond belief that the sacred olive trees were uprooted by the Spartans in this period, when we were unable to protect even our own property. Those of you who have a particular concern for such things, members of the Council, know that many places were then thickly covered both with private olive trees and with sacred olives. Most of these have now been uprooted, and the ground has become bare. Even though the same people had possession both in peacetime and during the war, you do not think it right to punish them when it is others who have done the uprooting. [8] But if you free from responsibility those who have cultivated the land throughout the entire period, then certainly you should not punish those who purchased it in peacetime.

[9] Anyway, members of the Council, I could tell you a lot about what happened earlier, but I think I have said enough. When I took over the estate, I rented it out to Callistratus before five days had passed, during the Archonship of Pythodorus. [10] He farmed it for two years,[6] and did not take over any private olive tree, or sacred olive, or *sēkos*. In the third year, Demetrius here cultivated it for one year.

---

[5] Possibly from its confiscation in 411, which would imply that it was granted to Apollodorus in 408.

[6] None of these tenants is otherwise known, but the dates are presumably as follows: Callistratus 404/3 and 403/2, Demetrius 402/1, Alcias 401/0, Proteas 400/399, 399/8, and 398/7, the speaker from 397/6. The question of whether such a turnover was typical is discussed in the Introduction.

In the fourth, I rented it to Alcias the ex-slave of Antisthenes, who is dead. After that, Proteas also rented it from me on similar terms for three years. Come forward, please, witnesses.

[WITNESSES]

[11] Since the end of this period, I have been cultivating it myself. My accuser claims that I uprooted a *sēkos* in the Archonship of Souniades.[7] However, the people who cultivated it before me and who rented it from me for many years have testified to you that there was never a *sēkos* on the estate. How can anybody prove more clearly that the accuser is lying? Someone who works the land afterwards cannot remove something that has not previously been there.

[12] In the past, members of the Council, I used to be annoyed whenever people said that I was clever and subtle and never did anything casually or without calculation. I thought this description of me was exaggerated. Now, however, I would be glad for you all to have that opinion of me—so that you would expect me, if I did attempt this sort of thing, to calculate what benefits would accrue to a person who removed it, what the punishment would be, what I would achieve if I managed to escape notice, and what I would suffer at your hands if I were found out. [13] People do not commit this sort of offense out of arrogance (*hubris*) but for profit. It would be reasonable for you to examine things in this way, and for litigants to frame their accusations on this basis, showing what benefit the offenders would derive. [14] My opponent, however, cannot demonstrate that I was forced by poverty to attempt such measures, or that the estate was spoiled so long as the *sēkos* existed, or that it obstructed any vines or was close to a house, or that I was unaware of the danger from your court if I did such a thing. I should emphasize that many severe penalties awaited me. [15] In the first place, it was during the day that I am supposed to have uprooted the *sēkos,* as if I did not need to avoid everybody's attention but wanted all Athens to know about it. If it had been simply a shameful act, then a passerby might not have cared, but I was in danger not of shame but of the severest penalty. [16] I would

[7] This is 397/6, when the speaker apparently resumed farming the estate (see previous note).

surely be the most wretched of human beings, if for the rest of my life my own attendants would be no longer my slaves but my masters, because they too would know about this act—so that even if they committed the greatest offenses towards me, I would not be able to punish them, because I would know full well that it was in their hands both to punish me and to gain their own freedom by denouncing me. [17] Moreover, even if I thought I could ignore my slaves, how on earth would I have dared to remove the *sēkos* when so many people had rented the estate, and all of them knew my secret? The profit would be tiny, and there was no time limit on the danger. All those who had cultivated the estate had an equal interest in ensuring that the *sēkos* was preserved, so that if anybody accused them, they would be able to pass the blame to the person to whom they handed it on. As it is, they have clearly acquitted me; and if they are lying, they have made themselves share in the guilt. [18] Even if I had managed to arrange that as well, how would I have been able to persuade[8] all the passersby, or the neighbors? Neighbors not only know things about each other that everyone can see, but they also find out about things we keep hidden from everybody else. Some of the neighbors are my friends, but others, as it happens, have disputes with me over my property. [19] He should have produced these people as witnesses, rather than simply making such audacious accusations. Instead, he claims that I was standing there, my slaves cut out the roots, and the ox driver loaded the wood on his cart and drove off with it.

[20] It was at that point, Nicomachus,[9] that you ought to have called the bystanders as witnesses and exposed the whole affair. You would have left me no defense. Assuming I was your enemy, in this way you would have punished me. If you were acting for the sake of the city, by convicting me in this way you would not have looked like a sykophant. [21] If you wanted to make a profit, it was then that you would have received the most money; for the case would have been clear, and I would have had no hope of safety other than to settle with you. But you did none of those things, and you now think you can destroy me by your speeches: you claim in your accusation that

[8] I.e., bribe, or possibly intimidate.

[9] Evidently the prosecutor; cf. the Introduction.

because of my influence and my money nobody is willing to be a witness for you. [22] But if you had called out the nine Archons, or else some other members of the Areopagus,[10] when you say you saw the sacred olive tree being removed, you would not have needed other witnesses; for in that case, the people who will decide the verdict in this trial would have known you were speaking the truth.

[23] So I am in a very awkward situation. Had he produced witnesses, he would have expected you to believe them; but since he does not have any, he thinks that this also ought to count against me. I am hardly surprised: as a sykophant, of course he will not be without witnesses and at the same time lack this sort of argument. But I do not expect you to share his attitude. [24] As you know, in the plain[11] there are many sacred olive trees and burnt stumps on my other estates. If I had wanted to, it would have been far safer for me to remove these or uproot them or encroach upon them: there are so many of them that the crime would have been less obvious. [25] But in fact I consider them as valuable as my fatherland and the rest of my property, and I think that the danger I face concerns both these things. As witnesses of this I shall produce you yourselves: you take up the matter every month,[12] and you send out investigative commissioners every year, none of whom has ever penalized me for working the land around the sacred olive trees. [26] And yet surely, if I treat these small penalties as so important, I can hardly pay no attention to the dangers affecting my person. Clearly I treat very well the many olive trees which I could more easily have damaged illegally—but I am now on trial for having removed a single sacred olive tree, which I could not have dug up without being noticed.

[27] Was it easier for me, members of the Council, to act illegally during the democracy or under the Thirty? I say this not as one who

[10] Or "some others, members of the Areopagus." This passage is not sufficient to determine whether Archons became members of the Areopagus on their entry into office or only at the end of their term.

[11] Either the plain surrounding Athens itself or the Thriasian plain around Eleusis.

[12] It is not clear what this refers to, but a similarity of wording here and at 7.7 suggests that there may have been two sets of inspections, a less detailed one every month and a more detailed one once a year.

was powerful then or is under suspicion now, but because it was much easier then than it is now for anybody who wanted to commit crimes. But it will be clear that not even under the Thirty did I do this sort of thing or any other offense. [28] Since you, the Areopagus, had such careful oversight, how on earth—unless I were my own worst enemy—could I have attempted to remove the sacred olive tree from this estate, which had not a single tree except the *sēkos* of one olive (or so he claims)? The road circled round the estate, neighbors lived on both sides, and it was unfenced and visible from all directions. Under such circumstances, who would have dared attempt something like this? [29] It seems to me quite remarkable that you, who have been granted supervision of sacred olive trees (*moria elaa*) in perpetuity by the city, have never punished me for encroaching, or put me on trial for removing any of them; whereas he, who does not farm nearby, and has not been elected as an inspector, and was not of an age to know about the events, is accusing me of having removed a sacred olive from the ground.

[30] I implore you not to regard speeches like his as more credible than actions. Do not accept the allegations of my enemies on matters about which you yourselves are knowledgeable. Remember what I have said, and the rest of my conduct as a citizen. [31] I have fulfilled all the duties laid upon me, more eagerly than was required by the city. As trierarch, as contributor to war taxes (*eisphorai*), as choregus, and in all the other liturgies, I have been as generous as any other citizen.[13] [32] And yet, if I had simply performed them adequately but not enthusiastically, I would not have faced a trial, risking exile and the remainder of my property.[14] I would have more possessions, without having committed any offenses or putting my life at risk. Whereas by doing what he accuses me of, I did not make any profit, and I put myself in danger. [33] You would all agree that it is fairer to use important evidence in important cases, and that you should consider

---

[13] Liturgies were a form of compulsory public sponsorship imposed on rich Athenians as a form of taxation. The most important of these were being trierarch (paying for the upkeep and commanding a warship for a year) and choregus (paying for the training of a chorus for a performance at a public festival; see Ant. 6).

[14] He presumably means that it is his prominence which has made him the target of an allegedly sykophantic prosecution.

things to which the whole city bears witness as more reliable than those for which he is the only accuser.

[34] There are other points to bear in mind as well, members of the Council. I went to him with witnesses and said I still had all the slaves belonging to me when I took over the estate,[15] and I was ready, if he wanted any of them, to hand them over for interrogation under torture, in the belief that this would be a more reliable test than his words and my actions. [35] He refused, claiming that there was nothing trustworthy about slaves. But it seems to me extraordinary that slaves who are under torture accuse themselves, in the full knowledge that they will die as a result, but in the case of their masters, to whom they are naturally very hostile, they may prefer to endure being tortured rather than denounce them and be released from their present sufferings. [36] I think it is clear to everybody, members of the Council, that if Nicomachus had asked me to hand over the slaves and I had refused, I would be seen to be conscious of my own guilt. But since it was I who offered and he who refused to receive them, it is only right that you should think the same about him, especially given that the danger for the two of us is not equal. [37] If the slaves said what my opponent wanted about me, I could not have defended myself. If they did not agree with him, he would not have been liable to any punishment. So it was far more his duty to receive them than my job to offer them. The reason I was so eager was that I thought I could arrange for you to find out the truth about the affair from testimony delivered under torture, and from witnesses, and from circumstantial evidence. [38] You need to consider, members of the Council, which side you should trust more: those whom many witnesses have supported or the one whom nobody has dared to support? Also, is it more likely that my opponent is lying without any risk or that I did a thing like this in the face of such great danger? And do you think he is trying to help the city or bringing a sykophantic accusation? [39] I am sure you realize that Nicomachus is undertaking this prosecution because he has been persuaded[16] by my enemies. He does not expect to show that I have done anything wrong, but hopes to receive money from

[15] In 404/3 or in 397/6?

[16] I.e., bribed.

me. Since these are the most unpleasant sorts of trial, and the most difficult to deal with, everybody tries to avoid these ones in particular. [40] But I did not think it was right to do that, members of the Council. Instead, as soon as he accused me, I offered myself for you to treat however you wished. I did not agree to terms with any of my enemies because of this trial, even though they insult me even more readily than they praise themselves. None of them has ever tried to harm me openly, but they send against me people like him—people you cannot rightly trust. [41] I would be the most wretched of all men, if I were unjustly forced into exile. I would be childless[17] and alone. My household would be made desolate. My mother would be stripped of everything. I would be deprived, on charges that bring extreme shame, of the native land which means so much to me, for which I have fought many battles on land and at sea, and have behaved well under both democracy and oligarchy.

[42] I do not know, members of the Council, why I need to mention these matters in your court. I have shown you that there was never a *sēkos* on the estate, and I have produced witnesses and circumstantial evidence. Remember this when you decide your verdict on the case. You should insist on hearing from my opponent why, when he could have convicted me in the act, he has forced me into so important a trial after such a long delay; [43] why he does not produce any witnesses but seeks to be persuasive on the basis of his speech, when he could have convicted me of wrongdoing by means of the actions themselves; and why, when I offered him all my slaves—who he claims were present—he refused to accept them.

---

[17] Or, "I am childless," etc.

8. AGAINST THE MEMBERS OF A *SUNOUSIA*[1]

INTRODUCTION

Lysias 8 is an odd piece of work, without parallel anywhere in the orators. It evidently created problems of interpretation even in antiquity: there are textual and linguistic difficulties throughout, presumably because ancient readers found it hard to work out what was going on. Admittedly there are other speeches that have no connection with the lawcourts. Lysias 2, for instance, is either a funeral oration or more probably a pamphlet modeled on a funeral oration. But the funeral oration was a well-known genre, whereas Lysias 8 is more like a resignation speech, or perhaps an open letter, addressed to (or perhaps against) the speaker's[2] former colleagues in a *sunousia* (lit. "association"). We hear vaguely of the existence in Classical Athens of a number of such informal groups, with a range of functions. In some cases the aims of the group were political, and usually oligarchic (e.g., Thuc. 8.54), but Andocides implies that his group of companions fulfilled also the social purposes of a drinking club (And. 1.61), and we hear frequently of groups of *eranistai,* whose etymology suggests that their primary function was to assist each other with mutual loans (*eranoi*).

To the modern reader, the most interesting feature of this speech is that it shows us something of the possible activities and tensions within such a group. Loans appear to be one of their major functions, but it is difficult to be sure of the precise details of what is going on.

[1] "Association": see below.

[2] If this is an open letter, it may never have been spoken, but it is more convenient to speak of "the speaker" than of "the speaker/author."

This is partly because none of the people mentioned here (all of them apparently members of the group) are otherwise attested. More importantly, no effort is made systematically to narrate the background to the dispute.[3] Instead, aspects of the story are mentioned as if to an informed audience (8.10–17), and although it is clear that there is a background of considerable backbiting (cf. 8.14–15), nevertheless the precise details are often unclear (see notes in the text).

One interesting question about Lysias 8 is why it has been included in our manuscripts and at this point in the corpus. In a papyrus containing fragments of summaries of speeches by Lysias (*P. Oxy.* 2537),[4] it is grouped together with Lysias 9, 10, and 11 under the heading *kakēgoria* (defamation). In fact only one of these four speeches (Lys. 10) was written to be delivered at a *dikē kakēgorias* (private prosecution for defamation), but there is evidently a loose thematic connection around the idea of people saying nasty things about other people.

8. ACCUSATION OF DEFAMATORY SPEECH, AGAINST THE MEMBERS OF A *SUNOUSIA* (ASSOCIATION)

[1] I think I have found a suitable moment for things I have long wanted to discuss. The people I am complaining about are present, and so are the ones before whom I want to censure those who are wronging me. And yet one is naturally more serious towards people who are present. I believe that the first group[1] will consider it insignificant if they seem to be unfriendly to their friends, because otherwise they would not be trying to wrong me in the first place. [2] However, I wish the other group would see that I am doing nothing wrong

---

[3] This may be because it really was delivered as a speech on a particular occasion to the members of the *sunousia* against whom it is directed (who would of course be familiar with the events), or because it was written as a pamphlet to criticize the members of the *sunousia* in front of an audience who could be assumed to be familiar at least with the names of those involved, or because the writer has not been particularly careful to think what future readers might not know.

[4] J. W. Barns, P. Parsons, J. Rea, and E. G. Turner, eds., *The Oxyrhynchus Papyri,* Vol. 31 (London, 1966), no. 2537.

[1] I.e., those he is complaining about; the other group is made up of those in front of whom he is complaining.

but am myself being wronged first. It is painful to be forced to speak about them, but it is impossible not to speak, when I suffer unexpected ill-treatment and find that those who seem to be friends are wronging me.

[3] In the first place, so that none of you can possibly collaborate in my opponent's actions and provide an excuse for his crime, let him say which of you I have slandered or injured, or which of you has asked me for something without receiving what he asked for, if I was in a position to grant it. Why then are you trying to hurt me with your words and actions, and to defame me in front of these people whom you are slandering in my presence? [4] And yet you were causing so much trouble that you considered it more important to appear to care for me, and instead to speak against me.[2] As to what he said, I would not tell you everything, because I was upset to hear it; nor would I, while accusing you, repeat what you said against me. I would be releasing you from my complaint if I said the same things to you on my part. [5] However, I will describe the outrage (*hubris*) that you thought you were committing against me, and how you made yourselves a laughingstock. You claimed that I forced you to associate with me and discuss things with me, and that while doing this you did not have any way to get rid of me, and finally that it was against your will that I had accompanied you on the sacred journey to Eleusis. You thought that by saying this you were slandering me, but you reveal yourselves as total incompetents, who were at the same time secretly insulting the same man whom you publicly considered as a friend. [6] Either you should have stopped slandering me, or you should have stopped associating with me and publicly renounced my company. If you regarded that as shameful, how was it shameful for you to associate with a man whose company you refused to renounce? [7] I have not myself discovered any reason why you could reasonably have despised my company. I was not aware that you were particularly wise and I was particularly stupid, or that you had plenty of friends and I was without any, or again that you were wealthy and I was poor, or indeed that you had a particularly good reputation and I was an object

[2] The meaning of the sentence remains obscure, even if we emend the text to read "that somebody should appear to care for me."

of derision, or that my affairs were at risk and yours were secure. On what basis, then, could I reasonably have suspected that you were upset with my company? [8] When you made these statements to the newest members,[3] you did not think to give this news to me. You thought it was a brilliant stroke of cleverness when you went around to everybody, but you were accusing yourselves of willingly consorting with criminals.

You would not succeed in finding out about the person who told me about this. In the first place, when you ask about the person who spoke to me, you already know him: how could you not know the identity of the person you spoke to?[4] [9] Secondly, I would be behaving disgracefully if I did the same to him as he did to you. He did not pass on the information to me with the same purpose that you spoke to him. He passed it on to my relatives[5] as a favor to me, whereas you spoke to him because you wished to harm me. If I did not believe this, I would try to test it. As it is, I do believe it, because these events agree with earlier ones, and confirm the others, just as the others confirm these.[6] [10] In the first place, it was through you that I conducted all my transactions with Hegemachus about pledging the horse.[7] When the horse fell sick, I wanted to return it to its owner, but Diodorus here tried to discourage me, saying that Polycles would not argue about the twelve minas but would repay the debt. That was what he said at the time, but after the horse's death, he eventually joined with these men like an opposing litigant, saying it would not be fair for me to recover the money. [11] And yet they were accusing themselves. If

---

[3] Lit. "the latest people," conceivably "your most recent hearers."

[4] A difficult sentence. He seems to be implying that they will not need to do any detective work to discover his informant, because his information comes from somebody to whom his opponents have themselves been slandering him.

[5] Or "close friends": *anankaioi.*

[6] The point of this sentence is obscure.

[7] The speaker has apparently lent twelve minas to Polycles, in return for a horse pledged by Polycles as security for the loan, which had been arranged by Hegemachus. He claims that when the horse fell sick he tried to cancel the loan, but was discouraged by Diodorus, on the grounds that Polycles would in due course repay the loan anyway; but that when the horse died, Diodorus changed his tune and argued that the speaker had no claim to recover his money.

it was wrong for me, as the injured party, to speak about what I had done together with them, how much more were they acting together improperly?[8] I believed that they were putting forward the opposite argument because they were quibbling[9] about the case. [12] However, they were not arguing against me but acting against me; and the reason they were acting against me was so that Polycles would know about my case. This became clear: Polycles lost his temper while the arbitrators were present, and said that even my friends were telling him that they thought I was behaving wrongly. Does this agree with the information they reported? The same person reported that you were promising to discourage those intending to speak on my behalf, and that you had already prevented some of them from doing so. What need is there for me to prove the case more clearly? [13] Come now: could that man[10] have known that I had asked unsuccessfully Cleitodicus[11] to speak in support? It was not possible for them. What profit was there for him in slandering me in front of you so enthusiastically that he was busy in inventing this story for the consumption of my relatives?

[14] I am aware that for a long time now you have been seeking a pretext, ever since you said it was on my account that Thrasymachus was slandering you. I asked Thrasymachus[12] if it was on my account that he was slandering Diodorus, and he was extremely critical of the phrase "on my account." He said it was totally untrue that he was slandering Diodorus on anybody's account. As I was pursuing the

---

[8] Reading *kakōs* in place of *kalōs* ("properly") in the manuscript.

[9] Lit. "being philosophers" (*philosopheō*). The use of the word here is interesting for its negative overtones.

[10] "That man" is possibly Polycles, and the phrase translated "it was possible for them" could also mean "he was not present with these people," but the meaning of this section is obscure. *Anankaioi,* here translated "relatives," may also denote "close friends," as in 8.9.

[11] The point of the reference to Cleitodicus here is unclear.

[12] To avoid the awkward and repetitious use of "that man," "this person," etc., I have rendered many of the Greek pronouns in this paragraph with the appropriate name, except in a few cases where the identifications are not entirely secure. The use of names for pronouns does mask the obscurity of the Greek. It should be noted that throughout this speech, "you" is always linguistically plural.

matter, Thrasymachus was eager to be examined about the things this man had said, but this man preferred a completely different arrangement. [15] After this, Autocrates told Thrasymachus in my presence that he had been informed by Menophilus that Euryptolemus was criticizing him and was claiming to have been slandered by him. Thrasymachus went with me to see Menophilus, and the latter stated that he had never heard the alleged slander and had not passed on the information to Euryptolemus. As if that was not enough, he added that he had not even spoken with Euryptolemus for a long time. [16] Clearly you have been putting forward pretexts like this, based in the past on the association between Thrasymachus and myself; but now, when pretexts have deserted you, you leave nothing undone in damaging me more openly. I should have recognized then that this fate was coming to me, when you were slandering each other even to me. In addition, I have told you all about Polycles, whom you are now assisting. [17] Why on earth was I so unguarded? I was rather naive. I believed that I was a special friend, exempt from being slandered[13] precisely because you were slandering the others in front of me, and that your criminal remarks about each other were a sort of security from each one of you.

[18] I therefore willingly withdraw from friendship with you—because, by the gods, I do not see what penalty I shall suffer if I cease to be your friend, and I have derived no benefit from being so. Shall I miss having somebody to speak for me and people to testify on my behalf when I am faced with some legal business? But at the moment, instead of speaking for me, you are seeking to prevent the one who is speaking, and instead of assisting me and testifying justly, you are associating with the opposing litigants and testifying for them. [19] Or will you say good things about me because you are well disposed to me? But at the moment, you are the only ones who are slandering me. There will be nothing in your way as far as I am concerned. Because it is your custom by word and action constantly to harm one of the members of your association, this is what will happen to your relations with each other: as soon as I am no longer one of you, you will turn against each other; then one by one you will become hateful to each

[13] The text here is uncertain, but this is the general sense.

other; and finally the only one who is left will resort to slandering himself.[14] [20] I will have this advantage, at any rate, that by getting rid of you first, I will suffer the least damage from you. Both in word and in deed you damage those who deal with you, but you have never damaged a single one of those who have no such dealings.

[14] An almost funny joke, which is unusual in the orators, though see Lys. 24 and Lys. Fr. 1 (*Aeschines*).

9. FOR THE SOLDIER

INTRODUCTION

The events behind this speech are narrated at 9.4–7. The speaker, whose name is apparently Polyaenus (9.5), claims that he had been called up unfairly for repeated military service, and had objected to the generals (who were responsible for the call up) but with no success. He had then discussed this with a private individual, and the generals had promptly punished him with a summary fine (*epibolē*) on the ground that he had slandered them. The speaker acknowledges that the generals had the power to impose such fines for slander, but claims that they could only do this if somebody insulted them "in the *sunedrion*" (see note on 9.6), whereas his criticisms had been made privately in a bank. No fine had been paid, and no attempt made to exact payment of the fine, during the generals' year of office. At the end of the year, they had attempted to report the alleged fine as an unpaid debt for the treasurers to collect, but the treasurers had refused to accept the report, on the grounds (according to the speaker) that the fine had been imposed irregularly and out of malice. Nevertheless, it is clear that the speaker is now being prosecuted by *apographē* (writ of confiscation): in other words, the prosecutors (whose identity is unknown) have submitted a written list of some or all of what he owns, alleging that it should be confiscated to pay the fine.[1]

---

[1] The speaker claims that the generals have prosecuted him on a capital charge (lit. "concerning the body": 9.15), and that his opponents have driven him out of the city (9.17). However, the penalty of death or banishment is not normal under this procedure, and these remarks are presumably exaggerated versions of the argument that if he now loses, he will in effect be forced into exile (9.21).

At first sight there is evidence that might suggest a late date for this speech, in the form of the phrase "the supporters of Ctesicles the *archōn*" at 9.6. The word *archōn* in its technical sense denotes one of the nine Archons, and particularly the first of these, the titular chief magistrate of Athens who gave his name to the year. The name of each year's Archon is known throughout the fourth century BC, and the only year in which the Archon was named Ctesicles was 333/2.[2] But it is by no means clear why the Archon, who dealt with matters involving inheritance and the family, would have been involved in a case like this, and Lysias elsewhere uses the word *archōn* in a less technical sense, specifically to denote military officials (Lys. 16.16). From the context, it is usually thought that Ctesicles is one of the generals. The office of General (unlike that of Archon) could be held repeatedly, and many of the holders are unknown. There is a Ctesicles who is known to have been general in 374/3. The name is not particularly rare, but if this is the same man, and if the speech is by Lysias or by a contemporary, it would seem likely that it dates from an otherwise unknown previous occasion on which he held the office.[3] The Corinthian War (395–387) would supply a plausible context.

There is a good discussion of the legal and historical problems in this speech by D. M. MacDowell, "The Case of the Rude Soldier (Lysias 9)," in G. Thür, ed., *Symposion 1993: Vorträge zur griechischen und hellenistischen Rechtsgeschichte* (Cologne and Vienna, 1994), 153–164.

9. FOR THE SOLDIER

[1] What on earth did my opponents have in mind when they ignored the point at issue and sought to defame my character? Are they unaware that they are supposed to keep to the point? Or do they recognize this, but devote more attention to other matters than they should, thinking that you will not notice? [2] I know for certain that they are delivering this speech not because they despise me but be-

[2] In which case of course the speech would be far too late to be by Lysias, whose last securely dated speech (Lys. 26) belongs to 382 BC.

[3] None of the other people mentioned in the speech is otherwise attested, not even Sostratus (see 9.13n): there is no reason to identify this man with the Sostratus of Lys. 1.22.

cause they despise the point at issue. But I would be surprised if they think that out of ignorance you can be persuaded by their slanders to vote for a conviction. [3] I had expected, gentlemen of the jury, that I would face trial on the basis of the indictment and not of my character. However, since my opponents are defaming me, I am forced to make my defense on the basis of all these topics. First of all, I shall tell you about the *apographē* (writ of confiscation).

[4] I returned to the city the year before last, and had not been living here two months when I was called up for military service. On discovering what had happened, I immediately suspected that I had been called up for no proper reason. I went to see the general and showed him that I had recently been on campaign, but I did not receive proper treatment. I was angry at being insulted, but I kept quiet. [5] Uncertain what to do, I was asking a fellow-citizen for advice about the matter, when I found out that they were threatening even to imprison me, claiming that "Polyaenus had been staying in Athens for as long as Callicrates." This conversation of mine that I have described had taken place at Philius' banking table.[1] [6] Nevertheless, the supporters of Ctesicles the official claimed the right to punish me when somebody mentioned that I was slandering them: this was illegal, because what the law forbids is if somebody insults an official in the *sunedrion.*[2] They imposed an *epibolē* (summary fine) but did not attempt to collect the money. Instead, when their term of office ended, they wrote it on a whitened board,[3] which they handed over to the treasurers. [7] That is what they did. The treasurers, on the other hand, did not share their opinions, but summoned those who had handed over the document, and tried to discover the reason for the charge. When they heard what had happened, and realized the sort of things I had suffered, they first tried to persuade them to let me off,

---

[1] An ancient Greek bank was literally a table at which the banker transacted business.

[2] *Sunedrion* means a "gathering." It may refer to a lawcourt presided over by the generals, or more generally to any meeting at which the generals were present in their official capacity. The significance of the word *archōn* (here translated "official") is discussed in the Introduction.

[3] Such wooden boards were regularly used for the type of public record that was intended to be less permanent than an inscribed stone.

arguing that it was not fair to register any citizen as a public debtor out of malice. When they could not find any way to persuade them, however, they took on themselves the danger at your hands[4] and ruled that the fine was invalid.[5]

[8] You now know that I was let off by the treasurers. In my view, I should properly be acquitted of the charge on the basis of this demonstration alone. However, I shall produce still more laws and other justifications. Please take and read the law for me.

[LAW]

[9] You have heard that the law explicitly orders a fine to be imposed on those who insult an official in the *sunedrion.* I have produced witnesses to testify that I did not go to the office of the officials; and that because I had a fine imposed on me unjustly, I do not owe it, and it is not right that I should pay it. [10] If it is clear that I did not go to the *sunedrion,* and the law states that those who offend there are to owe the fine, then clearly I have committed no offense, and have been punished without legal justification, fraudulently and maliciously. [11] The officials were aware that they had acted illegally, because they did not render accounts (*euthunai*), and they did not come to a lawcourt and confirm the validity of their actions with a jury's vote. Indeed, even if they had punished me in a lawful manner, and had ratified the summary fine (*epibolē*) in your presence, it would have been reasonable for me to be acquitted of the charge, since the treasurers had let me off the fine. [12] If the treasurers did not have the authority to decide whether to impose it or to let me off, I would properly owe the money, because I would have been legitimately fined. But if they do have the authority to let me off, provided they render an account of their actions in office, then they will certainly receive the appropriate penalty if they have done anything wrong.[6]

[13] You have learned how my name was handed over and I was fined, but you need to know not simply the reason for the indictment

---

[4] I.e., the risk of being punished when they submitted their accounts (*euthunai*) at the end of their own term of office.

[5] In view of the opening phrase of 9.8, and of what is said in 9.9, editors suspect that a reference to the testimony of witnesses has dropped out of the text here.

[6] I.e., they will be punished at their *euthunai;* cf. 9.7n.

but also the pretext for their hostility. Before their hostility developed, I was a friend of Sostratus,[7] because I knew that he had become prominent in public life. [14] Even while I was becoming well known through his influence, I did not take vengeance on an enemy or confer benefits on a friend. During his lifetime, I necessarily took no part in public affairs because of my age,[8] and after he died, I did not hurt any of my accusers in word or action. Indeed, I could recount events showing how I should much more justly receive benefits than suffer harm from my opponents. [15] Because of what has been mentioned, their anger grew, even though there was no reason for their hostility. After swearing to call up only those who had not been on campaign, they broke their oaths and brought my case before the People (*plēthos*) on a capital charge.[9] [16] By fining me on the pretext that I was slandering their authority, they treated justice with contempt, making every effort to hurt me. They would have done anything to damage me severely and to benefit themselves considerably, given that when neither of these was at issue, they reckoned everything else less important than injustice.[10] [17] These are men who despised your democracy and did not think it right to respect the gods. Instead, they have behaved so contemptuously and illegally that they have not even attempted to defend their behavior, and what is more, they have finally driven me out of the city,[11] in the belief that their revenge on me is not sufficient. [18] While behaving so lawlessly and violently, they have taken no trouble to hide their injustice. They are dragging me again into court

---

[7] Sostratus is described here in terms that suggest he is a major political figure. This may of course be an indication of the defective state of our knowledge, because it is certainly possible that there may be politically significant figures even in the first decades of the fourth century (a relatively well attested period) about whom we know nothing. On the other hand, it is quite likely that the speaker is exaggerating Sostratus' importance, to make it look as if the prosecutors are victimizing himself.

[8] This probably means that he was too young to hold public office (for which the minimum age was thirty).

[9] See the Introduction at n. 1.

[10] The manuscript has "justice," but the context suggests that this is a corruption.

[11] See the Introduction at n. 1.

on the same subject,[12] and are denouncing and defaming me when I have done nothing wrong. Their slanders are wholly inappropriate to my way of life but closely match their own behavior.

[19] These people[13] are keen to get me convicted in this case by any means possible. You must not be aroused by my opponents' slanders and convict me. Do not render invalid the better decision of those who decided justly. These people[14] have done everything lawfully and reasonably. Clearly they have committed no offenses but have had the greatest respect for justice. [20] I have been only moderately angry at my opponents' unjust behavior, because I believed that life was organized on a principle of hurting one's enemies and helping one's friends. I should be far more grieved, however, if I were deprived of justice at your hands, because I shall be seen to have suffered this fate not because of personal enmity but because of something wrong in the city. [21] I am on trial nominally over this *apographē* (writ of confiscation) but in reality over my citizenship. If I obtain justice—and I am trusting in your verdict—I could remain in the city; but if I were unjustly convicted after being brought before you by these people, I would run away. What hope would there be to encourage me to share in the life of the city? What would have to be my aim, given that I would know the eagerness of my opponents and would not know how to achieve any of my rights? [22] You should therefore pay the greatest attention to justice. Bear in mind that you regularly forgive even the most blatant offenses. Do not look on while those who have done no wrong are unjustly ensnared in the greatest misfortunes as a result of personal enmity.

---

[12] This may be a protest against the principle of double jeopardy.

[13] Presumably the generals.

[14] Presumably the treasurers.

10–11. AGAINST THEOMNESTUS FOR DEFAMATION

INTRODUCTION

Lysias 10 is an intriguing speech, which raises issues of law, of language, and of legal sociology. Sociologically what is most interesting about the speech is its position within an extended dispute, in which the present case is the fourth in the series to come to court; by no means is it necessarily the last. As usual, we do not know the result of the trial, or what happened afterwards, though it can be firmly dated to 384/3 BC (see 10.4n), making it one of the latest speeches in the corpus of Lysias.

The first of the sequence of cases had been brought by Lysitheus, alleging that Theomnestus had made a public speech while disqualified because he had previously thrown away his shield in battle (see 10.1n). Theomnestus, however, seems to have been acquitted,[1] and he retaliated by prosecuting one of Lysitheus' witnesses, apparently named Dionysius (10.24–25), who was convicted and disfranchised (10.22), and by prosecuting somebody else[2] for having slandered him with the story about the shield (10.12). The present prosecution is brought against Theomnestus by an unnamed plaintiff who had been involved as a witness alongside Dionysius (10.30) and therefore presumably at the original trial in support of Lysitheus. The procedure is a private prosecution for defamation (*dikē kakēgorias*). It is alleged that at that original trial, Theomnestus had characterized the speaker as a

[1] Nowhere stated, but implied by the wording of 10.3 and by Lysias' failure to mention a conviction.

[2] The manuscript says "Theon" (otherwise unknown), but it is widely if not universally accepted that this is a corruption of "Lysitheus."

parricide. The speaker and his father cannot be identified for certain, but what is said about the father's career at 10.27, together with the fact that the name Pantaleon is found in his family (10.5), has encouraged speculation that the father was Leon of Salamis, one of the Thirty's most prominent victims, who was executed despite Socrates' refusal of the Thirty's order to arrest him.[3] Nobody else in the speech is otherwise attested.

Several features of the Athenian law of defamation emerge from this speech. Particularly striking is the defendant's position, which can to some extent be inferred from the speaker's counterarguments. We might have expected Theomnestus, as defendant in a defamation case, either to deny that he had made the statement attributed to him, or alternatively to claim that he had done so because it was true. If either of these arguments had been the thrust of Theomnestus' defense, the speaker would presumably have concentrated on refuting them, but in fact he passes over them very briefly, with a simple assertion that Theomnestus had made the statement (10.1) followed by a brief argument that it cannot have been true (10.4–5).[4] Instead, the speaker focuses his attention on the claim that Theomnestus could be prosecuted only if he had used one of a number of prohibited words. The Athenian law of defamation seems to have banned any defamatory statements made in certain contexts (such as those made against an official in his *sunedrion;* cf. Lys. 9.9), or certain specific statements (the so-called *aporrhēta* or "things that must not be spoken") made in any context. The thrust of Theomnestus' defense appears to have been that this latter rule referred only to specific words (10.6), and that to claim that somebody had killed his father was not actionable, provided the speaker had not used the prohibited word *androphonos* ("man-slayer").

This is a clever if highly technical defense, which seems to reflect contemporary intellectual developments, and especially the sophists' interest in the use of language, to an extent that is unusual in the

---

[3] For Socrates' refusal to arrest Leon, see Plato, *Apology* 32c–d. Names in Athenian families sometimes shared the same core (which might account for the "-leon" ending in Pantaleon).

[4] The speaker claims that because he was only thirteen he was too young to understand the politics of his father's death, but this does not of course rule out the possibility that he had accidentally assisted those responsible.

orators. We may wonder how far Theomnestus could have expected the jury to sympathize with such a sophistic argument, but it is notable that the speaker feels the need to meet the defense head on, with a detailed and in places equally technical rebuttal. Specifically, he points out that a literal reading of this and of other laws leads to ridiculous conclusions (10.8–10). Moreover, he argues that the literal meaning has in fact been rejected implicitly by Theomnestus himself (10.12), because he had prosecuted Lysitheus (or Theon) for slandering him with the story about the shield, even though the latter had used not the prohibited verb *apoballō* (here translated "I throw away") but the synonymous term *rhiptō* ("I discard").

Legally more interesting, however, is the general argument that words in legal statutes should be interpreted so as to include their synonyms: an argument that is unique in the orators both for its didactic tone and for its conscious awareness of archaism. The speaker supports his case by discussing a series of quotations from what he describes as the "ancient (or possibly 'former') laws of Solon" (10.15–21). We cannot be certain that these laws are genuine products of the sixth-century lawgiver Solon, and the ambiguity of his phrasing means that we cannot be certain whether these laws are formally obsolete (i.e., "former") or simply "ancient." What is clear, however, is that they contain words which are no longer normally used but which (he claims) any reader of a legal statute must be expected mentally to translate into contemporary language.

Lysias 11 is a précis of Lysias 10. It used to be regarded as a late rhetorical exercise, because Harpocration, who wrote a *Lexicon to the Ten Orators,* probably in the second century AD, cites Lysias 10 by name on six occasions (more than any other speech in the corpus) for the use of rare legal terms, but he consistently describes it as if it were the only speech *Against Theomnestus* known to him, rather than the first of two. The inference was that Lysias 11 was not written until after Harpocration, but this conclusion has been undermined by the publication in 1966 of a papyrus containing fragments of summaries of speeches by Lysias (*P.Oxy.* 2537), which refers to both speeches.[5] For

[5] The papyrus (for which see the Introduction to Lys. 8 at n. 4) belongs to the late second or early third century AD, which hardly leaves time for a speech written after Harpocration's date to have become accepted into the corpus.

the modern reader, the main interest of Lysias 11 is that it indicates which bits of Lysias 10 were felt to be important by one ancient reader: the argument about obsolete terms in the law (10.15–21) is entirely omitted from Lysias 11, despite its being the source of all but one of Harpocration's citations from the speech.

There is a useful commentary by Usher on Lysias 10 in Edwards and Usher 1985. The sequence of trials underlying the speech, and some of the legal issues raised by the law of defamation, are discussed in more detail in Todd 1993: 258–262. On attitudes to written law in the fourth-century orators, there is a stimulating paper by R. Thomas, "Law and the Lawgiver in the Athenian Democracy," in R. G. Osborne and S. Hornblower, eds., *Ritual, Finance, Politics: Athenian Democratic Accounts Presented to David Lewis* (Oxford, 1994), 119–133.

10. PROSECUTION SPEECH AGAINST THEOMNESTUS: FIRST SPEECH [1]

[1] I do not expect to have any difficulty finding witnesses, gentlemen of the jury. I can see that many of you who are judging the case were among those present when Lysitheus denounced [2] Theomnestus, on the grounds that he was speaking in public when he was not permitted to do so because he had thrown away (*apoballō*) his shield. In the course of that litigation, Theomnestus asserted that I had killed my own father. [2] If he had accused me of killing his father, I would have forgiven him the statement, because I regard him as insignificant and unworthy of attention. Nor would I have taken proceedings against him if I had been called any other of the *aporrhēta* (prohibited words), because I believe that to prosecute for defamation is petty and over-litigious. [3] But it seems to me shameful not to punish the person who made that statement about my father, who has earned so much honor from you and the city. I want to know whether the de-

[1] For the relationship with speech 11, see the Introduction.

[2] According to the manuscript, the procedure was impeachment (*eisangelia*), which is not otherwise attested in such circumstances. I have therefore accepted the emendation *epangelia* (the preliminary denunciation necessary before bringing a *dokimasia* to scrutinize the qualifications of a public speaker). This procedure is paralleled in Aesch. 1 and would fit the context very well.

fendant is going to pay the penalty, or whether he alone of the Athenians will receive a special exemption to do and say anything unlawful he wishes. [4] I am thirty-two years old,[3] and this is now the twentieth year since you returned from exile,[4] so clearly I was thirteen when my father was killed by the Thirty. At that age I did not know what an oligarchy was, and I could not have assisted him when he was wronged. [5] Nor could I plausibly have been plotting against him for the sake of money, because Pantaleon my elder brother[5] took control of everything; he became guardian and deprived us of our inheritance. So I had many reasons, gentlemen of the jury, for wishing him alive. I need to remind you about these things, but there is no need for many words, because virtually all of you know that I am telling the truth. However, I shall produce witnesses to these facts.

[WITNESSES]

[6] He will perhaps make no defense on these points, gentlemen of the jury, but will say to you what he had the audacity to claim in front of the arbitrator, that it is not one of the *aporrhēta* if somebody says that I have killed my father, because the law does not forbid this but bans people from saying "*androphonos*" (man-slayer). [7] But in my view, gentlemen of the jury, you must decide on the basis not of the words but of their meaning: you all recognize that those who kill people are also *androphonoi,* and those who are *androphonoi* have also killed people. It would have been a considerable task for the lawgiver to write all the words that have the same meaning, but by talking about one of them, he made clear his views about them all. [8] I can hardly suppose, Theomnestus, that if somebody called you "father-beater" (*patraloias*) or "mother-beater" (*mētraloias*), you would expect to win a case against him, but that if somebody said that you hit the man or woman who gave you birth, you would think he should go unpunished because he had not spoken any of the *aporrhēta.* [9] I would be glad to hear you answer the following question, for you are

[3] The manuscript says "thirty," but editors emend this to "thirty-two," on the basis of Lys. 11.1.

[4] I.e., since the democratic restoration of 403/2 BC, which means that the speech is to be dated 384/3.

[5] Or possibly "his elder brother" (i.e., the speaker's uncle).

skilled and experienced in this matter, both in acts and in words. Would you not prosecute somebody who claimed that you had discarded (*rhiptō*) your shield, because it says in the law, "Anybody who says that a person has thrown away (*apoballō*) his shield may be prosecuted"? Or would you be happy to say that to discard it was no concern of yours, because discarding is different from throwing away? [10] Or assume, Theomnestus, that you were one of the Eleven:[6] if somebody arrested a criminal by *apagōgē* (summary arrest), claiming that the man had pulled off his cloak or stripped him of his tunic, presumably you would not accept the *apagōgē* but would release the man on the same principle, because the word "clothes snatcher" (*lōpodutēs*) was not used? Or presumably, if somebody was caught abducting a child, you would not describe him as a "kidnapper" (*andrapodistēs*), if you are going to squabble about words, rather than giving your attention to the acts for which everybody uses the words.

[11] Consider another point, gentlemen of the jury: it seems to me that the defendant is so lazy and slothful that he has not even climbed up onto the Areopagus hill. Everybody knows that when they judge homicide cases there, they do not use this word in constructing the litigants' oaths,[7] but they use the one with which I have been slandered. The plaintiff swears that his opponent has killed (*kteinō*), and the defendant that he has not killed. [12] Surely it would be ridiculous if they were to acquit a person who had committed murder and who admits that he is an *androphonos* (man-slayer), because the plaintiff swore that the defendant had killed. But how does that differ from this man's argument? You yourself prosecuted Lysitheus[8] for defamation, for saying that you had discarded (*rhiptō*) your shield. Yet nothing is said in the law about "discarding." Instead, the law orders anybody who says that a person has thrown away (*apoballō*) his shield to pay five hundred drachmas. [13] Is it not strange, Theomnestus, that you interpret the laws in the same way as I do when you want to punish your enemies for slandering you, but you do not think you

---

[6] The Eleven were the public officials in charge of prisons and executions.

[7] The *diōmosia,* for which see the Introduction to Lys. 3.

[8] The manuscript reading is "Theon," but editors generally emend this to "Lysitheus" in view of 10.1.

should pay the penalty when you slander somebody else unlawfully? Are you so skillful that you can manipulate the laws however you choose, or are you so powerful that you think those whom you wrong will never achieve justice? [14] Are you not ashamed to be so stupid that you think you ought to gain an advantage not because of any good you have done for the city, but because of crimes for which you have not paid the penalty? Please read the law for me.

[LAW]

[15] I think you all realize, gentlemen of the jury, that I am speaking the truth but that the defendant is so dull that he cannot understand what is being said. So I would like to clarify the point for him on the basis of other laws as well, in the hope that he may receive an education now at any rate on the speaker's rostrum, and not cause us trouble in future. Please read for me those ancient laws of Solon.[9]

[16] [LAW] . . . *Let him be confined for five days in the foot retainer, if the court* (hēliaia) *shall impose this additional penalty . . .*

This "foot retainer" (*podokakkē*), Theomnestus, is what is now called "being confined in the stocks." If somebody who had been confined were after his release to accuse the Eleven at their accounting (*euthunai*) because they had confined him not in the foot retainer but in the stocks, they would presumably regard him as an idiot. Please read another law.

[17] [LAW] . . . *Having abjured by Apollo, let him give security. If he is afraid on account of justice, let him abscond . . .*

This word "abjure" (*epiorkeō*) means "swear," and "abscond" (*draskazō*) is what we would call "run away."

. . . *Whoever debars by means of the door while the thief is inside . . .*

This word "debar" (*apillō*) is interpreted as "shut out," so please do not disagree about that.

[18] . . . *Let the money be placed at whatever amount the lender wishes . . .*

This word "placed" (*stasimos*), my good man, does not mean "put on a balance" but "to lend out" at whatever rate of interest one wishes. Please read me also the final part of this law.

---

[9] The interpretation of this phrase is discussed in the Introduction.

[19] . . . *All those women who go abroad overtly* . . . and . . . *For damage to a menial, let him owe double* . . .

Pay attention, all of you. "Overtly" (*pephasmenōs*) is "in public," "go abroad" (*pōleisthai*) is "walk around,"[10] and a "menial" (*oikeus*) is a "domestic slave."

[20] There are many other examples of this type, gentlemen of the jury. If this man is not made of iron, I suspect he has begun to realize that things are the same now as in the past, but that we do not use some of the same names now as previously. He can make clear his understanding by leaving the speaker's rostrum and departing in silence. [21] If he does not, gentlemen of the jury, then I ask you to vote in accordance with justice, bearing in mind that it is far worse to be accused of killing one's father than of throwing away one's shield. I myself would prefer to have thrown away every shield than to have had such thoughts towards my father.

[22] Although this man was liable to Lysitheus' charge, and the peril he faced was relatively minor, he did not simply receive pity from you but also disfranchised the witness.[11] I, on the other hand, have seen the defendant commit the action which you also know about, and have kept my own shield, but I have been accused of a sacrilegious and terrible crime. The disaster I face if he is acquitted is very great, whereas it does not matter for him if he is convicted simply of defamation. Surely I deserve justice from you. [23] What charge have you heard against me? Is it that I have been justly defamed? But you yourselves would not say that. Or that the defendant is better than I am and from a better family? But even he would not claim that. Or that I have thrown away my shield and am bringing a prosecution for defamation (*dikē kakēgorias*) against somebody who kept his? But that is not the story which has gone around the city. [24] Bear in mind that you have given Theomnestus that great and generous gift.[12] Who in

[10] The reference is apparently to prostitution.

[11] In the light of 10.24, this seems to imply that Theomnestus had brought a successful prosecution for false testimony (*dikē pseudomarturiōn*) against Lysitheus' witness, presumably Dionysius; cf. the Introduction.

[12] The "gift" here is apparently Theomnestus' success in having Dionysius disenfranchised for false testimony.

these circumstances would not pity Dionysius? He has had a terrible disaster, though he is the noblest of men in the face of danger. [25] As he left the courtroom, he said we had been engaged in a most disastrous campaign, in which many of us had died, and those who had kept their shields had been convicted of false witness by those who threw them away, and it would have been better for him to die in battle than to return home and suffer such misfortune. [26] So do not pity Theomnestus, if he has been described in unflattering but fitting terms. Do not forgive a person who behaves with arrogance (*hubris*) and who speaks unlawfully. What greater misfortune could I suffer than to be so shamefully accused in relation to such a father? [27] My father served as general on many occasions and faced many other dangers with you. He never fell into the hands of the enemy, and he was never fined when he presented his accounts[13] to the citizens. He was killed during the oligarchy at the age of sixty-seven, because of his goodwill towards your democracy. [28] Surely you should be angry at the person who said such things, and should assist my father, since he too is being slandered. What more wretched fate could befall him than to be killed by his enemies and to be accused by their children? Even now, gentlemen of the jury, the memorials of his bravery hang as dedications in your temples—whereas those of the defendant's cowardice and his father's are in the temples of your enemies, so inbred is their cowardice. [29] Indeed, gentlemen of the jury, the more impressive and youthful my opponents are in appearance, the more they deserve your anger, for clearly they are physically powerful but lacking in spirit.

[30] I understand, gentlemen of the jury, that he will resort to the argument that he made this statement because of anger that I had given the same testimony as Dionysius. You are aware, however, gentlemen of the jury, that the lawgiver does not offer any leniency towards anger: he punishes the speaker who does not show that the statement is true. Twice already I have been a witness about this, for I was not aware that you punish those who see the act but forgive those who throw away their shields.

---

[13] This may also mean "he never failed to present his accounts." For the accounting required of Athenian officials, see the Series Introduction.

[31] I do not know what more I can say about this. I ask you to convict Theomnestus, bearing in mind that no contest could be greater for me than this one. I am prosecuting him now for defamation, but in the same vote I am also defending myself on a charge of murdering my father—I, who on my own, as soon as I came of age,[14] brought proceedings against the Thirty before the Areopagus. [32] Remember this, and assist me, my father, the established laws, and the oaths you have sworn.

11. PROSECUTION SPEECH AGAINST THEOMNESTUS: SECOND SPEECH [1]

[1] Many of you are aware that he said I had killed my father, and are testifying for me. It is clear, however, that I did not do so: I am thirty-two, and this is the twentieth year since you returned from exile. [2] It is obvious that I was aged twelve when my father was killed by the Thirty, so I did not even know what an oligarchy was, nor was I capable of assisting him. Moreover, I did not plot against him for money, because my elder brother[2] took everything and deprived us.

[3] Perhaps he will say that it is not one of the *aporrhēta* (prohibited words) if somebody says I have killed my father, because the law does not forbid this but bans people from saying "*androphonos*" (man-slayer). In my view, however, you must decide not about the words but about the meaning of actions: you all recognize that those who kill people are also their *androphonoi,* and those who are somebody's *androphonoi* have also killed that person. [4] It would have been a considerable task for the lawgiver to write all the words that have the same meaning. Instead, by talking about one, he made clear his views about them all. I can hardly suppose that if somebody called you "father-beater" or "mother-beater," he is legally liable, but if some-

[14] Lit. "passed my *dokimasia,*" i.e., the judicial scrutiny faced by newly adult citizens. A prosecution before the Areopagus would presumably be for murder (i.e., the murder of the speaker's father), but it is hard to imagine how the Thirty would have been available for him to prosecute in 399/8, the year when he would have come of age.

[1] For the relationship with speech 10, see the Introduction.

[2] Or "his elder brother"; cf. Lys. 10.5n.

body said that you hit the man or the woman who gave you birth, he will be unpunished. [5] And I can hardly suppose that if somebody calls you "shield discarder," he will be immune, because the law sets out a penalty for anybody who says that a person has thrown away his shield but not for somebody who says a person has discarded it. Similarly, as one of the Eleven you would not accept the person arrested by *apagōgē* (summary arrest), because he had stripped off somebody's cloak or tunic, if he did not call him a "clothes snatcher." [6] And if anybody abducted a child, you would not accept his arrest as a "kidnapper." You yourself prosecuted for defamation the person who said you had discarded your shield. Yet this word is not written in the law, but only "if anybody says that a person has thrown away." Surely it is extraordinary that you interpret the laws in the same way as I do and seek vengeance on your enemies if somebody accuses you, whereas you claim you should not pay a penalty if you accuse me? [7] Help me, then, and remember that it is a greater disgrace if it is said that you killed your father than that you discarded your shield.[3] I myself would rather have thrown away every shield than to have had such thoughts about my father. And yet I have seen the defendant acting as you also know he did, and I kept my own shield. So why shall I not obtain justice from you? [8] What accusation has he brought against me? Have I have been justly defamed? But you yourselves would not say that. Or is he is better than I am? But even he himself would not claim that. Or have I thrown away my shield, and am prosecuting somebody who kept his? But that is not the story that has gone around the city. [9] Do not pity somebody who is being described in unflattering but fitting terms. Do not forgive a person who commits *hubris* and who speaks unlawfully—and this against a man who served many times as general and who faced many other dangers with you. He never fell into the hands of the enemy and was never fined when he presented his accounts to you.[4] He ended his life at the age of seventy under the oligarchy because of your goodwill. [10] It is right to be

[3] The verb here is *rhiptō,* whereas it ought logically to be *apoballō,* as at Lys. 10.21.

[4] For another possible meaning of this phrase, see the note to Lys. 10.27, though there the father is said to have been aged sixty-seven at the time of his death.

angry on his behalf. What more wretched name could he bear, if after being killed by his enemies, he were to be accused of having been killed by his children?[5] The memorials of his bravery hang as dedications in your temples—whereas those of the defendants' cowardice are in the temples of your enemies.

[11] He will say that he made this statement out of anger. You are aware, however, gentlemen of the jury, that the lawgiver does not offer any leniency towards anger: he punishes the speaker who does not demonstrate the truth of his statement. Twice already I have been a witness about this, for I was not aware that you punish those who see the act but forgive those who throw away their shields. [12] I am prosecuting now for defamation, but in the same vote I am also defending myself on a charge of murdering my father, and I could not be facing any more serious trial than that—I, who on my own, after I came of age,[6] brought proceedings against the Thirty before the Areopagus. Please assist him and me.

---

[5] Lys. 10.28 speaks of his being accused by the children of his enemies, which is rhetorically much more effective.

[6] Lit. "passed my *dokimasia*," as in Lys. 10.31.

12. AGAINST ERATOSTHENES

INTRODUCTION

This is the most famous of Lysias' speeches, not least because it directly concerns Lysias himself, not simply as author but also as speaker. It is an accusation against Eratosthenes, a former member of the Thirty (the oligarchic junta of 404/3), who is charged with the murder of Lysias' own brother Polemarchus.

In 403/2, democracy was restored at Athens, subject to a general amnesty to protect former supporters of the oligarchy. The terms of the amnesty are quoted in *Ath. Pol.* 39.1–6, and include specific provisions excluding the Thirty themselves, together with the holders of certain specified offices under the oligarchy, from the protection of the amnesty until and unless they successfully defended themselves at their accounting (*euthunai*);[1] if however they did this, they would receive the full protection of the amnesty, which prohibited anyone from "remembering wrongs" (or in other words from bringing a prosecution based on events before the restoration of democracy), except in cases where people were accused of killing with their own hands.

The legal context of Lysias 12 is nowhere explicitly stated in the speech, and modern scholars have debated at length whether it was at Eratosthenes' *euthunai* in 403/2, or at a subsequent prosecution for homicide, or indeed whether the speech was actually delivered. It is difficult, however, to see how it can have been at a subsequent

[1] Very few of those excluded seem to have take advantage of this opportunity. Most feared (probably correctly) that any examination would find them guilty.

homicide prosecution. If Eratosthenes had passed his *euthunai* and achieved the protection of the amnesty, he would have been able to protest that he was no longer liable for having brought about Polemarchus' death by arresting him, and Lysias makes no attempt here to argue that such action was somehow tantamount to killing with one's own hands (contrast Lys. 13.85–87).

More difficult is the question of whether the speech was delivered at Eratosthenes' *euthunai* or not delivered at all. This depends on whether Lysias, as a noncitizen, would have been entitled in his own right to bring a charge at such a hearing, and that is a question for which we do not have the evidence to give a direct answer. All we can say is that if Lysias was entitled to prosecute, it is difficult to think of reasons why he would not have done so, and there is nothing about the speech as it stands that would make it inappropriate for delivering at a trial. On the other hand, if Lysias was prevented by his status from appearing in person, he could have circulated this as a pamphlet and as a way of showing what he would have said, all the more so if he felt cheated at not having received the citizenship in return for his support for the democratic counterrevolutionaries in 404/3.[2]

The formal charge against Eratosthenes is covered in 12.6–36. No evidence is called, and the force of the argument rests on two things. The first of these is the careful construction of a narrative which assumes without stating it that the Thirty were corporately and individually corrupt. The second is the cross-questioning of Eratosthenes himself (12.25), as a result of which Eratosthenes appears[3] to be basing his defense on a plea that he was taking orders from superiors, which Lysias ruthlessly criticizes with many of the arguments that were put

---

[2] Immediately after the restoration of democracy, Thrasybulus successfully proposed a decree granting citizenship to all those who had joined him (including presumably Lysias), but it was judicially challenged and annulled apparently before taking effect.

[3] P. A. Krentz, in *Parola del Passato* 39 (1984): 23–32, has argued that this is an illusion created by manipulative questioning, and that Eratosthenes was really claiming to have acted out of fear not of his colleagues among the Thirty but of a counterrevolution among the metics against the Thirty. This, however, as A. H. Sommerstein notes in *Parola del Passato* 39 (1984): 370–372, would imply considerable naiveté on the part of Eratosthenes under questioning.

forward by the prosecutors at the Nuremberg trials. Nearly two-thirds of the speech, however, is devoted to material that is prejudicial rather than formally relevant (12.37–100), including an account of the previous career of Eratosthenes (12.42–52), which broadens into an attack on the rest of the Thirty and their hangers-on (12.53–61). It leads into a specific and extended attack on the controversial figure of Theramenes (12.62–78), the leader of one of the factions among the Thirty, who had been outmaneuvered and executed by his more extreme rival Critias (Xen., *Hellenica* 2.3).[4]

The attack on Theramenes is surprising, and it has often been used by modern scholars seeking to determine the result of the trial. Eratosthenes will presumably have been acquitted, so the argument runs, because he will have had the support of former supporters of Theramenes. But Theramenes does not seem to have been a uniformly popular figure at Athens, and although Lysias' caricature of his career is no doubt unfair, it is at least possible to invert the standard interpretations of its function: Lysias may be using the unpopularity of Theramenes to prejudice the audience against Eratosthenes. We have therefore no evidence for the result of the trial[5] (if, that is, the speech was actually delivered).

P. A. Krentz, *The Thirty at Athens* (Ithaca, 1982), is a stimulating if at times speculative attempt to see what the Thirty may have been trying to achieve. T. C. Loening, *The Reconciliation Agreement of 403/402 BC in Athens: Its Content and Application* (*Hermes* Einzelschrift 53, Stuttgart, 1987), is a useful account of the amnesty, though his views

[4] Theramenes had been one of the Four Hundred, but he engineered their downfall and his reinstatement as a democratic politician after 410, which gave him a name for always being on the winning side (Aristoph., *Frogs* 967–970). Some accounts written after his death, however, are rabidly positive: *Ath. Pol.* delivers a glowing eulogy and even suppresses his membership of the Thirty, and there exists a fragment known as the Theramenes papyrus (*P.Mich.* 5982, translated by Peseley in *Ancient History Bulletin* 3.2 [1989]: 30–31), which appears to be a conscious rebuttal of the account given in Lys. 12.62–78.

[5] Unless we accept the unlikely hypothesis (discussed in the Introduction to Lys. 1) that the defendant is to be identified with the Eratosthenes who was the victim of the killing which is the subject of that speech. In this case, Lys. 12 would have to be earlier and would have had to result in an acquittal.

on the dating of Lysias 12 have not won widespread acceptance. On the details of the speech, see Usher's commentary in Edwards and Usher 1985.

12. PROSECUTION SPEECH AGAINST ERATOSTHENES, FORMER MEMBER OF THE THIRTY: DELIVERED BY LYSIAS HIMSELF

[1] The difficulty I face, gentlemen of the jury, is not how to begin my prosecution but how to draw it to a close. The crimes committed by my opponent are so great and so numerous that even by lying I would not be able to accuse him of things more terrible than what happened, and if I stick to the truth, I cannot tell you everything: inevitably either the prosecutor will give up in exhaustion or his time will run out. [2] My situation seems to be the reverse of what has traditionally happened. Previously those prosecuting had to explain their hatred towards the defendants,[1] but in this case you should ask the defendants about their hatred towards the city, which has prompted them to dare to commit such crimes against it. Not that I cannot give an account of private enmity and suffering, but when there is such an abundance of enmity arising out of public concerns, then everybody should be angry. [3] For myself, gentlemen of the jury, I have never taken part in public affairs, either on my own or on anybody else's account, but because of what has happened, I am now compelled to prosecute this man. As a result, I have frequently become very nervous, lest out of inexperience I should produce a speech that was incompetent and unworthy of my brother and myself. Nevertheless, I shall attempt as best I can to tell you the story from the beginning.

[4] My father Cephalus was invited by Pericles to move to this land, and he lived here for thirty years.[2] Neither he nor the rest of the

---

[1] Personal enmity was regarded as a good motive for prosecuting, not least because prosecutions were normally brought by private individuals rather than public prosecutors. To prosecute somebody who was not your enemy laid you open to the suspicion of being a sykophant (for which cf. 12.5n).

[2] This is often assumed to be true, and is used to help date Lysias' family history. There is admittedly no contrary evidence, but we have only Lysias' word for it, and Pericles would have been a good patron to claim.

family was ever involved in any litigation, either as prosecutor or as defendant. We lived our lives under the democracy in such a way as to do no wrong to others and to suffer no harm from others. [5] Later on, however, the Thirty, who were criminals and sykophants,[3] established themselves in office, claiming that they needed to cleanse the city of wrongdoers and redirect the remaining citizens towards goodness and justice. But despite this assertion, they did not venture to do anything of the kind. I shall do my best to refresh your memories of this, by speaking first about my own affairs and then about yours. [6] It was at a meeting of the Thirty that Theognis and Peison raised the subject of the metics,[4] claiming that some were hostile to the new constitution. This would provide an excellent pretext for appearing to punish them while in reality making money, because the city was completely impoverished, and the regime needed cash. [7] They had no difficulty persuading their audience, who thought nothing of taking human life but were very keen to make money. They decided to arrest ten metics, two of them poor, so that they could plead in the case of the others that this had not been done for money but was for the benefit of the constitution—as if they had had valid reasons for any of their other actions! [8] They divided up the houses and set out. They found me entertaining guests at dinner, drove them out, and handed me over to Peison. The others went to the slave workshop (*ergastērion*) and began to draw up a confiscation list (*apographē*) of the slaves. I asked Peison whether he would be willing to take a bribe for rescuing me. He said yes, if it was a big one. [9] I replied that I was prepared to give him a talent of silver, and he agreed to this. I knew he had no respect for gods or for men, but given my situation, I thought it absolutely essential to get a pledge from him. [10] He swore an oath that he would rescue me if he received the talent, and he called down destruction on himself and his children. I then went into my bedroom and opened my treasure chest. Peison noticed this and came in, and seeing its contents, he called two of his attendants and told them to take what was in the chest. [11] He now had not

---

[3] A word normally used of malicious prosecutors and sometimes associated with alleged rabble-rousing democratic politicians; to predicate it of the oligarchs of 404/3 is a striking extension of its normal use.

[4] Lysias and his family were metics (noncitizens resident at Athens), some of whom were rich. Theognis and Peison were members of the Thirty.

simply the agreed amount, gentlemen of the jury, but three talents of silver, four hundred Cyzicene staters, one hundred Persian darics, and four silver cups.[5] So I asked him to give me some traveling money, but he said that I should be glad to save my skin. [12] As we were leaving the house, Peison and I ran into Melobius and Mnesitheides[6] coming out of the slave workshop. They met us just at the doors of the house and asked where we were going. Peison said to my brother's, to examine the contents of that house as well. They told him to carry on but ordered me to accompany them to Damnippus' house. [13] Peison came near me, and told me to stay quiet and keep my spirits up, because he would join us there. At Damnippus', we found Theognis keeping guard over various others. They handed me over to him and left. It seemed to me that the situation was so dangerous that death was already staring me in the face. [14] So I called Damnippus and said, "You are a close friend of mine, and I am in your house. I have done nothing wrong but am being killed for my wealth. Please help me in my suffering, and use your power to rescue me." He promised to do this, but he felt that it would be best to have a word with Theognis, who he thought would do anything for money. [15] While he was talking to Theognis—as it happened, I was familiar with the house and knew it had two doors[7]—I decided to try and save myself. I reckoned that if I was unnoticed I would be safe, and if I got caught, nothing worse would happen to me if Theognis had yielded to Damnippus' persuasion to accept money, whereas otherwise I would die anyway. [16] With this in mind, I began my escape while the others were engaged in guarding the outer door; the three doors I had to get through all happened to be open. I went to the house of Archeneus

[5] To the modern mind, it is extraordinary how much wealth even a very rich man like Lysias could claim to keep in cash, but we need to remember that although there were banks at Athens (see Lys. Fr. 1 [*Aeschines*], and Isoc. 17), nevertheless these were private institutions whose solvency was not guaranteed.

[6] Melobius and Mnesitheides were members of the Thirty. Damnippus (below) is not attested outside this speech.

[7] Presumably two outer doors leading into the street (otherwise the reference to three doors at 12.16 would be meaningless), whereas Athenian houses would normally have only one.

the shipowner and sent him to the town[8] to find out about my brother. He came back and told me that Eratosthenes had caught him in the street and dragged him off to prison.[9] [17] After hearing this, I sailed the following night to Megara. As for Polemarchus, the Thirty sent him their customary instruction to drink hemlock,[10] without telling him why he was to die. He did not even get a hearing and a chance to defend himself. [18] His body was brought back from the prison, but they would not allow us to conduct the funeral from any of our three houses. Instead, we had to hire a shed in which to lay him out. We owned plenty of cloaks, but when we asked, they would not give us a single one for the burial. Instead, one of our friends gave us the cloak for the burial, another the pillow, and others what each one happened to have. [19] The Thirty had seven hundred shields of ours. They had a huge amount of silver and gold, bronze and ornaments, and furniture and women's clothing, more than they had ever hoped to obtain; and also one hundred and twenty slaves, of which they kept the best but handed the remainder over to the Treasury. Such was the level of shamelessness and greed which they reached, and they made the following display of their true character: the moment Melobius first entered the house, he snatched from the ears of Polemarchus' wife the golden earrings she happened to be wearing. [20] We received not the smallest degree of pity from them; instead, because of our money, they behaved towards us just as others would have done if angered by very serious offenses. We did not deserve this sort of treatment at the hands of the city: we had sponsored all our choral performances[11] and contributed to many war taxes (*eisphorai*); we had conducted ourselves well and had done everything required of us; we had made no enemies

---

[8]The *astu,* or in other words the built-up area of Athens itself. Archeneus presumably lived in Piraeus (the port of Athens), and it is possible though not certain that Lysias and Polemarchus lived there also.

[9]The verb implies the procedure of *apagōgē* (summary arrest).

[10]Hemlock poisoning was regularly used by the Thirty as a means of execution, though it is not clear how widely it had been used before them.

[11]The *chorēgia,* or compulsory sponsorship of a choral production at a festival, was a liturgy to which metics were liable (though at only one of the two annual drama festivals, the Lenaea, whereas citizens were liable at the Dionysia as well).

but had ransomed many Athenians from the foe.[12] In these matters, they clearly did not believe that we as metics should behave in the same way that they behaved as citizens. [21] Many citizens they drove into the hands of the enemy; many they killed unjustly and deprived of burial; many of those who possessed full citizen rights they disfranchised; and many men's daughters they prevented from getting married. [22] And now they have reached such a pitch of audacity that they have come into court to defend themselves, and claim they have done nothing wrong and nothing shameful. For my part, I wish they were telling the truth, because I would be far better off in that case. [23] As it is, however, they are not treating me or the city in that way. For as I have already told you, gentlemen of the jury, Eratosthenes killed my brother. He had suffered no injury himself, nor did he see Polemarchus offending against the city. Instead, Eratosthenes himself was serving his own lawless desires.

[24] Gentlemen of the jury, I would like him to come up to the rostrum and answer questions.[13] My reason is that although I would regard it as impiety even to mention him to a third party if that was going to benefit him, nevertheless, when it will contribute to his downfall, I regard it as a sanctified and holy act even to speak directly to him. So go up and answer whatever questions I put to you.

[25] SPEAKER: Did you summarily arrest Polemarchus or not?

DEFENDANT: I obeyed the orders of those in power, because I was afraid.

SPEAKER: Were you present in the Council-chamber during the discussion about us?

DEFENDANT: I was.

SPEAKER: Did you speak in support of those demanding our execution or against them?

---

[12] I.e., during the Peloponnesian War.

[13] Litigants at Athens had the right to cross-question each other, and the opponent was apparently obliged to answer. (This was not the case for a witness.) Other examples of interrogation (*erōtēsis*) can be found at Lys. 22.5 (again with the questions and answers reported in the text), and at Lys. 13.30–32 (though in that case the questions and answers are not reported).

DEFENDANT: I spoke against, to try to prevent you being killed.
SPEAKER: Was this in the belief that we were suffering injustice?
DEFENDANT: Yes.

[26] Do you mean to say, you shameless villain, that you spoke against the proposal in an attempt to save our lives but joined in the arrest with the aim of getting us killed? That you spoke against those who wanted to kill us when the majority of your colleagues were in control of our fate, but that when it was in your hands alone to rescue Polemarchus or not, you summarily dragged him off to prison? Do you really deserve to be regarded as an honorable man because (so you say) you spoke against the proposal without achieving anything, but do not deserve to pay the penalty to me and to the jury for having arrested and murdered him? [27] In fact, if he is telling the truth when he says he spoke in opposition, there is no reason to trust his claim that he was acting under orders—because it was hardly in the case of the metics that the Thirty would have tested his loyalty. For who is less likely to have been ordered to arrest us than the man who had spoken in opposition and had thereby made clear his intentions? Who is less likely to have obeyed such an order than the man who spoke against what they wanted done? [28] The rest of the Athenians, it seems to me, could have a plausible excuse for what happened by laying the blame on the Thirty—but if the Thirty lay the blame on themselves, how can you reasonably accept this excuse? [29] If there had been any higher authority in the city who had ordered Eratosthenes to execute men unjustly, then perhaps it would be reasonable for you to pardon him; but where will you get justice, if the Thirty are allowed to plead that they were acting on the orders of the Thirty? [30] What is more, Eratosthenes seized and arrested him not at home but in the street, where he could have left both Polemarchus and the Thirty's instructions unviolated. You are angry against all the Thirty, because they invaded your houses and carried out searches for you or any of your families. [31] But if you must pardon those who killed others to save themselves, then it would be more legitimate to pardon those who conducted house arrests, for it was dangerous for them not to go or to deny it once they had carried out the arrest. Eratosthenes, on the other hand, could have said he did not meet Polemarchus or

that he never saw him: there was no means of verifying this,[14] and so it could not be disproved if his enemies had wanted to. [32] Had you been an honest man, Eratosthenes, you should far sooner have warned those about to die unjustly, rather than arresting those who were to be unjustly executed. As it is, your actions are clearly those of someone who is enjoying what has happened, not trying to remedy it. [33] The jurors should cast their votes on the basis of your actions, not your words,[15] taking the actions—which they know to have been done—as evidence for what was said at the time, since it is impossible to provide witnesses for what was said: not only could we not be present at their debates, but we could not even be present in our own houses. As a result, those who did all the harm to the city can say everything good about themselves. [34] I am not trying to evade this problem. If he wants, I accept his denials. But I do wonder what he would have done if he had spoken in favor of Polemarchus' death, given that he claims to have spoken against it before killing him!

Imagine for a moment that you are the brothers or sons of the defendant. What would you have done? Acquitted him? Gentlemen of the jury, Eratosthenes must demonstrate one of two things: either that he did not arrest him or that he was justified in doing it. But he has himself agreed that he arrested him unjustly, and so he has made your decision easy. [35] Many people have come here, both citizens and foreigners, to find out your attitude towards these men. Before they leave, those onlookers who are your fellow-citizens will discover either that they will be punished for any offenses they may have committed; or else that by achieving what they desire, they will become tyrants over the city, but if they fail, they will still obtain leniency from you. As for the foreigners living here, they will discover whether they are acting justly or unjustly in proclaiming the banishment of the Thirty from their cities. If those who have themselves suffered harm

---

[14] This ignores the probability that Eratosthenes still had with him the attendants mentioned at 12.10, who would have been in a position to denounce him if he had let Polemarchus off.

[15] The contrast between *logos* (word) and *ergon* (action) is a commonplace in Greek thought (cf., e.g., 14.34).

get their hands on the offenders but let them go free, then these foreigners will think it a waste of time to look after your interests. [36] Is it not striking that you imposed the death penalty on the generals who won the sea battle,[16] when they claimed that because of the weather they could not rescue the men in the water, since you believed it was essential to exact revenge from them for the bravery of those who had died? The defendants, on the other hand, did their best as private citizens to ensure your defeat in the sea battle, and they admit that once in office, they deliberately executed many of the citizens without trial. Should you not punish them and their descendants with the heaviest penalties available?

[37] My original opinion, gentlemen of the jury, was that the accusations I have made were sufficient. I believe that one should prosecute only to the point where it is clear that the defendant has done things that deserve death, because this is the most extreme penalty we can exact from them. I see no need, therefore, for lengthy prosecution speeches against men like this, who would not be able to pay a sufficient penalty even if they died twice for each of their crimes. [38] Nor can he even do what has become the custom in this city, whereby defendants make no defense against the charges, but sometimes deceive you with irrelevant statements about themselves, showing you that they are fine soldiers, or have captured many enemy ships while serving as trierarchs,[17] or have made hostile cities into friendly ones. [39] You must insist that he show you where they have killed as many of the enemy as they have citizens, or where they have captured as many ships as they have betrayed, or what city they have won over to match their enslavement of yours, [40] or that they have stripped as many shields from the enemy as they stole from you, or that they have captured walls as good as those they tore down in their own fatherland. They have even destroyed the guard posts surrounding Attica—

[16] The reference is to the battle of Arginusae in 406, after which six of the generals were executed for failing either to pick up the bodies or perhaps to rescue those clinging on to pieces of wrecked ships (cf. 21.8n).

[17] The trierarch was a rich citizen who paid for the upkeep of a warship for a year and was expected to command it.

thereby showing that it was not on the instructions of the Spartans that they stripped Piraeus of its protection, but because they believed that in this way their power would be more secure.[18]

[41] I have frequently been amazed at the impudence of those who speak for the defendant, except when I realize that it is natural for those who commit all sorts of offenses to praise others like them. [42] This is not the first occasion on which he has acted against your democracy. At the time of the Four Hundred, he established an oligarchy in his military camp, and he fled from the Hellespont, a trierarch deserting his ship, accompanied by Iatrocles and others whose names I need not mention.[19] After returning here, he acted in opposition to those who supported democracy. I will provide you with witnesses for these claims.

[WITNESSES]

[43] I will pass over his manner of life here in the intervening period, but after the sea battle took place which was a disaster for the city,[20] while the democracy was still in existence (this was the point at which they began the civil strife), the so-called companions (*hetairoi*)[21] appointed five men as "ephors," whose task was to incite the citizens,

---

[18] Precisely what Lysias is getting at here is unclear, though the Thirty are known to have sold the dockyards at Piraeus for scrap, and the Long Walls linking Piraeus to Athens had been pulled down under the terms of surrender at the end of the Peloponnesian War.

[19] The first oligarchy, that of the Four Hundred, held power for four months in 411 BC. Iatrocles is not otherwise known.

[20] A euphemism for the decisive defeat at Aegospotami in 405, which led to the siege of Athens.

[21] The word has aristocratic connotations, and *hetaireiai* were typically oligarchic clubs. The ephors (five in number) were public officials at Sparta, and this passage could suggest that the oligarchs were deliberately modeling themselves on a Spartan pattern (with the Thirty themselves being modeled on the Spartan *gerousia,* which comprised twenty-eight members plus the two kings). There is, however, no other evidence for the existence of ephors at Athens in 404, and this may be simply an attempt by Lysias to imply treasonable pro-Spartan motives and to associate Eratosthenes with the pro-Spartan extremist leader Critias.

to lead the conspirators, and to oppose your democracy. Among these were Eratosthenes and Critias. [44] These men appointed Phylarchs[22] in charge of the tribes, and they gave instructions about what Assembly motions were to be voted for and who was to hold office, and they had full power over anything else they might wish to do. As a result, you were the victims of a plot not simply by the enemy but by these men, your fellow-citizens, to prevent you from voting through any good proposal and to ensure that you would suffer serious shortages. [45] They understood clearly that otherwise they could not prevail, but that if things went badly, they could achieve it. They reckoned that because of your desire to escape existing sufferings, you would give no thought to future ones.

[46] As to the claim that he was one of the ephors, I will provide you with witnesses—not his accomplices, because I could not produce them, but those who heard it from Eratosthenes himself. [47] And yet if the accomplices were wise, they would act as witnesses against those men and would harshly punish the teachers of their own crimes; if they were wise, they would not regard as trustworthy the oaths that were designed to harm the citizens,[23] and they would willingly break them for the good of the city. I have finished what I have to say against these men, so kindly call my witnesses. Please go up on the podium.

[WITNESSES]

[48] You have heard the witnesses. In the end, once in office, he did nothing that was good but much that was not. If he had been an honest man, he should in the first place never have held office illegally; secondly, he should have laid information before the Council about

---

[22] The term Phylarch literally means "commander of a tribe (*phulē*)," but a Phylarch normally commanded a tribe's cavalry contingent only, whereas its hoplite contingent was commanded by a Taxiarch (cf. 13.79n). It is not clear why the Phylarchs are mentioned here, though the Thirty do seem to have drawn support from the cavalry (cf. Lys. 16).

[23] I.e., the oaths that the oligarchs are assumed to have sworn as conspirators at 12.43.

all the impeachments (*eisangeliai*), showing that they were false: that Batrachus and Aeschylides[24] were bringing denunciations that were untrue, but were initiating impeachments that had been concocted by the Thirty and were designed to harm the citizens. [49] What is more, gentlemen of the jury, those who were ill disposed to your democracy lost nothing by remaining silent. Others were saying and doing unsurpassable evils to the city. As for those who claim to be well disposed, how did they fail to demonstrate this at the time, by producing the best advice and deterring those who were in error?

[50] Perhaps he can claim that he was afraid, and to some of you this will seem an adequate defense. But he will need to ensure that he was not seen opposing the Thirty in debate. Otherwise it will be clear that to this extent he was pleased with their activities and that he was powerful enough to oppose them without suffering any harm. He should have devoted this enthusiasm towards your security rather than towards Theramenes,[25] who had repeatedly wronged you. [51] This man[26] treated the city as his enemy and your enemies as his friends. I shall bring a lot of evidence to prove both these claims, and also that the disagreements between them took place not for your sake but for their own, to decide which of them was going to control affairs and rule the city. [52] If they really had been quarreling on behalf of those who were being wronged, what better occasion was there for a man in office to show his goodwill towards you than when Thrasybulus captured Phyle?[27] And yet instead of doing or proclaiming anything to benefit those at Phyle, the defendant marched out with his colleagues to Salamis and Eleusis, dragged off three hundred citizens to prison, and condemned them all to death by a collective vote.[28]

---

[24] For Batrachus as an informer, see Lys. 6.45 with note. Aeschylides is otherwise unknown.

[25] This paves the way for the attack on Theramenes at 12.62–78, the function of which is discussed in the Introduction.

[26] Presumably Eratosthenes, but it is not clear whether the disagreements here are general disagreements among the Thirty, or specific but otherwise unattested disagreements between Eratosthenes and Theramenes.

[27] The capture of Phyle in 403 was the first stage in what became the democratic counterrevolution against the Thirty (cf. 12.53n).

[28] The massacres at Salamis and Eleusis were two of the Thirty's most notorious actions and are alluded to also at Lys. 13.44. There is a detailed account of the

[53] When we came to Piraeus, and the disturbances took place, and there were discussions about the peace terms, we had many hopes on each of the two sides (as both groups demonstrated) of concluding a settlement with each other.[29] Those from Piraeus were victorious and allowed the others to leave. [54] The latter returned to the town (*astu*) and expelled the Thirty (except for Pheidon and Eratosthenes). They elected as officials those who were most hateful to the former Thirty, thinking that it was reasonable for those who hated the Thirty to prefer those at Piraeus. [55] In this group were Pheidon, and Hippocles, and Epichares of the deme Lamptrae, and others who seemed to be particularly hostile to Charicles and Critias and their faction;[30] but once they took office, they organized a much more extensive civil war between those in the town and those in Piraeus. [56] In this way they made clear that they were not fighting the civil war on behalf of those in Piraeus or those who had been unjustly slaughtered. Neither the fact of past deaths nor the prospect of future ones concerned them—only how to achieve greater power and more rapid enrichment. [57] Once they had taken office and controlled the city, they made war against both sides: against the Thirty, who had done every kind of evil, and against you, who had suffered it. Yet everybody recognized that if the Thirty had been justly exiled, then your exile was unjust, and if yours was just, then the Thirty's was unjust: it was because they had been held responsible for these deeds, rather than any

---

Salamis massacre in Xen., *Hellenica* 2.4.8–10, and a briefer mention of both massacres in Diodorus Siculus 13.32.4.

[29] "We" in this passage denotes the democratic counterrevolutionaries of 403/2 led by Thrasybulus, who had initially occupied Phyle and had then marched to Piraeus. They defeated the Thirty there at a skirmish in Munychia (a hill near Piraeus), in which Critias, the extremist leader of the oligarchs, was killed, and the Thirty were promptly deposed by their supporters and replaced by a board of Ten. Lysias claims that the Ten were elected with the task of making peace (12.58), but it is equally possible that their mandate was to conduct the civil war more efficiently.

[30] *Hetaireia:* cf. 12.43 and note. Critias (cf. 12.43) and Charicles were, like Eratosthenes and Pheidon, members of the Thirty, but unlike them were among the extremist oligarchs. Of Pheidon's new colleagues, Epichares had served on the Council under the Thirty, but neither he nor Hippocles (otherwise unknown) had been members of the Thirty themselves.

others, that the Thirty had been expelled from the city. [58] So you should be very angry that Pheidon,[31] who was elected to draw up peace terms and to bring you back from exile, nevertheless joined in Eratosthenes' activities. He shared Eratosthenes' aims, and was prepared to use you to damage those on his own side who were more powerful, but was not willing to restore the city to you, who had been unjustly exiled. Instead, he went to Sparta and tried to persuade them to send troops, slanderously claiming that the city was about to become a Theban possession, and making other assertions that he thought would be most convincing. [59] He failed, either because the sacrificial omens prevented it or because the Spartans themselves were unwilling. But he borrowed one hundred talents to hire mercenaries, and he asked for Lysander[32] as governor. Lysander was particularly favorable to the oligarchy and hostile to Athens, and above all he hated those at Piraeus. [60] After hiring all sorts of people to help destroy Athens, they roused the other cities, and finally the Spartans and those of their allies that they could persuade. They were getting ready not to draw up peace terms, but to destroy the city, had it not been for the activities of honest men;[33] and you must make it clear to these men, by punishing their opponents, that you are giving thanks to them also. [61] You yourselves also are aware of this, and I do not know what need there is for me to produce witnesses, but nevertheless I will. I need to pause, and for some of you it will be easier to hear the same story from many speakers.

---

[31] Pheidon is the only member of the Ten who is known previously to have been a member of the Thirty, and the only member of the Thirty apart from Eratosthenes himself who is known to have remained in Athens after the regime's collapse (cf. 12.54). It is not clear whether he is being singled out for criticism because he is present or because he is for some unknown reason a particularly unpopular target.

[32] The former Spartan admiral, who had defeated the Athenians at Aegospotami in 405 and had established the Thirty. His appointment was a clear signal of Spartan intentions to reimpose oligarchy, but he was superseded in command by King Pausanias, who allowed democracy to be restored subject to the amnesty of 403/2, and whose role is suppressed in the vague reference to "honest men" at 12.60 below.

[33] See previous note.

[WITNESSES]

[62] I would like to tell you something also, as briefly as I can, about Theramenes.[34] I want you to listen both for my sake and for the city. Let nobody claim that I am making irrelevant charges against Theramenes, when it is Eratosthenes who is on trial, because I hear that he will defend himself by claiming he was an ally of Theramenes and shared in the same activities. **[63]** And yet given that he was at Theramenes' side in ensuring that the walls were knocked down, I assume that he would claim he was a political ally of Themistocles in ensuring they were built.[35] But I do not think the two things deserve equal consideration: it was against Spartan opposition that Themistocles built the walls, but Theramenes destroyed them by deceiving the citizens. **[64]** So the reverse of what was expected has befallen the city. It would have been fitting for Theramenes' friends to die with him, unless any of them happened to be acting in opposition to him. As it is, I see defendants referring to him, and his associates trying to grab honor, as if he had been responsible for great benefits rather than great evils. **[65]** In the first place, he had prime responsibility for the earlier oligarchy, when he persuaded you to vote for the constitution based on the Four Hundred. His father was one of the Probouloi[36] and behaved in the same way as Theramenes; he himself was elected general by them, because he seemed particularly well disposed to their regime. **[66]** As long as he was being honored, he proved to be faithful to them. But when he saw that Peisander and Callaeschrus and others were being placed ahead of him, and the democracy was no longer

---

[34] The diatribe against Theramenes that follows is discussed in the Introduction.

[35] The walls of Athens itself had been built by Themistocles in the 470s after the Persian invasion, whereas the Long Walls joining Athens to Piraeus had been pulled down in 404 under the terms of the surrender to Sparta that Theramenes had negotiated. Plutarch (*Lysander* 14) offers a pro-Theramenes response to this charge of undoing the work of Themistocles.

[36] A board of public officials created under the democracy in 413 BC, who were subsequently regarded as having paved the way for the oligarchic revolution of the Four Hundred. They were ten in number and included Theramenes' father Hagnon.

willing to obey them, he began to collaborate with Aristocrates, either because he envied them or because he feared you.[37] [67] He wanted to appear faithful to your democracy, so he prosecuted Antiphon and Archeptolemus, his closest allies, and had them executed. His wickedness was such that he simultaneously reduced you to slavery to prove his reliability to them, and destroyed his friends to prove the same to you. [68] Although he received honors and was very highly valued, when instructed to save the city he destroyed it all by himself.[38] He claimed he had found a magnificent and worthy plan, and promised to make peace without giving up any hostages, destroying the walls, or surrendering the ships, but he refused to explain his plan to anybody, telling you to trust him. [69] The Areopagus Council, men of Athens, was working to achieve your safety. Many people spoke against Theramenes. You yourselves knew that whereas other people keep secrets from the enemy, Theramenes refused to tell a meeting of his own fellow-citizens what he intended to say to the enemy,[39] but you still entrusted him with your fatherland, your children, your wives, and yourselves. [70] He accomplished none of the things he had promised, but, convinced that the city should be made small and weak, he persuaded you to do things that no enemy had even contemplated and no citizen had expected. He was not forced to act by the

---

[37] Peisander was one of the extremist leaders among the oligarchy of the Four Hundred in 411 BC (Thuc. 8.68), who fled into exile after the collapse of their regime (his property was then confiscated, and is under discussion in Lys. 7). Antiphon (the first of the Ten Orators) was another of the extremist leaders named by Thucydides, but he remained in Athens with Archeptolemus and was executed under the intermediate regime. Part of his defense speech survives on papyrus (Ant. Fr. 1) and mentions Theramenes by name as one of his accusers. Little is known of Callaeschrus and Aristocrates.

[38] During this sentence Lysias moves, without indicating the transition, from Theramenes' role in overthrowing the Four Hundred in 411 to his role in negotiating the surrender of Athens in 404 prior to the establishment of the Thirty. The effect is to accentuate the impression of a man who is constantly changing sides.

[39] The Theramenes papyrus (cf. the Introduction at n. 4) attributes to Theramenes' contemporaries a charge that is phrased in almost identical terms to this (*P.Mich.* 5982, lines 5–10), and responds with a long and detailed rebuttal placed in the mouth of Theramenes himself (lines 10–33).

Spartans, but himself gave them instructions that the walls around Piraeus should be destroyed and the constitution repealed. He did this in the full knowledge that if you had not been deprived of all your hopes, you would rapidly have punished him. [71] In the end, gentlemen of the jury, he prevented the Assembly from meeting until the moment which had been agreed by these men, and which he was carefully looking out for. He summoned Lysander's fleet from Samos, and the enemy's camp was in the city. [72] It was then, under these conditions and in the presence of Lysander and Philochares and Miltiades,[40] that they summoned the Assembly to debate the constitution. Their aim was that no orator would oppose or threaten them, and that you would not choose proposals that were good for the city but would vote for those they had decided on. [73] Theramenes stood up and demanded that you entrust the city to the control of thirty men and adopt the constitution proposed by Dracontides.[41] But even though you had been reduced to such despair, you began to protest that you would not do this. You realized that the Assembly you were holding that day would decide between slavery and freedom. [74] Theramenes responded—I call on you yourselves to be my witnesses of this, gentlemen of the jury—that he was not in the slightest concerned by your outcry, because he knew that many Athenians were trying to achieve a similar solution, and he said that this was what Lysander and the Spartans had decided on. After him, Lysander stood up and stated among other things that he held you guilty of breaking the truce, and that unless you did what Theramenes commanded, it would be a matter not of your constitution but of your lives. [75] Those members of the Assembly who were honest citizens recognized conspiracy and compulsion: some of them remained and stayed silent, while others got up and left, having the consolation at least of knowing that they had not voted for any harm against the city. But a few evil-minded scoundrels voted the proposal through. [76] Instructions were given to vote for ten men identified by Theramenes, ten whom the previ-

---

[40] Philochares and Miltiades were Lysander's subordinates in command of the Spartan fleet.

[41] Dracontides of the deme Aphidna, identified in *Ath. Pol.* 34.3 as the proposer of the resolution establishing the Thirty.

ously established "ephors"[42] should appoint, and ten more from those at the meeting. They were so aware of your weakness and so confident of their own power that they knew in advance what would happen at the Assembly. [77] It is not my version of events that you should trust, but Theramenes': in his defense speech before the Council, he mentioned everything I have said.[43] He reproached the exiles, because it was through him that they had returned, when the Spartans had showed no concern for this. He reproached those who had shared in the activity of government,[44] because he was suffering such a terrible fate even though he had been responsible for everything that had been accomplished in the ways I have described: his actions had provided them with many indications of his loyalty, and he had received oaths from them in return. [78] This man was responsible for evils as great as that, and for other shameful ones, some done long ago and others recent, some great and some small—and yet these men will have the impudence to claim friendship with him, although he died not for your interests but because of his own crimes. It was right that he paid the penalty under an oligarchy, given that he had already betrayed one; it would also have been right under a democracy. Twice he reduced you to slavery, because he despised what was present and longed for what was not. He used beautiful language to make himself a teacher of shameful deeds.

[79] The accusations I have made against Theramenes are sufficient. For you, gentlemen of the jury, the moment is coming when you must have no pardon or pity in your minds but must instead punish Eratosthenes and his fellow officials. You were better than the enemy in war: do not prove weaker than your opponents in voting. [80] Do not let gratitude for the things they promise to do overcome your anger at what they have done. Do not make plans against the Thirty when they are absent, only to acquit them when they are pres-

---

[42] For the "ephors," see 12.43 with note.

[43] We possess a version of Theramenes' defense speech when prosecuted by Critias under the Thirty (Xen., *Hellenica* 2.3.35–49), but it does not support either these or the following allegations.

[44] In other words, the Thirty themselves. Or it could mean "shared in the citizenship," which would imply the Three Thousand who enjoyed full civil rights under the Thirty.

ent. Do not defend yourselves less strongly than does fortune, which has delivered these men into the hands of the city.

[81] This prosecution has been directed against Eratosthenes and his friends, whom he will use to support his defense, and with whose help he acted. However, the contest between him and the city is not on level terms: he was both accuser and judge of those who were condemned, whereas we are now in a situation of accusing and defending. [82] These men executed without trial those who had done nothing wrong, whereas you have decided to judge according to the law those people who destroyed the city—and yet even if you wanted to punish them illegally, you would not be able to impose a punishment to match the crimes they committed against the city. What penalty could they suffer that was worthy of their actions? [83] Would executing them and their children be a suitable penalty for the murders—for our fathers, sons, and brothers whom they executed without trial? Would confiscating their visible property[45] be a good thing either for the city, from which they stole so much, or for private individuals whose households they destroyed? [84] But since even by doing this you would not be able to exact an adequate punishment, it is surely shameful for you to leave unused any penalty that anybody wishes to impose on them.

A man who comes here now, to speak in his own defense against those who are witnesses of his crimes, when the jurors are none other than those he oppressed, seems to me to show utter impudence: either this is the extent to which he despised you, or that to which he trusted in other people. [85] You must be on guard against both alternatives. Bear in mind that they would not have been able to do what they did without others to assist them. Nor would they have attempted to come here, except in the hope of being rescued by those same people, who have come not to help them, but in the belief that if you acquit those who are responsible for the greatest evils, they themselves will have virtual impunity for what they did and might wish to do in future. [86] It is right to wonder at his supporting speakers. Is it as honorable citizens that they are going to plead for him, displaying their own merits as something more worthy than the defendants'

[45] I.e., land and houses, as opposed to cash.

crimes (because I would be glad if they were as keen on saving the city as the defendants are on destroying it!)? Or will they be clever speakers for his defense, claiming that these men's actions were highly meritorious? And yet none of them has ever tried to deliver a speech that is just or in your interests.

[87] It is also right to look at the witnesses, who by testifying for the defendants accuse themselves. They must think that you are extraordinarily forgetful and stupid, if they believe they can rescue the Thirty without fear under your democracy, when under Eratosthenes and his colleagues it was dangerous even to attend a funeral. [88] And yet if these men are rescued, they would again be able to destroy the city, whereas those they destroyed have ended their lives and are beyond taking vengeance on their enemies. Is it not terrible that the friends of those who were unjustly killed perished with them, whereas many people (or so I suppose) will attend the funerals of those who destroyed the city, given that so many are prepared to help their defense? [89] It would I think be far easier to speak against them on behalf of what you have suffered than to deliver a defense on behalf of what these men have done. And yet they claim that Eratosthenes did the least wrong out of the Thirty, and for this reason, they argue, he should be spared. But do they not realize that he should be executed because he wronged you more than all the other Greeks?[46] [90] You must show your opinion about these matters. If you vote to convict this man, it will be clear that you are angry at what has occurred. If you vote to acquit, you will be regarded as having the same aims as the defendants, and you will not be able to claim that you acted under orders from the Thirty. [91] At the moment, nobody is forcing you to vote against your conscience, so I would advise you not to condemn yourselves by voting to acquit these men. And do not think that your vote is secret, because you will be making your opinion known to the city.

[92] I want to remind both sides—those from the town (*astu*) and those from Piraeus[47]—of several other things, and then step down, so

---

[46] Presumably this should not be taken to include his former colleagues among the Thirty.

[47] Respectively the former supporters of the Thirty and the democratic counterrevolutionaries.

that when you cast your votes, you will regard as precedents the disasters that you endured because of the defendants. First, then, you who are from the town should realize that the defendants ruled you so badly that you were compelled to fight a war against your brothers, your sons, and your fellow-citizens, in which defeat brought you equality with the victors, whereas had you won, you would have enslaved them. [93] The defendants made their own private households great at the expense of public business, while your fortunes were reduced on account of the civil war. They did not want you to share in their profits but forced you to share their bad reputation. They were so contemptuous that they did not gain your loyalty by sharing their proceeds, but instead they thought you would support them if you shared in their shame. [94] In return for this, be confident now, as far as you can be, and punish them, both on your own behalf and on behalf of those from Piraeus. Realize that you were ruled by the defendants, who were the worst of men; realize too that you now share the government with good men, you are fighting against external enemies, and you are taking counsel for the city; and remember the mercenaries that the defendants established on the Acropolis as guardians of their power and of your slavery.

[95] That is all I say to you, although I could say much more. As for those who are from Piraeus, I want you first to remember your weapons. After fighting many wars on foreign soil, you were deprived of them not by the enemy but by the defendants in time of peace. Next, remember how you were banished from the city that our fathers handed down to us; and when you were in exile, they demanded your extradition from other cities. [96] In return for this, display your anger as you did when you were in exile. Remember also the other evils you suffered at their hands. They executed people after forcibly seizing them, some from the Agora and others from shrines; they dragged others away from children, fathers, and wives, compelling them to be their own killers,[48] and did not allow them to have the customary funeral rites, in the belief that their own authority was more powerful than the gods' vengeance. [97] Those who escaped death found danger in many places. They wandered to many cities and were banished from all of them. They lacked the necessities of life. Some left their

---

[48] By drinking hemlock, as in Polemarchus' case (12.17).

children behind in a hostile fatherland, others in foreign territory, and it was against considerable opposition that you came to Piraeus. The dangers were many and great, but you were honest men. You set the one group free and led the others back to their fatherland. [98] If you had suffered misfortune and had failed to achieve your aims, you yourselves would have fled into exile, fearing that you would suffer the same things as before. Because of these men's behavior, no shrines or altars would have helped you, though these provide sanctuary even for criminals. Your children who were in Athens at the time would have suffered outrageous violence (*hubris*) at the defendants' hands; those who were abroad would have been enslaved for petty debts, without anybody to help them.

[99] But I do not want to talk about what would have happened, and I cannot describe what these men have done. That is a task not for one or two prosecutors, but for many. Nevertheless, there is nothing lacking in my zeal—zeal for the sanctuaries that the defendants either sold or polluted by entering; zeal for the city that they weakened, for the shipyards that they destroyed, and for the dead: you may not have been able to defend them during their lifetime, but you can assist them in death. [100] It is my belief that they can hear us and that they will recognize you as you cast your ballots. In their view, those who vote to acquit the defendants will thereby be passing a death sentence on them, their victims, whereas those who exact justice from the defendants will have avenged them.

Here I shall end my prosecution. You have heard, you have seen, you have suffered, and you have them in your grasp. Give your verdict!

13. AGAINST AGORATUS

INTRODUCTION

This speech is in some ways parallel to Lysias 12, which may explain why they have been placed together in our manuscripts. They are the two longest speeches in the corpus, they both deal with murders committed under the Thirty in 404/3 BC, and they both seek the death penalty. There are, however, significant differences. In the first place, the defendant Agoratus was a man of much lower status than Eratosthenes in Lysias 12. He seems to have been born a slave (a point which is repeatedly emphasized, e.g., at 13.18 and 13.64), but he evidently claimed—and was probably entitled to claim—that he had been granted Athenian citizenship, either because of his part in the assassination of the oligarch Phrynichus in 411 BC (a claim that Lysias unconvincingly seeks to rebut at 13.70–72; cf. 13.70n), or alternatively because he had joined the democratic counterrevolutionaries at Phyle in 404/3 (a claim that Lysias conveniently sidesteps at 13.77–79; cf. 13.77n).

Whereas Eratosthenes had been a member of the Thirty, Agoratus was an alleged informer, whose denunciations had eased their path to power by enabling the arrest and execution of a number of their political opponents in the Spring of 404. His victims (13.13) included Strombichides, who had been general on several previous occasions and was possibly holding that office again at the time of his death, and Dionysodorus, who is otherwise unknown. It is for the killing of Dionysodorus that Agoratus has now been summarily arrested by *apagōgē*,[1] on grounds that are not entirely clear.

---

[1] Thus M. H. Hansen, *Apagoge, Endeixis and Ephegesis* (Odense, 1976), 130–131, on the basis of the description of the procedure at 13.86. As Hansen rightly

Apagōgē was a procedure regularly used against people who were subject to *atimia* (i.e., those whose civic rights were somehow restricted, normally as a consequence of a previous offense) and who broke the terms of this restriction. It was sometimes used against homicides (cf. Ant. 5), presumably on the grounds that they were appearing in public despite the pollution that had automatically resulted from the killing, and that may be the explanation for its use against Agoratus, although no attempt is made to prove that he has appeared in public places. The prosecution has been brought in the name of Dionysius (13.86), the brother of Dionysodorus (13.41), but the speaker is an unnamed cousin who is also the brother of Dionysodorus' wife (13.1, 13.40). Given the length of the speech and the trouble taken to cover the background to the case, it is reasonable to infer that the speaker is doing the bulk of the work. Unlike a formal prosecution for homicide, which could be brought only by the next of kin, *apagōgē* could in theory be brought by any citizen concerned at the defendant's allegedly illegal behavior. But as next of kin, Dionysius is the obvious person to lend his name to the charge, even if his role in court was in practice confined to standing up and asking the jury to let his cousin speak for him.

One of the problems facing the prosecutors was the date of the trial. This cannot be precisely determined but was clearly some time after the event. Indeed, the speaker expects Agoratus to complain about undue delay, to which he himself responds by insisting that crimes like that of Agoratus are not protected by any statutory time limit (13.83). Since the time limit in other types of case was often five years (e.g., Dem. 36.27, 38.27), the speaker's failure to add "and anyway the delay has been less than that" suggests that the case was heard no earlier than the Spring of 399.[2] The latest possible date for Lysias 13 is more difficult to determine, but there are some close parallels with

---

points out, this description is far more reliable than the reference to the related procedure of *endeixis* (indictment) in the manuscript title of the speech, which need be no more than a copyist's conjecture and is therefore omitted in the translation below.

[2] The execution of Menestratus, which has already taken place, is similarly described as taking place "much later" than his denunciations (13.56), but this in itself need not imply a delay of more than a few years since the Spring of 404.

Lysias 30 (delivered in 399), which may suggest a similar date for the two cases.[3]

We cannot be sure why the prosecutors waited so long before arresting Agoratus, but part at least of the reason was presumably the amnesty of 403/2. This, as we saw in the introduction to Lysias 12, allowed prosecutions to be brought for previous homicide only in cases where people were accused of killing with their own hands. This possibility did not apply in the case of Agoratus, who had caused death by denunciation and should therefore have been protected by the amnesty. Indeed, the speaker has to resort to extremely specious arguments at 13.88–90, to evade Agoratus' expected objection that he is so protected. Moreover, it seems that the Eleven, who were the public officials in charge of prisons and executions and who were responsible for accepting cases of *apagōgē* and bringing them to trial, had themselves been dubious about the legal validity of the prosecution (13.85–87): we do not know why they had insisted on Dionysius rephrasing his *apagōgē* to include the words *ep' autophōrōi*—a phrase of disputed significance, which was regularly associated with *apagōgē* but which hardly seems appropriate here (see 13.85n)—but part of their reason may have been a wish to cover their backs against future charges of illegal behavior in office by throwing the responsibility for the creative use of language onto the speaker.

In law, the prosecutor would seem to have a very weak case, and scholars have sometimes inferred that Agoratus must therefore have been acquitted. But once again, as with Lysias 12, such an argument can be inverted: we can in fact only guess at the result of the trial, but if Lysias' client dared appear in court with a case as weak as this, he may have guessed that feeling against the Thirty and their former helpers was for the moment at least running so high that a jury would be prepared to convict even on this basis. The year 399 was notable for a number of political show trials, including that of Socrates, and a

[3] Most obviously the account of Cleophon's death (13.8–12, 30.10–13) and the interest in the death of Strombichides (13.13, 30.14). For a speculative reconstruction of the relationship between the two speeches, see S. C. Todd, "Lysias *Against Nikomakhos:* The Fate of the Expert in Athenian Law," in L. Foxhall and A. D. E. Lewis, *Greek Law in Its Political Setting* (Oxford, 1996), 101–131, at 117–120.

temporary surge of feeling might explain why the prosecution chose to bring proceedings at this date.

Given the scale and the importance of the speech, it is perhaps surprising that there is no modern specialist treatment in English. The nineteenth-century commentary by E. S. Shuckburgh (*Lysias: Sixteen Speeches* [London, 1882]) is still useful on some points of detail.

13. PROSECUTION SPEECH AGAINST AGORATUS [1]

[1] Gentlemen of the jury, it is fitting that you should all take vengeance for the men who are dead, because they supported your democracy. But it is particularly fitting that I should do so, because Dionysodorus was my cousin and brother-in-law. So I have the same enmity towards the defendant Agoratus as does your democracy. Because of what he has done, he is now rightly hated by me, and (god willing) he will be justly punished by you. [2] He killed my brother-in-law Dionysodorus in the time of the Thirty, and many others whose names you shall hear, men who were loyal to your democracy, by serving as an informer against them. By doing this, he seriously injured me as an individual and each of their relatives, and also, in my opinion, caused no small damage to the whole city collectively, by depriving it of men like these. [3] So, gentlemen of the jury, I consider it a legitimate and righteous action for me and for all of you to take vengeance as far as each of us can, and I believe we would derive benefits, both from the gods and from men, if we did this. You need to hear the entire story from the beginning, men of Athens, [4] so that you can understand, first, how and by whom your democracy was overthrown; and secondly, how these men were killed by Agoratus, and what instructions they gave us when they were about to die. If you knew the whole story accurately, your vote to condemn this man Agoratus would be more pleasant and more righteous. So I shall begin to tell you the story from the point at which it is easiest for me to narrate and you to hear it.

[5] Not long after your ships were destroyed,[2] and the situation in

---

[1] See the Introduction at n. 1.

[2] At the battle of Aegospotami in 405, which led to the siege of Athens and the surrender to the Spartans in 404. As often in Lysias, this battle is alluded to without being named.

the city had deteriorated, the Spartan fleet arrived at Piraeus, and peace talks with the Spartans began at the same time. [6] Meanwhile, those who wanted a political revolution in the city were making plots. They thought they had found a particularly attractive opportunity and that this was the best time to reorganize public affairs in the way they wanted. [7] They believed no other obstruction stood in their way, except for the leaders of the common people (*dēmos*), the generals, and the Taxiarchs.[3] They wanted to get these men out of the way by some means or other, so that they could organize things easily as they wished. So first of all they took action against Cleophon,[4] as follows: [8] during the first Assembly to discuss peace, when the envoys from Sparta stated the terms on which the Spartans were ready to make peace—the terms were that ten stades of each of the Long Walls[5] were to be pulled down—at that point, men of Athens, you could not bear to hear about the destruction of the walls, and Cleophon stood up on behalf of all of you and objected that there you could not possibly do this. [9] After this, Theramenes, who was plotting against your democracy, rose and said that if you chose him as delegate with power to negotiate over the peace terms,[6] he would arrange things in such a way that you would not have to destroy the walls or cause any other loss to the city, and he thought he would be able to extract some other

[3] Regimental commanders; cf. 13.79n.

[4] Cleophon was a well-known "demagogue" or popular leader, who is frequently lampooned in Aristophanes' *Frogs* (produced in 406/5), and whose political prominence is alluded to in Lys. 19.48. There is a parallel account of his death at Lys. 30.10–13.

[5] The Long Walls were those linking Athens to the port of Piraeus, which had made the city invulnerable to land attack. A stade is the length of a racecourse, about 200 yards, so ten stades is just over a mile (Piraeus is about 4–5 miles from Athens).

[6] I translate *autokratōr* as "with power to negotiate," because the context makes clear that any settlement negotiated by Theramenes would have to be referred for ratification to the Assembly. (The literal translation "with full powers" would misleadingly imply that he could himself conclude a binding settlement.) The Theramenes papyrus (*P.Mich.* 5982, for which see the Introduction to Lys. 12 at n. 4) is evidently drawing on this passage when it similarly describes Theramenes as delegate with power to negotiate, but it gives a much more favorable explanation of his delay by insisting that he went to see Lysander at Samos before being sent by him to Sparta (lines 33–45).

concession as well for the city from the Spartans. [10] You were convinced and elected him as delegate with power to negotiate: a man whom you had rejected at his *dokimasia*[7] the previous year, after he had been elected general, in the belief that he was hostile to your democracy. [11] So he went to Sparta and stayed there a long time, leaving you here under siege. He knew that your democracy was in a difficult situation and that most of the necessities of life were running short because of the war and because of hardship. He acted in this way in the belief that if he could make you as desperate as he did, you would gladly agree to make peace on any terms.

[12] Those who remained here and were plotting to overthrow your democracy brought Cleophon to trial. Their pretext was that he did not go to the camp when he wanted to take a rest,[8] but in reality it was because he spoke out on your behalf against destroying the walls. They rigged up a lawcourt for him, and those who wanted to establish an oligarchy came into court and executed him on that pretext. [13] Theramenes subsequently arrived from Sparta. Some of the generals and the Taxiarchs—among them were Strombichides and Dionysodorus, and several other citizens who supported you, as they later showed—went to see him and protested vigorously. He came back bringing peace, and we know from experience what it was like: we lost many good citizens, and we ourselves were banished by the Thirty. [14] Instead of ten stades of the Long Walls, the peace terms were to destroy their entire length. Instead of the "other concession" that he was to have obtained for the city, we were to hand over the fleet to the Spartans and to destroy the wall around Piraeus. [15] When these men saw what was nominally called a peace, but was in reality the destruction of the democracy, they said that they would not allow this to happen. It was not that they felt pity for the walls because they were to fall, men of Athens, nor were they anxious about handing the ships over to the Spartans. Neither of these affected them any more than it did each one of you. [16] But they realized that in this way your democracy was going to be destroyed. It was not, as some say, that they had no desire to make peace, but they wanted to make a

---

[7] The judicial scrutiny of an incoming public official, a procedure that is discussed in the Introduction to Lys. 16.

[8] Evidently a charge of evading military service.

better peace than this for the Athenian People. They believed they could accomplish this—and they would have done so, if they had not been destroyed by this man Agoratus.

[17] Theramenes knew, and so did the others who were plotting against you, that there were some people who would prevent the democracy being destroyed and would oppose this in the interests of liberty. They decided that before the Assembly met to discuss the peace, they would first expose these men to slander and peril, so that nobody at the meeting would speak in opposition on behalf of your democracy. [18] So they concocted a plot. They persuaded this man Agoratus to become an informer against the generals and the Taxiarchs. It was not that he knew any of the conspirators' plans, men of Athens. They were not so naive or so friendless that in matters of this sort they would have called on Agoratus—a slave and the son of slaves[9]—treating him as a faithful and reliable friend. They simply thought he was a useful informer. [19] They wanted him to appear an unwilling rather than a willing informer, so that his information might seem more reliable. But I think that you too will recognize from what happened that he did inform willingly. They sent Theocritus, known as the son of Elaphostictus,[10] to the Council; this Theocritus was a friend and comrade of Agoratus.

[20] The Council that held office prior to the Thirty[11] was corrupt, and had (as you know) a strong desire for oligarchy. The evidence for this is that many members of this Council served on the next Council, the one that held office under the Thirty.[12] Why am I telling you this? So that you can regard the earlier Council in an appropriate light, recognizing that all the decrees passed by them were not the result of goodwill towards you but were aimed at the destruction of your

[9] One of several attacks on the origins and status of Agoratus (cf. the Introduction).

[10] The name Elaphostictus literally means "the deer tattoo." Tattooing was practiced in Thrace, which was not part of the Greek world in antiquity, and it has been suggested that Theocritus was of Thracian extraction.

[11] I.e., the Council of Five Hundred for the year 405/4 BC. (The Thirty held office in 404/3.)

[12] The implication is that this was improper: under the democracy, an individual was allowed to serve on the Council twice in his lifetime but not in consecutive years.

democracy. [21] Theocritus came before this Council in secret and informed them that certain people were gathering to oppose the regime that was being established. He refused to give their names individually, because, he said, he had sworn the same oaths as them, and because there were others who would give the names, but he himself would never do that. [22] If Theocritus had not become an informer as a result of intrigue, why on earth did the Council not compel him to reveal the names, instead of bringing a nameless denunciation? In fact they passed the following decree:

[DECREE]

[23] When this decree had been passed, selected members of the Council went down to see Agoratus at Piraeus. They happened to find him in the Agora[13] there, and were about to arrest him, when Nicias and Nicomenes[14] and various others came by. Seeing that affairs in the city were not going as well as they might, they said that they would not let them[15] arrest Agoratus. Instead, they defended his freedom, gave guarantees, and agreed to produce him in front of the Council. [24] The members of the Council wrote down the names of those who were providing surety and preventing the arrest, and went back to the town. Agoratus and his guarantors sat down at the altar in Munychia,[16] and as soon as they had done this, they began discussing what to do. The guarantors and the others decided that they should get Agoratus away as soon as possible. [25] They brought two boats to anchor nearby, and pleaded with him to flee Athens by any means possible. They said they would sail with him, until the situation became stable, and they pointed out that if he were brought in front of the Council, he would perhaps be compelled under torture to reveal the names of such Athenians as might be suggested by people wanting to cause trouble in the city.

[26] That was what they pleaded. They had prepared the boats and were themselves ready to sail with him, but Agoratus here refused to follow their advice. And yet, Agoratus, unless you were in the plot and

[13] Evidently the Agora at the port of Piraeus, not the one in Athens.

[14] Nicias and Nicomenes are otherwise unknown. There is no reason to identify this Nicias as a relative of the famous Nicias.

[15] I.e., the members of the Council.

[16] A low hill at the edge of Piraeus, the site of an important shrine of Artemis.

knew that you would suffer no harm, why you did not leave, given that the boats had been prepared and your guarantors were ready to sail with you?[17] You still could have done this, given that the Council had not yet got you into its power. [27] In fact the situation was not the same for you as for your guarantors. In the first place, they were Athenians, so they did not have to fear being tortured.[18] Secondly, they were prepared to leave their fatherland and sail with you, thinking this would be better than for you to kill many good citizens unjustly. You, on the other hand, risked being tortured if you stayed. [28] Moreover, you would not be leaving your own fatherland. In every respect, therefore, it suited you more than them to sail—unless you had something to rely on. In fact you pretend you were unwilling, but you killed many good Athenians willingly. To prove that the whole affair was planned as I say, there are witnesses, and the Council's own decree will bear witness against him.

[WITNESSES]

[DECREE]

[29] When this decree had been passed, and the Council's representatives came to Munychia, Agoratus got up willingly from the altar—though he now claims that he was dragged away by force. [30] When he was brought before the Council, Agoratus provided the following names in a written denunciation: first his own guarantors, then the generals and Taxiarchs, and then various other citizens. This was the beginning of all the trouble. I think that even he will agree that he did provide the names, but if not, I shall convict him in the act.[19] Answer me.

---

[17] One plausible reason for Agoratus' refusal is that he would have had to run the Spartan blockade of Athens, which seems still to have been continuing, though Lysias suppresses this possibility.

[18] The innuendo is part of Lysias' repeated attempt to undermine Agoratus' claim to citizenship (cf. the Introduction).

[19] *Ep' autophōrōi* is a technical phrase meaning "in the act of committing a crime" or "in such circumstances as to make denial impossible," which is a necessary condition for certain types of *apagōgē* (summary arrest; cf. 13.85–87 and note). If it has any meaning here, it is presumably "in the act of lying," which is hardly an indictable offense.

[INTERROGATION[20]]

[31] They wanted him, gentlemen of the jury, to provide the names of even more people. The Council was determined to do some harm, and they did not think this man had made a full and true accusation. He provided all these names willingly, and no compulsion was used. [32] When the Assembly met in the theater at Munychia, some people expressed so much concern that a denunciation about the generals and the Taxiarchs was made in the Assembly meeting as well[21]—for the others, it was enough for denunciation to be made only in the Council—and as a result, they brought Agoratus there before the Assembly. Answer me, Agoratus: I do not believe that you will deny what you did in front of all the Athenians.

[INTERROGATION]

[33] He himself admits it. Nevertheless, the decree of the Assembly will be read to you as well.

[DECREE]

I am sure you are all aware that this man Agoratus provided the names of these men—both those he denounced in the Council and those in the Assembly—and that he is their killer. But I think I should demonstrate to you briefly that he was responsible for all the evils suffered by the city and does not deserve anybody's pity. [34] When his victims had been arrested and imprisoned, at that moment[22] Lysander sailed into your harbors, your ships were handed over to the Spartans, the walls were pulled down, the Thirty were appointed, and all possible evils fell on the city. [35] When the Thirty took office, they immediately arranged a trial for these men before the Council—

---

[20] For the procedure of *erōtēsis* (interrogation of the opponent), see Lys. 12.24n.

[21] I.e., the Assembly refused to ratify the Council's decision in these cases without hearing Agoratus themselves (so there is plenty of evidence of what he said there), whereas they would have been prepared to approve the other denunciations unheard.

[22] A striking example of the *post hoc, propter hoc* fallacy (cf. also 13.43), designed to suggest that Agoratus' denunciations were the cause of the surrender and the disasters that followed.

whereas the Assembly had decreed "in a lawcourt manned by two thousand."[23] Read me the decree.

[DECREE]

[36] If they had been tried in a lawcourt, they would easily have gone free. All of you had already realized that the city was in trouble, but you were no longer able to help in any way. Instead, they brought them before the Council that held office under the Thirty. The trial took place in a way that you yourselves know well. [37] The Thirty were seated on the benches where the Prytaneis[24] now sit. Two tables were set out in front of them, and one had to cast one's vote not into voting urns but openly on these tables, with the vote to convict going on the further table: so how could any of them be rescued? [38] In a word, the death penalty was passed on all who went to the Council-chamber to face trial. They did not acquit a single one, except this man Agoratus. They let him off, on the grounds that he was a "benefactor." I want to read out to you the names, so that you can see how many people were killed by this man.

[NAMES]

[39] When the death sentence had been passed, gentlemen of the jury, and it was time to die, each of them summoned to the prison his sister, or his mother, or his wife, or whoever was most closely related to each one. They did this so as to greet their families for a final time before dying. [40] Dionysodorus summoned to the prison my sister, who was his wife. Hearing the summons, she arrived dressed in a black cloak,[25] as was appropriate for one whose husband had been struck down by such a terrible fate. [41] In the presence of my sister, Dionysodorus made arrangements for his household in the way he thought best. He identified this man Agoratus as the cause of his death, and he directed me and his brother Dionysius here, and all his friends, to take

---

[23] The normal size of a jury panel in a public case was five hundred *dikastai,* but particularly important trials could be heard by multiple panels sitting together, as was envisaged here.

[24] The executive committee of the Council.

[25] The text is not entirely satisfactory at this point, and there may be one or two words missing.

vengeance against Agoratus on his behalf. [42] Believing that his wife was carrying his child, he directed her too, if she bore him a boy, to tell him as he grew up that Agoratus had killed his father, and to encourage him to take vengeance on Agoratus as a murderer for his father's sake. I shall produce witnesses that I am telling the truth.

[WITNESSES]

[43] These, men of Athens, were the men who were denounced and killed by Agoratus. I suspect you know full well that when the Thirty had removed them, many terrible things immediately happened to the city,[26] and this man is the cause of all those things, because he killed them. I am sorry to recall to mind the disasters that befell the city, [44] but in the present situation it is necessary, gentlemen of the jury, so that you can see just how much Agoratus deserves your pity. You know the citizens from Salamis[27] who were taken away—their characters, their numbers, and how they were destroyed by the Thirty. You know the ones from Eleusis: many of them suffered this fate. You remember also those here in Athens who were arrested and dragged to prison as a result of private hatreds. [45] These men had done no harm to the city but were forced to die a particularly shameful and inglorious death. Some left elderly parents behind, who had expected to be cared for in old age by their children and buried by them when they died. Others left unmarried sisters, while others left small children who still needed a lot of looking after. [46] What sort of opinion, gentlemen of the jury, do you think these people have about the defendant, and what sort of verdict would they reach if the decision were in their hands, since on his account they have been deprived of what is sweetest? In addition, you remember how the walls were pulled down, and the ships handed over to the enemy, and the shipyards destroyed, and the Spartans took possession of our Acropolis, and all the city's power was exhausted, so that our city was no different from the weakest of cities. [47] Moreover, you lost your private property, and as a final touch, you were all collectively expelled

[26] A more explicit use of the *post hoc, propter hoc* fallacy than at 13.34.

[27] For the Thirty's massacres at Salamis and (below) Eleusis, cf. Lys. 12.52 with note.

from your fatherland by the Thirty. Those good men recognized this and refused to allow the peace to be made. [48] But you, Agoratus, killed them, when they wanted to do something good for the city. You denounced them for plotting against the city, and you were the cause of all the disasters that happened to the city. So each of you, gentlemen, should remember both your private sufferings and those that were common to the city, and take vengeance on the man who caused them.

[49] I wonder, gentlemen of the jury, what on earth Agoratus will find to say to you in his defense. He needs to demonstrate that he did not denounce these men and was not the cause of their death—which he would never be able to show. [50] In the first place, the decrees of the Council and the one passed by the Assembly bear witness against him, because they explicitly say, "concerning the people whom Agoratus has denounced." Secondly, the verdict that was passed under the Thirty, and that acquitted him, explicitly states, "because it appeared that his information is true." Please read them for me.

[DECREES]

[VERDICT]

[51] So in no way could he demonstrate that he did not denounce them. As a result, he must show that he acted justly in denouncing them, presumably because he saw them acting in an improper and criminal fashion towards your democracy. But I suspect that he will not even attempt to show this. For if Agoratus' victims had done any harm to the Athenian People (*dēmos*), the Thirty can hardly have been frightened that the People were being overthrown and have killed them as a way of defending the People. In fact, I think it would have been precisely the opposite.

[52] Perhaps he will claim that he did all this damage unwillingly. But in my view, gentlemen of the jury, when a man has done you such unsurpassable evil—even if it is totally against his will—you still have a duty to defend yourselves on this account. And remember also that this man Agoratus could have been rescued before he was taken before the Council, when he was sitting at the altar at Munychia. Boats had been prepared, and his guarantors were ready to leave with him. [53] If you, Agoratus, had been persuaded by them and had been

willing to sail with them, you would not have killed all these Athenians, willingly or otherwise. But in fact you were persuaded by people who won you over at the time, and you believed that you would win a substantial reward from them if only you mentioned the names of the generals and of the Taxiarchs. This excuse does not entitle you to any mercy at our hands, because the men you killed did not receive any mercy from you either. [54] Hippias of Thasos and Xenophon of Curium,[28] who were summoned by the Council on the same charge as you, were both put to death, Xenophon after being tortured on the rack, while Hippias was simply[29] executed. They were executed because they did not seem to the Thirty to be worth rescuing, since they had not killed any Athenians. Agoratus, however, was let off, because they thought he had done very well for them.

[55] I understand he is trying to put some of the blame for these denunciations on Menestratus. But the fact is that this Menestratus was denounced by Agoratus, and was arrested and imprisoned. It was Hagnodorus of Amphitrope,[30] who belonged to the same deme as Menestratus and was related by marriage to Critias (one of the Thirty), who wanted Menestratus to be rescued. He also wanted to cause as many as possible of those who had been denounced to be executed, so when the Assembly took place in the theater at Munychia, he brought Menestratus before the People, and they voted him immunity according to the following decree.

[DECREE]

[56] When this decree had been passed, Menestratus became an informer and made a fresh denunciation against other citizens. The Thirty let him off, as they did this man Agoratus, because it appeared that his information was true. Much later, however, you convicted[31]

---

[28] Thasos is an island in the north Aegean, and Curium a city in Cyprus, so neither Hippias nor Xenophon was an Athenian citizen.

[29] Lit. "in this way," i.e., without being tortured.

[30] Otherwise unknown, but the fact that he belonged to the Athenian deme Amphitrope shows that both he and therefore also Menestratus must have been Athenian citizens.

[31] Or possibly "arrested" (Gk. *labontes*): the text could mean that Menestratus was arrested because he tried to take part in a trial as a juror, in breach of the ban against murderers from appearing in public places.

him in a dikastic court as a murderer. You quite rightly condemned him to death and handed him over to the executioner, and he suffered death by *apotumpanismos.*[32] [57] And yet if Menestratus was executed, then Agoratus too will be justly executed: he was the man who denounced Menestratus and was responsible for his death—and who is more responsible for the deaths of those denounced by Menestratus than the person who put him under such compulsion?

[58] What happened to Aristophanes of the deme Cholleidae[33] seems to me entirely different. He was at the time one of the defendant's guarantors, who prepared the boats at Munychia and was ready to sail with him. As far as he was concerned, Agoratus, you would have been rescued, you would not have destroyed any Athenians, and you would not yourself have faced such a dangerous situation. [59] As it was, you were so bold as to denounce your own would-be rescuer, and by denouncing him you killed both him and your other guarantors. There were people who wished to have Aristophanes tortured, on the grounds that he was not a pure-bred Athenian, and they persuaded the Assembly to pass the following decree.

[DECREE]

[60] After this, those who then were in control of public affairs came to Aristophanes and begged him to make a denunciation and save himself. They advised him not to risk being put on trial at a *graphē xenias*[34] and suffering the ultimate penalty, but he said that he would never do what they asked. He had such a high sense of duty, both towards those who had been imprisoned and towards the Athenian People, that he preferred to die rather than to denounce and destroy anybody unjustly. [61] That was the sort of man that he turned

---

[32] *Apotumpanismos* was a form of bloodless crucifixion, used in certain contexts as a more painful alternative to hemlock. It appears to have been employed in cases of *apagōgē* (summary arrest), which is the procedure used against Agoratus and presumably also against Menestratus (hence the dikastic court), so *apotumpanismos* may be the penalty Agoratus is facing if convicted.

[33] Otherwise unknown, and certainly not the comic poet. The mention of his deme implies that he had some claim to Athenian citizenship, though 13.59 suggests that there was something suspect about his citizen status.

[34] A public prosecution for pretending to be a citizen (as in Dem. 59). The normal penalty was enslavement.

out to be, Agoratus, and you destroyed him. You, on the other hand, knew nothing that would discredit your victims. You were won over by the promise that if they were destroyed, you would have a share in the constitution that was being established at the time. And so you denounced and murdered many good Athenians.

[62] Gentlemen of the jury, I would like to show you the sort of men you were deprived of by Agoratus. If there were not so many, you could hear about them one by one, but as it is I shall praise them collectively. Some of them had frequently been your generals and had handed on a greater city to their successors. Others had held major public offices, and served often as trierarchs,[35] and had never been criticized by you. **[63]** Still others survived and escaped safely—though this man killed them just as effectively, since they were condemned to death. But fortune and the gods protected them. They fled from here, were not arrested, and did not remain to stand trial. They have returned from Phyle[36] and are honored by you as good men.

[64] These were the sorts of men Agoratus killed or drove into exile from Athens. And who is Agoratus? You need to realize, gentlemen, that he is a slave and the descendant of slaves,[37] to see the sort of person who has injured you. For the defendant's father was Eumares, and this Eumares belonged to Nicocles and Anticles.[38] Let my witnesses come forward.

[WITNESSES]

[65][39] It would be a considerable task to tell you the rest, gentlemen of the jury: the shameful and disgusting acts practiced by the defendant and his brothers. But there is no need to talk in detail about his sykophancy—all the private prosecutions he has brought as a sy-

---

[35] The trierarch was a rich citizen who paid for the upkeep of a warship for a year and was expected to command it.

[36] Cf. 13.77n.

[37] One of several attacks on the origins and status of Agoratus (cf. the Introduction).

[38] Nothing is otherwise known about Eumares or his alleged joint owners Nicocles and Anticles.

[39] The sequence of thought here is odd, though not impossible. Some editors think that 13.65–66 should be deleted or that they belong between 13.68 and 13.69.

kophant, or the public prosecutions, or the denunciations. All of you together, both in the Assembly and in the lawcourt, convicted him of sykophancy, and he was fined one thousand drachmas.[40] [66] So you have all given sufficient testimony to this at least. And although he is that kind of person, he has also attempted to commit adultery with the wives of the citizens, and to corrupt freeborn women, and has been caught as an adulterer—something for which the penalty is death.[41] Call witnesses that I am telling the truth.

[WITNESSES]

[67] The defendant, gentlemen of the jury, is one of four brothers. The eldest was caught by Lamachus[42] in Sicily making secret fire-signals to the enemy, and was executed by *apotumpanismos.*[43] The next one smuggled a slave from here to Corinth; there he was caught attempting again to smuggle out a slave girl, and he was locked up in prison and died. [68] The third one was arrested here by Phaenippides for stealing clothes:[44] you, gentlemen, tried him in the lawcourt, sentenced him to death, and handed him over to be executed by *apotumpanismos.* I think Agoratus will himself admit that I am telling the truth, and I shall also produce witnesses.

[WITNESSES]

[69] How can there be any doubt that you all have a duty to convict this man? If each of his brothers was thought to deserve death for a single offense, it is absolutely essential that you condemn Agoratus to death, since he has committed many offenses both publicly against the city and individually against each one of you, and the penalty in law for each offense is death.

[70] Agoratus will attempt to deceive by claiming, gentlemen of

---

[40] An apparent allusion to the procedure of *probolē,* which according to *Ath. Pol.* 43.5 could be brought against sykophants (malicious prosecutors). It involved a preliminary vote in the Assembly, which had no binding effect but could encourage the proposer to bring a formal charge before a lawcourt.

[41] Not the only penalty, though it was a possible one.

[42] One of the commanders of the Athenian expedition to Sicily in 415 BC.

[43] For *apotumpanismos* as a method of execution, see 13.56n.

[44] A *lōpodutēs* (clothes stealer) was one of the categories of offender liable to *apagōgē* (summary arrest); cf. 10.10.

the jury, that he assassinated Phrynichus at the time of the Four Hundred and that for this deed the People made him an Athenian citizen.[45] But this is a lie, gentlemen: he did not kill Phrynichus, and the People did not make him an Athenian. [71] The death of Phrynichus, gentlemen, was planned jointly by Thrasybulus of Calydon[46] and Apollodorus of Megara, who came upon him when he was out on a walk. Thrasybulus struck Phrynichus and knocked him down with the blow, but Apollodorus did not touch him. Meanwhile, however, a disturbance arose, and they ran off. This man Agoratus was not called upon to help them, he was not present, and he did not know anything about the affair. The decree itself will show you that I am telling the truth.

[DECREE]

[72] That Agoratus did not kill Phrynichus is clear from the terms of the decree. Nowhere does it say, "Agoratus is to be an Athenian," as it does for Thrasybulus and Apollodorus. And yet if he really killed Phrynichus, then it would necessarily have been recorded that he was to be an Athenian, on the same inscribed stone where this is said about Thrasybulus and Apollodorus. But by offering bribes to the proposer, some people arranged to have their own names added to the inscription as "benefactors." The following decree will prove that I am telling the truth.

[DECREE]

[73] However, gentlemen, the defendant despised you to such an extent that even though he was not an Athenian, he took part in the

[45] Phrynichus (mentioned also in Lys. 20.11) was one of the leaders of the Four Hundred, and his assassination by two foreigners sparked off the overthrow of the regime. Contradictory accounts of the event are given in Thuc. 8.92 and Lyc. 1.112. Our evidence does not allow us to determine Agoratus' role or reward in the affair, although we possess a decree of 410/09 (translated in Fornara 1983: no. 155), parts of which may be the source of one or other of the documents quoted at 13.71 and 13.72, naming him and others as "benefactors" and giving citizenship to Thrasybulus: for detailed discussion, see M. J. Osborne, *Naturalization in Athens,* Vol. 2 (Brussels, 1982), 16–21.

[46] No relation either to Thrasybulus of Steiria, leader of the democratic counterrevolution in 404/3 (cf. Lys. 12.52 and 28.4), or to Thrasybulus of Collytus (cf. Lys. 26.13, 21).

lawcourts and the Assembly, and initiated public prosecutions of all types, recording his name with the additional description "of the deme Anagyra."[47]

There is one powerful additional piece of evidence that he did not kill Phrynichus (for which he claims to have been made an Athenian citizen). This man Phrynichus set up the Four Hundred, and after his death, most of the Four Hundred went into exile. [74] Do you think that the Thirty and the Council that held office under them, who had themselves all been members of the exiled Four Hundred, would have released the killer of Phrynichus after getting hold of him, or would they have punished him both for Phrynichus' sake and for the exile they themselves had suffered? I certainly believe they would have punished him. [75] If, as I claim, he pretends to have killed Phrynichus when he did not, then he is behaving unjustly.[48] But if, Agoratus, you dispute this and claim that you did kill Phrynichus, then it is clear that you can only have escaped liability at the hands of the Thirty on Phrynichus' account by having done some greater harm to the Athenian People. You are never going to persuade anybody that you killed Phrynichus and were let off by the Thirty, unless you had done some great and incurable harm to the Athenian People. [76] So if he claims to have killed Phrynichus, remember this, and punish him for what he has done. If he denies it, ask him how he claims he was made an Athenian. If he cannot show how, then punish him for having taken part in the lawcourts and in the Assembly, and for having maliciously prosecuted many people, while adding to his name the description "Athenian."

[77] I hear that he is arranging to defend himself by claiming that he went to Phyle[49] and that he returned from Phyle with the others—and I hear that this is the main trick in his defense. What actually happened was this. He did indeed go to Phyle, but what sort of person

---

[47] I.e., he identified himself in the *graphē* (the written statement of the charge) as "Agoratus of the deme Anagyra" and therefore as a citizen rather than a metic.

[48] I.e., by claiming Athenian citizenship.

[49] I.e., that he joined the democratic counterrevolution at a very early stage, before the march on Piraeus (cf. 12.53n). Citizenship was subsequently voted to all those foreigners who had been present at Phyle, which would presumably have included Agoratus if he had not already been given citizenship for killing Phrynichus—a point that the speaker conveniently sidesteps here (cf. the Introduction).

could be more blood-cursed? He knew that some of the men at Phyle were among those he himself had driven into exile, and yet he dared to go and join them. [78] As soon as they saw him, they seized him and took him immediately to kill him at the place where they slit the throats of others also, whenever they happened to catch a bandit or a criminal. But Anytus,[50] who was general, said they ought not to do this. He told them that things were not in a fit state for them to punish any of their enemies and that for the moment they should remain at peace. If they ever returned home from exile, that would be the time to punish wrongdoers. [79] By saying this, Anytus was responsible for the defendant's escape at Phyle, for they had to listen to a man who held the generalship, if they wanted to survive. But there is another point: it is clear that nobody shared his food or his tent with the defendant, and the Taxiarch did not assign him to his tribe.[51] Instead, no human being spoke to him—it was as if he were polluted. Please call the Taxiarch.

[TESTIMONY]

[80] When the peace settlement took place between the two sides, and those from Piraeus held their procession up to the Acropolis with Aesimus[52] leading, the defendant behaved just as outrageously. He took up arms and tried to accompany the procession up to the town (*astu*), joining in with the hoplites. [81] When they were in front of the gates, standing at arms before entering the town, Aesimus noticed him. He came up, seized his shield and tore it away, and told him to go to hell. He said that Agoratus, as a murderer, could have no part in

---

[50] A leader of the democratic counterrevolutionaries. In 399 BC (about the time of this trial) he was one of the prosecutors of Socrates.

[51] The ten Taxiarchs (regimental commanders) each commanded the hoplites (heavy infantry) of one tribe (*phulē*).

[52] We would expect the amnesty to have been accompanied by a symbolic act of reconciliation, but what is described here sounds more like a victory procession. There is a brief allusion to the same event in Xen., *Hellenica* 2.4.39, but it gives no details. Aesimus was one of the leaders of the democratic forces: he is less well attested than Anytus (cf. 13.78n), but is mentioned in the context of an Assembly debate in 397/6 (*Hellenica Oxyrhynchia* 6[1].2: ed. with trans. and comm. by P. R. McKechnie and S. J. Kern [Warminster, 1988]).

the procession to Athene. That is how he was driven away by Aesimus. I will provide witnesses to show that I am telling the truth.

[WITNESSES]

[82] These, gentlemen of the jury, are the dealings he had with the hoplites at Phyle and in Piraeus. Nobody spoke to him, since he was a murderer, and only Anytus kept him from being killed. If he uses in his defense the journey to Phyle, you need to ask whether Anytus kept him from being killed when people were ready to punish him, and whether Aesimus tore away his shield and refused to let him join in the procession.

[83] Do not accept these excuses from him, and do not accept the argument that we are seeking vengeance long after the event. I do not believe there is any statutory time limit for offenses like this.[53] Indeed, I think that whether a person seeks vengeance immediately or later, the defendant must demonstrate that he did not do the things he is accused of doing. [84] So let him demonstrate either that he did not kill his victims, or that he did so justly because they were harming the Athenian People. Suppose we are seeking vengeance later, when we ought to have done so long ago: if so, then the intervening time during which he has stayed alive has been a benefit he does not deserve—and the men he killed are no less dead.

[85] I hear that he intends to rely on this point as well, that the phrase "in the act"[54] is written in the arrest document (*apagōgē*). But I think this is the most naive of all his arguments. Are we to suppose that if the phrase "in the act" had not been added to the document, he would have been liable to arrest (*apagōgē*), but because this phrase was added, he thinks that he has an easy escape? That is simply to

---

[53] The implications of this argument for the dating of the speech are discussed in the Introduction.

[54] The phrase *ep' autophōrōi,* which forms the basis of the discussion in 13.85–87, literally means "in the act" (though there is some dispute as to whether this means "caught in the act of committing a crime" or "caught in such circumstances as to make denial impossible"). The phrase is closely associated with the procedure of *apagōgē* or summary arrest, but whichever of the two meanings we adopt, it hardly seems appropriate here. The Eleven's insistence on having it included in the arrest document is discussed in the Introduction.

admit that he did the killings, but not in the act, and to base his case on this—as if he deserves to be acquitted simply because he killed but not in the act. [86] It seems to me that the Eleven,[55] who accepted this arrest, did not want to make things easier for Agoratus, who was even then relying on this point. So they very properly compelled Dionysius, who was making the arrest, to add this particular phrase "in the act." How could Agoratus not have been caught in the act, given that first in front of five hundred, and again later in front of all the Athenians,[56] he killed several people by denouncing them? [87] Do you seriously believe, Agoratus, that the phrase "in the act" applies only if a man strikes another with a club or a knife and knocks him down? On the basis of your argument, it will appear that nobody killed the men whom you denounced, for nobody struck them or slit their throats; instead, they were compelled to die by your denunciation. Surely "in the act" denotes the person responsible for their deaths—and who else is responsible other than you who denounced them? So if you are the killer, how can you not be "in the act"?

[88] I gather that he also intends to speak about the oaths and the agreements, and to claim that he is being prosecuted contrary to the oaths and the agreements which those of us who were at Piraeus made with those in the town (*astu*).[57] By asserting this point, he is virtually admitting he is a murderer. He throws up as obstacles the oaths or the agreements or the passage of time or the phrase "in the act," but he has no confidence that he can defend himself properly on the real issue. [89] You should not accept his arguments on these points, gentlemen of the jury, but should force him to plead either that he did not denounce the men or that they are not dead. Anyway, I do not believe the oaths and the agreements apply to our relationship with the defendant. The oaths were sworn by those in the town towards those in Piraeus. [90] If the defendant had been in the town and we

[55] The Eleven were the public officials responsible for prisons and executions, who therefore presided over cases of *apagōgē*.

[56] I.e., the Council and the Assembly.

[57] I.e., the general amnesty of 403/2. The text of the amnesty as quoted in *Ath. Pol.* 39.5 makes it clear that it did not in fact cover only offenses committed by members of one faction against members of the other. For other similarly restrictive misinterpretations of the amnesty, see Lys. 6.37–41 and 26.16–20.

had been in Piraeus, the agreements would have had some value for him. As it is, however, he was in Piraeus, and so was I, and Dionysius, and all those who are seeking to punish him, so this presents no obstacle to us: those in Piraeus did not swear any oath towards those in Piraeus.

[91] It seems to me that in every way he deserves not just one death. He claims to have been adopted as a citizen by the People (*dēmos*), but it is the People—whom he describes as his father—that he is shown to have wronged, and he treacherously betrayed those who were making the community (*dēmos*) greater and stronger. If a person struck down his natural father and failed to provide him with the necessities of life, or if he robbed his adoptive father of the things he already possessed—surely such a person deserves the death penalty for this reason, according to the law on maltreatment of parents.

[92] It is as fitting for all of you, gentlemen of the jury, as for each one of us, to avenge these men. When they were dying, they laid the responsibility on us and all their friends to take vengeance for their sake against this man Agoratus, their killer, and (to put it briefly) to do him as much harm as each of us could. So if it is clear that these men have done some good either to the city or to your democracy—as you yourselves acknowledge—you must all necessarily be their close friends, so they have laid the responsibility on each one of you just as much as on us. [93] For you to acquit this man Agoratus would be unholy and illegal. Act now! At the time his victims were killed, men of Athens, you could not assist them, because of the political situation, but now, when you have the opportunity, you should punish their killer. Take care, men of Athens, that you do not commit the most outrageous act of all. If you acquit this man Agoratus, that is not all you are doing: by the same vote, you also condemn to death those men whom you agree were your supporters. [94] By acquitting the person who was responsible for their deaths, you are simply deciding that they were justly killed by him. So they would suffer the most terrible of all fates, if they had laid the responsibility on you as their friends to avenge them, and you cast the same vote against them as the Thirty did. [95] By the Olympian gods, gentlemen of the jury, do not sentence these men to death as the result of any skill or trickery. They did you much good, and for that they were killed by the Thirty and by this man Agoratus. Remember all your sufferings, both those

common to the whole city and the private ones that affected each one of us when these men died, and punish the man responsible for them. It has been shown to you in full detail, from the decrees and the denunciations and everything else, that Agoratus is responsible for their deaths.

[96] Moreover, it is fitting that you should vote in opposition to the Thirty. You should acquit those whom they condemned to death, and convict those whom they did not. The Thirty condemned to death these men, who were your friends, whom you must acquit. They acquitted Agoratus, because he appeared eager to destroy these men, so it is fitting that you should convict him. [97] If you vote the opposite way to the Thirty, then first of all you are casting a different vote from your enemies; secondly, you will have avenged your own friends; and finally, you will appear to all mankind to have voted according to the demands of justice and of religion.

14–15. AGAINST ALCIBIADES

INTRODUCTION

Lysias 14 and 15 deal with a prosecution brought against Alcibiades the younger (son of the famous Alcibiades) for dereliction of military duty. The younger Alcibiades was probably born around 416 or 415 BC, because he was left a child at the time of his father's death in 404, but had reached adulthood some time in the early 390s. He evidently inherited many of the liabilities, both financial and personal, that had been incurred by his flamboyant father, but without also inheriting his father's personal and political power. We possess the young man's own speech (Isoc. 16) in an unrelated case brought against him around 397 BC by a plaintiff who claimed that the elder Alcibiades had cheated him by entering in the Olympic Games under his own name a chariot team allegedly belonging to the plaintiff, and it is clear from the present dispute that the young man had many enemies, some of whom (including the speaker of Lys. 14) he had inherited from his father. The present case is heard by a special jury of soldiers presided over by the generals, probably in 395 BC.[1] The penalty if convicted is *atimia* or deprivation of civic rights, together with confiscation of property (14.8–9). The result of the case is unknown: we hear nothing of the younger Alcibiades after this trial, but that need not signify a conviction.

The formal charge against the defendant is that he was called up to serve as a hoplite[2] but has instead served in the cavalry, despite

[1] It is described at 14.4 as the first such case to be heard since the peace (i.e., the peace with Sparta at the end of the Peloponnesian War). The first war fought by Athens after this date was the Corinthian War, which began in 395.

[2] Hoplites are heavy-armed infantry.

the requirement that prospective cavalry pass a *dokimasia* (scrutiny),[3] which he failed to do. The law on which the prosecutors have based their case is summarized at 14.5, where they appear to be relying on an idiosyncratic, not to say implausible, interpretation of a crucial phrase: the law provides for the prosecution of anybody who absents himself from the ground forces (*pezē stratia,* lit. "foot army"), a term that was probably intended to designate the land army as opposed to the fleet, but the speaker uses it in a narrower sense to designate the infantry as opposed to the cavalry.

It is at first sight surprising that we possess two speeches by co-prosecutors (*sunēgoroi*), and not by the main prosecutor Archestratides (referred to by name at 14.3 and at 15.12). This has given rise to speculation that Lysias 14 may be the only one that is a genuine speech, with Lysias 15 being a rhetorical exercise based on it. Such speculation has been encouraged by the different titles of the speeches in our manuscripts, with Lysias 14 describing itself as a prosecution "for deserting the army" (*lipotaxion*) and Lysias 15 as "for failing to undertake military service" (*astrateia*), as if they were unable to make up their minds what the charge was. (Since both speeches refer to Archestratides as the main prosecutor, it is very unlikely that they belong to separate trials.) However, it is not wholly clear that *lipotaxion* and *astrateia* were regarded as different offenses, and the titles in our manuscripts are sometimes the product of speculation by copyists. Moreover, each speech deals with very different aspects of the case.[4] Lysias 14 covers the charge (14.4–15) and includes a wide-ranging attack on Alcibiades' family and upbringing (14.16–40). Lysias 15 is much shorter and is directed specifically against the generals (who are presiding at the trial), some of whom are expected to appear in support of Alcibiades and to defend him by saying it was they who had ordered him to serve in the cavalry. It is indeed precisely because Alcibiades has apparently been obeying orders, rather than disobeying them, that the prosecution seems so vindictive.

Evidence for the career and family of Alcibiades is collected and discussed by Davies 1971: no. 600, esp. pp. 17–21 (the elder Alcibiades,

---

[3] For this procedure, see *Ath. Pol.* 49.1–2.

[4] So clearly Lys. 15 is not based on Lys. 14 in the way that Lys. 11 is based on Lys. 10.

whom he identifies for convenience as Alcibiades III) and pp. 21–22 (his son Alcibiades IV, the defendant in this trial). On the Athenian cavalry, see I. G. Spence, *The Cavalry of Classical Greece: A Social and Military History with Particular Reference to Athens* (Oxford, 1993). There is no recent commentary on Lysias 15, but on the details of Lysias 14, see Carey 1989.

14. FIRST PROSECUTION SPEECH AGAINST ALCIBIADES, FOR DESERTING THE ARMY[1]

[1] In my view, gentlemen of the jury, you require no explanation from those who want to prosecute Alcibiades. From the start, he has shown himself to be the sort of citizen that you should treat as your enemy on the basis of his general behavior, even if he has injured nobody personally. [2] His crimes are not small and do not deserve forgiveness. They do not offer hope that he will improve in the future, but have been committed in such a way and have reached such a level of depravity that even his enemies are ashamed at some of the things he takes pride in. There was in the past, gentlemen of the jury, a long-standing enmity between our fathers, and since I have long considered this man a criminal, and have now been badly treated by him, for all these reasons I shall attempt with your help to punish him for all his actions. [3] Archestratides, my fellow-prosecutor, has dealt sufficiently with the general charges. He has shown you the laws and has produced witnesses about everything. I shall explain to you point by point some things that he omitted.[2]

[4] Given that you are deciding a case of this type for the first time since we made peace,[3] gentlemen of the jury, it is appropriate that you should be not simply jurors (*dikastai*)[4] but lawgivers (*nomothetai*).

---

[1] Gk. *lipotaxion.*

[2] The manuscript here adds "Please read the law for me. [LAW]," but this seems out of place here.

[3] The implications of this phrase for dating are discussed in the Introduction.

[4] The argument here is the opposite of the one deployed by the speaker's colleague at Lys. 15.9. Although the translation "juror" for *dikastēs* is conventional and convenient, it should be remembered that the Athenian *dikastēs* combined the role of the modern juror (who decides the facts) with that of the judge (who interprets the law and passes sentence).

You are fully aware that in the future the city will treat such matters in whatever way you decide today. The task of a responsible citizen and of a just-minded juror, it seems to me, is to interpret the laws in the way that will benefit the city in future. [5] Some people dare to claim that nobody is liable to charges of desertion or cowardice, since no battle took place, whereas the law says that if somebody deserts the ranks in retreat because of cowardice while others are fighting, the soldiers are to judge the case. However, the law deals not simply with these cases but also with anybody who absents himself from the ground forces.[5] Please read me the law.

[LAW]

[6] You hear, gentlemen of the jury, that it deals with both categories: those who retreat when there is a battle and those who are absent from the ground forces. Now consider who are obliged to present themselves. Is it not those who are of an appropriate age? Is it not those whom the generals call up? [7] In my view, gentlemen of the jury, the defendant alone is liable to the whole of the law. He could legitimately be convicted of refusing to serve (*astrateia*), because he was called up as a hoplite and did not march out with you; of deserting the ranks (*lipotaxion*), because he alone did not offer himself to serve with the other hoplites; and of cowardice (*deilia*), because he preferred the cavalry when it was his duty to face danger with the hoplites.

[8] Nevertheless, people tell me that he is going to make the following defense: that he did no harm to the city when he served in the cavalry. But I think you would rightly be angry with him for this, because he dared to serve in the cavalry without passing his *dokimasia* as a cavalryman, even though the law says that if anybody serves in the cavalry without passing his *dokimasia,* he is to suffer *atimia.*[6] Please read me the law.

[LAW]

[9] This man had reached such a level of wickedness, he so despised you, he so feared the enemy, he was so keen to be in the cavalry, and

---

[5] For the ambiguity of *pezē stratia,* see the Introduction.

[6] For the *dokimasia* (judicial scrutiny) of prospective cavalry, and the penalty of *atimia* (loss of civic rights), see the Introduction.

he was so contemptuous of the laws that he disregarded these dangers and preferred to suffer *atimia,* to have his property confiscated, and to be liable to all the statutory penalties, rather than to serve as a hoplite alongside the citizens. [10] There were other people who had never been hoplites but had on previous occasions served in the cavalry and had done a lot of damage to the enemy. They did not dare join the cavalry, because they respected you and the law. They based their plans on the expectation not that the city was going to be destroyed but that it would survive and would punish wrongdoers. Alcibiades, on the other hand, dared to join the cavalry, not because he was loyal to your democracy (*plēthos*), or had previously served in the cavalry, or was at the time particularly skilled, or had been approved by you at his *dokimasia,* but in the expectation that the city would not be in a position to punish criminals. [11] You should bear in mind that if everybody is allowed to do whatever he likes, there will be no point in having laws, or meeting as an Assembly, or electing generals. I am surprised, gentlemen of the jury, that anybody thinks it right to convict someone assigned to the front line who retreats to the second line under enemy attack, but to pardon a person assigned to the hoplites who is found in the cavalry. [12] In my opinion, gentlemen of the jury, you are judging cases not simply on account of individual defendants but so as to encourage improvement among those whose discipline is poor. If you punish those who are unknown, none of the others will behave better, because nobody will hear about the offenses you have condemned; but if you punish the most prominent among the criminals, everybody will know, and as a result, the citizens will heed this example and become better. [13] So if you convict my opponent, not only will those in the city hear about it, but the allies also will find out, and the enemy will know. They will regard the city as worthy of greater respect, if they see that you are particularly angry about these sorts of crimes, and that those who lack discipline in war receive no forgiveness. [14] Bear in mind, gentlemen of the jury, that some of the soldiers were sick, and others lacked the necessities of life. The former would gladly have remained and been treated in their communities, the latter would gladly have returned home to look after their affairs, others would gladly have fought as light-armed troops, and others would gladly have faced the danger among the cavalry. [15] Nevertheless, you did not dare to abandon the ranks or choose what you pleased. Instead, you feared the laws of the city much more than the danger of facing the enemy. Now you must remember this and cast your vote, and make clear to everybody that those Athenians who are unwilling to fight the enemy will suffer very severely at your hands.

[16] In my opinion, gentlemen of the jury, my opponents will have nothing to say about the law and about the facts of the case. Instead, they will stand here begging and beseeching you, and will ask you not to convict the son of Alcibiades of such great cowardice, claiming that his father was responsible for much good rather than much evil. But if you had executed the father when he was the same age as the defendant, when you first discovered him committing crimes against you, the city would not have suffered disasters on such a scale. [17] It seems to me extraordinary, gentlemen of the jury, that you condemned the father to death but will for his sake acquit his criminal son, who did not himself have the courage to fight beside you, whereas his father decided to campaign on the side of the enemy. When the defendant was a child, and it was not yet clear how he would turn out, he was almost handed over to the Eleven because of his father's crimes.[7] Do you really think it is right to spare him for his father's sake, now that you know about his own crimes in addition to his father's? [18] Surely it is a terrible thing, gentlemen of the jury, that my opponents are so privileged that when they are caught committing crimes, they are spared because of their family, whereas if we suffer misfortune because of those who lack discipline, no plea to the enemy will succeed, not even one based on the deeds of our ancestors. [19] And yet these deeds were many and famous, and were performed on behalf of all the Greeks. They are in no way comparable to what these men have done to the city, gentlemen of the jury. If they are seen as virtuous because they rescue their friends, it is obvious that you too will be seen as virtuous if you punish your enemies. [20] If any of Alcibiades' relatives try to demand his acquittal, gentlemen of the jury, I think you should

---

[7] The Eleven were the public officials in charge of prisons and (here) executions. The speaker is presumably referring to the elder Alcibiades' involvement in the religious scandals of 415 (see the Introduction to Lys. 6), when the son would have been at most three or four years old. There had evidently been some talk at the time of sentencing not just the father but his descendants to death (cf. Isoc. 16.45).

be angry that they did not attempt to plead with him to obey the city's commands—unless they pleaded but were unable to win him over—and are now seeking to persuade you that there is no need to punish criminals. [21] If any of the public officials[8] assist him, making a display of their own power and boasting that they can rescue even those who are manifestly guilty, you must understand first, that if everybody had been like Alcibiades, there would have been no need of generals, because there would have been nobody to lead; and secondly, that it is far more appropriate for them to prosecute those who desert the ranks than to defend such people. What hope will there be that other people will do what the generals command, when the generals themselves seek to rescue those who behave badly? [22] So if those who are speaking and pleading for Alcibiades demonstrate that he fought among the hoplites, or served in the cavalry after passing his *dokimasia,* I ask you to acquit him. But if, without any justice on their side, they command you to do them a favor, you must remember that they are telling you to break your oath and disobey the laws, and that their eagerness to assist criminals makes many others keen to do the same things.

[23] I am particularly surprised, gentlemen of the jury, that any of you might decide to spare Alcibiades because of those who are helping him, and not to destroy him because of his criminal nature. You need to hear about this, so that you will realize he does not deserve acquittal on the pretext that despite these offenses, he has been a useful citizen in other respects. In fact you could legitimately condemn him to death for his other actions, [24] and you ought to know about them. Since you listen to defendants recounting their own merits and the benefactions performed by their ancestors, you should listen to prosecutors as well, if they can show that the accused have committed many offenses against you and that their ancestors have been responsible for much harm. [25] When my opponent was a child, he used to drink at the house of Archedemus[9]—the man with the runny eyes, who had embezzled a great deal of your property—reclining together under the

[8] *Archontes,* here presumably the generals, whose support for the defendant is criticized in detail in Lys. 15.

[9] A politician who is described as a "demagogue" in Aristoph., *Frogs* 420–425, with further jokes about his eyesight in *Frogs* 588.

same cloak, in the sight of many people. He used to dance the *kōmos*[10] during the day and maintained a courtesan (*hetaira*) before reaching adulthood. Clearly he was emulating his ancestors, in the belief that he could become famous when older only if he showed himself to be the worst of criminals while he was young. [26] He was sent for by Alcibiades[11] because he was behaving scandalously in public. How do you think you should regard a person whose behavior had scandalized even the man who taught other people such things? He plotted with Theotimus against his own father, and betrayed Orni[12]—and Theotimus, on taking over the site, first of all committed *hubris*[13] against him (now that he was in the prime of his youth), and eventually imprisoned him and tried to exact a ransom. [27] However, his father hated him so much that he declared he would not even collect his bones if he died. After his father's death, Archebiades[14] became his lover and paid the ransom. Not much later, after gambling away his property, he began to raid his friends' ships, using Leuke Akte as his base.[15] [28] It would be a lengthy task, gentlemen of the jury, to recount all his crimes against citizens or foreigners, in respect to his own friends or other people. However, Hipponicus[16] summoned many witnesses and

---

[10] It was said of the *kōmos* (a type of dance normally performed at night) that a respectable man ought to be ashamed to participate without a mask (Dem. 19.287).

[11] I.e., his father, the elder Alcibiades. On the latter's career, see Davies 1971: 17–21.

[12] One of the forts in Thrace controlled by the elder Alcibiades after his final exile from Athens in 406 BC. Theotimus is not otherwise known.

[13] *Hubris* is aggravated assault or outrageous violence, and in this context it probably implies rape.

[14] Given that the name is not common, he is probably to be identified with the Archebiades who was denounced together with Alcibiades in 415 (And. 1.13); he may also be the man of the same name who was the plaintiff in Lys. Fr. 5 (*Archebiades*).

[15] Lit. "drowned (*katapontizō*) his friends." For the connection with piracy, see Carey's commentary on this passage. There were many promontories known as Leuke Akte ("white cliff"), but the lexicographer Harpocration suggests that this one was in the Propontis.

[16] We are told elsewhere (Dem. 59.87) that a husband who caught an adulterer with his wife had to divorce her, but the force of the allegation here is not just

dismissed his own wife, claiming that the defendant had entered his house not as her brother but as her husband. [29] He has committed offenses like this, and has done many other outrageous things, but he has no regrets for the past and no concerns for the future. He ought to be the most discreet of the citizens, making his own life a defense against his father's crimes, but instead he seeks to commit *hubris* against others, as if he could transfer much of his own shame onto other people—[30] and this when he is the son of Alcibiades, who persuaded the Spartans to fortify Decelea,[17] sailed to the islands to make them revolt, was a teacher of evil for the city, and campaigned more often with the enemy against his fatherland than with the citizens against the enemy. In return for this, you and your descendants have a duty to punish any members of the family you can get your hands on. [31] He has become too accustomed to saying that whereas the Assembly rewarded his father with gifts on his return from exile, we have unfairly used this exile as an excuse to slander the son.[18] But it seems extraordinary to me if you are going to acquit this criminal on the grounds that his father was of service to the city, when you took away those gifts from the latter on the grounds that they were unjustly given. [32] Furthermore, gentlemen of the jury, besides many other reasons, you should convict him in particular because he is using your meritorious deeds as examples for his own crimes. He dares to claim that Alcibiades did nothing wrong by campaigning against his own fatherland, [33] because you yourselves as exiles captured Phyle and cut down trees and assaulted the walls, and by doing this, you did

---

adultery but incest, because Hipponicus' wife was the younger Alcibiades' sister. (This Hipponicus was the son of Callias the Torchbearer, who was the enemy of Andocides; cf. the Introduction to Lys. 6.)

[17] After his defection in 415/4, the elder Alcibiades advised the Spartans to fortify Decelea (an Athenian deme nearly fifteen miles northeast of the city) as a permanent base in Attica, and to build a fleet in order to challenge Athens' control of its subject allies. These two things together did more than anything else to ensure Athenian defeat.

[18] The younger Alcibiades puts forward a version of this argument in another speech (Isoc. 16.11), ignoring the point made in the next sentence here, that the gifts made after Alcibiades' return from exile in 407 had apparently been confiscated again at some time after his second exile in 406.

not bequeath shame to your descendants but gained honor from all mankind[19]—as if the two groups deserve the same reputation, those who as exiles campaigned with the enemy against the land and those who were returning from exile when the Spartans controlled the city! [34] I think it is clear to everybody that my opponents sought to return in order to hand over command of the sea to the Spartans, and themselves to rule over you, but when your democracy returned, it drove out the enemy and liberated even those citizens who wished to be slaves. So he is making speeches, but the actions of the two groups were in no way similar.[20] [35] Despite the many great misfortunes that have befallen him, he prides himself on his father's criminal nature and asserts that his father was so powerful that he was the cause of all the evils which afflicted the city. But who is so ignorant about his own fatherland that if he did want to be a criminal, he could not explain to the enemy which parts of the territory are essential to capture, which of the guard-posts are poorly defended, what aspects of public affairs are in trouble, and which of the allies are prepared to revolt? [36] It is hardly a sign of the elder Alcibiades' power that he was able to harm the city when in exile, but that when (by deceiving you) he had returned from exile and controlled many triremes, he could not expel the enemy from our territory, or make the people of Chios (whose revolt he had caused)[21] into our friends again, or benefit you in any other way. [37] So it is not difficult to recognize that Alcibiades' power was no greater than other people's, but he is foremost among the citizens for wickedness. He became an informer for the Spartans about those aspects of your affairs he knew were in trouble, but when he had to serve as general, he could not harm them in any way. He promised that for his sake the Great King of Persia would provide money, but he embezzled more than two hundred talents from the city. [38] He was aware of having committed so many crimes

[19] These activities are ascribed to the democratic counterrevolutionaries in 404/3 by Xenophon (*Hellenica* 2.4.25). The younger Alcibiades puts forward elsewhere (Isoc. 16.13) a version of the argument rebutted here.

[20] For the contrast of *logos* (word) and *ergon* (action), see, e.g., 12.33.

[21] With Alcibiades' assistance, Chios had been the first subject ally to revolt in 411 after the loss of the Athenian expedition to Sicily (cf. Thuc. 8.14).

against you that he never dared to offer his accounts (*euthunai*)[22]—even though he was a capable speaker, and had friends, and possessed money—but condemned himself to exile and preferred to be a citizen of Thrace, and every other city, rather than his own fatherland. Eventually, gentlemen of the jury, surpassing his previous criminal behavior, he dared together with Adeimantus to betray the fleet to Lysander.[23] [39] So if any of you pities those who died in the sea battle, or feels shame for those enslaved by the enemy, or is angry about the destruction of the walls, or hates the Spartans, or detests the Thirty—for all these things you must regard the defendant's father as responsible. You must remember that your ancestors twice ostracized both the defendant's great-grandfather Alcibiades, and Megacles his father's maternal grandfather,[24] and that the older ones among you condemned the defendant's father to death. [40] So now you should regard my opponent as a hereditary enemy of the city, and convict him. You should not regard pity or forgiveness or mercy as more important than the established laws and the oaths you swore.

[41] You must consider, gentlemen of the jury, why anybody should spare people like this. Is it because although their relations with the city are unfortunate, nevertheless they are in other regards decent

---

[22] This presumably refers to Alcibiades' refusal to return to Athens after the Athenian defeat at Notium in 406.

[23] Adeimantus was the only Athenian general captured at Aegospotami not to be executed by the Spartans, and Demosthenes (19.191) claims that he was charged with treason more than ten years later on this account. As is normal in Lysias, the battle itself is glossed over here. For a less prejudiced account of the elder Alcibiades' behavior immediately before the battle, see Xen., *Hellenica* 2.1.25–26.

[24] Ostracism was a ballot, which could be held annually but became obsolete in the second half of the fifth century, to exile any one political leader for ten years. Votes were cast by scratching names on pieces of broken pottery (*ostraka*). Surviving *ostraka* suggest that an Alcibiades, apparently the grandfather of the elder Alcibiades, was ostracized around 460, and *Ath. Pol.* 22.3 dates Megacles' ostracism to 487/6, but there is no reliable supporting evidence that either of them was ostracized twice. (The phrase "his father's maternal grandfather" is a restoration of a corrupt text, but it is a plausible restoration, because this Megacles was the father of Deinomache, the mother of the elder Alcibiades.)

and well behaved? But have not many of them prostituted themselves, while others have slept with their sisters and others have had children by their daughters? [42] Have not others enacted the Mysteries, mutilated the Herms, behaved impiously towards all the gods, and committed crimes against the whole city?[25] Have they not behaved unjustly and illegally both towards other people in public and in their relations with each other? Have they not indulged in every outrage, such that there is nothing outrageous in which they are not expert? They have suffered all things and have done all things.[26] Their character is such that they are ashamed at what is good and pride themselves on what is evil. [43] Admittedly, gentlemen of the jury, you have previously acquitted people you realized were criminals but believed would be useful to you in future. But what hope is there that the city will benefit in any way from this man? You will realize he is totally worthless when he makes his defense—and you have already recognized that he is a criminal from his general behavior. [44] What is more, he would not be able to harm you even if he left the city, because he is a coward, a poor man, unskilled in public affairs, engaged in disputes with his friends, and hated by everybody else. [45] So not even for these reasons does he deserve cautious treatment. You ought instead to make an example, especially for his friends, who do not want to obey orders but enjoy behaving like him. They have been badly advised about their own affairs and are delivering public speeches about yours.

[46] I have made my prosecution speech as best I can. I realize that my audience is wondering how on earth I have been able to identify these men's offenses so precisely, while my opponent is sneering at me because I have not recounted even the smallest part of their crimes. [47] When you weigh both what has been said and what has been left out, you should be the more ready to convict him, realizing that he is liable to the terms of the indictment (*graphē*), and that getting rid of citizens like this is a great blessing to the city. Please read the laws, the

---

[25] The Herms and Mysteries scandals of 415 (which led to the elder Alcibiades' first exile) are discussed in the Introduction to Lys. 6.

[26] The text is corrupt here, and this is an ancient copyist's guess at what Lysias may have written.

oaths, and the indictment to the jurors. Let them bear these in mind and deliver a just verdict.

[LAWS, OATHS, INDICTMENT [27]]

15. SECOND PROSECUTION SPEECH AGAINST ALCIBIADES, FOR FAILING TO UNDERTAKE MILITARY SERVICE[1]

[1] I ask you, gentlemen of the jury, to vote in accordance with justice. In particular, given that throughout their tenure of office they have done much for the city,[2] I ask the generals to be evenhanded to the prosecutor and the defendant in public prosecutions for failure to undertake military service (*graphai astrateias*), and not to make every attempt to ensure that you vote contrary to justice by supporting the side they want to win. [2] You[3] should bear in mind that you would be extremely angry if the Thesmothetae were to stand up during your *dokimasia* and ask for a conviction. You would think it terrible if those conducting the trial and putting the issue to the vote should recommend the acquittal of some defendants and the conviction of others. [3] What custom could be more shameful in the city, what event more terrible, than for the Archon[4] in private cases involving heiresses to

---

[27] To end a speech with the reading of documents is unusual (there is no parallel in any of Lysias' surviving speeches), but it serves here to focus attention on the speaker's plea for the rigorous application of what he claims is the letter of the law.

[1] Gk. *astrateia.*

[2] Lit. "been worth much to the city."

[3] Addressed apparently to the generals, who are chairing the court. The Thesmothetae were the six junior Archons (see the Series Introduction), who presided over various public cases, evidently including the generals' own *dokimasia* (the judicial scrutiny faced by incoming public officials; cf. the Introduction to Lys. 16).

[4] The Archon presided over family and inheritance matters involving citizens (including disputed claims to an *epiklēros,* here loosely translated "heiress"); his colleague the Polemarch presided over similar cases involving metics. The Eleven were the officials in charge of prisons and executions, who presided over cases of *apagōgē* (summary arrest, as in Lys. 13).

dare to beg and beseech the jurors as to how they should vote, or for the Polemarch and the Eleven to make requests in the cases introduced by them—as is happening now? [4] You should have the same attitude towards your own situation, and bear in mind that for you to assist somebody on a personal basis in a case involving failure to undertake military service will be no different from any of these other officials making requests while themselves putting the issue to a vote. [5] Ask yourselves, gentlemen of the jury, whether the evidence is not sufficient to prove that none of the officials in the camp had supported Alcibiades. For if they are telling the truth, they should have summoned Pamphilus,[5] because by taking away Alcibiades' horse, he deprived the city of a cavalryman; they should have imposed a fine (*epibolē*) on the Phylarch, because by expelling Alcibiades from the tribal cavalry contingent,[6] he had rendered ineffective their own authority; and they ought to have ordered the Taxiarch[7] to rub out Alcibiades' name from the list of the hoplites. [6] In fact they did none of these things. Instead, in the camp they took no notice while he was insulted by everybody and while he served as cavalryman among the mounted archers (*hippotoxotai*);[8] but now, when you have to punish the offenders, they obligingly testify that he served in that rank under their orders. And yet it is a dreadful thing, gentlemen of the jury, that whereas the generals themselves, who are elected by the Assembly, would never dare lead us before they had passed their *dokimasia* in accordance with

---

[5] Evidently a subordinate commander, probably serving as Hipparch (cavalry commander). Pamphilus later became general in 389/8 (Xen., *Hellenica* 5.1.2).

[6] Lit. "from the tribe (*phulē*)." The Phylarch was the commander of the tribal cavalry contingent, just as the Taxiarch (below) commanded the tribe's hoplites. Evidently the Phylarch and the Taxiarch of Andocides' tribe had both agreed that he should serve as hoplite rather than in the cavalry.

[7] Regimental commander: see previous note.

[8] Archers, even mounted archers, are liable to allegations of cowardice since they generally fight at a distance, and the present passage may imply that they have lower prestige than the cavalry, though cf. Loomis, *Zeitschrift für Papyrologie und Epigraphik* 107 (1995): 230–236, at p. 233, who suggests that the passage should be translated "even though he was serving . . . ," which would imply the opposite (cf. the Introduction to Lys. Fr. 10 [*Theozotides*] at n. 9 and n. 10).

the laws, nevertheless Alcibiades dares to be enrolled by them contrary to the laws of the city. [7] In my view it is terrible, gentlemen of the jury, that although the generals cannot at whim enroll among the hoplites any cavalryman who has passed his *dokimasia,* nevertheless it is to be within their power that any hoplite they wish, who has not undergone *dokimasia,* may serve as a cavalryman. [8] You would not be justified in gratifying them, gentlemen of the jury, if they had this power and allowed nobody else to serve in the cavalry even though many wanted to. If, however, they admit they did not have the power to enroll him, then bear in mind that you have sworn to decide what is just, not to vote for whatever these men tell you. You should therefore pay more attention to yourselves and your oath than to any of those making requests. [9] Furthermore, gentlemen of the jury, if anyone thinks that the penalty is substantial and the law too severe, you need to remember that you have not come here to be lawgivers[9] but to vote according to the established laws, not to have pity on wrongdoers but rather to be angry with them and to assist the city as a whole. You are fully aware that by punishing a few people for what has happened, you will improve the discipline of many of those who will face danger in the future. [10] Just as the defendant took no notice of the city and looked only to his own safety, gentlemen of the jury, in the same way you must take no notice of the defendant and vote as is best for the city—particularly because you have sworn oaths, and are due to vote about Alcibiades, who will go away laughing at the city if he deceives you. He will not repay you with gratitude if he benefits secretly in your vote, for he is a man who does harm to those of his friends who have benefited him in public. [11] You must regard his pleas as less important, gentlemen of the jury, and vote for what is just. It has been proved that Alcibiades was enrolled among the hoplites; that he deserted his position; that he served in the cavalry without passing his *dokimasia,* even though the laws forbid this; and that as a private individual he has given himself authority over matters concerning which the laws explicitly state that neither general nor Hipparch nor anybody else is to have more power than the laws them-

[9] Contrast Lys. 14.4.

selves. [**12**] I am assisting Archestratides[10] because he is a friend of mine, and taking vengeance on Alcibiades because he is an enemy. I beg you to vote justly. You must vote with the same attitude as when you thought that you were about to face the ultimate danger against the enemy.

---

[10] Evidently the main prosecutor; cf. Lys. 14.3.

16. FOR MANTITHEUS

INTRODUCTION

The word *dokimasia* (pl. *dokimasiai,* Eng. "scrutiny") denotes the judicial examination of a person's right to hold an office or to receive a privilege. There were various types of *dokimasia* in Athenian law,[1] but Lysias 16 involves the *dokimasia* that had to be undergone by anybody who had been appointed, whether by election or by lot, to public office.[2] No fewer than four of the speeches and one of the papyrus fragments of Lysias belong definitely or probably to such *dokimasia* hearings: Mantitheus here, and Philon in Lysias 31, are prospective Councilors; Lysias 26 is an attack on Euandrus, who has been chosen as Archon; the anonymous speaker in Lysias 25, and Eryximachus in Lysias Fragment 9, have apparently been appointed to other offices.

We have no *dokimasia* speeches among the works of any other orator, and we hear of very few contested cases outside the period 403–380. What is at issue in Lysias' *dokimasia* speeches is consistently the

[1] We hear elsewhere in Lysias of the *dokimasia* of those who were disabled, which they had to pass before receiving a pension (such a case is the subject of Lys. 24), of prospective cavalry before service (which Alcibiades is charged with failing to undergo at Lys. 14.8, and cf. Lys. 16.13), and of young men before becoming adult citizens, such that "I passed my *dokimasia*" becomes a synonym for "I came of age" (frequent throughout the corpus, as at Lys. 10.31 and 21.1).

[2] Jurisdiction varied according to the prospective office (for the rules, see *Ath. Pol.* 45.3 and 55.2–5): the nine Archons received a unique double *dokimasia,* first before the Council (as in Lys. 26) and then before a court, the Council alone (i.e., the outgoing Council) heard the *dokimasia* of their prospective successors (as in Lys. 16 and Lys. 31), and all other officials were scrutinized simply by a lawcourt (as probably in Lys. 25 and Fr. 9 [*Eryximachus*]).

way in which the prospective official behaved under the oligarchy of 404/3, as in the present case, where Mantitheus has to defend himself against an accusation of having served in the cavalry under the Thirty. Such behavior was not illegal, and indeed the amnesty of 403/2 prohibited the "remembering of wrongs," which should have made it impossible for anybody to prosecute Mantitheus for it. On the other hand, if Mantitheus came before a judicial body on another charge or for other reasons, he became a standing target for any allegation. The particular prevalence of contested *dokimasiai* during the generation following the restoration of democracy may reflect a way of evading the amnesty, so as to gain revenge on some former supporters of the oligarchy. It was not that such people would necessarily fail their *dokimasiai,*[3] and indeed we do not know the result of this case, but clearly Mantitheus' opponents were taking their chances to make things unpleasant for him, in a way that might not have happened a generation earlier or later.

The name of the defendant Mantitheus is found not in the speech itself but in the manuscript title.[4] Mantitheus cannot be identified for certain: it has been suggested that he is related to the family of Mantias and Mantitheus in Demosthenes 39–40, but there are difficulties in constructing a family tree.[5] What can be inferred from the present speech is that he is a young man (not likely to be much more than the minimum age of thirty required for public office), that he has an excellent military record and sufficient wealth to serve in the cavalry, that he is politically ambitious, and that he wears his hair in a style that was characteristic of those young aristocrats who admired Sparta (cf. 16.18 with note). It is interesting that he feels he can afford to do

---

[3] We know the outcome of only one of Lysias' *dokimasia* cases: Euandrus won his *dokimasia* but only had the chance to do so because of the rejection of the previous candidate Leodamas (see the Introduction to Lys. 26).

[4] Only two titles in the manuscripts of Lysias contain apparently reliable information that could not simply have been inferred from the text. The other is Lys. 26, where the speaker's opponent Euandrus is not named in the extant portions of the speech (but may have been named in the opening, which is lost). Lys. 16, on the other hand, appears to be a complete text.

[5] For a full statement of the problems, see Davies 1971: no. 9667, at pp. 364–365.

this, even at a time when Athens and Sparta are at war. The speech cannot be precisely dated, but the background to Mantitheus' military career is the Corinthian War (395–387), and specifically the campaigns of 395 (16.13–14) and 394 (16.15–17). It is generally thought that the jibe at 16.15 is directed against Thrasybulus of Steiria, the leader of the democratic counterrevolutionaries in 403; if so, the tone suggests that Thrasybulus, who died in 389, was either still alive or at least a recent memory.

So far as the specific allegation of cavalry service under the Thirty is concerned, Mantitheus' rebuttal is inconclusive. He claims that he had returned to Athens only five days before Thrasybulus' march from Phyle to Piraeus, which led rapidly to the fall of the Thirty (16.4–5). He also objects that the documentary evidence for his alleged cavalry membership is weak, because the list with his name on it is unreliable, and preference should be given to the absence of his name from the list compiled when the Thirty's cavalry were forced to repay their equipment allowance (16.6–7). But we know that the Thirty ran short of money towards the end of their time, and it is conceivable that there would not have been enough to supply the allowance for somebody enlisting late. Moreover, Mantitheus is very coy about why he returned to Athens when he did, and at least one possibility is that his father had summoned him back to help man the barricades. Perhaps he is wise to claim that his candidature should stand or fall not on the specific allegations but on his general character (16.9).

The interpretation of the *dokimasia* and the amnesty put forward here is argued in more detail in Todd 1993: 285–289. On the Athenian cavalry, see I. G. Spence, *The Cavalry of Classical Greece: A Social and Military History with Particular Reference to Athens* (Oxford, 1993). For the details of the speech, see Usher's commentary in Edwards and Usher 1985.

16. AT THE COUNCIL-MEETING: DEFENSE SPEECH FOR MANTITHEUS AT HIS *DOKIMASIA* (SCRUTINY)

[1] If I were not aware, members of the Council, that my accusers wish to hurt me in every possible way, I would be very grateful to them for this accusation. The people who force those who are unjustly accused to undergo an investigation of their life's record are in my view

responsible for great benefits. [2] I am so utterly confident in myself that I expect even someone badly disposed towards me to change his mind when he hears me speak about what happened and to think much better of me in the future. [3] I do not claim any special merit, members of the Council, if I demonstrate to you merely that I am loyal to the existing constitution and have been compelled to share in the same dangers as you. But if it is clear that I have lived an orderly life in other respects also, contrary to the opinions and the statements of my enemies, I ask you to approve me at my *dokimasia* and to think worse of my opponents. I shall demonstrate first that I did not serve in the cavalry, and was not even present in Athens, under the Thirty, nor did I have a share in the constitution that existed at that time.

[4] Before the disaster on the Hellespont,[1] our father sent us to live at the court of Satyrus in the Pontus.[2] We were not in Athens either when the walls were being destroyed or when the constitution was being changed. We came back only five days before the men from Phyle returned from exile to Piraeus.[3] [5] It was hardly likely that after arriving at such a critical time, we should have wanted to share in other people's dangers, or that the Thirty would have wanted to grant a share in the activity of government to those who were living abroad and not committing any crimes. They preferred to remove the citizen rights even of those who had joined them in overthrowing the democracy. [6] Moreover, it is naive to search in the *sanidion*[4] for those who served in the cavalry. Many of those who admit to being members of the cavalry are not present on it, and some of those who were abroad are listed. This is a particularly important argument. When you returned from

---

[1] Euphemism (as often in Lysias) for the Athenian defeat at Aegospotami in 405 BC.

[2] Satyrus was a Thracian king in the area of the modern Crimea, a long-term supporter of Athens and a major supplier of grain. Affairs at his court form the backdrop to Isoc. 17.

[3] I.e., the democratic counterrevolutionaries. The argument here is discussed in the Introduction.

[4] A *sanis* or (as here) *sanidion* was a wooden tablet used for keeping public records more temporary than those inscribed on stone. The relative reliability of the documents mentioned here is discussed in the Introduction.

exile, you voted that the Phylarchs[5] should provide a list of those who had served in the cavalry, so that you could recover the equipment allowance (*katastasis*) from them. [7] Now nobody would be able to demonstrate that my name was handed over by the Phylarchs, or that it was passed on to the Revenue Commissioners (*sundikoi*), or that I had to repay the allowance. And yet it is easy for everybody to determine this, because the Phylarchs themselves had to pay a fine if they did not reveal the names of those who had had the allowance. It would be far more just for you to trust these documents than the other ones: anybody who wishes can easily have his name erased from the *sanides,* whereas in their lists the Phylarchs had to declare the names of those who have served in the cavalry. [8] What is more, members of the Council, if I had served in the cavalry, I would not deny it, as if I had done something terrible. Instead, after showing that no citizen had suffered harm at my hands, I would claim the right to pass my *dokimasia.* I see that you take the same attitude as well, and that many of those who served in the cavalry then are now members of the Council, and many others have been elected generals and Hipparchs.[6] So do not think I am making this defense for any other reason than because they dared to fabricate patent lies against me. Please come forward for me and testify.

[TESTIMONY]

[9] Concerning the accusation itself, I cannot think of anything more that needs saying. However, members of the Council, it seems to me that although in other trials it is appropriate to defend oneself simply on the charges, in *dokimasiai* it is fair to give an account of one's whole life. I ask you, therefore, to listen to me with goodwill, and I shall make my defense as briefly as I can.

[10] First of all, because of the disasters that happened to my father and the city,[7] I did not inherit much property. Nevertheless, I gave away two sisters in marriage, each with a dowry of thirty minas. I

---

[5] Commanders of the ten tribal cavalry contingents (cf. 12.44n). They were under the authority of the Hipparchs (16.8n).

[6] The two Hipparchs (cavalry commanders) were in overall charge of the cavalry (cf. 16.6n).

[7] Yet another euphemism for Aegospotami; cf. 16.4.

divided the estate with my brother in such a way that he admits that he received more than I have, and in my dealings with everybody else, I have lived my life in such a way that I have never been involved in any legal action (*enklēma*) against even a single individual. [11] That is how I have lived my private life. As far as public life is concerned, I believe the strongest proof of my good conduct is this: you will see that those of the young men who spend their time playing dice, drinking, and participating in that sort of unruliness are all hostile to me, and these in particular are the ones fabricating false rumors about me. It is clear that they would not take that attitude towards me if we had the same interests. [12] What is more, members of the Council, nobody could show that I have been involved in any shameful private or public litigation,[8] and yet you see others frequently involved in such lawsuits. Consider also my conduct towards the city, in facing military campaigns and dangers from the enemy. [13] In the first place, when you made the alliance with the Boeotians, and there was a need to send help to Haliartus, I was called up by Orthobulus for cavalry service.[9] I saw that everybody believed the cavalry were bound to be safe but thought the hoplites were bound to face danger. Other people were joining the cavalry illegally, without having passed the *dokimasia*,[10] but I told Orthobulus to erase my name from the list. I thought it shameful to take care of my own safety on campaign, when the majority were going to face danger. Please come forward, Orthobulus.

[TESTIMONY]

[14] Now when the members of my deme assembled together before setting out, I knew that some of them were honorable and enthusiastic citizens but lacked supplies, so I suggested that those who were well off should provide what was necessary for those who were

---

[8] Lit. "any shameful *dikē* (private case), or *graphē* (public prosecution), or *eisangelia* (impeachment)."

[9] The skirmish at Haliartus in 395 was a minor one, though the former Spartan admiral Lysander was killed, and King Pausanias exiled for failing to rescue him (Xen., *Hellenica* 3.5). Orthobulus is probably to be identified with the Orthobulus who was sent on a delegation to Byzantium in 378/7.

[10] Mantitheus' attitude is ostentatiously the opposite of that ascribed to Alcibiades in Lys. 14–15.

in need. Not only did I recommend this to other people, but I myself gave thirty drachmas each to two men as well. Not that I did this as somebody who was rich, but so that it would be an example for the others. Please come forward.

[WITNESSES]

[15] After this, members of the Council, came the expedition to Corinth.[11] Everybody knew in advance that this would certainly be dangerous. Other people were drawing back, but I arranged to be put in the front rank for fighting the enemy. Our tribe (*phulē*) suffered particularly heavy losses, and very many died there. But I retreated later than the pretentious man from Steiria[12] who had been reproaching everybody with cowardice. [16] Not many days after this, some strong positions at Corinth had been occupied, with the effect that the enemy could not pass. Agesilaus had pushed on into Boeotia, and the commanders (*archontes*) voted to detach some companies to provide assistance.[13] Everybody was afraid—which was reasonable, members of the Council, because it was an alarming prospect to face another danger when they had narrowly escaped a short time before. However, I went to see the Taxiarch and told him to send our company without casting lots.[14] [17] If any of you are angry at those who claim the right to manage the affairs of the city but who run away from its dangers, you could not justly hold that opinion about me. I not only fulfilled my duties enthusiastically, but also had the courage to face danger. I did this not because I treated lightly the prospect of

---

[11] The Nemea campaign of 394 (Xen., *Hellenica* 4.2), at which the Athenian losses were far heavier than at Haliartus.

[12] The most famous member of the Athenian deme Steiria is Thrasybulus, the leader of the democratic counterrevolutionaries of 403, and it is generally thought that he is being referred to here.

[13] They were trying to prevent the Spartan king Agesilaus from bringing back his army overland from his campaigns in Asia Minor. This attempt led to the battle of Coronea in 394 (Xen., *Hellenica* 4.3).

[14] The Taxiarch (regimental commander) was the officer in charge of the tribal contingent of hoplites (heavy-armed infantry). We may wonder how the other members of the company (*taxis*) felt about Mantitheus' action, and whether any of them were present to hear his speech.

facing the Spartans, but so that if ever I were unjustly forced into litigation, I would be better received by you because of this and would receive full justice. Please come forward as witnesses of these facts.

[WITNESSES]

[18] I have never been found wanting in any of the other campaigns and garrisons. Instead, I have always managed to begin the expeditions in the front rank and retreat with the rearguard. You ought to examine those who play an ambitious but responsible role in the city on these criteria, and not dislike a person simply because he wears his hair long.[15] Such habits harm neither individuals nor the city as a community, but you all benefit from those who are willing to face danger against the enemy. [19] It is not right, members of the Council, to like or dislike anybody on the basis of his appearance, but you should examine his actions instead. Many who talk little and dress in an orderly fashion have been responsible for great harm, whereas others who take no interest in such things have brought you many benefits.

[20] I have already noticed, members of the Council, that some people are also irritated with me because I sought to speak in the Assembly while I was relatively young. But in the first place, I was forced to deliver an Assembly speech for the sake of my own interests, though I also suspect that I was inclined to be more ambitious than was necessary. I did this partly because I realized that my ancestors never ceased from engaging in public affairs, [21] and also because at the same time I realized that you yourselves (the truth needs to be told) thought that only people like this had any value. Who, therefore, on seeing that you take this attitude, would not be inspired to work and speak on behalf of the city? How could you be annoyed with such people? After all, it is you yourselves, not anybody else, who are the judges in their case.

---

[15] This translation is the result of a textual emendation (*komai* "wears his hair long" for *tolma* "is daring"), which is accepted by the overwhelming majority of editors. The significance of long hair is discussed in the Introduction.

17. ON THE PROPERTY OF ERATON

INTRODUCTION

This is the first of a group of three speeches dealing with the confiscation of property. In this case the property belongs to three brothers, Erasiphon, Eraton, and Erasistratus, the sons of another Eraton, who is now dead (17.3). For convenience in this translation, the two Eratons are distinguished as Eraton I (the father) and Eraton II (the son), though no distinction is drawn in the Greek text.[1] The background to the speech is that property is being confiscated on the grounds that it belongs to the Treasury. The reason for the confiscation is not stated: simply that a number of people have brought *apographai,* or written claims that items belonging to the family should be confiscated (17.4). The date cannot be precisely determined, but it is probably around the mid-390s BC.[2] It is clear that the confiscation affects the property of all three brothers (17.4), though if the manuscript is correct at a crucial point, it appears that the property being confiscated is that of Erasiphon (17.6 with note). It is difficult to see why such a confiscation would affect the property of his brothers. A possible explanation (if not a wholly satisfactory one) is that the confiscation has happened because of an offense that Erasiphon has committed, but that the brothers are affected because the estate had never been formally divided between them.

---

[1] These are the only people named in the speech, and none of them is otherwise known.

[2] Three years have passed (17.5, 17.8) since an adjudication in the Archonship of Xenaenetus in 401/0 (17.3), but the opponents have allegedly been engaged in various delaying tactics (17.5), so the case may be a year or two later than 397.

The speaker (whose name is unknown to us) has challenged the Treasury's right to part of the confiscated property,[3] on the grounds that he has himself a prior legal claim arising from a verdict his father had previously obtained against Erasistratus (17.3), when the speaker's father had sued to recover a substantial sum of money that Eraton (I) had allegedly borrowed from the speaker's grandfather (17.2). The speaker implies that he is being extremely generous by claiming only the two pieces of property to which he has already staked a claim in the litigation against Erasistratus (17.6). His own calculations represent these two pieces of property together as worth only a quarter of the family's total assessed wealth, and a far smaller proportion of the original alleged debt (cf. 17.7n). He states that he is giving up two-thirds of what he would be entitled to claim (17.6), presumably so as to suggest that whereas previous litigation has given him an overwhelming right to Erasistratus' real or imagined share of the property, he is generously waiving his claim to that of the other two brothers.

This may be a sensible attempt not to antagonize the jury, whose interests lie in maximizing the public revenue. It is, however, striking that nothing is said about the reason for the confiscation (though of course the jury may know this already), and no attempt is made to attack the brothers as criminals who have defrauded the city just as they have defrauded the speaker. Nor is anything said about the reason why the money had originally been borrowed. There is always the possibility that the debt either never existed or has been artificially inflated, and that the speaker and the brothers are colluding to invent a debt and to share the proceeds.[4]

Two well-preserved inscriptions record the results of other cases dealing with prior claims to confiscated property: G. V. Lalonde, M. K. Langdon, and M. B. Walbank, *The Athenian Agora,* XIX, *Inscriptions: Horoi, Poletai Records, Leases of Public Lands* (Princeton, 1993), offers a

---

[3] The procedure he is using is not stated, but it is presumably an *enepiskēpsis* or *enepiskēmma* (presentation of prior claim), which would lead to a *diadikasia* or *diadikasma* (adjudication of disputed property; cf. 17.1 and 17.10) between the speaker and the Treasury. The case is heard by a dikastic court presided over by the Revenue Commissioners (*sundikoi*).

[4] For two other cases of apparent collusion in the confiscation of property, see R. G. Osborne, "Law in Action," *Journal of Hellenic Studies* 105 (1985): 40–58, at p. 45.

brief discussion at pp. 58–60, and reedits the texts as nos. P.5 and P.12 (but without translation, for which see respectively *Hesperia* 10 [1941]: 17–18, and *Hesperia* 5 [1936]: 406–407).

17. ON THE PROPERTY OF ERATON, AGAINST THE TREASURY [1]

[1] Because of my desire to make a name for myself, gentlemen of the jury, some of you may think I could also speak better than other people. In fact I am so far from being competent to speak about things that do not concern me that I fear I may be incapable of saying what is necessary even about matters I must talk about. Nevertheless, if I give you a full account of our dealings with Eraton and his children, I think you will easily discover what attitude you should take towards this adjudication (*diadikasia*). Please listen to the story from the beginning.

[2] Eraton (I) the father of Erasiphon borrowed two talents from my grandfather. To show that he received the money, and that this was the amount that he asked to borrow, I will produce for you witnesses in whose presence it was handed over. As to how he used it and how much he benefited from it, those who know more than I do, and who have been close to his affairs, will tell you the story and testify. Please call witnesses for me.

[WITNESSES]

[3] While Eraton was alive, we continued to receive the interest payments and the other amounts as agreed. But after he died, leaving three sons—Erasiphon and Eraton (II) and Erasistratus—these men stopped fulfilling any of their legal obligations towards us. During the war,[2] because no private cases (*dikai*) took place, we were not able to recover from them what they owed; but when peace was made, as soon as the private cases of citizens[3] were being tried, my father initiated a

[1] The manuscript title "Of Public Injustices" is obviously corrupt, and this is a plausible restoration.

[2] By "the war," he certainly means the Peloponnesian War (which ended in 404), though he may also have in mind the civil war of 404/3.

[3] "Private cases of citizens" is a plausible but not conclusive interpretation of the obscure phrase *astikai dikai*.

case for the whole debt against Erasistratus, who was the only brother residing here, and obtained a verdict against him in the Archonship of Xenaenetus (401/0).[4] I shall produce witnesses for you about this as well. Please call witnesses for me.

[WITNESSES]

[4] It is easy to see from this that the property of Eraton (I) is rightly ours. It is also easy to recognize from the *apographai* (writs of confiscation) themselves that the entire property is being confiscated,[5] because three and four people have listed each item for confiscation. And yet it is clear to everybody that if they could have confiscated any other item of Eraton's (I) property, those who were listing the whole of Eraton's property—including that which I have long possessed—would not have omitted it. So it seems obvious to me that we will not be able to recover our money from anywhere else, if you confiscate this property. [5] You need to hear in detail how I have conducted the dispute with you and with private individuals. As long as Erasiphon's relatives were disputing with me about this money, I claimed that the whole estate was mine, because Erasistratus had been defeated in a lawsuit brought by my father for the entire debt. I have been renting out the property at Sphettus for three years already, and I was engaged in litigation with those in possession over the property at Cicynna and the house there.[6] Last year they had my case struck out by claiming to be import traders; the Nautodikae have not yet decided the case, even

---

[4] It has been inferred from this passage that the suspension of private cases lasted until 401/0 (thus D. M. MacDowell in *Revue Internationale des Droits de l'Antiquité* 18 [1971]: 267–273, who uses this as the basis for an important reconstruction of the dates of other speeches and legal innovations during the period 403–400), but given the continual hints throughout this speech about the brothers' delaying tactics, I am not sure that the inference is safe.

[5] I.e., the property of the family rather than simply that of one brother.

[6] Sphettus and Cicynna were neighboring Athenian demes about eight miles in a direct line southeast of the city but separated from it by Mount Hymettus. The speaker has evidently taken possession of the estate at Sphettus, but possession of the one at Cicynna is still contested. Presumably these are the estates valued at one thousand drachmas and at five minas (five hundred drachmas) respectively in 17.7.

though I brought it in the month of Gamelion.[7] [6] Because you have decided to confiscate the property of Erasiphon,[8] however, I am surrendering two-thirds of my rights to the city, and am claiming only that the property of Erasistratus should be adjudicated to me, since you have already decided on a previous occasion that it belongs to us. I have therefore marked out for myself one-third of their property: I have not examined the precise details but have left far more than two-thirds to the Treasury. [7] This is easy to recognize from the assessment that has been calculated, for they[9] have assessed the entire estate at more than one talent, but I am claiming one property worth five minas and the other worth one thousand drachmas.[10] If they are worth more than this, the city will receive the surplus after they are auctioned. [8] To assure you that these things are true, I shall produce the following witnesses: first, those who have rented the estate at Sphettus from me; secondly, the neighbors of the estate at Cicynna, who know that we have been involved in litigation for three years now; and finally, last year's officials, before whom the cases were initiated, and the current Nautodikae. [9] The various *apographai* will also be read out for you. From them you will recognize clearly that our claim that the money belongs to us is not a recent one, and that our current dispute with the Treasury is not about more money than our previous dispute with private individuals. Please call witnesses for me.

---

[7] The Nautodikae (lit. "judges of seafarers") were a little-known board of public officials. Gamelion was the seventh Athenian month, which usually fell in December/January.

[8] Some editors emend this to read Eraton (I), on the grounds that it is easier to see why the confiscation of the father's property would affect the three sons than it is to see why the confiscation of one brother's property would affect the rest (cf. the Introduction). But it is difficult to see why the scribe copying the manuscript would have made this mistake.

[9] Presumably the people who have brought the *apographai* against the family's various properties.

[10] Lit. "I am involved in litigation for one . . . , I have calculated the other. . . ." On his figures, the speaker is claiming 1,500 drachmas out of a total property of 6,000, leaving only slightly more than two-thirds for the Treasury (cf. the Introduction). He claims elsewhere that the size of the original debt was 12,000 drachmas or two talents (17.2).

[WITNESSES]

[10] It has been demonstrated, gentlemen of the jury, that I am not arguing unjustly that this adjudication (*diadikasma*) should be decided in my favor, but that I am claiming that the property should be returned to me only after surrendering to the city much of what is mine. It is in my view reasonable to lay this request before you and before the Revenue Commissioners (*sundikoi*) in your presence.

18. ON THE PROPERTY OF NICIAS' BROTHER

INTRODUCTION

Like Lysias 17 and 19, this speech deals with the confiscation of property, but the family whose affairs are under discussion had been one of the best known in Athens. At its head was Nicias, an extremely rich man who had been a leading politician and (until his defeat and death when leading the disastrous Sicilian Expedition of 415–413, during the Peloponnesian War) a more than usually successful military commander.[1] The achievements of Nicias himself are summarized eulogistically at 18.2–3, but rather more is said about his two brothers, who were evidently much younger and are less well attested elsewhere. One of these was Eucrates, who had been elected general to fill one of the vacancies left by the crushing defeat at Aegospotami in 405/4, and whose opposition to the rise of the Thirty in 404/3 had led to his death (a point the speaker predictably emphasizes at 18.4–5). The other brother was Diognetus, whose earlier career is rather glossed over. The speaker admits at 18.9 that Diognetus was in exile before 404, but he fails to clarify whether this was the result of a judicial sentence, or perhaps of complicity with the previous oligarchy in 411. Diognetus evidently remained in Athens under the Thirty, but the speaker is able to emphasize his role in winning over the support of the Spartan king Pausanias for the democratic restoration (18.10–12).

[1] Thucydides' account of the Sicilian expedition fills books 6–7 and concludes with a possibly ironic obituary of Nicias himself (Thuc. 7.86.5). The bulk of Nicias' wealth, according to Plutarch (*Nicias* 4.2) had come from the ownership of silver mines. For the family, see Davies 1971: no. 10808, pp. 403–407.

Lysias 18 is spoken by one of the two sons of Eucrates, who appear from the anecdote in 18.10 both to have been children in 403.[2] The date of the speech cannot be precisely determined, but the speaker must necessarily have come of age, and most scholars infer from 18.15 that Sparta and Athens are still at peace, which suggests a date before rather than after the Corinthian War (395–387 BC). It is clear that the speaker is defending himself against an attempt to confiscate his family's property. Because the speech is incomplete,[3] however, the grounds for such a proposed confiscation are less clear, although it seems that what is being confiscated is nominally the property of his father Eucrates (hence the manuscript title), which may suggest that the complaint is about Eucrates' financial activities while in office.[4] Even less clear is the procedure, because the meaning of the crucial passage (18.13–14) is obscure, and the text may well be corrupt. The opponent is evidently called Poliochus, and there has been a previous but unsuccessful attempt to confiscate the property, but different proposed texts leave it uncertain whether Poliochus was or was not responsible for the previous attempt, or indeed whether the previous one-thousand drachma fine was the punishment for a failed prosecution or the result of a successful counterprosecution.

The anecdote about the Spartan king Pausanias (18.10–12, mentioned above) is interesting, because it hints at one of the reasons for his astonishing reversal of Spartan policy towards Athens in 403.

---

[2] That Eucrates was the speaker's father is clear from 18.4, and that the speaker had one brother is implied at 18.21. Other members of the family mentioned in the speech are Nicias' son Niceratus, who was killed under the Thirty, leaving his own infant son (evidently younger than the speaker and his brother; cf. 18.10), and the speaker's cousin Diomnestus, the son of Diognetus (18.21). For the relationships, see Davies 1971: 404–406.

[3] We have no way of telling whether a preceding statement of the defense case has been lost or whether the concluding appeal for the jury's sympathy based on the speaker's family history (which is all that survives) was all that was commissioned from the orator.

[4] This hypothesis would raise some awkward conflicts between the prosecution and the amnesty of 403/2, but these would apply to any prosecution aimed at Eucrates, who had died before the date of the amnesty and should therefore be protected by it, since the wording of the amnesty implies that it covered any event before 403/2, not simply events under the Thirty.

When the Thirty appealed to Sparta for military assistance against Thrasybulus' attempted counterrevolution, the Spartan admiral Lysander had himself appointed governor of Athens with the evident aim of restoring the Thirty in power. After Lysander left for Athens, however, Pausanias arranged for the army of the Peloponnesian League to be sent out under his command, superseded Lysander's authority, and permitted the democratic restoration subject to a general amnesty. Narrative sources see Pausanias' motives in terms of jealousy (e.g., Xen., *Hellenica* 2.4.29) and imply that he came to Athens with the intention of supporting the democrats (*Hellenica* 2.4.35). Jealousy, or in other words fear of Lysander's power, is a plausible motive for Pausanias' desire to supersede Lysander, but the speaker's anecdote here implies that what swayed him against the Thirty may have been a realization that their victims had been not simply lower-class rabble-rousers, but had included Eucrates, Niceratus, and others like them: these were, after all, members of the family of Nicias, who had negotiated the Peace of 422/1 between Athens and Sparta and will therefore have established hereditary ties of hospitality with leading Spartans (cf. 18.10n).

For Spartan policy towards Athens in 403/2, see C. D. Hamilton, *Sparta's Bitter Victories: Politics and Diplomacy in the Corinthian War* (Ithaca, 1979), and P. A. Cartledge, *Agesilaos and the Crisis of Sparta* (London, 1987). Hereditary ties of hospitality are the subject of G. Herman, *Ritualised Friendship and the Greek City* (Cambridge, 1987).

18. CONCERNING THE CONFISCATION OF NICIAS' BROTHER'S PROPERTY: PERORATION (*EPILOGOS*)

[1] Bear in mind, therefore,[1] gentlemen of the jury, what sort of citizens we ourselves are, and also our ancestors. We claim the right to be pitied by you and to receive justice for the wrongs we have suffered. We are on trial not simply for our property but also for our *politeia* (civic status),[2] to discover if we will have a place in the city under the democracy. First of all, therefore, you should recall to mind our uncle

[1] On the incompleteness of the speech, see the Introduction.

[2] The word *politeia* is important in this speech and has a wide range of meanings (civic status, constitution, the process of government), some of which I have attempted to indicate by means of glosses as appropriate.

Nicias. [2] In everything he did on behalf of your democracy using his own judgment, it will be clear that in each case he was responsible for many benefits to the city and did a lot of damage to the enemy. In everything he was compelled to do not willingly but involuntarily, he himself suffered a significant part of the damage. But those who persuaded you should justifiably shoulder the blame for the disaster, [3] because in your good fortune and your enemies' misfortunes, he demonstrated his goodwill towards you and his own merits. It would be a lengthy task to describe individually the many cities he captured as your general and the many glorious trophies he set up over the enemy.

[4] Eucrates, who was his brother and my father, demonstrated clearly his loyalty towards your democracy when the final sea battle had already been fought.[3] After your defeat in the sea battle, he was elected your general, and although he was invited to share in the oligarchy by those who were plotting against the democracy, [5] he rejected their request. He was caught in the kind of crisis in which most men shift their ground in the light of circumstances and yield to the pressure of fortune. The democracy was in a weak condition, he was not being driven out of the *politeia* (government),[4] and he did not feel any personal enmity towards those who were coming to power. Indeed, it would have been possible for him to have become one of the Thirty and to have been as powerful as any of them. Instead, he preferred to die while working for your safety rather than see the walls being destroyed, the ships handed over to the enemy, and your democracy enslaved.

[6] Not long afterwards Niceratus, my cousin and the son of Nicias, who supported your democracy, was arrested and executed by the Thirty. In birth, wealth, and age, he appeared worthy to share in the *politeia* (government);[5] however, his and his ancestors' relationship towards your democracy was felt to be such that he could never desire

---

[3] As usual in the corpus of Lysias, the decisive Athenian defeat at Aegospotami in 405 is not mentioned by name.

[4] I.e., the process or activity of government (similarly at 18.6), or possibly here "public life." Greek has no concept of "the Government" in the sense of a group of people holding official posts.

[5] See previous note.

a different type of *politeia* (constitution). [7] The oligarchs were aware that the whole family were respected by the city, for they had faced danger on your behalf in many places, had contributed to many war taxes (*eisphorai*) and performed liturgies[6] excellently, and had never shirked any of the other tasks that the city had laid on them but had eagerly fulfilled such duties. [8] Who would be less fortunate than ourselves, if under the oligarchy we were to be killed for favoring the democracy, and under the democracy we were to be deprived of our property on the pretext that we were hostile towards it?

[9] As for Diognetus, gentlemen of the jury, he went into exile because he was slandered by the sykophants,[7] but was one of very few of the exiles who did not fight against the city and did not go to Decelea.[8] He has not been responsible for any harm to your democracy, either while in exile or on his return. Instead, his behavior was so honorable that he was more angry with those who had committed offenses against you than with those who had been responsible for his return from exile. [10] He held no public office under the oligarchy. Instead, as soon as Pausanias and his Spartans arrived at the Academy,[9] he took us, who were children, and the son of Niceratus. He placed Niceratus' son on the lap of Pausanias and set us by his side. Then he described to him and to the others present all that we had suffered and the sorts of misfortune that had befallen us. He called on Pausanias to assist us and to punish those who had wronged us, because of the friendship and the *xenia*[10] that existed between Pausanias and our-

---

[6] A form of compulsory public sponsorship imposed on rich Athenians (cf. the Introduction to Lys. 21).

[7] Malicious prosecutors. The term is used particularly by those who claim to be the rich and inoffensive victims of rabble-rousing democratic politicians.

[8] I.e., to join the Spartans during the period when Decelea was a Spartan garrison (413–404). The circumstances of Diognetus' exile are discussed in the Introduction.

[9] In 404/3; cf. the Introduction. The Academy was the grove of the hero Academus, on the outskirts of the town. It later became the site where Plato established his famous school (from which derive the word's educational connotations).

[10] *Xenia* was the term used to denote the hereditary ties of hospitality that linked together elite families from different cities. These ties were reinforced by exchange of guest-gifts (themselves called *xeniai,* which is the plural of *xenia*).

selves. [11] It was from that moment that Pausanias began to favor the democracy. He used our sufferings as an example to the rest of the Spartans of the Thirty's criminal nature. It became clear to all the Peloponnesians who had accompanied him that the Thirty had been killing not the worst criminals among the citizens, but those who most deserved to be honored because of their birth, their wealth, and their general merits. [12] Such was the pity felt for us, and the terrible things everybody could see we had suffered, that Pausanias refused to receive the guest-gifts (*xeniai*) of the Thirty but accepted them from us. It would be extraordinary, gentlemen of the jury, if we were pitied as children by the enemy, who had come to assist the oligarchy, but now that we have become adults, you were to deprive us of our property, though our fathers died on behalf of the democracy.

[13] I am fully aware, gentlemen of the jury, that Poliochus would place a very great value on getting a favorable result in this trial. He believes that for him this would be an excellent demonstration both to citizens and to foreigners that he has so much power at Athens that he can make you contradict yourselves in the way that you vote on matters about which you have sworn the dikastic oath. [14] Everybody knows that previously you punished him with a one-thousand drachma fine when he wanted to make our land into public property.[11] Now he has won by ordering you to confiscate it. Concerning both these matters, Athenians have contradicted themselves in the way they voted, even though on both occasions the same person was defending himself on a charge of making an illegal proposal.[12] [15] Is it not

---

[11] The text is uncertain at a crucial point: the version adopted here makes the speaker's opponent Poliochus the person who proposed the confiscation, but several editors prefer "you punished the person who wanted" (implying that it was somebody other than Poliochus).

[12] If the text is sound, this may explain the thousand-drachma fine as resulting from the prosecution and conviction of Poliochus (or whoever; cf. previous note) at a *graphē paranomōn* on a charge of making an illegal proposal to confiscate. Another possible explanation of the fine, however, is that such fines were imposed on prosecutors who failed to obtain one-fifth of the vote in certain cases. Yet another possibility is that the text should read "on both occasions the same person (i.e., the speaker himself) was illegally prosecuted," making this a protest against double jeopardy. See further the Introduction.

shameful, if you are going to strengthen the agreements you made with the Spartans but are going to destroy so readily those you voted to make with yourselves?[13]—if you are going to make binding the agreements with the Spartans but are going to invalidate the ones with yourselves? You are angry if any other Greeks place a higher value on the Spartans than on you: are you yourselves going to be seen as more faithful to the Spartans than to yourselves? [16] It is right to be particularly angry that those people who control the city's affairs are already behaving in such a way that the orators do not propose what would be best for the city, but instead, you are voting for proposals from which they themselves will benefit. [17] If it helped your democracy for some people to possess their own property, but for the property of others to be unjustly confiscated, it would be reasonable for you to ignore what we are saying. But in fact everybody would agree that consensus (*homonoia*) is the greatest good for the city, whereas civil strife (*stasis*) is responsible for all evils, and that mutual disagreements arise particularly when one group desires what belongs to other people, and the other group is ejected from its property. [18] You yourselves recently acknowledged this when you returned from exile, and you were well advised. You still remembered the earlier disasters, and you prayed to the gods to restore the city to consensus rather than to leave it in a condition of civil strife, with people turning to vengeance over what had happened, and with the orators rapidly becoming rich. [19] It would be more forgivable to bear grudges when you had recently returned from exile and your anger was still fresh, rather than to turn to vengeance so long afterwards for what had happened. You have been persuaded to seek vengeance by the sort of people who, after remaining in the town, think that they are giving you a guarantee of their goodwill not by showing themselves to be good citizens but by making others into bad ones.[14] They are now enjoying the prosperity of the city but did not in the past share in your perils.

[20] If you saw, gentlemen of the jury, that the properties confis-

---

[13] Evidently a rather obscure appeal to the protection of the amnesty of 403/2.

[14] Some editors would change the text to read "by harming other people." The expression "remaining in the town (*astu*)" refers to those who had supported the oligarchs in 404/3.

cated by my opponents were being preserved for the city, you would forgive them. As it is, you know that part of the confiscated property is being made to disappear by my opponents, while the rest, which is worth much, is being sold for little. If you follow my advice, however, you will derive no less profit from it than we who possess it. [21] At the moment Diomnestus, I, and my brother, three of us from a single household, are serving as trierarchs,[15] and we are contributing to war taxes (*eisphorai*) for you from this estate whenever the city is short of money. Spare us, therefore, because we have this attitude and because our ancestors were the sort of people we have described. [22] There would be nothing to prevent us from being the most wretched of men, gentlemen of the jury, if after being left as orphans under the Thirty, we were deprived of our property under the democracy—we, who while still children were allowed by fortune to go to the tent of Pausanias and help the democracy. To what judges should we have wished to flee for protection in such circumstances? [23] Surely to judges who lived under the type of *politeia* (constitution) for which my father and my relatives gave their lives. So now we beg this token of gratitude from you in return for everything. Do not look on while we become destitute and are stripped of the necessities of life, and do not destroy the prosperity that belonged to our ancestors, but instead, create for those who wish to benefit the city an example of the rewards they will receive from you when they are in danger.

[24] I do not have anybody, gentlemen of the jury, that I can bring forward to plead on my behalf. Some of my relatives have died in war, after showing themselves to be honorable men and making the city great. Others have died on behalf of the democracy and your freedom, by drinking hemlock under the Thirty. [25] As a result, the merits of our kinsmen and the misfortunes of the city are the cause of our iso-

[15] The trierarchy was a form of liturgy (compulsory public sponsorship) and involved paying for the upkeep of a warship for a year. If indeed two brothers and a cousin are simultaneously undertaking independent trierarchies, and if this speech belongs before 395 (cf. the Introduction), then this passage would imply that although the Athenians were still formally subject allies of Sparta, nevertheless they were already asserting a degree of independence by manning a much larger fleet than the twelve permitted following the surrender to Sparta in 404 (Xen., *Hellenica* 2.2.20).

lation. It is right that you should remember them and should enthusiastically assist us, by taking the view that those who shared a part of your sufferings during the oligarchy deserve to receive benefits from you under the democracy. [26] I ask the Revenue Commissioners (*sundikoi*) also to support us, and to remember the time when you were expelled from your fatherland and lost your property. You regarded those who were dying on your behalf as the best of men, and you prayed to the gods to be able to give a token of gratitude to their children. [27] We are sons and relatives of those who ran the first risks on behalf of freedom. We ask you now for that token of gratitude. We call on you not to destroy us unjustly but rather to assist those who shared in the same misfortunes. I beg and entreat and implore you, and I think it is right that I should receive this help from you. We are facing danger not about any small matter but about our entire property.

19. ON THE PROPERTY OF ARISTOPHANES

INTRODUCTION

Aristophanes, whose property forms the subject of this speech, is not the comic poet but a minor politician active in the 390s BC. Together with his father Nicophemus, he had benefited from the patronage of Conon, who had been one of the few Athenian generals to be moderately successful in the final years of the Peloponnesian War. Conon had escaped from the final Athenian defeat at Aegospotami in 405/4, but did not return to Athens, except briefly in 393–392. Instead, he operated as a freelance naval commander first for the Great King of Persia (for whom he won a decisive victory over the Spartan fleet at the battle of Cnidus in 394, early in the Corinthian War) and later for Euagoras of Salamis in Cyprus, who nominally governed the island on behalf of the Persians but was effectively independent and finally in open revolt. At some time around 390,[1] Aristophanes and Nicophemus fell out of favor and were executed.[2] The reasons for this are unknown but are likely to relate to the failure of some diplomatic or military initiative with which they were associated.[3]

[1] In 19.28–29, Aristophanes' death is placed "four to five years" after Cnidus, which in context is likely to be a conservative figure, as the speaker is trying to minimize the time period for his expenditures.

[2] We do not know where this happened and whether it was carried out by Athens or by Euagoras, though it would be easier to understand the details in, e.g., 19.7, if the execution took place in Cyprus.

[3] Conon by this date had probably already died a natural death in Cyprus (19.39–41), but it is notable that there seems to have been no threat to his son Timotheus (cf. 19.34, 19.38), so clearly not all Conon's policies were being repudiated.

Execution was followed by the confiscation of their property at Athens. This seems to have been proposed by somebody called Aeschines and to have been challenged unsuccessfully by *graphē paranomōn* (public prosecution for proposing an illegal decree), if we can trust the title of a lost *Prosecution Speech against Aeschines, Concerning the Confiscation of the Property of Aristophanes,* which is attributed to Lysias by the lexicographer Harpocration. The confiscation took place, but the value of the property confiscated did not meet popular expectations. Suspicion arose that some of Aristophanes' wealth had been salted away by his marriage-relatives. A prosecution[4] was brought against Aristophanes' father-in-law, but the latter died before the trial (19.62), leaving the case to be defended by his son, the brother-in-law of the dead Aristophanes. We cannot identify the speaker or his father, but they are clearly members of a prominent family: the speaker lists his other relatives by marriage at 19.12–17, in order to argue that his father would never have arranged a marriage to make money in the way that he is accused of having profited from Aristophanes' estate, and the list includes several prominent Athenians.

The aim of the defense is twofold. In the first place, there are repeated attempts to distance the speaker's father from Aristophanes, so as to imply that there are other people in whom the latter was more likely to have trusted and to whom he would have entrusted his affairs. This is done by representing the speaker's father as a patriot willing to fulfill his obligations to Athens, but as one who had no ambitions for public office (e.g., 19.18, 19.57). Secondly, there are arguments to minimize the scale of Aristophanes' wealth, in order to suggest that the confiscation has in fact yielded as much as could reasonably have been expected. To this end the speaker emphasizes the levels of the expenditure Aristophanes had had to undertake as a newly rich man seeking to buy himself into social respectability after Cnidus (19.28–29). He also gives a list of examples, including not only Conon himself (19.34–41) but also a number of other recently deceased prominent Athenians, many of them known to us from other sources (19.46–52), to

[4] Probably an *apographē* (a written list of property being denounced for confiscation; cf. the Introduction to Lys. 17), heard by a dikastic court presided over probably by the Revenue Commissioners (*sundikoi:* 19.32), though the text at 19.55 speaks of a *graphē* (public prosecution).

demonstrate with figures that rich men can turn out at their deaths to be a lot poorer than they or their fathers or grandfathers were reputed to be.

We must of course bear in mind that the speaker has a point to argue here, and his figures may be unreliable or rhetorically distorted. They are, however, of considerable interest to the historian, as a way in which patterns of wealth and of economic behavior could be represented as reasonable to a jury. Also of considerable interest, but this time to the student of law and rhetoric, is the contrast between this speech and Lysias 29. The latter is a prosecution speech, delivered in very similar circumstances—Ergocles, a politician and general, has been executed, and his subordinate Philocrates is now on trial because Ergocles' confiscated property has not fulfilled expectations—and although we do not know the result of the present case, the arguments used in Lysias 29 may give some indication of what could be said against the defendant in Lysias 19.

On the aspects of the speech that concern Athenian foreign policy, see C. J. Tuplin, "Lysias 19, the Cypriot War, and Thrasyboulos' Naval Expedition," *Philologus* 17 (1983): 170–186. Two older commentaries are still useful on points of detail: E. S. Shuckburgh, *Lysias: Sixteen Speeches* (London, 1882), and especially C. D. Adams, *Lysias: Selected Speeches* (Norman, Okla., 1905).

19. ON THE PROPERTY OF ARISTOPHANES: DEFENSE SPEECH AGAINST THE TREASURY

[1] This trial, gentlemen of the jury, places me in a very awkward situation. I am aware that if I myself do not speak effectively on this occasion, then not only I but my father too will be regarded as criminals and deprived of all our property. So even though I am not skilled at this task, I must defend my father and myself in whatever way I can. [2] The plotting and the eagerness of my enemies are things that you can see, and I need say nothing about them. My own inexperience is recognized by all my acquaintances. So I shall ask you to show me the kindness—something that is both just and easy to do—of listening without anger to us too, as you also did for the prosecutors. [3] Even if you grant us an equal hearing, the defendant is necessarily in a worse position. The opponents have delivered their prosecution speech after

preparing it for a considerable time, and with no risk to themselves. We, on the other hand, are defending ourselves in a context of fear and defamation and the greatest danger. So it is reasonable that you should show greater favor to the defendants. [4] I am sure you all know that often in the past people have made many serious accusations but have at once been so clearly convicted of lying that they have left the court hated by all who were present. Others have given false testimony and have only been detected after destroying people unjustly, when there was nothing more that could be done for their victims. [5] Given that such things have often happened, or so I hear, it is reasonable for you, gentlemen of the jury, not to regard the prosecutors' speeches as trustworthy until we too have spoken. I for my part have heard, and I believe many of you are aware, that defamation is the most terrible of all things. [6] You can see this most clearly when many people face trial on the same charge, because what generally happens is that those who are tried last are acquitted. You hear their cases after you have quenched your anger, and by then you willingly accept their counterarguments.

[7] Please bear in mind that Nicophemus and Aristophanes were put to death without trial, before any of their friends could be present when they were found guilty of wrongdoing.[1] Nobody even saw them after their arrest. The authorities did not even hand over their bodies for burial: their fate was so terrible that they were deprived of this as well, in addition to everything else. [8] But I shall leave that issue aside, because I would not be able to finish it. It is the children of Aristophanes who seem to me far more wretched. Although they had wronged nobody, either privately or publicly, not only have they lost their ancestral property (which is against your laws), but their one remaining hope, that their upbringing would be funded from their grandfather's property, has been placed in terrible jeopardy. [9] What is more, we have been deprived of our relations by marriage, deprived of the dowry, forced to bring up three children—and on top of that, we are being attacked by sykophants[2] and are on trial for the property

[1] These events, and the careers of Aristophanes, Nicophemus, and Conon, are briefly discussed in the Introduction.

[2] Malicious prosecutors.

which our ancestors justly possessed and handed down to us. And yet throughout his life, gentlemen of the jury, my father spent more on the city than on himself and the members of his family: twice what we now possess, as I often heard him calculate. [10] Do not convict prematurely of wrongdoing the person who spends little on himself but a great deal every year on you. Instead, convict those who have been accustomed to lavish on their disgusting pleasures not only their ancestral property but anything they may have acquired from elsewhere. [11] It is difficult, gentlemen of the jury, to defend oneself against the opinion some people have of Nicophemus' wealth, and against the current shortage of money in the city—all the more so when the case is a defense against the Treasury. Nevertheless, even under such circumstances you can easily realize that the accusations are untrue. I ask you to give us a favorable hearing with full care and attention right to the end, and then to vote as you think would be most advantageous to yourselves and most in keeping with your oath.

[12] Let me explain to you first of all how we became related by marriage. Conon was serving as general around the Peloponnese[3] and had for a long time been friends with my father, who was serving as trierarch. He asked my father to give my sister in marriage to the son of Nicophemus, who was requesting this. [13] Seeing that Nicophemus' family was trusted by Conon, and that they had become prominent and were (at least at that time) in favor with the city, my father agreed to do so. He did not know of the defamatory accusation that was to follow. His decision was made at a time when any one of you would have been pleased to become related to them by marriage. That it was not done for money, you can easily tell from my father's whole life and his accomplishments. [14] When he was a young man he had the chance to marry somebody with a lot of money, but he took my mother, even though she brought no dowry, because she was the daughter of Xenophon son of Euripides,[4] who was not simply recognized as honorable in his private affairs, but whom you chose to serve

[3] Probably in 393 BC, when he is known to have been active there (Xen., *Hellenica* 4.8.7–8).

[4] This Xenophon (not the same person as the author, just as his father is not the same person as the poet) was general on several occasions between 441 and 430 and was killed in battle in 429.

as general, or so I have heard. [15] Several very rich people wanted to marry my sisters without dowries, but my father refused, because these suitors seemed of too low birth. Instead, he gave one to Philomelus of the deme Paeania,[5] whom most people would describe as honorable rather than rich, and the other to his own nephew, Phaedrus of the deme Myrrhinus,[6] a man who had become poor not because of any wickedness. He gave him a dowry of forty minas, and later the same to Aristophanes. [16] Moreover, when I could have received a very large dowry, he advised me to accept a smaller one, so that he could be sure I would have respectable and discreet marriage-relatives. So now I am married to the daughter of Critodemus of the deme Alopece,[7] who was killed by the Spartans when the sea battle took place at the Hellespont.[8] [17] And yet, gentlemen of the jury, a man who himself married without receiving any money, who gave considerable sums as dowries for both of his daughters, and who accepted a small dowry for his son—surely it is reasonable to believe that it was not for money that he entered into a marriage alliance with Nicophemus' family.

[18] What is more, it is easy to tell that although Aristophanes was now married, he would have had closer dealings with many other people than with my father. Their age was very different, and their character even more so. It was in my father's nature to mind his own business, whereas Aristophanes wanted to be involved in not only his own but public affairs also. Whatever money he had, he spent it in his

---

[5] Philomelus may be the Philomelus who acts for the speaker in Isoc. 17.45, but several members of his family are more firmly attested. His father Philippides appears as an incidental character in Plato, *Protagoras* 315a; his son, another Philippides, is the subject of a long honorific decree (*IG* II² 649).

[6] The friend of Socrates, after whom Plato's *Phaedrus* is named: he was exiled for participation in the scandal of the Herms and Mysteries in 415 BC (a point that is carefully glossed over here). By implication, Phaedrus is now dead or divorced, since his widow (apparently) remarried Aristophanes.

[7] Critodemus is otherwise unknown, but his son Aristomachus appears as a witness in what may be a genuine document quoted in Dem. 59.25 and is attested as a minor politician in Dem. 23.13, 110.

[8] The Athenian defeat at Aegospotami in 405. As usual in Lysias, it is unnamed.

desire for glory. [19] You can tell from his actions that I am speaking the truth. In the first place, when Conon wanted to send somebody to Sicily, Aristophanes volunteered and went with Eunomus, who was both a personal and a hereditary friend of Dionysius[9] and had brought considerable benefits for your democracy, as I understand from those who were present at Piraeus. [20] The object of the voyage was to persuade Dionysius to conclude a marriage alliance with Euagoras,[10] and to become an enemy of the Spartans and the friend and ally of your city. They accomplished this, despite considerable dangers facing them by land and by sea, and persuaded Dionysius not to send the triremes that he had already prepared for the Spartans. [21] Later on, when the envoys came from Cyprus to seek assistance, Aristophanes did not relax his passion for activity. You gave them ten triremes and voted for other expenditures, but they lacked money for the expedition. They had arrived with little money and needed a lot more, not simply for the ships but because they had also hired peltasts[11] and had purchased weapons. [22] Aristophanes personally supplied most of their money, and when this was insufficient, he persuaded his friends, by pleading and offering guarantees. He also took forty minas belonging to his half-brother, which had been left on deposit with him, and used that. The day before he sailed, he came to see my father and asked him to lend whatever money he had, because he said he needed more to pay the peltasts. We had seven minas at home, and he took that as well and used it. [23] Do you think that this man, gentlemen of the jury, who was eager for honor, who had letters arriving from his father saying that he would have no financial problems in Cyprus, who had been elected envoy and was about to sail to join Euagoras, would have left behind any of his property? Do you not think he would have supplied everything he possibly could, to gratify Euagoras and procure a larger return? To show that I am telling the truth, please call Eunomus for me.

---

[9] The delegation was sent in 394 or 393 to Dionysius I, tyrant of Syracuse. Aristophanes' colleague Eunomus is otherwise attested as a naval commander in 389/8 (Xen., *Hellenica* 5.1.5, 7), and the speaker is predictably keen to emphasize his credentials as one of the democratic counterrevolutionaries of 403 ("those present at Piraeus"). For hereditary friendship (*xenia*), see Lys. 18.10n.

[10] Tyrant of Salamis in Cyprus; cf. the Introduction.

[11] Light-armed troops.

[TESTIMONY[12]]

[24] You have heard the witnesses—not simply that they lent the money when he asked for it, but also that they have recovered it, because it was returned to them on the trireme.

So it is easy to tell from what has been said that when such crises occurred, he would not have spared any of his property. The strongest proof of that is as follows. [25] Demus son of Pyrilampes[13] was about to go to Cyprus as trierarch and asked me to see Aristophanes. Demus said that he had received a gold cup as a pledge (*sumbolon*) from the Great King and that he would give it to Aristophanes as security for a loan of sixteen minas, so that he would be able to pay for the trierarchy. He explained that Aristophanes would be in a position to redeem it for twenty minas when he arrived at Cyprus, since that pledge would enable him to obtain cash and many other benefits throughout the mainland.[14] [26] Aristophanes listened to Demus' proposal and my request, and although he was to take the gold cup and receive four minas as interest, he replied that it was not possible, and swore that he also had had to borrow from elsewhere for the mercenaries:[15] otherwise he would have been the first person to accept this pledge and satisfy our request. [27] I shall produce witnesses for you that I am telling the truth.

[WITNESSES]

From what has been said and what has been testified, it is easy to be certain that Aristophanes left no silver or gold behind. As for bronze, he possessed only a small assortment: when he gave a dinner for the envoys from Euagoras, he had to use borrowed bronze vessels. The clerk will read out the list of what he did leave behind.

---

[12] "Witnesses" in 19.24 implies that others besides Eunomus were called at this point, and some editors change the text so that other witnesses are explicitly summoned.

[13] Demus' hereditary links with the Great King of Persia arose from his father Pyrilampes' diplomatic activities on repeated Athenian missions to Persia in the fifth century (Plato, *Charmides* 158a).

[14] Presumably this refers to Asia Minor.

[15] I.e., the peltasts mentioned at 19.21.

[LIST OF BRONZE VESSELS]

[28] To some of you, gentlemen of the jury, this list perhaps seems short. Bear in mind, however, that before Conon won the sea battle at Cnidus, he possessed no land apart from a small estate at Rhamnous.[16] The sea battle occurred in the Archonship of Eubulides (394/3). [29] Given that he previously had no property, gentlemen of the jury, it was no easy matter in four or five years to serve as choregus[17] for tragedy twice (on his father's behalf and on his own), to serve as trierarch for three years continuously, to have contributed to many war taxes (*eisphorai*), to purchase a house for fifty minas, and to acquire more than seventy acres of land[18]—do you think that on top of all this he must have had many personal effects to leave behind? [30] Even those who are thought to have been wealthy for a long time may not be able to produce personal effects worth mentioning. Sometimes it is impossible, even for somebody who very much desires it, to purchase the sorts of things that would in the future give their owner pleasure. [31] Bear in mind also that in all the other cases of property confiscation, not only could the property not be sold, but even the

---

[16] It is unclear (perhaps deliberately so) whether the property in question is that of Aristophanes alone, or of Aristophanes and his father Nicophemus together. If the latter, Rhamnous (on the northeast coast of Attica, some twenty-five miles from Athens) is probably their ancestral deme. The battle of Cnidus was Conon's great achievement, which restored his political credibility at Athens, and it evidently had similarly dramatic effects on his subordinates' careers.

[17] The *chorēgia* (funding the training of a chorus, here for the performance of a tragedy) and the trierarchy (paying for the upkeep of a warship for a year) were two of the most important liturgies (a form of compulsory public sponsorship imposed on rich individuals). The *eisphora* was a war tax, imposed at times of need on everybody with sufficient property.

[18] Lit. "three hundred *plethra.*" A *plethron* is a measure of area, nominally ten thousand square feet. Three hundred *plethra* would make this equal to the largest estate to be identified by area in our sources (the elder Alcibiades inherited one of the same size, according to Plato, *Alcibiades 1,* 123c). Assuming that 19.42 refers to the same piece of property, it was valued at more than five talents (thirty thousand drachmas), which makes it by far the most expensive single piece of property in the orators. (The next most expensive is the one at Is. 11.42, valued at two and a half talents.)

doors were stripped from the buildings. In our case, as soon as the property was confiscated and my sister had left, we set a guard on the empty house, so that neither doors nor storage jars nor anything else would disappear. People reported personal effects worth more than one thousand drachmas, and you have never previously received this amount from anybody. [32] In addition, we previously offered in front of the Revenue Commissioners (*sundikoi*), and we now offer again, to give whatever pledge[19] is most binding on mankind, that we do not possess any of Aristophanes' property, but that my sister's dowry, and the seven minas he borrowed from my father when he left, are both owing to us. [33] How could humans be more wretched than if they were to lose what was their own and to be thought to possess the property of those people?[20] Worst of all, we must receive back my sister with her many children, and bring them up—even though, if you confiscate our property, we ourselves will have nothing.

[34] By the gods of Olympus, look at it this way, gentlemen of the jury: suppose one of you had given his daughter or his sister to Timotheus son of Conon,[21] and suppose Timotheus had been slandered when he was absent from the city, and his property had been confiscated, and suppose when everything had been sold, the city had gained only four talents of silver. Would you argue that Timotheus' children and relatives ought to be ruined simply because his property was found to be vastly smaller than had been rumored here? [35] But you all know that Conon was commander, and Nicophemus did what he said. It is likely that Conon passed on only a small proportion of his takings to anybody else, so that if people think Nicophemus acquired a lot, they would agree that Conon's share was more than ten times that much. [36] Moreover, there seems never to have been any disagreement between them, so it is likely that they took the same attitude towards money as well: that each should leave a sufficient

[19] The Greek word is *pistis,* which here presumably denotes an oath (in whatever form the Revenue Commissioners choose to specify).

[20] I.e., those whose property has been confiscated.

[21] Timotheus son of Conon had probably not yet begun his political career at this date (he held his first attested public office in 378/7), but in due course he became if anything an even more important political figure at Athens than his father.

amount here at Athens with his son and keep the rest in his own hands in Cyprus. Conon had a wife and son in Cyprus, and Nicophemus a wife and daughter, and they believed that what was in Cyprus was just as safe for them as what was here. [37] Bear in mind also that even a man who had not himself acquired his property, but had inherited it from his father and had divided it among his sons, would have retained the greater portion for himself. Everybody wants to be wealthy and properly treated by his sons, rather than being poor and having to beg from them.

[38] Imagine that you were to confiscate the property of Timotheus—I very much hope that this will not happen, unless some great disaster is about to befall the city—and that you received less money from it than from Aristophanes' estate. Would you think that because of this, his relatives should lose what belongs to them? [39] That would be wholly unreasonable, gentlemen of the jury. The death of Conon, and his will (which he drew up in Cyprus), made it clear that his property was many times smaller than you had expected. He set apart five thousand staters[22] for dedications to Athena and to Apollo at Delphi. [40] To his sister's son, who acted as his guardian and steward for all his property in Cyprus, he gave about ten thousand drachmas, and three talents to his brother. He left the rest, seventeen talents, to his son.[23] The total of these bequests comes to roughly forty talents.[24] [41] Nobody can claim that the estate was plundered or that it was not properly accounted for: Conon himself drew up the will during his illness, while his mind was sound. Please call me the witnesses of this.

---

[22] The stater was a large-denomination coin, probably worth some 20–30 drachmas, but we do not know whether the reference here is to the Attic or the Cyzicene stater (for the latter, cf. the Introduction to Lys. 32, Table 2), and we do not have enough evidence to be sure of the exchange rate in Athens at this date.

[23] In theory, a man with legitimate sons did not have the legal right to leave his property to other people. This text may suggest that the law did not match social realities, but Conon may have also felt that he had greater freedom because the will was drawn up away from Athens.

[24] Given the uncertainty over the value of the staters (above), we cannot say how accurately this calculation adds up, but it is in the right order of magnitude.

WITNESSES

[42] Before the two sets of figures had been made public, gentlemen of the jury, anybody would have thought that Nicophemus' property was only a fraction the size of Conon's. But Aristophanes had purchased land and a house worth more than five talents. He served as choregus both on his own and on his father's behalf, at a cost of five thousand drachmas, and as trierarch he spent eighty minas.[25] [43] No less than forty minas was contributed to war taxes (*eisphorai*) for the two of them.[26] He spent one hundred minas on the voyage to Sicily. For the equipping of the triremes, when the Cypriots came and you gave them ten ships, he supplied thirty thousand drachmas towards the hiring of peltasts and the purchase of weapons. The total of all these amounts comes to fifteen talents or slightly less.[27] [44] So you could not reasonably hold us responsible, because the property of Aristophanes is found to be worth more than one-third the value of that of Conon, which was thought to be very much larger and which is acknowledged to have been properly accounted for by Conon himself—and we are not including the amounts that Nicophemus himself kept at Cyprus, where he had a wife and a daughter.

[45] I do not think that after producing so much weighty evidence, gentlemen of the jury, we should be unjustly ruined. I have heard from my father, and from other older men, that not just now but also previously you have been much mistaken about property: people who during their lifetimes were thought rich, but when they died were shown to be very different from your expectations. [46] For example, everybody (as I hear) thought during his lifetime that Ischomachus[28] had seventy talents, but after his death his two sons did not share even ten talents each. Stephanus son of Thallus[29] was said to have more

[25] For these various expenditures, see 19.29 and notes.

[26] I.e., Aristophanes and Nicophemus.

[27] The calculation is broadly accurate. The figures quoted in 19.42–43 add up to fourteen talents, thirty minas, but he does claim that the land cost "more than" five talents, which would account for some at least of the difference.

[28] Ischomachus can presumably be identified with Socrates' interlocutor in Xenophon's *Oeconomicus* (a treatise on estate management).

[29] Stephanus is otherwise unknown.

than fifty talents, but after his death his property was found to be about eleven talents. [47] The household of Nicias[30] was expected to be worth no less than a hundred talents, with most of this being kept at home; but Niceratus, when he was dying, said that he had no silver and gold to leave, and the property he left to his son is worth no more than fourteen talents. [48] Callias son of Hipponicus,[31] soon after his father's death, was thought to have owned the most of any Greek. People say that his grandfather valued his own property at two hundred talents. But Callias' present tax assessment (*timēma*) is not even two talents. You all know how Cleophon[32] controlled all the affairs of the city for many years and was expected to make a large amount from his official position. But when he died, this property could not be found anywhere; even his relatives by blood and by marriage, in whose hands he would have left it, are acknowledged to be poor men. [49] Clearly we have been greatly deceived both about those whose wealth is inherited and about those who have recently come into prominence. I think the explanation is that people too easily venture to say that an individual is receiving many talents from his official position. I am not particularly surprised that they make such claims about the dead, because this cannot be refuted by those concerned; but I am surprised that they try to tell such lies about those who are alive. [50] You yourselves recently heard it said in the Assembly that Diotimus[33] had received forty talents more from the owners of merchant ships (*nauklēroi*) and from the import traders (*emporoi*) than he

---

[30] Nicias is the fifth-century general and politician whose family history (including Niceratus' execution by the Thirty) is the subject of Lys. 18.

[31] Callias is the man allegedly behind the prosecution of Andocides (cf. the Introduction to Lys. 6). Xenophon (*Poroi* 4.14–15) brackets Nicias (cf. previous note) and Callias' father Hipponicus together as men who made substantial wealth from the silver mines.

[32] Cleophon is the "demagogue" whose execution in 404 is reported in Lys. 13.7–12 and 30.10–13 (we may wonder whether his property was confiscated, which might undermine the argument here by providing an alternative explanation for his relatives' poverty).

[33] Diotimus is attested as general commanding a fleet in the Hellespont in the early 380s (Xen., *Hellenica* 5.1.25), though the dating of this speech may imply that he had already held similar office slightly earlier.

himself had admitted. When he arrived, he submitted accounts in writing and was angry that he had been slandered in his absence. Nobody challenged him, even though the city was short of money and he was willing to render an account. [51] But consider what would have happened if, after all the Athenians had heard that Diotimus had received forty talents, he had suffered some accident before returning here. His relatives would have been in very great danger, if they had had to defend themselves against so great a slander, since they would not have known anything about what had happened. Those who easily venture to tell lies, and who long to bring sykophantic charges against people, are responsible for deceiving you about many people in the past and for causing some to perish unjustly.[34] [52] I believe you know that Alcibiades served as general for four or five years in succession,[35] during which he defeated the Spartans and maintained control, and the allied cities decided to give him twice what they had given to any other general. As a result, some people thought he had more than one hundred talents, but when he died, he showed that this was untrue: he left less property to his sons than he himself had received from his guardians.

[53] It is easy to recognize that such things happened in the past. But people say that the best and wisest men are most willing to change their minds. If therefore we seem to speak sensibly and to have produced sufficient evidence, gentlemen of the jury, you should pity us with all your power and ability. Although the slander was so serious, we always expected to overcome it with the help of truth; but if you are not prepared in any way to be persuaded, it seems that we have no hope of survival. [54] By the Olympian gods, gentlemen of the jury, please be willing to deliver us justly instead of ruining us unjustly, and trust these people to tell the truth, who even while remaining silent show themselves to be prudent and honest in their whole life.

[55] You have heard about the indictment[36] itself, and how we became related by marriage, and how Aristophanes' property was not

---

[34] This is the general sense, but the text of this sentence is obscure.

[35] From 411/10 (initially elected by the fleet, without this being accepted at Athens) until the battle of Notium in 407/6. Some editors place 19.52 directly after 19.47.

[36] *Graphē:* see the Introduction at n. 4.

sufficient for the naval expedition, but he had to borrow from other sources, and witnesses have confirmed all this for you. However, I want to say a few words about myself. I have now reached the age of thirty, and I have never in any way spoken against my father. Nor has any citizen prosecuted me, and although I live close to the Agora, never until this misfortune occurred was I seen either in court or in the Council-chamber. [56] That is what I have to say about myself, but about my father—since the prosecution speeches have treated him as a criminal—please forgive me if I report what he has spent on the city and his friends. I am doing this not from a desire for glory, but as evidence that the same man does not both spend a great deal voluntarily and want to steal part of the public property despite very great danger. [57] Some people admittedly spend money in advance, not merely for the sake of altruism but so that they will be chosen by you for public office, and will be able to carry off twice as much. My father, on the other hand, never wanted to hold office but fulfilled all his *chorēgiai,* served on seven occasions as trierarch, and made many large contributions to war taxes (*eisphorai*).[37] The clerk will read an itemized list, so that you too may know about this.

[LITURGIES]

[58] You hear the quantity, gentlemen of the jury. For fifty years my father performed liturgies for the city, both in person and with his money. Given that he had from the start the reputation of being wealthy, he presumably did not avoid any expenditure in all this time, but I will produce witnesses for you as well.

[WITNESSES]

[59] The total of all these benefactions is nine talents and two thousand drachmas. In addition to this, he privately helped some of the poorer citizens by contributing to their daughters' and sisters' dowries, ransomed others from the enemy, and provided money for others for their burial. He did this in the belief that an honorable man should help his friends, even if nobody would know about it. But now it is

---

[37] For liturgies such as the *chorēgia* and the trierarchy, and for the *eisphora,* see 19.29n.

fitting that you too should hear about it from me. Please call that man, and the other one, for me.

[WITNESSES]

[60] You have heard the witnesses. Bear in mind that although a person could create a false character for a short period, nobody could conceal being a criminal for a period of seventy years. Now, one might perhaps make other complaints about my father,[38] but not even his enemies would dare complain about his money. [61] Do not trust the prosecutors' words; instead, trust the actions he performed throughout his life, and the passage of time, which you yourselves recognize as the most accurate test of truth. If he had not been this sort of person, he would not have left only a small amount out of much wealth—for if today you are deceived by these men and confiscate our property, you will receive not even two talents. So it is to your advantage to vote for acquittal, not only for your reputation but also for financial reasons: you will derive greater benefit if we continue to possess our property. [62] Consider how much is shown to have been spent on the city in the past. At the moment, too, I am paying as trierarch out of what is left, and my father was serving as trierarch when he died. In the future I shall attempt little by little to set aside small amounts for the common good, just as I saw him doing, with the effect that our property has for a long time belonged in reality to the city: I shall not feel robbed by being deprived of it, and in this way you will benefit more than if you were to confiscate it. [63] Moreover, you should bear in mind my father's character. In every instance that he wanted to spend money beyond what was necessary, clearly these were things from which the city also would gain honor. For instance, when he took up horse breeding, he produced horses that were not simply handsome but champions, who won victories at the Isthmus and at Nemea.[39] As a result the city was named in the proclamation,[40] and he himself won the wreath. [64] So I beg you, gentlemen of the

---

[38] An intriguing admission.

[39] These were two of the four sets of Panhellenic Games (the others were the Pythian Games at Delphi, and the Olympics).

[40] I.e., the herald's announcement of his victory identified him as an Athenian. Whereas athletes in the modern Olympics compete as members of national teams,

jury, remember these and all the other things that have been said, come to our help, and do not let us be destroyed by our enemies. If you do this, you will be bringing in a just verdict, and one that will benefit you yourselves.

---

ancient contestants did not represent their cities but themselves. However, the *Odes* of Pindar celebrate not simply individual glory but also the glory that a city could derive from its citizens' victories at the games. The modern parallel would perhaps be golf or tennis stars, who compete as individuals but are nevertheless the objects of national pride.

20. FOR POLYSTRATUS

INTRODUCTION

The background to this speech is the oligarchy of the Four Hundred, who held power for four months in the Summer of 411 BC. Their collapse was followed by an intermediate regime (a moderate oligarchy), which lasted until full democracy was restored following the battle of Cyzicus in the Spring of 410. Lysias 20 is a defense speech on behalf of an elderly man named Polystratus, on a charge that is never made explicit but is clearly connected with his membership in the oligarchy.[1] The wording of 20.17 implies a date soon after the restoration of full democracy, probably 410 or possibly 409, and at any rate considerably earlier than 403/2, which is generally thought to be the start of Lysias' career as a speechwriter. Because of the early date, but also because of the style and composition (which is sometimes awkward), modern scholars have generally concluded that this is probably a real speech, or possibly parts of two real speeches,[2] but almost certainly not by Lysias.

Leaving aside questions of literary quality, the main value of this speech is as a historical source. It provides us with early and

[1] There has evidently been an earlier trial, resulting in a substantial fine, though it is not clear that this has been paid and there is no reference to the threat of proceedings for nonpayment (20.14, 20.18, 20.22). The attractive suggestion has been made that this was a fine imposed under the intermediate regime, which will have lapsed with that regime's collapse.

[2] From 20.11 onwards, the speaker is clearly one of Polystratus' sons (he refers consistently to "my father"), but this does not seem to be the case in the earlier part of the speech (cf. 20.4).

independent, if tendentious, information about the oligarchy of the Four Hundred, which is one of the few events in Athenian history for which we possess alternative and contradictory narrative accounts (Thuc. 8.63–72, 89–98, and *Ath. Pol.* 29–33). This allows us to confirm or question some of the details. The task of the defense was difficult, because it was impossible to deny Polystratus' involvement as a member of the Four Hundred. Indeed, it was impossible to deny that he had served also as one of the Registrars (*katalogeis*), though it is not clear whether these were simply the hundred men chosen to register the Five Thousand who were allegedly to form the wider electorate for the oligarchic regime (*Ath. Pol.* 29.5), or whether they were also responsible for selecting the Four Hundred themselves (also a task for which a hundred men were chosen, according to Thuc. 8.67.3). The speaker implies the former and represents Polystratus as being torn between duty and generosity: on the one hand, he acted only when forced to do so by the threat of punishment (20.14), but he is also said to have registered nine thousand in place of five thousand, because of his unwillingness to disappoint anybody (20.13). It is, however, difficult to match this latter assertion with the repeated claim that he served on the Council—a careful euphemism for membership of the Four Hundred—only for eight days (20.10, 20.14, 20.16) before sailing off to Eretria (20.14), because there would not have been time for him to do much registration.

Given the weakness of Polystratus' position, it is hardly surprising that considerable attention is devoted to the record of the sons whom he had brought up to be such a credit to Athens and whose military activities are recounted at 20.23–29. Particularly interesting is what is said about the speaker himself, which casts light on the situation in Sicily following the collapse of the Athenian Expedition of 415–413 BC. This is a topic about which we know little, but he claims to have been active in continuing resistance to the victorious Syracusans from a base at Catana, and he gives vivid if not always comprehensible detail (20.24–26).

We have no direct evidence for the result of the case, but it apparently did not produce the consequences envisaged at 20.35, where the speaker suggests that conviction would lead to the loss of citizenship for the whole family (presumably as a result of an unpayable fine, which would be hereditary). Nothing further is heard of the defendant himself, but two sons of a Polystratus who is evidently the same man are commemorated in a series of fourth-century memorial stones, all of which are elaborately carved and evidently costly pieces of work. The implication is that the family not only continued to enjoy full citizen rights at Athens but also retained considerable wealth.[3]

The value of Lysias 20 as near-contemporary (if highly misleading) evidence for the revolution of the Four Hundred is discussed in an excursus on "Sources for the Revolution," in A. W. Gomme, A. Andrewes, and K. J. Dover, *A Historical Commentary on Thucydides* (Oxford, 1981), vol. 5, pp. 201–206.

20. ON BEHALF OF POLYSTRATUS: DEFENSE SPEECH ON A CHARGE OF OVERTHROWING THE DEMOCRACY

[1] In my opinion, you should not be angry at the name of the Four Hundred but at the actions of some of them. Some were engaged in plots, but others served on the Council[1] not to harm either the city or any of you but with good intentions. Polystratus here was one of these. [2] He was selected by the members of his tribe (*phulē*) because he was honest in his dealings both with the members of the deme and with your democracy. The prosecution are now accusing him of being hostile towards your democracy, but he was chosen by the members of his tribe, who could best distinguish the characters of their own members. [3] Why would he have desired an oligarchy? Was he of an age to achieve success among you as a speaker or to trust in his physical strength, so that he could commit violent outrages (*hubris*) against any of you? But you can see how old he is: it would be more appropriate for him to restrain other people from such actions. [4] Admittedly if a person desired a different constitution when he had suffered *atimia*[2] for a previous offense, then he would be doing this for his own sake because of his earlier misdeeds. But this man had not

[3] The memorial stones are *IG* II[2] 12499, 12658, and 12967. Identification is made overwhelmingly probable because all three were found near Keratea, within a couple of miles of the family's deme Deiradiotai (cf. 20.12n).

[1] Lit. "entered the Council-chamber," a frequent phrase throughout the speech. The reference is to the oligarchic junta of Four Hundred rather than to the democratic Council of Five Hundred.

[2] Loss of citizen rights, as a judicial penalty or in consequence of an unpaid debt to the city.

committed any offense that would make him hate your democracy for his own or his children's sake. One of them was in Sicily, and the others in Boeotia, so he did not desire a different constitution for their sakes either. [5] The prosecution accuse him of holding many public offices, but nobody can show that he behaved improperly in office. It is not, in my opinion, people like this who act wrongly in such situations. Instead, what is wrong is if somebody holds few offices but acts against the interests of the city. It was not those who held office properly who betrayed the city, but those who did so unjustly. [6] In the first place, when this man was a public official at Oropus,[3] he did not betray the city and set up a different constitution—even though all the other officials betrayed their responsibilities. They did not await trial, and so convicted themselves of wrongdoing. He believes that he has done nothing wrong, and is paying the penalty. [7] In the case of the criminals, the prosecutors are accepting bribes and stealing them away,[4] but they denounce as guilty those from whom they could not profit. They bring similar accusations against those who made proposals in the Council and those who did not. [8] But the defendant did not make even a single proposal concerning your democracy. Those who were well disposed to you, but were not hated by the oligarchs, do not in my opinion deserve to suffer any harm at your hands. Some of those who spoke against the oligarchs went into exile, and others were executed, so even if somebody wanted to oppose them for your sake, fear and dread at their sufferings deterred everyone. [9] As a result, most of them gave up entirely, because the oligarchs were expelling some of them and executing others. They[5] placed in power those who would obey them and not plot or pass information to the enemy: so you could not easily change the constitution. It is not right that such people should be punished for the support they gave you. [10] It seems outrageous to me if somebody who made no proposals is going to suffer the same as those who made proposals that were against the

---

[3] Oropus was a piece of disputed territory on the northern border between Attica and Boeotia. It does not appear to have been in Athenian hands at this time (Thuc. 8.95.3), and some scholars change the text to Oreus, which was the only city in Euboea to remain loyal to Athens after the failure of Thymochares' expedition (Thuc. 8.95.7).

[4] I.e., helping them escape justice.

[5] I.e., the oligarchs.

interests of your democracy. He committed no offense against you for seventy years but allegedly did so in eight days. Some people, who have been criminals throughout their lifetime, win over their prosecutors and become honest at the office of the *logistai,*[6] whereas others, who have always behaved honorably towards you, become criminals.

[*Many editors believe that there is a change of speaker here (see the Introduction).*]

[11] In their previous accusations, the prosecutors made many false allegations against my father, including the claim that Phrynichus was a relative of his.[7] Anybody who wishes can testify during my speech that he was closely connected with Phrynichus. But in fact their accusation was false. Not even in childhood were they friends. Phrynichus was a poor man, and worked as a shepherd in the countryside, but my father was brought up in the town (*astu*). [12] When he reached adulthood, my father became a farmer, whereas Phrynichus came to the town and became a sykophant.[8] So their styles of life have nothing in common. For example, when Phrynichus was paying off a fine to the Treasury, my father did not contribute money for him, and yet situations like this reveal most clearly who one's friends are. It is not right that my father should suffer simply for being a member of Phrynichus' deme[9]—unless you also are criminals because he was a fellow-citizen of yours. [13] How could anybody do more for the common people than the man who served as Registrar (*katalogeus*)[10] after you had voted to hand over public affairs to five thousand people and who registered nine thousand. He did this to avoid quarreling with

---

[6] The *logistai,* together with the *euthunoi,* were the public officials who presided over the judicial audit of the accounts (*logoi, euthunai*) of every outgoing official at the end of his term of office.

[7] Phrynichus was one of the extremist leaders among the Four Hundred. His assassination (discussed at Lys. 13.70–76) sparked off the regime's collapse.

[8] Malicious prosecutor. The term is used particularly by those who claim to be the rich and inoffensive victims of rabble-rousing democratic politicians.

[9] Rather a specious argument, given that Deiradiotai (the deme of Phrynichus and therefore also of Polystratus) was a fairly small deme. It had three seats on the Council, which may imply a total size of about 120–180 adult males.

[10] The function of the Registrars is discussed in the Introduction.

any of the deme members, but so that he could register anybody who wanted it, and could do it as a favor if there was a problem about any individual. Surely the people who overthrow the democracy are not those who make more people into citizens but those who make fewer out of more. [14] He was unwilling either to swear the oath or to act as Registrar, but they compelled him to do so by imposing fines (*epibolai*) and punishing him. After he had given way to pressure and had sworn the oath, he served on the Council for eight days and then sailed off to Eretria.[11] He displayed no cowardice[12] in the sea battle, and returned here wounded, by which time the regime had already collapsed. So the defendant, who made no proposals and served on the Council for no more than eight days, has had a massive fine imposed on him,[13] whereas many who spoke against your interests and remained in the Council-chamber to the end were acquitted. [15] I do not speak from envy of those men but out of pity for ourselves. Some people, who were thought to be guilty, were saved by the pleas of those who in public affairs had eagerly supported your interests. Others, who had done wrong, bought off their accusers and did not even appear guilty. How could our situation be other than appalling? [16] The prosecution accuse the Four Hundred of being criminals. But you yourselves were persuaded by them to hand over power to the Five Thousand—and if you, who were so many, were persuaded, then surely each of the Four Hundred could similarly have been persuaded. It is not these men who are doing wrong, but the people who deceive and damage you. The defendant shows his loyalty[14] to you in many ways; in particular, if he had wanted there to be a revolution of some sort against your democracy, he would never have sailed off after spending eight days on the Council. [17] Somebody may object that he sailed away because he was keen to make money, just as some

[11] Possibly as part of Thymochares' disastrous expedition, which precipitated the fall of the Four Hundred (Thuc. 8.95.2), but more likely before it.

[12] Or "no criminal intentions."

[13] The language here implies that a fine has been imposed but not necessarily that it has been paid or is still owing (cf. the Introduction).

[14] "His loyalty" is a conjecture. The manuscript reads, "The defendant shows you in many ways that if he had wanted . . . ," but it is hard with this text to make sense of the "many ways."

people went robbing and pillaging. However, nobody could identify anything of yours in his possession. They accuse him of anything else more readily than of what he did in office. Moreover, at the time, the prosecutors did not show themselves loyal to the democracy in any way, nor did they help it. Now, however, when the democracy itself is claiming particular loyalty to itself, they are nominally helping you, but in reality themselves. [18] Do not be surprised, gentlemen of the jury, that he was sentenced to such a large fine. They caught him unprotected and won a conviction by accusing both him and ourselves. Even somebody who had testimony to give in his favor would not have been able to testify, through fear of the prosecution; but people testified falsely for the prosecutors because they were afraid. [19] We would suffer terribly, gentlemen of the jury, if you acquit those who cannot deny being in possession of your property simply because somebody asks you to, but will not show mercy to us, who have been eager supporters of your democracy and whose father has done you no wrong. If some foreigner arrived here and asked you for money or claimed that he should be recorded as a benefactor, you would grant it to him. Will you not grant to us that we ourselves may have citizen rights among you? [20] Even supposing some people were hostile to your system of government and made unsuitable proposals, the people who were absent should not be held responsible, given that you have acquitted those who were actually present. Supposing somebody here won you over with an ill-advised speech, you yourselves are not responsible, but the one who deceived you. [21] The real criminals have convicted themselves of guilt in advance, and have fled to avoid paying the penalty. If there are others who are guilty—less than the real criminals, but guilty nonetheless—their fear of you and of the accusers makes them go on campaign rather than stay at home, so that they can either mollify you or win over the prosecutors. [22] Even though the defendant committed no offense against you, he has submitted himself to a trial immediately after the events, when you had the clearest memory of what happened and he expected to face rigorous examination, trusting that he had done nothing wrong and would succeed in court with justice on his side.[15]

[15] Some of the phrases in this sentence allow different interpretations: "submitted himself to a trial," for instance, could be "paid the penalty," and "expected

I shall demonstrate to you that he supported the common people. [23] In the first place, the members of his deme would be able to say from personal knowledge how often he served on campaign without a break. He could have made his property invisible[16] and given you no assistance, but instead he wanted you to know about it—so that even if he did want to be a criminal that would not be possible, but he would have to contribute to war taxes (*eisphorai*) and to perform liturgies. Moreover, he brought us up to be of great help to the city. [24] He sent me to Sicily, and to you I was not . . .[17]—with the result that while the expedition was safe, the cavalry knew what sort of character I had. When it was destroyed, and I escaped to Catana, I made my base there and devoted myself to damaging the enemy by raiding them, with the result that more than thirty minas was set apart as a tenth share for the goddess and towards ransoming all those soldiers who were in enemy hands. [25] When the people of Catana made me serve in the cavalry, I did so. Not even in that context did I avoid any danger, with the result that everybody knew my character both as cavalryman and as hoplite. I shall provide you with witnesses of these things.

[WITNESSES]

[26] You have heard the witnesses, gentlemen of the jury. I shall now show you how I have behaved towards your democracy. A man from Syracuse had arrived at Catana with an oath. He was ready to make people swear it and was going individually to each one of those

---

to face rigorous examination" could be "was bound to be convicted." (It is not even clear whether the reference is to a previous trial or to the present one.) It is impossible to retain these ambiguities in English.

[16] The point of making his property "invisible" (selling his land and turning the proceeds into cash or liquid assets) would have been to avoid the obligation to liturgies (a form of compulsory public sponsorship imposed on rich Athenians) by not appearing wealthy enough to be liable.

[17] Editors agree that at least one word has dropped out of the text here. The historical value of the speaker's account of his activities in Sicily after the collapse of the Athenian expedition of 415–413 is discussed in the Introduction.

present. I immediately spoke against him. I went to Tydeus[18] and explained the situation, and he held a meeting, at which various speeches were delivered. I shall call witnesses about what I said.

[WITNESSES]

[27] Consider also my father's letter, which he gave somebody to deliver to me: were its contents good for your democracy or not? It contained matters of domestic concern and also the advice that I should return when the situation in Sicily was going well. And yet the same things were advantageous both to you and to those who were there, so he would never have sent such a letter if he had been hostile to the city or to you.

[28] Next, I shall discuss my youngest brother's attitude towards you. During the raid by the exiles, who not only did whatever damage they could but also continued to ravage and plunder you from the fortress,[19] he rode forward from the rest of the cavalry and killed one of the enemy. I shall produce those who were themselves present as witnesses of this.

[WITNESSES]

[29] As for my eldest brother, those who actually campaigned together know him—I mean those of you who were in the Hellespont with Leon.[20] So you know that his character is the equal of anybody's. Please come forward for me.

---

[18] Tydeus cannot be identified with certainty (though Lamachus, one of the Athenian generals who had been killed during the expedition, had a son with this name). Indeed, it is not even clear whether this man is an Athenian commander of a raiding band or a public official in Catana.

[19] The specific context of this raid is unknown, but the reference is presumably to Athenian oligarchs in exile assisting the Spartans in their occupation of Decelea ("the fortress"), for which see 18.9n.

[20] Evidently the Leon whom Thucydides (8.23) names as a general in 412/1: probably to be identified with Leon of Salamis, the victim of the Thirty. For the possibility that the latter might be the father of the speaker of Lys. 10, see the introduction to that speech.

[WITNESSES]

[30] Since this is the sort of people we are, it must surely be right for us to receive a reward from you. Is it right for us to be destroyed because of slanders you have heard against our father but to have no benefit for our loyalty towards the city? No, it is not right! If we must suffer anything because of the slanders against the defendant, we deserve to rescue both him and ourselves because of our loyalty. [31] The reason we treated you well was not to receive money, but so that if we were ever in trouble, you would grant our request for acquittal as a fitting reward. You should do this to influence others also, recognizing that you will be benefiting not just us but yourselves as well, if anyone is loyal to you in future. You have tested us to find out what sort of people we are, even before we requested your favor, but you will make others more loyal by rewarding appropriately whatever good anybody does you. [32] Do not in any way strengthen the position of those who put forward the most wicked argument of all: it is claimed that those who are treated badly have better memories than those who are treated well. Who will still want to behave honorably, if those who do you good are defeated by those who harm you? For you, gentlemen of the jury, the situation is as follows: your vote is about us, not property. [33] So long as peace continued, we possessed land,[21] and our father was a successful farmer. However, we were deprived of all this when the enemy began their invasions.[22] So for these reasons we have been loyal towards you. We knew we did not have the money to pay a fine, and we believed that we ought to receive a reward for our own loyalty towards you. [34] Nevertheless, gentlemen of the jury, we see that if somebody brings forward his children and weeps and laments,[23] you take pity on the children if they are to lose their citizen rights on his account, and you pardon the father's crimes on account of the children, without knowing whether they are going to turn out well or badly when they grow up. In our case, you know that we have been loyal to you and that our father has done nothing wrong. So it will be

[21] Lit. "visible property," which would include house(s) as well as land.

[22] Perhaps "began their occupation (of Decelea)," i.e., in 413.

[23] A technique sufficiently common to be parodied in Aristoph., *Wasps* 976–978.

far more just for you to reward those whom you have tested, rather than people whose future development is unknown to you. [35] Our predicament is the opposite of other people's: they bring forward their children and plead with you; we bring forward our father and ourselves, and beg you not to deprive us of citizen rights and of citizenship. Take pity on our father, who is an old man, and on us. If you destroy us unjustly, how will he take pleasure in our company, or we in each other's, given that we will have been judged unworthy of yourselves and the city? There are three of us, and we beg you to allow us to be still more loyal in future. [36] We beg you for the sake of whatever is most dear to each of you. Those of you who have children, take pity on us for their sakes. Those who are the same age as ourselves or as our father, take pity and acquit us. Do not yourselves obstruct our desire to benefit the city. We would be suffering a terrible fate if we were rescued by the enemy[24] (who could reasonably have prevented our being rescued) but failed to find safety at your hands.

---

[24] The point of this remark is obscure.

21. ON A CHARGE OF ACCEPTING BRIBES

INTRODUCTION

The opening words make clear that what we have here is not a complete speech but simply a part of one. The charges have already been dealt with, and what follows is first a statement of the anonymous defendant's services towards Athens (21.1–11) and then a peroration (21.11–25). It is possible that the first part of the speech has been lost, but there is no evidence for a gap in the manuscripts, and it is equally possible that this is all that was commissioned from the orator, with the litigant himself being responsible for the rest.[1]

The case is being heard before a dikastic court, presumably soon after the democratic restoration in 403/2 (which is the most recent date explicitly mentioned in the catalogue at 21.4). The speaker hints that he may have remained in Athens under the Thirty (21.4n), which is likely to have prejudiced the court against him, although it is not clear that it formed the basis of the charge. The title claims that the speaker has been accused of accepting bribes, but this may be an invention by a copyist faced with the incompleteness of the speech. The phrasing of 21.16, however, implies that he is charged with possessing public property, and perhaps that the property in question has been denounced by *apographē* (writ of confiscation) before a special commission of investigators (*zētētai*). The allegation that the opponents have themselves previously been prosecuted for impiety (21.20) may imply that a related charge (for instance, the embezzlement of sacred funds) underlies the present case also; but this could simply be a per-

[1] A possible parallel would be Isoc. 16, which similarly begins by referring back to the subject of the case.

sonal innuendo about the prosecutors, which might make sense to us if we knew who they were.

The services rendered towards Athens consist mainly of liturgies (21.1–5), though the speaker does give us some interesting incidental information about his war record at the naval battles of Arginusae (406) and Aegospotami (405). "Liturgy" is the conventional translation of the Greek word *leitourgia* (lit. "public work"), but the latter has none of the ecclesiastical overtones of its English equivalent. Athenian liturgies were a form of compulsory sponsorship imposed on rich men because of their wealth, such that they had to spend a fixed minimum, but they could spend more in the hope that the prestige so bought would lead to political success. The most common liturgies were the *chorēgia* (paying for a choral production at a festival) and the trierarchy (paying for the crew and upkeep of a warship for a year and normally commanding it).

Even allowing for exaggeration, the scale and frequency of the speaker's liturgies (tabulated for convenience below [Table 21.1]) is enormous, but we should not necessarily take it as typical. Davies (1971: no. D.7, pp. 592–593) discusses what can be inferred about the various individual payments and also analyzes the pattern of expenditure: he suggests that the speaker's family were heavily implicated in the oligarchy of the Four Hundred in 411 BC and that the speaker himself had at once engaged in a program of massive expenditure in the hope of buying his way back into political favor under the restored democracy. This is a highly plausible reconstruction, but if so, we have no way of telling whether he was ultimately successful.

21. DEFENSE SPEECH ON A CHARGE OF ACCEPTING BRIBES:[1] UNNAMED

[1] On the subject of the accusations, gentlemen of the jury, the position has been made sufficiently clear to you. However, I ask you to listen to me on other matters as well, so that you may know the sort of person you are going to be voting about. I came of age[2] in

[1] See the Introduction.

[2] Lit. "passed my *dokimasia*" (the judicial scrutiny faced by young men before they could become adult citizens).

TABLE 21.1

Expenditures Claimed in 21.1–5

Year[1]	*Event*	*Month*[2]	*Liturgy*	*Expenditure Claimed*	*Drachma Equivalent*
411/10	Great Dionysia?	9 (March)	tragic chorus	30 minas	3,000
411/10	Thargelia	11 (May)	men's dithyrambic chorus*	2,000 drachmas	2,000
410/9	Great Panathenaea	1 (July)	pyrrhic dance*	800 drachmas	800
410/9	Great Dionysia?	9 (March)	men's chorus*	5,000 drachmas	5,000
409/8	Lesser Panathenaea	1 (July)	dithyrambic chorus	300 drachmas	300
411/0–405/4?			trierarch	6 talents	36,000
?			*eisphora* (war tax)	30 minas	3,000
?			*eisphora*	4,000 drachmas	4,000
405/4	Prometheia	?	gymnasiarch*	12 minas	1,200
404/3?	?	?	boys' chorus	15+ minas	1,500+
403/2	Great Dionysia?	9 (March)	comic chorus*	16 minas	1,600
?	Lesser Panathenaea	1 (July)	boys' pyrrhic dance	7 minas	700
?	Panathenaea?	?	trireme race*	15 minas	1,500
?			others	30 minas	3,000

*victory in competition.

[1] The Athenian calendar year ran from midsummer to midsummer: underlining is used in this column to denote the half of the calendar year in which an event fell (thus 411/10 is the second half of the Athenian calendar year, and corresponds to our January–June 410).

[2] For convenience, Athenian months are numbered in this column from the start of the year in midsummer, with approximate modern equivalents given in brackets.

the Archonship of Theopompus (411/10), was appointed choregus for tragedy, and spent thirty minas.[3] Two months later, I was victorious at the Thargelia with a men's chorus, at a cost of two thousand drachmas. I was also victorious, spending eight hundred drachmas, in the pyrrhic dancing competition[4] at the Great Panathenaea in the Archonship of Glaucippus (410/09). [2] I was again choregus in the same year with a men's chorus at the Dionysia,[5] and won the victory: including the dedication of the tripod, I spent five thousand drachmas. In the year of Diocles (409/8), I spent three hundred drachmas on a cyclic chorus[6] at the Lesser Panathenaea. In the meantime I was serving as trierarch for seven years[7] and spent six talents. [3] Even though I undertook all these expenditures, running daily risks on your behalf and remaining abroad,[8] nevertheless I contributed thirty minas to one war tax (*eisphora*) and four thousand drachmas to another. On sailing back to Athens, in the Archonship of Alexias (405/4), I immediately served as gymnasiarch[9] at the Prometheia and won the victory at a cost of twelve minas. [4] Afterwards[10] I was appointed choregus of a boys' chorus and spent more than fifteen minas. In the Archonship of Euclides (403/2), I won the victory at the competition for comedy with a play written by Cephisodorus and spent sixteen minas, includ-

---

[3] The Thargelia, Panathenaea, Dionysia, and Prometheia were all religious/civic festivals. For a tabulation of the expenses reported in 21.1–5, see the Introduction.

[4] A dance in which the dancers are men (or, as in 21.4, boys) wearing armor.

[5] Presumably the Great Dionysia or City Dionysia, on which see A. W. Pickard-Cambridge, *The Dramatic Festivals of Athens* (Oxford, 2d ed., 1988), 57–125. (The Rural Dionysia is possible but unlikely.)

[6] A chorus that performs a dithyrambic ode, for which see Lys. 4.3 and note.

[7] Presumably the seven years inclusive from 411/10 to 405/4. A continuous trierarchy on this scale is unusual and may indicate that Athens was under considerable financial pressure in this period.

[8] Presumably as commander of his trireme; cf. previous note.

[9] A form of liturgy analogous to the *chorēgia,* but which in this case involved preparing the runners for the torch-races that were held at a number of festivals, including the Prometheia.

[10] If the list is in sequence, this presumably denotes the Archonship of Pythodorus (404/3), which he is careful not to mention, because it would imply that he had been active in Athens under the Thirty.

ing the cost of dedicating the equipment. I also served as choregus at the Lesser Panathenaea with a chorus of beardless pyrrhic dancers and spent seven minas. [5] I have won the trireme race to Sunium,[11] at a cost of fifteen minas. This is leaving aside the leadership of sacred delegations (*architheōria*), the *errhēphoria*,[12] and other things of that sort, on which I have spent more than thirty minas. All in all, if I had wanted to spend on liturgies only what is required by law, I would have paid not even one quarter of the sums mentioned. [6] Moreover, during the time I was serving as trierarch, my ship was the best equipped in the whole fleet. I can give you very strong evidence of this: first, there was Alcibiades.[13] I would have given a great deal not to have him sailing with me in my ship, because he was neither a friend nor a relative nor a member of my tribe (*phulē*). [7] However, I am sure you all realize that he was general, with the power to do whatever he liked. Since he himself was going to face danger, he would never have sailed on any ship other than the best-equipped one. When you suspended him and his colleagues from office, [8] and elected the ten who included Thrasyllus,[14] all of these wanted to sail on my ship, but after considerable disagreement among them, it was Archestratus of Phrearrhii who came aboard. After his death at Mytilene, Erasinides sailed with me.[15] And yet how much money do you think I spent on a ship that was so well equipped? How much damage did it do to the enemy? How much good did it do to the city? [9] The best evidence for this is as follows: in the final sea battle, when the ships were

[11] The southernmost point on the coast of Attica, about 35 miles by sea from Piraeus. Such races are attested at the Panathenaea.

[12] The *errhēphoria* or *arrhēphoria* was a procession of young women carrying sacred baskets at the Panathenaea.

[13] Alcibiades was general from 411/0 until he was deposed after being defeated in his absence at the battle of Notium early in 406.

[14] Thrasyllus, together with Erasinides (below), was among the six generals executed after the battle of Arginusae in the summer of 406 (cf. 12.36n).

[15] Comparison of three passages in Xenophon's account of the battle of Arginusae (Xen., *Hellenica* 1.5.16, 1.6.15–18, 1.6.29–30) suggests that Archestratus may have been killed in the course of a preliminary skirmish in which part of the Athenian fleet was blockaded on Mytilene and that his colleague Erasinides may have replaced him on the speaker's ship in time for the battle itself.

destroyed and I had no general sailing with me—I mention this to emphasize the point, because you were angry with the trierarchs as well as with the generals because of the disaster that took place[16]—I brought away my own ship and rescued that of Nausimachus of Phaleron. [10] This happened not by chance but because of my preparedness: I had Phantias as my pilot[17] throughout this period, because I made it worth his while, and he was held to be the best pilot among the Greeks. I also provided a crew to match him, and the rest of the rowers to accompany them. All of you who were there as soldiers know I am telling the truth, but please call Nausimachus as well.

[TESTIMONY]

[11] So, then, twelve ships in all were rescued, of which I brought away two: my own trireme and that of Nausimachus.

Even though I have run so many risks on your behalf, and have accomplished so much for the city, I am not now asking, as others do, for a gift in return. Instead, I ask not to be deprived of my own property, because I regard it as a disgrace to you as well to take it from me, with or without my consent. [12] It is not so much the prospect of losing my property that concerns me, but I would not be able to endure the insult (*hubris*). Nor could I put up with those who avoid their liturgies, if the money spent on you wins me no gratitude, and their decision to spend none of their resources on you is thus regarded as sensible. If you accept my argument, you will be voting for what is just and choosing what is beneficial to yourselves. [13] You can see, gentlemen of the jury, how small the revenues of the city are and how these are being stolen by those in charge of them. It is right, therefore, that you should regard the property of those willing to undertake

---

[16] A more than usually circumspect reference to the disastrous battle of Aegospotami (405). Given that the Spartan admiral Lysander is said to have captured at anchor all but a handful of the Athenian fleet of 180 ships—all but 12 (21.11), or all but 9 (Xen., *Hellenica* 2.1.28–29)—it is striking how many of Lysias' clients claim to have been among the few who were quick-witted enough to escape (2 ships here, and another at Fr. 9 [*Eryximachus*], lines 102–104).

[17] The pilot had a role closer to that of a modern naval captain, because the trierarch, though formally in command of the ship, held this position not because of military skill but because he was paying for the ship's upkeep.

liturgies as the most secure revenue for the city. If you accept good advice, you will take no less care of our money than you do of what belongs to you individually, [14] because you are aware that you will have the use of all our money in the future, just as you have had in the past. I am sure you all realize that I will be a far better steward for you of my property than those who are your stewards of the city's property. If you reduce me to poverty, you will hurt yourselves as well: other people will divide up this property, just as they have divided up the other properties also.

[15] You should bear in mind that it is far more fitting for you to give me part of your property than to argue with me about mine, and to pity me for becoming poor rather than envy me for being rich. You should pray to the gods for other people to be the same sort of citizens as I am, so that they do not covet your property but spend their own property on you. [16] In my view, gentlemen of the jury,—please do not be annoyed at this suggestion—it would be far more just for you to face an *apographē* (writ of confiscation) in front of the commission of investigators (*zētētai*) on a charge of possessing my property than for me now to be prosecuted for possessing property belonging to the Treasury. The attitude I take towards the city is that in private life I am frugal, but in public I am pleased to undertake liturgies. I do not boast about the money that is left over but about what is being spent on yourselves, [17] because I consider myself responsible for the expenditure, whereas other people left me the property; the property is the reason my enemies unjustly bring malicious prosecutions against me,[18] whereas the expenditure is the reason I am justly being rescued by yourselves. There is no good reason, therefore, for other people to obtain my acquittal from you.[19] Indeed, if any of my friends were facing such a court hearing, I would expect you to repay your gratitude to me, and if I were on trial in front of anybody else, I would expect you to plead on my behalf. [18] Nobody could claim that I have held many public offices and have profited from your property,

---

[18] Lit. "for this reason I experience unjust sykophancy at the hands of my enemies."

[19] I.e., his liturgies have been so substantial that he needs no friends to plead for him but would indeed be in a position to offer them some of the surplus gratitude that he has earned.

or have been prosecuted in shameful litigation, or am responsible for anything disgraceful, or was glad to see the disasters suffered by the city. I believe that in all my activities, both private and public, I have—as you well know—served the public interest to such a degree that there is no need for me to defend myself on this score. [19] I ask you, gentlemen of the jury, to have the same attitude towards me as in the past. Do not simply remember the public liturgies, but bear in mind also my private activities. You should realize that the most difficult liturgy is to behave respectably and prudently at every moment, right to the end of your life, and not to be overcome by pleasure or inspired by gain, but to behave in such a way that no citizen either criticizes you or contemplates prosecuting you.

[20] It is not right, gentlemen of the jury, that you should believe prosecutors of this type and vote to convict me. They have spent a very long time on trial for impiety; and although unable to defend themselves over their own offenses, they now dare to accuse others. My opponents display indignation about the city's affairs—even though Cinesias,[20] with his notorious character, has served on more campaigns than they have. They do not contribute to things that will make the city prosper, but they do everything to ensure that you will be angry at those who benefit it. [21] If only my opponents would speak to you in the Assembly, gentlemen of the jury, about their own activities! No worse fate than this could I wish upon them. I beg and beseech and implore you not to convict me of accepting bribes. Do not think there is any amount of money so great that I would be willing to harm the city for the sake of it. [22] I should be mad, gentlemen of the jury, if out of ambition for glory I spent my ancestral property on you, but then accepted bribes from other people to damage the city. I cannot think of anybody besides yourselves, gentlemen of the jury, whom I would want as judges in my case, if we are supposed to pray that those who have received benefits should judge the cases of those who have performed those benefits. [23] In addition, gentlemen of the jury,—I want to emphasize this point particularly—

---

[20] A minor poet, with a reputation for cowardice that is alluded to repeatedly by Aristophanes. Lys. Fr. 4 (*Cinesias*) is directed against him and focuses on his alleged impiety.

when liturgies had to be performed on your behalf, I never considered that I would be leaving my children that much poorer. Instead, I was much more worried that I might not eagerly perform my duties. [24] If at any time I was about to face danger in a sea battle, I did not pity myself and weep and mention my wife or children, and I did not regard it as terrible if I should leave them behind as orphans, deprived of their father, after ending my life in the service of my fatherland. Instead, I regarded it as far more terrible if I should inflict shame on myself and on them by escaping danger disgracefully. [25] In return, I now ask you for a mark of gratitude. Because I displayed this attitude towards you in times of danger, I think it right that now that you have regained your confidence, you should place a high value on myself and these children. You should realize that it will be terrible for us and shameful for you if we are forced to lose our civic rights on charges like these, or to lose our property and become paupers, wandering about as vagabonds, with few possessions, and suffering a fate that is unworthy of ourselves and unworthy of what has been done for you. Do not let this happen, gentlemen of the jury. Acquit us, and continue benefiting from the sort of citizens we are, as you have previously.

22. AGAINST THE RETAILERS OF GRAIN

INTRODUCTION

A recent and authoritative study of ancient food supply argues persuasively that modern scholars have traditionally underestimated the productivity of Athenian agriculture, but it nevertheless concludes that Athens needed to import substantial amounts of grain from abroad.[1] The grain trade was subject to a series of special regulations in Athenian law, designed both to maximize imports and also, as in the present case, to prevent manipulation of the price.[2]

Neither the speaker (who is the prosecutor) nor his opponents in this speech are named, but the latter are a group of grain dealers, or more specifically retail traders in grain, who evidently face the death penalty if convicted (cf. 22.5, 22.13). They live at Athens as metics (resident aliens, a point that is stressed at 22.5), and towards the end of the speech they are unfavorably contrasted with the wholesale importers, who are assumed to be foreigners based elsewhere (22.17, 22.21). Their case had initially been referred to the Council, and the speaker (himself a Council-member) claims that that it was he who had persuaded his colleagues to follow normal practice and refer the case for its present hearing in a dikastic court,[3] even though they had

---

[1] Garnsey, *Famine and Food Supply* (cited below), e.g., p. 105.

[2] For details of these regulations, see Todd 1993: 320–321.

[3] This two-stage process, first before the Council and then before a lawcourt, is characteristic of *eisangelia* (impeachment), which is probably the procedure being used.

been on the verge of executing the defendants without trial.[4] He alleges that he is now obliged to prosecute in order to avoid allegations that his intervention had served the interests of the defendants rather than of justice (22.2–4), but this expression of reluctance may be designed primarily to avoid the imputation of sykophantic or improper prosecution (22.1).

The charge against the defendants is clear in outline (they are accused of profiteering) but obscure in detail. Part of the problem lies in the law which they are accused of having broken, and which forbids them from "buying together" (*sunōneisthai* or *sumpriasthai*) more than fifty *phormoi*[5] of grain (22.5–6). It is not clear whether the prefix *sun-* ("together") refers to the grain and so constitutes a ban on hoarding, or whether it refers to the purchasers and so constitutes a ban on operating a cartel; and it has indeed been suggested that the rhetoric of this speech depends on manipulating this ambiguity.[6] The situation is complicated by the obscurity of another crucial passage (see 22.12n), where it is not clear whether the allegation is of exceeding the permitted markup or of fraudulently varying the price by claiming that each sale was from a separate stock.

The background to the speech is evidently a period of short-term grain crisis. The mention of Anytus as one of the public officials in charge of the grain trade (the Grain Guardians or *sitophulakes:* 22.8–9) gives us no help with the date. It is possible though not certain that he is to be identified with the Anytus who was one of the leaders of the democratic counterrevolution in 403, but even if so, we know too

---

[4] He does not explicitly say that summary execution would have been illegal, merely that it was dangerous and inappropriate (22.2). It is certainly true that the Council could not execute citizens on its own authority, but it is possible that they did have this power over noncitizens.

[5] The word *phormos* (pl. *phormoi,* lit. "basket") seems to be a measure of grain, but we should beware of assuming that it is identical with a *medimnos* simply because that is what Lysias implies at 22.12.

[6] Thus R. Seager, "Lysias *Against the Corndealers,*" *Historia* 15 (1966): 172–184, who sees the law as intended to ban hoarding, whereas T. Figueira, "*Sitopōlai* and *Sitophulakes* in Lysias' *Against the Graindealers:* Governmental Intervention in the Athenian Economy," *Phoenix* 40 (1986): 149–171, sees it as banning cartels.

little of his subsequent career for it to be a useful indication. The alleged rumors of 22.14, however, would fit a date early in 386, during the negotiations leading up to the Peace of Antalcidas, which ended the Corinthian War. The background to these negotiations lies in Thrasybulus' naval campaign in 390–389, which was perceived as an attempt to reconstitute an Athenian maritime empire.[7] This was a threat to Persia and led in due course to rapprochement between Persia and Sparta, the result of which was Persian support for Antalcidas as Spartan naval commander in blocking the Hellespont in 387, and in cutting off the supply of grain from the Black Sea, so forcing Athens to negotiate. The resulting crisis would help to explain the legacy of bitterness against the grain retailers that the speaker is manipulating throughout this speech, his attempts to marginalize them from the interests of the city as a whole, and perhaps also his insistence that they are the guilty parties who are undermining the heroic achievements of the wholesale importers. The strident use of anti-metic rhetoric is particularly striking (e.g., 22.16). This is one of the few speeches where it would be interesting if we knew for certain that the speech was written by Lysias, because Lysias was of course a metic himself.

On all aspects of food supply in antiquity, see P. D. A. Garnsey, *Famine and Food Supply in the Graeco-Roman World: Responses to Risk and Crisis* (Cambridge, 1988). There is a useful commentary on Lysias 22 by Usher in Edwards and Usher 1985, and the legal background—including the disputed interpretations of 22.5–6 and 22.12—is discussed further in one of the case studies in Todd 1993: 316–320.

22. PROSECUTION SPEECH AGAINST THE RETAILERS OF GRAIN

[1] Many people have come to me, gentlemen of the jury, expressing surprise that I accused the grain retailers in the Council-meeting. They say that even though you are sure the defendants are as guilty

---

[7] This campaign forms the background to Lys. 28–29 and is discussed further in the Introduction to those speeches.

as it is possible to be, nevertheless you also believe that those who are delivering speeches about their case are engaging in sykophancy.[1] So I wish first to explain why I have been forced to accuse them.

[2] When the Prytaneis[2] referred their case to the Council, there was such anger against them that some speakers said we ought to hand them over without trial to the Eleven[3] to put to death. I believed that it was dangerous for the Council to get into the habit of doing this, so I stood up and said that in my view we ought to try the grain retailers according to the law. I took the view that if they had committed actions that deserved death, you would dispense justice no less than the Council, but if they were doing nothing wrong, it was not appropriate to kill them without trial. [3] After the Council agreed to do this, some people tried to slander me, saying I had made this speech with the aim of saving the grain retailers. I defended myself by my actions in the Council, when their preliminary hearing took place.[4] Whereas other people stayed silent, I stood up and accused them, and made clear to everybody that I was not speaking on behalf of these men but was supporting the established laws. [4] This was why I began my involvement in the prosecution, because I feared the allegations. However, I considered it shameful to withdraw before you have the chance to vote about their case.

[5] First of all, please go up onto the rostrum.[5]

SPEAKER: Tell me, are you a metic?

DEFENDANT: Yes.

SPEAKER: Is your aim in residing here as a metic to obey the laws of the city or to do whatever you please?

DEFENDANT: To obey.

SPEAKER: Do you accept that you deserve a death sentence, if you violate the laws for which the penalty is death?

DEFENDANT: I agree.

---

[1] Malicious prosecution.

[2] The executive committee of the Council.

[3] The public officials in charge of prisons and (here) executions.

[4] The implications of this two-stage process for identifying the judicial procedure used in this case are discussed in the Introduction.

[5] For the procedure of *erōtēsis* (interrogation of the opponent), see Lys. 12.24n.

SPEAKER: Tell me if you agree that you bought together[6] more grain than fifty *phormoi,* which the law says is allowed?

DEFENDANT: I did so because the public officials ordered me.

[6] If he can demonstrate, gentlemen of the jury, that there is a law that orders grain retailers to buy grain together if the officials order this, then you should acquit him. If not, it is right that you should convict. We[7] have presented you the law forbidding any of the inhabitants of the city to buy together more than fifty *phormoi* of grain.

[7] The accusation already made ought to have been sufficient, gentlemen of the jury, because the defendant admits that he bought the grain together, and the law clearly prohibits this. Nevertheless, I must say more about the case, so as to convince you that my opponents are lying about the officials as well. [8] When the defendants brought up this accusation against them, we called the officials together and questioned them. Two of them[8] denied knowing anything about the affair, but Anytus said that during the previous winter, when grain was expensive with the defendants bidding against each other and contending among themselves,[9] he had advised them to stop competing, in the belief that their buying it at the best price possible would benefit you as their future customers—for it was obligatory for them to sell at a price that was higher only by an obol. [9] I will produce Anytus himself for you as a witness that he did not tell them to buy

[6] *Phormos* (lit. "basket") is evidently a measure of volume, but its size is unknown. For the two possible meanings of *sunōneisthai/sumpriasthai* ("hoarding" or "operating a cartel"), see the Introduction.

[7] This may imply that the speaker is one of several prosecutors, but the plural is often used for the singular in such contexts.

[8] This is the manuscript reading, but nowhere else in our sources is the number of Grain Guardians (*sitophulakes;* see the Introduction) put at three, so we should probably change the text. Scholars have suggested either "four of them" (cf. *Ath. Pol.* 51.3 for the number five) or else "the current ones" (implying that Anytus was a member of the previous year's board). The identity of Anytus is discussed in the Introduction.

[9] This translation is an attempt to retain the ambiguity of whether the competitiveness is simply an accompanying consequence of the high price (which is probably what happened) or a cause of it (which is presumably what Lysias wishes the audience to infer).

together and hoard the grain but simply advised them not to compete against each other in their purchasing.

[TESTIMONY]

Anytus made these statements during the term of the previous Council, but these men have clearly been buying together during the current one.

[10] You have heard that they did not buy the grain together on the instructions of the officials. In my opinion, even if they tell the truth as far as possible on this point, they will be accusing the officials, not defending themselves. In situations where the laws are explicitly written, it is surely necessary to punish both those who disobey and those who tell them to do the opposite of what the law says.

[11] I do not expect, however, gentlemen of the jury, that they will resort to this argument. Instead, they will perhaps say, as they did in the Council-meeting, that they were buying the grain together out of goodwill towards the city, so that they could sell it to you as cheaply as possible. But I will tell you the strongest and clearest evidence that they are lying: [12] if they really were acting for your sake, they ought to have been seen selling at the same price for several days, until the stock they had bought together ran out. But in fact they sometimes sold it on the same day for a drachma more, as if they were buying together by the *medimnos*.[10] [13] I produce you yourselves as witnesses of this. It seems strange to me that whenever it is necessary to contribute to a war tax (*eisphora*), which everybody will know about, they are reluctant and put forward the pretext of poverty; but when the penalty is death and it suited them to remain secret, they claim they committed these offenses out of goodwill towards yourselves. You are all aware that the defendants have the least right to make speeches like this. What suits them is the opposite of what suits other people: they

---

[10] Traditionally this sentence has been glossed as "at a profit of a drachma" (i.e., six times the permitted markup of one obol mentioned at 22.8), but it may mean that they have been varying their prices by up to one drachma in a day, presumably by claiming that each sale was from a separate stock, or in other words that they had been purchasing on a scale more appropriate to a householder than a trader. (The *medimnos,* like the *phormos,* was a measure of volume.) This interpretation, however, raises further problems, for which see Todd 1993: 319.

make their greatest profits at precisely the time when some disaster has been reported to the city and they can sell their grain at a high price. [14] They are so pleased to see your misfortunes that in some instances they learn about them before other people do, and in others they themselves create rumors—that your ships in the Pontus have been lost, that they have been captured by the Spartans while sailing out, that the trading ports (*emporia*) have been blockaded, or that the truce is about to collapse.[11] [15] They have reached such a level of hatred towards you that they take the same opportunities to plot against you as do the enemy. Whenever you are most in need of grain, these men snatch it up and refuse to sell it, so that we will not challenge their price but will be happy to come away after buying from them at any cost. On occasions, therefore, even in time of peace, we find ourselves besieged by them. [16] The city has recognized the unscrupulousness and ill will of the defendants for so long that whereas you have established the post of Market Regulators (*agoranomoi*) to supervise all the other traders, you appoint Grain Guardians (*sitophulakes*) separately by lot to oversee this one single trade. You have already frequently exacted the most severe penalty from the Grain Guardians, even though they were citizens, for being unable to control the criminal activity of these men. And yet what should the wrongdoers themselves suffer at your hands, when you are executing even those who cannot keep watch on them?

[17] You must realize that it is impossible for you to vote for an acquittal. If you acquit those who themselves acknowledge having collaborated against the import traders, you will yourselves be seen as plotting against those who sail here with goods. If they were constructing any other defense, nobody would be able to blame those who voted for acquittal, since it would be your decision which side you wanted to trust. As it is, however, you will certainly be seen as acting outrageously, if you release without punishment those who admit breaking the law. [18] Bear in mind, gentlemen of the jury, that many people accused of this offense in the past have denied it and produced witnesses, but you condemned them to death because you

[11] For the relevance of these rumors to the dating of the speech, and their significance in understanding the prosecutor's strategy, see the Introduction.

found the accusers' statements more reliable. It is surely extraordinary if, in judging the same offenses, you are more eager to punish those who deny than those who admit their guilt. [19] Furthermore, gentlemen of the jury, I imagine it is obvious to everybody that trials about such matters are of general interest to those in the city. So they will find out your attitude toward these cases, in the belief that if you condemn the defendants to death, the other grain retailers will be better behaved. If, however, you release them unpunished, you will have granted them a considerable immunity to do whatever they please. [20] It is essential to punish them, gentlemen of the jury, not simply because of what has happened but also to set an example for the future—even so they will be scarcely bearable. Remember that most of those involved in this trade have been on trial for their lives. They make such massive profits from it that they prefer to risk their lives on a daily basis rather than to stop making unjust gains at your expense. [21] Even if they beg and beseech you, you would not be justified in taking pity on them. You should far sooner pity those of the citizens who died because of these men's crimes, and the import traders against whom they collaborated. By exacting punishment from these men, you will be pleasing and encouraging those import traders. What attitude do you think they will take otherwise, when they discover that you have acquitted the market traders who have admitted plotting against those who sail here with goods?

[22] I do not know what more I need say. When you deliver your verdict on other offenders, you need to hear from their accusers, but you all know the criminal behavior of these men. If you convict them, you will be doing what is just, and you will buy grain more cheaply; if not, it will be more expensive.

23. AGAINST PANCLEON

INTRODUCTION

The connection between Plataea and Athens has been discussed in the Introduction to Lysias 3. In that speech there are incidental problems of interpretation arising from the status of Theodotus, the male prostitute who forms the object of the dispute and who does not appear to be an Athenian citizen even though he seems unquestionably to be from Plataea.[1] In Lysias 23, on the other hand, the status of the speaker's opponent Pancleon is central, in that he is evidently claiming to be an Athenian citizen by virtue of being a Plataean, a claim that the speaker is contesting.

Despite the manuscript title, Lysias 23 is not in fact a prosecution speech, but a defense against what it describes as an *antigraphē* brought by Pancleon (23.5). This procedure is not otherwise attested, but it appears to be a variant form of *paragraphē.* A *paragraphē* was a counterprosecution, brought by the defendant in a *dikē* (private prosecution) against the plaintiff, on the grounds that the latter's *dikē* was not admissible for one of a number of reasons, including the plea that the *dikē* had been brought before the wrong court. That is apparently the basis of Pancleon's argument here (23.2). When the speaker initially summoned him before the court of the Polemarch, the Archon who dealt with most cases involving metics (resident aliens), Pancleon asserted that as a Plataean he was an Athenian citizen. Private prosecutions against citizens had to be brought before the tribal judges, and

[1] Athenian citizenship was granted to those citizens of Plataea who chose to register for it after the destruction of Plataea by Thebes in 427 BC.

the speaker had therefore demanded to know Pancleon's deme,[2] partly to know how to issue the correct summons, but also by implication to be in a position to challenge the veracity of Pancleon's claim.

In an elaborate and fascinating account of his detective endeavors, the speaker recounts how he had questioned first of all the members of Decelea at the barber's shop which they use as an informal meeting place (23.3), and then the citizens of Plataea at what appears to be their monthly plenary meeting (23.6). This account highlights the continuing existence of the Plataeans as an identifiable group at Athens at the date of the speech,[3] with regular meetings serving to maintain this identity despite the dispersal of their members among the various Athenian demes, and the role of oral memory rather than a written membership list in identifying members of the group.

The narrative leads inexorably and with superficial plausibility to the attempted seizure of Pancleon by Nicomedes (23.9–11), who claims that Pancleon is his slave. Nicomedes is introduced with a studied impression of casualness: he has evidently appeared as one of the witnesses in 23.8 but without being named. The inference that we are clearly intended to draw from 23.9–11 is that Nicomedes' claim is justified, and it has indeed been suggested that the speaker is colluding with Nicomedes to this end, or in other words that the speaker is aiming not so much to win his original case but to have the satisfaction of watching Nicomedes seize Pancleon the moment the verdict makes it clear that Pancleon is lying about his status.[4] This hypothesis is not capable of proof, but it would account for one very peculiar feature of the speech: whereas all the other extant speeches from *paragraphē* disputes (Isoc. 18 and Dem. 32–38) deal not only with the technical question of whether the case is admissible but also (and ex-

---

[2] Each of the 139 Athenian demes was allocated to one of the ten tribes. For the tribal judges, see 23.2n.

[3] Evidently after the introduction of *paragraphē* in or soon after 403, and presumably before the rebuilding of Plataea in 386.

[4] For this interpretation, originally proposed by Wilamowitz, see Todd 1993: 168–169. Against it, see E. E. Cohen, "Status and Contract in Fourth-Century Athens: A Reply to S. C. Todd," in G. Thür, ed., *Symposion 1993: Vorträge zur griechischen und hellenistischen Rechtsgeschichte* (Cologne and Vienna, 1994), 141–152, esp. 147–148.

haustively) with the dispute itself, in this speech uniquely the speaker displays no interest in that whatever.

One other odd feature of this speech is the persistent reference to the waterclock, used to regulate the time allotted to each litigant, when introducing witnesses (23.4, 23.8, 23.11, 23.14, 23.15).[5] This is mentioned nowhere else in the corpus of Lysias but occasionally in the speeches of other orators (e.g., Is. 3.12, 3.76 and Dem. 54.36). The use of the formula here is regarded by some scholars as evidence that this speech is not really by Lysias but by another orator, though it is also possible that there may be tactical reasons for its use, for instance to create an impression that the speaker has no time to waste.[6]

Lysias 23 is discussed as one of the case studies in Todd 1993: 167–170.

23. PROSECUTION SPEECH AGAINST PANCLEON, SHOWING THAT HE WAS NOT A PLATAEAN

[1] I would not be able to speak at length about this case, members of the jury, and there seems to me no need to do so. But I shall attempt to show you that I have acted correctly in initiating this *dikē*[1] against Pancleon here, since he is not a Plataean.

[2] Because for a long time he would not stop doing me wrong, I went to the fuller's where he worked; and thinking that he was a metic, I served him with a summons to appear before the court of the Pole-

[5] For the waterclock (*klepsudra*), see Boeoghold 1995: 31, 77–78, 226–230, and plate 13.

[6] For which cf. the emphasis at 23.1 and 23.11 on not talking at length and the use of no fewer than five sets of witnesses (who do not use up the speaker's time) in such a short speech. The argument for spurious authorship is set out most clearly by S. Usher, "The Speech against Pancleon," *Classical Review* 16 (1966): 10–12, but there seems to be no reason for doubting that this is a genuine speech, even if not by Lysias.

[1] A *dikē* (pl. *dikai*) is a private prosecution, or in other words one that could only be brought by the aggrieved party. See the Series Introduction. The phrase "to initiate proceedings," etc., is used in this translation to render *dikēn lanchanō* (lit. "to obtain by lot the opportunity to bring a *dikē*"), and "to summon" or "to serve with a summons" to translate *proskaleō*.

march. On his claiming that he was a Plataean, I asked him his deme, because one of the bystanders advised me to issue an additional summons before the court of whatever tribe he claimed to belong to. When he replied that he was from Decelea, I summoned him also before the judges for the tribe Hippothontis.[2] [3] I went to the barber's near the Herms, which is frequented by the members of Decelea,[3] and asked those of the Deceleans I met there whether they knew any deme member from Decelea called Pancleon. None of them claimed to know him—and I discovered that there were other *dikai* before the Polemarch, in which he was defending himself or had already been forced to pay damages—and so I too initiated proceedings in that court.

[4] I shall produce for you as witnesses first those of the Deceleans whom I questioned, and then any of those present who have initiated proceedings against him before the Polemarch or have won their *dikai* against him. Please stop the water for me.[4]

[WITNESSES]

[5] I trusted this information and initiated the *dikē* against him in the court of the Polemarch. However, when Pancleon brought an *antigraphē,*[5] claiming that my *dikē* was not admissible, I was very concerned that I should not appear eager to behave with arrogance (*hubris*) rather than simply wanting to obtain satisfaction for the wrongs done to me. So I first asked Euthycritus, who I knew was the oldest of the Plataeans and I thought would be the best informed, whether he knew a Plataean called Pancleon, the son of Hipparmodorus. [6] He replied that he knew Hipparmodorus but was not aware of any son,

---

[2] Hippothontis is the tribe (*phulē*) that includes the deme Decelea. The tribal judges (the Forty) were divided equally between the ten tribes, and cases were allocated to those dealing with the tribe of the defendant.

[3] For Herms, see the Introduction to Lys. 6. The relationship between the deme Decelea and the "House of the Deceleieis" mentioned in the contemporary Demotionidae decree is discussed by S. D. Lambert, *The Phratries of Attica* (Ann Arbor, 1993), 115–116.

[4] Speeches in court were timed by a waterclock, which was normally stopped for the reading of laws, witnesses' testimonies, etc. See the Series Introduction, n. 25.

[5] For the use of this "counterprosecution," see the Introduction.

either Pancleon or anybody else. So I then asked also those others whom I knew to be Plataeans. None of them knew his name, but they said I would obtain the most accurate information by going to the fresh-cheese market on the first day of the month, because the Plataeans assemble there on a monthly basis. [7] So I went on that day to the cheese market and asked them whether they knew somebody called Pancleon, a fellow-citizen of theirs. The others said they knew nothing, but one man stated that although he was not aware that any of the citizens had this name, nevertheless he said he had a slave called Pancleon, who had run away. He told me the slave's age, which was that of the defendant, and the occupation (*technē*), which was the one that the defendant practices. [8] As witnesses that this is true, I shall produce Euthycritus whom I first asked, and the other Plataeans I met, and the one who claimed to be the defendant's master. Please stop the water for me.

[WITNESSES]

[9] Not many days later, I saw the defendant Pancleon being arrested by Nicomedes, who has testified to being his master. I went up to them, wishing to know what exactly was happening about him. When they stopped fighting, some of those with the defendant said he had a brother who would vindicate his status as a free man. They departed after pledging themselves as sureties that they would produce the brother the next day. [10] So next day, in view of this *antigraphē* and the *dikē* itself, I decided I should be present with witnesses, so that I would be aware of the person who was due to vindicate his status, and what he would say when he did. Neither brother nor anybody else turned up to fulfill the pledges, but a woman came, claiming that he was her slave.[6] She began an argument with Nicomedes and refused to allow him to take Pancleon away. [11] It would be a lengthy account to describe everything that was said there, but the defendant himself and those accompanying him reached such a level of violence that although Nicomedes on the one hand, and the woman on the

[6] It is interesting that a woman can claim this in her own right, even if only in the informal context of a street dispute rather than the formal context of a lawcourt.

other, were both willing to let him go if anybody vindicated his status as a free man or arrested him claiming he was his slave, they did none of these things but left, taking him with them. I shall produce witnesses for you that sureties were pledged on these conditions the previous day, and that on the day in question they carried him off by force. Please stop the water for me.

[WITNESSES]

[12] It is easy therefore to be sure that not even Pancleon believes in himself—not simply that he is not a Plataean but that he is not even free. If somebody is willing to be forcibly carried off and so render his close friends liable to prosecution for violence, rather than to have his status as a free man vindicated according to the laws and to exact a penalty from those who arrest him, it is not hard for anybody to recognize that such a person knew full well that he is a slave, but was afraid to appoint sureties and stand trial on the question of his status.

[13] I imagine you are pretty clear from this that he is far from being a Plataean. Moreover, you will easily discover from his own actions that even the defendant himself, who is in the best position to know his own affairs, did not expect you to regard him as a Plataean. At the pretrial oath[7] in the *dikē* that Aristodicus here initiated against him, when he was claiming that *dikai* involving him should not be brought before the court of the Polemarch, he was the object of a *diamarturia*[8] that stated that he was not a Plataean. [14] He gave a formal undertaking (*episkēpsis*) that he would prosecute the *diamarturia* witness, but failed to do so. Instead, he allowed Aristodicus to win the *dikē* against him. When he defaulted on the debt,[9] he paid off the penalty on whatever terms he could persuade Aristodicus to ac-

[7] The *antōmosia,* which was sworn by the rival litigants.

[8] A procedure by which, in the legal preliminaries before a trial, a litigant (in this case Aristodicus) produces a witness formally to testify to a fact that has procedural consequences that are binding on the court until and unless the opponent succeeds in convicting the witness of giving false testimony. In this case the formal testimony is that Pancleon, as a non-Plataean, is subject to the jurisdiction of the Polemarch's court.

[9] Presumably referring to a debt arising out of a judgment won by Aristodicus.

cept. I shall produce witnesses for you that these events are true. Please stop the water for me.

[WITNESSES]

[15] Before coming to this agreement with him, Pancleon moved away and lived as a metic at Thebes, because he was afraid of Aristodicus. I imagine you realize that if he really was a Plataean, it would be more sensible for him to live as a metic anywhere else rather than Thebes[10]—so I shall produce witnesses to show you that he lived a long time there. Please stop the water for me.

[WITNESSES]

[16] I believe that my arguments are sufficient, gentlemen of the jury. If you bear them in mind, I know you will vote for justice and truth, which is precisely what I ask of you.

---

[10] Thebes had been responsible for the destruction of Plataea in 427 and for the massacre of those inhabitants who had surrendered.

24. FOR THE DISABLED MAN

INTRODUCTION

The procedure in this case is probably *dokimasia*[1] (lit. "scrutiny"). The use of *dokimasia* to examine the qualifications of those who have been appointed to public office is common in the speeches of Lysias,[2] but in this instance the issue is not an office but a privilege, or more specifically a disability pension. Neither the speaker (who is defending his right to continuance of his pension) nor his opponent is named, and there are no indications of date except for a reference back to the speaker's actions at the time of the Thirty in 404/3, which would fit a date for the speech at any time within the career of Lysias (403–380).

The rules governing the payment of disability pensions are outlined in *Ath. Pol.* 49.4, written in the 330s or 320s BC: those who possess capital of less than three minas, and who are so badly maimed that they cannot do any work, receive a daily payment of two obols, subject to a *dokimasia* conducted by the Council. One clear discrepancy between the system outlined in the *Ath. Pol.* and the situation presupposed in Lysias 24 is that the speaker refers throughout to a payment of one obol rather than two (24.13, 24.26), but presumably the level of payment has been raised in the half-century or so between the speech and the *Ath. Pol.* More difficult to avoid are the speaker's implied ad-

[1] The manuscript title describes it as an *eisangelia* (impeachment), but that is probably an erroneous guess by a copyist.

[2] Discussed in the Introduction to Lys. 16, with reference to other cases at Lys. 25, 26, 31, and Fr. 9 (*Eryximachus*).

mission that he is able to do some work (he claims it is not enough to support him: 24.6) and his failure adequately to discuss the capital value of his property (despite a passing claim not to have inherited wealth: 24.6). It is possible that the regulations for eligibility have been tightened during the intervening period, but perhaps it is easier to infer that the speaker is doing his best to conceal the weaknesses of his case.

Overall, the speech is both evasive and irreverent. An example of the former is the response to the allegation about horse riding (24.10–12), which was presumably intended by the opponent to prove that the speaker was fitter than he admits, but which is manipulated by the speaker into an allegation about his wealth. Throughout the speech there is an undertone of parody, of which one example will suffice: this speech, like Lysias 16, begins by thanking the opponent for creating the opportunity for the speaker to talk about himself, a claim that is appropriate for a proud and ambitious aristocrat like Mantitheus at his *dokimasia* but is faintly ridiculous in the present context.

The tone of Lysias 24 is one reason why several scholars have argued that it must be a rhetorical exercise rather than a genuine speech; another reason is that if the speaker is really poor, it is difficult to see how he could have afforded to commission Lysias as his speechwriter, or indeed whether this would have been worth his while for the amount at issue. But it is equally possible that a speechwriter like Lysias may have decided to adopt unusual tactics to deal with a patently weak case, by attempting to win the Council's support for his client's personality and encouraging them to laugh the case out of court.[3] As for the speechwriter's fees, it is worth bearing in mind not only that the speaker may be better off than he admits, but also that people will sometimes spend more than is justifiable in strictly economic terms to avoid the shame of losing something they have previously held. But perhaps a more likely explanation would be that the

[3] It is worth bearing in mind the possibilities of visual theater in this case. A lot could be done to exaggerate the speaker's disability by the way he walked to the podium with the use of two sticks (cf. 24.13), if he trained himself to use them for the day.

orator (whether Lysias or somebody else) might be prepared to reduce or waive his fees in the light of a personal connection with the speaker. This is pure speculation, the more so given that we know nothing about the normal charges for a speechwriter's services, but clearly the speaker had a craft or trade that brought him into contact with many rich people (24.5), even though he nowhere admits what it is, and it is conceivable that Lysias or one of his friends was among them.[4]

There is a useful commentary on the speech by Usher in Edwards and Usher 1985. See also the reading by C. Carey, "Structure and Strategy in Lysias 24," *Greece & Rome* 37 (1990): 44–51.

24. FOR THE DISABLED MAN

[1] I am almost grateful to my accuser, members of the Council, for having devised these proceedings against me. In the past, I had no reason to give an account of my life, but now, because of him, I have one. In my speech, I shall attempt to show that he is a liar and that up to this very day I have been living a life worthy of praise rather than envy—because it seems to me that envy is the only explanation for his having devised this danger for me. [2] And yet, if somebody envies those whom others pity, what wickedness do you think such a man would shrink from? Could he possibly be bringing charges against me for money as a sykophant?[1] If on the other hand he claims that he is seeking vengeance on me as his enemy, then he is lying: I have never had anything to do with him either as friend or as enemy, because of his criminal nature. [3] So it is clear, members of the Council, that he is envious of me for being a better citizen than he is, even though I am afflicted with such misfortune. In my view, members of the Council, one should remedy physical weakness with mental qualities. If in the future I can maintain an attitude and lead a life that matches my misfortune, how will I be inferior to this man?

[4] I have said enough on these matters, so I shall speak as briefly

[4] The other possibility, of course, is that the speaker's rich friends or clients are paying Lysias on his behalf.

[1] Malicious prosecutor.

as I can about the points I need to discuss. The accuser claims that it is not right for me to receive money from the city. He alleges that I am physically healthy, not disabled, and that I have a *technē*[2] such that I could live even without this income. [5] As evidence of my physical strength, he cites my riding of horses; as evidence of my prosperity in my *technē,* my consorting with those who have money to spend. I believe you all know about the alleged prosperity from my *technē,* and my livelihood[3] in general, but all the same I too will discuss them briefly. [6] My father left me nothing, I only ceased to be responsible for my late mother two years ago, and I do not yet have any children who will support me. I have acquired a *technē* that is able to help a little, but already I can perform it only with difficulty, and I have not yet been able to obtain the services of somebody to take it over.[4] I have no other income apart from this, and if you take it away from me, I would be in danger of facing a very difficult situation. [7] Do not unjustly destroy me, members of the Council, when it is in your power to rescue me justly. Now that I am older and weaker, do not take away from me what you gave me when I was younger and stronger. In the past, you were seen to be full of pity, even for those who had suffered no harm. Do not now for my opponent's sake treat savagely those who are objects of pity even to their enemies. Do not have the hard-heartedness to wrong me, and so cause others in my position to despair. [8] It would be extraordinary, members of the Council, if I were shown to have been receiving this money when I had a single misfortune, but should be deprived of it now, when I am afflicted by age and illness and the sufferings that accompany them. [9] It seems to me that my accuser could demonstrate the scale of my poverty more clearly than anybody else. If I were to be appointed

---

[2] The word *technē* (pl. *technai*) denotes a "skill" or "craft" or "trade." It is very difficult to see precisely what the speaker's occupation is (cf. 24.5), which may be deliberate fudging on his part, because he is equally cagey about the precise nature of his disability.

[3] Or "life," "lifestyle," Gk. *bios.*

[4] Presumably a slave. The reference to children is vague enough to leave it unclear whether he is married, so it is not necessarily significant that nothing is made of the labor power of a hypothetical wife.

choregus for tragedy, and were to challenge him to an *antidosis,*[5] he would prefer to serve ten times as choregus rather than to complete the *antidosis* once. Surely it is disgraceful for him to allege that because of my great prosperity I can consort on equal terms with the very rich—whereas if any of the things I am describing were to happen to him, he would recognize that my condition is like that, or even worse.[6]

[10] My opponent has dared to draw to your attention my horse riding, because he does not respect fortune and feels no shame towards you. In this matter, my account can be brief. I am sure, members of the Council, that all those who experience misfortune take as their aim and object of study how to cope with their existing condition with the minimum of discomfort. I am one of those, and because I have encountered such misfortune, I discovered this means of comfort for myself on the longer journeys I have to undertake. [11] The most important evidence, members of the Council, that I do this because of my misfortune, and not—as he claims—because of arrogance (*hubris*), is that I ride horses; if I possessed property, I would travel on a mule with a padded saddle rather than riding other people's horses. As it is, I cannot afford to possess anything of the sort, so I am forced to make frequent use of other people's horses. [12] Surely it is extraordinary, members of the Council, that this man would remain silent if he saw me traveling on a saddled mule—what would he be able to say?—but because I ride borrowed horses, he seeks to persuade you that I am capable.[7] Surely it is extraordinary that he uses my horse riding as evidence that I am able-bodied, but does not also accuse me of being able-bodied in that I use two sticks, whereas others use one. But it is for the same reason that I use both.

---

[5] The *chorēgia* was one of the most important forms of liturgy (compulsory public sponsorship), and entailed funding a choral production at a festival. A person appointed to perform a liturgy could get out of it by challenging somebody richer either to take it over or to accept an *antidosis:* that is, to exchange all his property with the challenger.

[6] The text is corrupt, and this translation is merely a guess at the original meaning.

[7] "Capable" is used here to translate *dunatos* (used with its derivatives frequently in this speech), which has connotations both of "powerful" or "able-bodied."

[13] To such an extent does he surpass the whole human race in shamelessness, that he is attempting by himself to persuade you who are so many that I am not one of the disabled. But if he succeeds in persuading some of you, members of the Council, what would prevent me from drawing lots to be one of the nine Archons?[8] What is there to prevent you from taking away my obol on the pretext that I am in good health, and voting it to him out of pity on the pretext that he is disabled? Surely the same man cannot have his grant taken away by you on the grounds that he is able-bodied, and be prevented by the Thesmothetae[9] from drawing lots on the grounds that he is disabled. [14] However, you do not share the same opinions as him, and he is not in his right mind. He has come here to argue about my misfortune, as if for an heiress,[10] and he is seeking to persuade you that I am not the sort of person that you can all see. You, on the other hand, should act like those in their right mind and believe in your own eyes rather than in my opponent's words.

[15] My opponent claims that I am full of *hubris,* violent, and totally dissolute—as though he would be telling the truth if he used frightening words but not if he used gentler language and refrained from lying. But I think, members of the Council, that you should distinguish clearly between those people for whom to commit *hubris* is natural and those for whom it is not appropriate. [16] It is not the poor or the genuinely needy who are likely to commit *hubris* but those who possess far more than the necessities of life; not the disabled but those who are over-confident in their own strength; not those who have already progressed in age but those who are still young and who think the thoughts of young men. [17] The rich buy off danger with their money, but the poor are compelled by their immediate needs to

---

[8] The implication is that those classified as disabled were not eligible for this office (which like most others at Athens was selected by lot).

[9] The Thesmothetae (the six junior members of the college of nine Archons, who presided over the selection of at least some public officials) are not in the manuscript, but are a plausible supplement accepted by most editors.

[10] "Heiress" is a loose translation of the Gk. *epiklēros,* which denotes a woman whose father had died without male descendants, leaving the property vested in her, though she did not herself own it. Several claimants might compete (in court) for the hand of an *epiklēros* from a rich family.

behave responsibly. Young men believe they will be forgiven by their elders, but both young and old alike criticize those older men who commit offenses. [18] Those who are strong can generally commit *hubris* against anybody they wish, without suffering anything themselves; but the weak cannot ward off aggressors when they suffer *hubris,* nor can they overcome those they are trying to hurt, if they themselves wish to commit *hubris.* So it seems to me that the accuser is not speaking seriously about my *hubris* but is joking. He does not wish to persuade you that I am that sort of person, but seeks to caricature me, as if he is doing something clever.

[19] He also claims that people who are criminals meet together on my premises—people who have wasted their own property and are plotting against those who want to keep what is their own. You should all bear in mind that by saying this, he is not accusing me any more than all those others who have *technai,*[11] nor is he accusing those who come to my premises any more than those who visit the premises of other tradesmen (*dēmiourgoi*). [20] Each of you is accustomed to visit tradesmen: the perfume seller, the hairdresser, the leather cutter, and wherever you might happen to go. Most of you visit the tradesmen who have set up shop nearest to the Agora, and very few visit those that are furthest away from it. So if any of you is going to condemn the criminal tendencies of those who come to my premises, you will clearly be condemning also those who spend time with the other tradesmen; and if them, then all Athenians, because you are all accustomed to visit one place or other and spend time there.

[21] I do not see what need there is for me to drag out more time defending myself in excessive detail against everything that has been said. If I have already spoken about the most important points, what need is there to treat seriously the minor ones, as he has done? I ask you all, members of the Council, to have the same attitude towards me as in the past. [22] Do not, for the sake of my opponent, deprive me of the only thing in my fatherland of which fortune has given me a share. Do not let this one man persuade you to take away what you all collectively gave me in the past. It is because god has deprived us of the best things, members of the Council, that the city has voted

---

[11] See 24.4n.

to grant us this money, in the belief that both good- and ill-fortune are common to all. [23] I would surely be the most wretched of men, if because of my misfortune I should have been deprived of what is greatest and best, and if because of my accuser I were to be stripped of what the city has given out of consideration towards those in my condition. Do not cast your votes in this way, members of the Council. Why should I find you so disposed? [24] Is it because anybody has ever been put on trial because of me and has lost his property? But not even one person would be able to show this. Or because I am a busybody, or aggressive, or fond of feuds? But I do not, as it happens, use for that purpose such means of livelihood as I have. [25] Or is it because I indulge in excessive *hubris* or violence? But not even my opponent would say so, unless he wanted to lie about this too, just as he lies about other things. Or is it because I was in power under the Thirty and harmed many of the citizens? But I went into exile at Chalcis[12] with your democracy, and although I could have shared in the *politeia*[13] with them, I preferred to share in the danger with all of you. [26] Do not treat me in the same way as those who have committed many offenses, members of the Council, for I have committed none. Instead, cast the same vote for me as your predecessors have done. Remember that I am not giving an account after administering public funds, and I have not held any public office for which I am now undergoing the audit of my accounts (*euthunai*); but instead, I am making this speech simply for a single obol. [27] With this in mind, you will all decide justly; I shall accept your decision and give you thanks. My opponent will learn for the future not to plot against those who are weaker than himself but to overcome only those who are like him.

---

[12] A city in Euboea (the large island immediately north of Attica). Going into exile in 404/3 is of course precisely the basis of the speaker's attack on Philon in Lys. 31.8–14.

[13] *Politeia* may here denote either "citizenship" (a fairly outrageous claim, given that the Thirty restricted citizen rights to three thousand of the wealthiest Athenians) or possibly "the activity of government" (an even more outrageous claim).

25. ON A CHARGE OF OVERTHROWING THE DEMOCRACY

INTRODUCTION

The title given to this speech in the manuscripts is "Defense on a Charge of Overthrowing the Democracy," but this can hardly be correct, because there is no suggestion in the speech of any specific charge against the speaker or of any penalty he might be facing if convicted. The only allegation made against him, to which he refers incessantly, is that he remained in Athens under the oligarchy of the Thirty. Scholars have generally inferred that this is a defense in a *dokimasia* (that is, that the speaker is undergoing judicial scrutiny of his right to hold a public office to which he has been appointed[1]) because defeat at the *dokimasia* was unique in leading to no penalties, and behavior under the Thirty is the subject of all of Lysias' surviving *dokimasia* speeches.

The speech as we have it is incomplete, and breaks off in midsentence because some pages are missing in the Palatinus manuscript.[2] We can calculate the total amount that has been lost (cf. the Introduction to Lys. 26) but without being sure how much of it belonged to this speech. The date of the speech appears to be later than the recapture of Eleusis by the restored democracy, which took place in 401/0 (*Ath. Pol.* 40.4) and which seems to be referred to in 25.9; there is no

[1] For the *dokimasia,* see the Introduction to Lys. 16. For other *dokimasia* speeches, see Lys. 26, 31, and Fr. 9 (*Eryximachus*). We do not know the speaker's prospective office here, but it cannot be membership of the Council of Five Hundred because the speech is addressed to a dikastic court, and the absence of reference to a previous hearing by the Council suggests that he has not been chosen as one of the nine Archons.

[2] For the Palatinus manuscript, see the Introduction to Lys. 5 at n. 1.

obvious reference to any subsequent event. We do not know the name of the speaker, and all that we can infer about him from the speech is that he is wealthy enough to have undertaken liturgies on a scale that suggests political ambitions (25.12–13). The trouble he takes to rebut the allegations that he had been a member of the Four Hundred and that he had held office under the Thirty (25.14) may imply that he was the sort of person about whom such allegations could plausibly have been made. As for his accuser or accusers, it is possible that these are the people criticized by name at 25.25, but the names in the manuscript here (Epigenes, Demophanes, and Cleisthenes) cannot be positively identified with known individuals.[3]

One of the striking features of this speech is the tone. The speaker is surprisingly explicit about alleged abuses of power under the democracy (25.19, 25.27, 25.30), to an extent that might have been expected to provoke hostility from a democratic jury. Moreover, the theory of political motivation developed at 25.7–11 is notable for the cynicism with which the speaker claims that politicians are motivated purely by self-interest, for the generalization with which he assumes that this applies in every case, and for the didactic tone with which he expounds his views. One possible explanation is to see this as a hypothetical defense, written not for a real case but to be circulated as a pamphlet.[4] Such a reading would carry the interesting implication that the *dokimasia* was seen as a suitable subject for a model speech, and therefore presumably as the typical threat to former supporters of the oligarchy under the restored democracy. It may be better, however, to see Lysias 25 as a real speech, but one in which the speaker was deliberately broadening his case into a defense not simply of himself but of all those former supporters of the oligarchy who could plausibly dissociate themselves from the worst excesses of the Thirty.[5] This

[3] Some scholars have emended the text to read Demophantus and Cleigenes (minor democratic politicians mentioned at And. 1.96).

[4] Thus Dover (1968: 188–189). Dover supports this hypothesis by noting that the reference to the speaker's liturgies at 25.12 is far less specific than the one at 21.1–10, but other references to liturgies in the corpus (e.g., 3.47, 7.31, 12.20) more closely resemble 25.12 than 21.1–10.

[5] For a reading of the speech from this perspective, see T. M. Murphy, "Lysias 25 and the Intractable Democratic Abuses," *American Journal of Philology* 113 (1992): 543–558.

would be a high-risk strategy, but one that might perhaps be worth adopting by somebody with a sufficiently high profile.

There is a useful commentary by Usher on Lysias 25 in Edwards and Usher 1985.

25. CONVENTIONALLY, "DEFENSE ON A CHARGE OF OVERTHROWING THE DEMOCRACY" [1]

[1] I could easily forgive you, gentlemen of the jury, for being angry without discrimination against all those who remained in the town (*astu*),[2] when you listen to speeches like these and recall what has happened. But the accusers are neglecting their own affairs and taking an interest in those of other people, and I am surprised that even though they can distinguish clearly between those who are doing no wrong and those who have committed many crimes, they are nevertheless seeking to persuade you to have the same opinion about all of us. [2] If they believe they have accused me of everything the city suffered at the hands of the Thirty, then I regard them as incompetent speakers, because they have not even mentioned the tiniest part of the damage those men did. But if they are speaking about these events on the grounds that this is somehow relevant to me, then I shall make clear that their speeches are false in every respect and that I behaved just as the most honorable of those at Piraeus would have done, if he had remained in the town. [3] I beg you, gentlemen of the jury, not to share the attitude of the sykophants.[3] It is their task to incriminate also those who have not committed any crimes, because from them they can best obtain money. It is your task, however, to grant an equal share in public life (*politeia*) to those who commit no crimes, for in this way you would secure the most allies for the established order. [4] If I show that I was not responsible for any disaster, gentlemen of the jury, but in fact performed many services for the city both in person and with my money, I believe you should give me those rewards which not only benefactors but also those who are not criminals have

---

[1] For the title, see the Introduction.

[2] I.e., the former supporters of the Thirty who stayed in Athens in 404/3, contrasted with the democratic counterrevolutionaries, who are regularly described as "those at (or 'from') Phyle (or 'Piraeus')."

[3] Malicious prosecutors.

a right to receive. [5] A powerful argument, in my view, is that if my accusers were able to convict me personally of wrongdoing, they would not be accusing me of the crimes of the Thirty. They would not think it necessary to slander other people for what the Thirty did, but to punish those who were themselves guilty. As it is, they believe that your anger towards the Thirty is sufficient to destroy even those who have done nothing wrong. [6] If certain people are responsible for many benefits to the city, I do not think it fair that others should receive from you the honor or gratitude for those deeds—nor, if certain people are responsible for many evils, would it be reasonable for those who do nothing wrong to be humiliated and slandered on their account. For the city has enough enemies already, who regard it as highly advantageous that people are being unjustly slandered.

[7] Let me try to explain to you which of the citizens in my view are likely to prefer oligarchy and which democracy. This is the basis on which you will make your decision, and I will make my defense by showing that I had no reason to be hostile to your democracy because of what I did either during the democracy or during the oligarchy. [8] In the first place, it is important to remember that no human being is by nature either oligarchic or democratic: instead, he wants that constitution (*politeia*) to be established which would most benefit himself. So you have no small responsibility to ensure that as many people as possible prefer the system that now exists. The truth of this proposition you will discover without difficulty from what happened in the past. [9] Consider how often the supporters of each of the two types of constitution changed their allegiances, gentlemen of the jury. Did not Phrynichus, Peisander,[4] and their friends the demagogues establish the first oligarchy because they were afraid of punishment for the many crimes they had committed against you? Did not many of the Four Hundred return from exile together with those from Piraeus? Did not some of those who had driven the Four Hundred into exile subsequently become members of the Thirty? Among those who had

[4] Phrynichus and Peisander were among the extremist leaders of the revolution which set up the first oligarchy, the Four Hundred, in 411 BC. For Peisander's previous democratic credentials, see And. 1.36. In Lysias, Phrynichus is mentioned also at 13.70–76 (his assassination) and 20.11–12 (his relationship with the speaker), and Peisander at 7.4 (the confiscation of his property) and 12.66 (Theramenes' attitude towards him).

registered their names for Eleusis,[5] there were some who marched out with you and besieged those on their own side. [10] It is not difficult to recognize, gentlemen of the jury, that differences with each other are not about a constitution but about what is personally beneficial to each individual. So you should conduct a *dokimasia* of the citizens on this basis: consider their politics under the democracy, and examine whether there was any advantage for them in the constitution being overthrown. In this way you will reach the fairest verdict about them. [11] My own opinion is that the people who are likely to have desired an alternative constitution, in the hope that the change would bring some benefit to them, were those who had suffered *atimia* (loss of civic rights) under the democracy after failing to submit their accounts,[6] or had their property confiscated, or suffered some other similar disaster. But those who performed many good deeds for the democracy, and never any evil ones, deserve to receive your thanks rather than to be punished for their actions; it is not right that you should accept slanders against them, not even if all the people in charge of the city's affairs should describe them as oligarchs.

[12] In my case, gentlemen of the jury, during that period I never suffered any misfortune, either private or public, that would have made me keen to escape from immediate difficulties and eager for a different state of affairs. I have served as trierarch[7] on five occasions, fought in four sea battles, contributed to many war taxes (*eisphorai*) during the war, and performed the other liturgies as well as any of the

---

[5] I.e., former supporters of the Thirty. Anybody who did not wish to remain in Athens under the restored democracy in 403 was permitted under the terms of the general amnesty (*Ath. Pol.* 39.1–5) to register for membership of what was to be an independent oligarchic state at Eleusis, a town in Attica some twelve miles west of Athens, and the home of the Eleusinian Mysteries. This independent state was forcibly reincorporated into Athens in 401/0 (the date is given at *Ath. Pol.* 40.4, and the treacherous diplomacy used by the democrats during the siege is described in Xen., *Hellenica* 2.4.43).

[6] Or after failing to have them approved. For the accounting process (*euthunai*) imposed on public officials at the end of their term of office, see the Series Introduction.

[7] Liturgies were a form of compulsory public sponsorship imposed on rich Athenians. A trierarch paid for the upkeep of a warship for a year and normally commanded it. See Lys. 21.6–11.

citizens. [13] But the reason I spent more than was required by the city was to improve my reputation among you and to be able to defend myself better if I were to encounter any misfortune.[8] Under the oligarchy, I was deprived of all this. The oligarchs did not think that those who had been responsible for benefiting the democracy should receive a reward at their hands. Instead, they honored those who had done you the most harm, as if they had taken this as a pledge of loyalty from us. All of you should bear this in mind: do not trust the words of my opponents, but look at the actions performed by each individual. [14] As for me, gentlemen of the jury, I was neither a member of the Four Hundred—let any accuser who wishes come forward and refute me—nor again can anybody show that I served as a member of the Council or held any office when the Thirty were in power. But if I was unwilling to hold office when I could have done so, it is right that I should now be honored by you.[9] If those who held power at that time did not think that they should give me a role in public affairs, how could I demonstrate more clearly than this that my accusers are lying?

[15] It is also right, gentlemen of the jury, to look at other things I have done. During the city's misfortunes,[10] I showed myself to be the sort of person that if everybody had had the same attitude as me, none of you would have experienced any misfortune. For it is clear that during the oligarchy, nobody suffered summary arrest (*apagōgē*) at my hands, none of my enemies was punished, and none of my friends was rewarded. [16] (There is no cause to be surprised at this, because it was difficult to do good during that period, and easy for anybody who wanted to commit offenses.) It is also clear that I did not place anybody on the catalogue of the Athenians,[11] or obtain an arbitration verdict at anybody's expense, or become rich because of your misfor-

---

[8] Euphemism for "if I were to be prosecuted."

[9] I.e., with public office.

[10] Perhaps an even more than usually vague reference to the crushing Athenian defeat at Aegospotami in 405 BC, or perhaps an allusion to the rule of the Thirty (as follows).

[11] There is a similar passage in Lys. Fr. 9 (*Eryximachus*), lines 116–118, from which it appears that this catalogue was a list of Athenians called up for military service under the Spartan admiral Lysander, in the period after 404, when Athens became a subject ally of Sparta.

tunes. But if you are angry at those responsible for the evils that took place, it is reasonable also that those who committed no crimes should improve their reputation among you. [17] What is more, gentlemen of the jury, I believe that I have given the democracy the greatest pledge of my loyalty: I committed no crimes during that period when considerable opportunity was available. Surely I shall be particularly eager to be a model citizen now, when I know for certain that I will immediately be punished if I do anything wrong. But in fact I have consistently followed this principle: during oligarchy not to covet other people's property, and during democracy to spend my own property eagerly on yourselves.

[18] In my opinion, gentlemen of the jury, it would not be right for you to hate those who merely suffered no evil under the oligarchy, when you can display your anger at those who committed offenses against the democracy. You should regard as enemies not those who did not go into exile but those who sent you there; not those who wished to preserve their own property but those who stole the property of others; not those who remained in the town for the sake of their own safety but those who took a part in public affairs because they wanted to destroy other people. If you think it is your duty to destroy the men whom those criminals left untouched, not one of the citizens will be left.

[19] You should also consider things from the following perspective, gentlemen of the jury.[12] You all know that under the previous democracy many of those in charge of the city's affairs were stealing public property. Some received bribes at your expense, and others provoked the allies into revolt by being sykophants.[13] Even you would have regarded the Thirty as honorable men if they had punished only those people. But in fact you became angry at the Thirty, because they decided to punish the democracy for the crimes committed by those men, and you thought it terrible that the crimes of a few were held collectively against the entire city. [20] It is not right to do the same things which you regarded as crimes when other people committed them. Nor is it right to consider justifiable, when you do them to

[12] The extraordinary nature of the following critique of the pre-404 democracy is discussed in the Introduction.

[13] Malicious prosecutors; cf. 25.3n.

others, the things you regarded as unjustifiable when you were suffering them. Instead, you should have the same attitude towards other people after your return home from exile as you had towards yourselves when you were exiles. By this means you will create the greatest possible unanimity, the city will be as strong as possible, and you will be voting in a way that is most distressing to your enemies.

[21] Bear in mind also, gentlemen of the jury, what happened under the Thirty, so that the crimes of your enemies may encourage you to make better plans about your own affairs. Whenever you heard that those in the town were unanimous, you had little hope of returning from exile, because you realized that our unity was the greatest hindrance in your exile. [22] But when you heard that the Three Thousand[14] were in a state of civil strife (*stasis*), that the other citizens had been formally expelled from the town, that the Thirty were no longer united, and that the people who feared for you outnumbered those who were fighting against you—it was from that moment that you began to look forward to returning from exile and punishing your enemies. You prayed to the gods for the things you saw your enemies doing, because you expected to be rescued by the wickedness of the Thirty, far more than to return because of the power of those in exile.

[23] You should therefore, gentlemen of the jury, make your plans for the future using the past as an example. You should regard as the best democrats those who want you to be united and who therefore keep to the oaths and the agreements,[15] believing that this will be the most satisfactory safeguard for the city and the greatest punishment for its enemies. Nothing could be more bitter for them than to discover that we have a role in public affairs, and to realize that the citizens are behaving just as if no charges had been laid against each other. [24] You ought to be aware, gentlemen of the jury, that those who are now in exile want as many as possible of the remaining citizens to be slandered and deprived of citizen rights, because they hope that those wronged by you will become their allies. They would welcome the sykophants being popular among you and having great power in the

---

[14] The Thirty restricted full citizen rights to three thousand of the richest Athenians.

[15] "The oaths and the agreements" is a phrase frequently used to denote the amnesty of 403.

city, because they believe that the criminal behavior of these men will be their own salvation.

[**25**] You should also remember what happened after the Four Hundred, for you will realize clearly that what my opponents advise has never benefited you, but that what I am recommending is always advantageous to both types of constitution (*politeia*). You know that Epigenes, Demophanes, and Cleisthenes[16] profited privately from the misfortunes of the city and were responsible for great damage to the community. [**26**] They persuaded you to condemn some people to death without trial, to confiscate unjustly the property of many more, and to expel others and deprive them of citizen rights. They were the sort of people who took bribes and let go those who were criminals, but came before you and destroyed those who had done nothing wrong. They did not stop until they had reduced the city to civil strife and very great disaster, while they themselves went from poverty to wealth. [**27**] But you decided to receive back the exiles, you restored citizen rights to those who had lost them, and you swore oaths about unanimity with the remainder. In the end, you would more readily have punished those who were sykophants under the democracy than those who had held office under the oligarchy. This was perfectly reasonable, gentlemen of the jury, for it is by now clear to everybody that democracy comes into being because of those who exercise power unjustly under the oligarchy, and that oligarchy has twice been established because of those who were sykophants under the democracy. It is not right, therefore, to use these men frequently as your advisers, when you have never profited even once from following their advice. [**28**] Bear in mind that of those from Piraeus[17] also, the ones who have the finest reputation, who have faced the greatest danger, and who have done you the most good, have already frequently advised your democracy to keep the oaths and the agreements,[18] because they think that this is a safeguard for the democracy: it would create immunity about the past for those from the town, and in this way the constitution would remain secure for the longest time for those from Piraeus.

---

[16] None of these three can be identified, though some scholars have suggested changing the text (cf. the Introduction at n. 3).

[17] See 25.1n.

[18] See 25.23n.

[29] You would be far more justified in placing your trust in these men rather than in my opponents, who as exiles were rescued on account of other people,[19] and after returning from exile have begun to behave as sykophants. In my opinion, gentlemen of the jury, out of those who remained in the town, the ones who have the same opinions as myself have made clear under both oligarchy and democracy what sort of citizens they are. [30] As for my opponents, it is legitimate to wonder what they would have done if somebody had allowed them to become members of the Thirty, since under the democracy they are now doing the same things as the Thirty did. Out of poverty, they have rapidly become rich. They have held many public offices but have submitted no accounts (*euthunai*). Instead, they have created suspicion among us instead of unanimity. They have proclaimed war instead of peace, and on their account we have lost the trust of the Greeks. [31] They are responsible for such great evils and for many others also. They are no different from the Thirty—except that the Thirty under an oligarchy desired the things my opponents do, whereas my opponents even under a democracy desire the same things as the Thirty. Nevertheless, they think they have a right to do evil to whomever they wish as readily as if everybody else were guilty and they themselves were totally respectable. [32] (You should not be shocked at my opponents but at yourselves—for believing that a democracy now exists, whereas what actually happens is whatever my opponents wish, and it is not those who have wronged your democracy, but those who refuse to give up their property, who pay the penalty.) They would prefer the city to be weak rather than for others to make it powerful and free. [33] They believe that because of the dangers at Piraeus, they can now do whatever they wish; but that if in the future you are rescued by other people, they themselves will lose power, whereas the others will grow stronger. So they are all similarly obstructive, if you become aware of any benefit from anybody else. [34] Anybody who wishes can easily recognize this. These men do not try to hide, but are ashamed at not being perceived as criminals. You can see part of the situation yourselves and hear about the rest from

[19] The implication (whether justifiably or otherwise) is that the speaker's opponents may have been in exile under the Thirty, but were not among the democratic counterrevolutionaries at Piraeus.

many other people. In our opinion, however, gentlemen of the jury, you should keep your agreements and your oaths towards all the citizens. [35] Nevertheless, when we see those who are responsible for evils paying the penalty, we forgive you because we remember what was done to you in the past; but when you are seen to be punishing those who are in no way responsible equally with those who are guilty, by the same vote you reduce us all to a state of suspicion . . .

26. AGAINST EUANDRUS

INTRODUCTION

The beginning of this speech is missing, because a quaternion of eight pages, which will have contained roughly four thousand words, has been lost from the Palatinus manuscript.[1] The title "Concerning the *Dokimasia* of Euandrus" is provided by a list of titles at the front of the Palatinus (which also makes clear that the gap contained not only the end of what we call Lysias 25 and the start of what we call Lysias 26, but between them another speech, *Against Nicides,* which is now lost).

The name of the candidate Euandrus, against whom the speech is directed, is not found in the extant portions of the text; the name may, however, have appeared in the lost opening of the speech, and it is likely to be correct (see below). The present hearing is repeatedly described as a *dokimasia,*[2] and although the speech is addressed to the Council of Five Hundred (e.g., 26.1), nevertheless the implication of

---

[1] For the Palatinus manuscript, see the Introduction to Lys. 5, at n. 1. The number of pages lost here has implications for the scale of the three affected speeches, because the remaining portions of Lys. 25 and of Lys. 26 in the Greek are roughly 2,000 words and roughly 1,400 words respectively. The addition of 4,000 words would give a total of 7,400 to be divided among three speeches, which implies either three medium-length speeches (2,500 words is about the length of Lys. 1, 6, or 14) or else at least one that was significantly longer than this.

[2] The judicial scrutiny of a man's right to hold a public office. There is a fuller discussion of *dokimasia* in the Introduction to Lys. 16; the other *dokimasia* speeches are Lys. 25, 31, and Fr. 9 (*Eryximachus*).

26.6 is that there will have to be a further hearing before a dikastic court. Such a double *dokimasia* was required only in the case of the nine Archons (*Ath. Pol.* 55.2), which would fit the reference to a sacrifice due to be conducted by the nine Archons as a college (26.8). At first sight this passage would seem to imply that the opponent has been selected as Basileus (the one of the nine Archons who presided over homicide cases in the Areopagus and elsewhere, and who is envisaged as conducting the sacrifice in question), and this would seem to be supported by the candidate's prospective jurisdiction over homicide cases (26.12).

A more careful reading, however, suggests that the office in question is that of the Archon himself, the member of the college who gave his name to the year. This is confirmed by the mention of orphans and heiresses (*epiklēroi:* 26.12), who were the unique concern of the Archon. Presumably the candidate will have jurisdiction over homicide not as Basileus but as member of the Areopagus (to which all former Archons belonged), and the Basileus will sacrifice not in his own right but on behalf of his colleague if no Archon has yet been confirmed in office. The reason for the delay that has allowed this situation to become a serious prospect is that the opponent is evidently not the person originally selected for the post: Leodamas, the first candidate, has already been rejected at his *dokimasia* (26.13–15), and Euandrus is now put forward as his *epilachōn* ("alternate" or "substitute"), but there will be no time for a further choice before the start of the new year (26.6).

Internal evidence gives some help in dating the speech, because of the attack on the candidate's supporter Thrasybulus at 26.23. The details here make clear that this is not the famous Thrasybulus of Steiria, who led the democratic counterrevolution in 403 and who died in 389/8 (see Lys. 28), but his namesake Thrasybulus of Collytus, who was a lesser-known though still important politician. At least one of the activities ascribed here to Thrasybulus can be dated to 387 (cf. 26.21n), and the speech must therefore be later than 387, and presumably earlier than the end of Lysias' career around 380 BC. Two pieces of external evidence, however, provide further information. The first is the list of Athenian Archons, which is fully preserved for this period and in which the name Euandrus appears for 382/1. Given the conjunction of dates and names, it is difficult to avoid the conclusion that this Euandrus is the opponent in Lysias 26, which would imply that the speaker's attack on his candidature was unsuccessful.

The other piece of external evidence is an anecdote in Aristotle (*Rhetoric* 2.23.25 = 1400a32–36), which reports the clever if evidently unsuccessful response made by Leodamas (presumably to be identified with the previous candidate mentioned at 26.13–15) to the allegation by Thrasybulus (presumably of Collytus) that he had been named (presumably as a traitor) on an inscribed stone on the Acropolis but that this had been destroyed at the time of the Thirty. This is interesting for two reasons. In the first place, it joins together a set of motives that the speaker in Lysias 26 (whose identity is unknown) is keen to separate: that Thrasybulus' support for Euandrus may have been the reason for his attack on Leodamas, and that the speaker (despite his denials at 26.13–15) may therefore have been an ally of Leodamas motivated by sour grapes. It also suggests that allegations of antidemocratic behavior before the amnesty of 403/2 could be used to destroy Leodamas as candidate at his *dokimasia* more than twenty years later, even if the similar allegations that the speaker brings against Euandrus were more vague, more farfetched, and ultimately unsuccessful. The speaker's case consists largely of an attempt to blacken Euandrus by association as one of "these men" (26.2, 26.3, 26.13, 26.14) who are to be held responsible for unspecified conspiracies. There is suspiciously little detail about the crimes (26.10, 26.20), arrests (26.18), and bereavements (26.12) for which he was allegedly responsible, or about the offices he may have held (26.9–10). Moreover, the attempt to evade the amnesty by distinguishing between "nice" and "nasty" former supporters of the oligarchy (26.16–20) seems to our minds extraordinarily specious: what is an amnesty for except to protect those who are otherwise vulnerable?

Lysias 26 is discussed as one of the case studies in Todd 1993: 285–289.

26. CONCERNING THE *DOKIMASIA* OF EUANDRUS [1]

[1] . . . instead, you[2] believe that because of the time remaining, they will not conduct a detailed *dokimasia,* because you are conscious

[1] For the title and the lost opening of the speech, see the Introduction.

[2] Evidently Euandrus ("you" in this first sentence is singular).

that you have committed many terrible crimes against them, which you expect some of them to disregard or even not to remember. That is what I am particularly angry about, if he has come before you, members of the Council, trusting in this hope—just as if those wronged by him were one group of people, and a different group were going to give a verdict about the case, instead of it being the same people who had been the victims and who were going to hear him. [2] You yourselves are responsible for this situation. You are forgetting that when the city was ruled by the Spartans, these men did not even see fit to share collective slavery with you but actually drove you out of the city. You, on the other hand, after you had made the city free, shared with them not only your freedom but also the right of sitting in justice and in assembly on matters of common concern. So they can reasonably convict you of naiveté in this matter. [3] My opponent is one of these men, and he is not content if somebody allows him to share in those activities,[3] but also claims the right to hold public office again, before paying the penalty for his crimes. I hear that today he will defend himself only briefly on the charges against him, skimming over the issues and evading the charges in his defense: he will say that they have spent a great deal of money on the city, that they have performed liturgies[4] in a spirit of competitive enthusiasm and have won many glorious victories under the democracy, and that he himself is a responsible person, and is not seen doing what other people here have the audacity to do but believes in minding his own business. [4] I do not think it difficult to refute such statements. Concerning the liturgies, for instance, it would have been better for his father not to undertake them than to spend so much of his money, because by means of them he won the trust of the People (*dēmos*) and overthrew the democracy, so that these actions are more memorable than the dedications arising out of his liturgies.[5] [5] Concerning this man's alleged love of quiet, there is no point in examining whether he is respectable

---

[3] I.e., justice and assembly; cf. 26.2.

[4] A system of compulsory public sponsorship imposed on rich Athenians (see the Introduction to Lys. 21). This included the *chorēgia* (funding a choral performance at a competitive festival), which is presumably the point of "glorious victories" here and of the "dedications" mentioned at 26.4.

[5] Cf. previous note.

now, when there is no opportunity for him to behave badly, but we should instead look at the period when he could behave as he wished, and he chose to take part in an illegal regime. That he is not at present committing any crimes is due to those who have prevented this; but my opponent's own character, and those who decided to entrust power to him, are responsible for what happened in the past. So this is the view you must take if he claims to pass his *dokimasia* on that basis; otherwise he will regard you as naive.

[**6**] Perhaps they will resort to the following argument, that there is not sufficient time for you to choose another candidate by lot, and that if you reject him at his *dokimasia,* the ancestral sacrifices will not be performed. If so, you must bear in mind that the time is already long past. Tomorrow is the only remaining day of the year. On that day, a sacrifice is performed to Zeus the Savior (*Sōtēr*), and it is not possible to man a dikastic court in contravention of the laws.[6] [**7**] If my opponent has contrived all these things in this manner, what must we expect him to do after he has passed his *dokimasia,* if he has persuaded the outgoing official to break the law for his sake? Will he contrive only a few things like that during the year? I certainly would not think so. [**8**] In addition, you need also to consider, first, whether it is better on religious grounds for the Basileus and his fellow Archons to conduct the sacrifices on behalf of the Archon-to-be,[7] as has already happened in the past, or whether my opponent also should conduct the sacrifice, even though those who know the truth have testified that he does not have clean hands;[8] and secondly, whether you have sworn to appoint to public office[9] a person who has not passed his *dokimasia,* or else to conduct a *dokimasia* first and then to garland the person who is worthy of office. That is what you should consider. [**9**] Bear in

---

[6] This argument is not as specious as might appear, because whatever the result of the present hearing, Euandrus will have to undergo a second *dokimasia* before a court, and it might not be possible to hold both hearings on the same day. The charge that the delay has been occasioned by Euandrus corrupting the outgoing officials, however, seems farfetched, given that the rejection of the previous candidate Leodamas will have held matters up.

[7] The significance of this is discussed in the Introduction.

[8] I.e., that he is polluted by blood-guilt because of the people he has killed.

[9] Or "to the Archonship."

mind also that the person who created the law about *dokimasiai* did so not least because of those who had held office under an oligarchy. He thought it would be a terrible thing if those on whose account the democracy had been overthrown should again hold office under that constitution and should gain control of the laws and of the city, which they had so shamefully and terribly mistreated when they previously took charge of it. So it would be wrong to take the *dokimasia* lightly or to think the issue is a small one and not to pay attention to the *dokimasia.* Instead, you should guard it, because the constitution and the rest of your democracy owes its security to each person holding office legitimately. [10] If he were now undergoing his *dokimasia* before becoming a member of the Council, and his name had been written on the *sanides*[10] as having served in the cavalry under the Thirty, you would reject him even if there were no accuser. But now that he is shown not merely to have served in the cavalry and as a former member of the Council,[11] but also to have committed offenses against the democracy, it would be extraordinary for you not to show the same attitude towards him. [11] What is more, if he had passed his *dokimasia* as a member of the Council, he would have served on the Council as one of five hundred along with the others for only one year. So even if he wanted to commit an offense during that period, he would easily be prevented by his colleagues. But if he is found worthy of this position, he will hold office on his own, and will gain control permanently of matters of the greatest importance, as a member of the Council of the Areopagus.[12] [12] It is important therefore that you make the *dokimasia* for this office more detailed than for the other offices. Otherwise, how do you think the rest of the citizens will

---

[10] Tablets of wood used for keeping public records where these did not need to be permanently carved on stone. The argument here is the one attacked by Mantitheus, the speaker of Lys. 16.6–7.

[11] This is the manuscript reading, but the text has been doubted, because there is no other indication that Euandrus served in the Council under the Thirty.

[12] To which members (or at least former members) of the college of nine Archons belonged for life. The jurisdiction of the Areopagus over homicide trials, and the responsibility of the Archon for cases of family law (including orphans and *epiklēroi,* here loosely translated "heiresses"), is discussed in the Introduction.

feel, when they see that a person who ought to be paying the penalty for his crimes has instead been approved by you for this type of office? Or that the man who ought himself to be on trial before the Areopagus is instead judging homicide cases? Or when they see he has been garlanded and has taken charge of heiresses and orphans, for some of whom he was himself responsible for their orphaned state? [13] Do you not believe that they will be angry, and hold you responsible, when they think back to those times when many of them were summarily dragged off to prison, were executed by these people without trial, were forced to flee their own country—and when they further realize that this same man [13] is responsible for Leodamas being rejected at his *dokimasia* and for Euandrus [14] being accepted at his, because he was the accuser of the former and plotted to defend the latter. What is Euandrus' attitude towards the city? For how many crimes has he been responsible? [14] If you are persuaded by these men, what sort of criticism would you expect? Previously, people thought you had rejected Leodamas at his *dokimasia* because you were angry, but if you approve this man, they will recognize clearly that you have not shown a fair attitude towards Leodamas. My opponents are facing a judicial hearing in your court, but you are on trial in the court of the whole city, and the city is now discovering what attitude you will take towards it. [15] None of you should think that I am accusing Euandrus as a favor towards Leodamas, simply because he happens to be my friend. Instead, I am doing it out of consideration for you and for the city. That is easy to recognize from the case itself. It is in Leodamas' interests that this man should pass his *dokimasia,* because in that way you will be heavily criticized, and you will be seen to be putting oligarchs in office ahead of those who support the People. But it is in your interests to reject Euandrus, because you will be perceived justly to have rejected Leodamas as well; whereas if you do not reject Euandrus, then you will appear to have rejected Leodamas unjustly.

[16] And yet I hear he will argue that the *dokimasia* is not about him alone but about all those who remained in the town, and he will

[13] Evidently Thrasybulus of Collytus; cf. 26.21–24 below. His role in the rejection of the previous candidate Leodamas is discussed in the Introduction.

[14] Lit. "this man," as also in the following sentence.

remind you of the oaths and the agreements,[15] in the hope that these will help him gain the approval of those who remained in the town. On behalf of the democracy, I would like to respond briefly as follows: the People (*dēmos*) does not take the same attitude towards all who remained in the town; instead, in the case of those who committed crimes like this, it takes the attitude that I say is necessary; but towards the remainder, the opposite attitude. [17] The evidence is as follows: the city has honored these men[16] no less than it has honored those who returned to Phyle and captured Piraeus.[17] And rightly so: in the case of the latter, the *dēmos* knows what sort of men they are only under a democracy, and has not experienced what sort of people they would be under an oligarchy.[18] For the former group,[19] the *dēmos* has had a sufficient indication under both constitutions, such that it is reasonable to trust them. [18] The *dēmos* believes it was due to men like these[20] that people were arrested and executed during that period, and due to the others that people escaped, because if everybody had shared the same attitude, neither the exile nor the restoration nor any of the other past events would have befallen the city. [19] What to some people seems inexplicable—how it was that those who were numerous[21] were defeated by the few at Piraeus—came about precisely

[15] I.e., the amnesty of 403/2. The people who "remained in the town (*astu*)" were those who supported the Thirty in 404/3, whereas "those who returned to Phyle and captured Piraeus" (26.17) were the democratic counterrevolutionaries. There are other attempts to evade the amnesty in Lys. 6.37–41 and 13.88–90, but this is the most specious. See further the Introduction.

[16] I.e., those oligarchs who committed no crimes.

[17] I.e., the democratic counterrevolutionaries of 404/3 (though "honored . . . no less" is a textual emendation).

[18] The argument here is obviously tendentious, but it does nevertheless display an unusually disparaging attitude towards the heroes of the democratic restoration.

[19] I.e., those oligarchs who committed no crimes.

[20] I.e., those oligarchs who had committed crimes, such as Euandrus and his supporters.

[21] In context this means the supporters of oligarchy, who probably outnumbered the democratic counterrevolutionaries in the fight at Munychia near Piraeus in 403 and were certainly better armed, but it is nevertheless paradoxical to contrast the many oligarchs with the few democrats.

because of the foresight of these men.[22] They preferred to share the *politeia*[23] with the returning exiles rather than to be slaves to the Spartans alongside the Thirty. [20] That is why the *dēmos* has honored them with the greatest honors, ahead of the exiles. It has chosen them to be Hipparchs (cavalry commanders), generals, and delegates (*presbeutai*) on its own behalf, and has never regretted this. It is on account of those who committed many crimes that the *dēmos* has established *dokimasiai,* but it made the agreements[24] for the sake of those who did nothing like that. That is the sum of my response on behalf of the *dēmos.*

[21] It is your task, members of the Council, to consider whether you would make a better decision in this *dokimasia* by placing your trust in me or in Thrasybulus,[25] who is going to defend him. This man will not be able to find any indication of hatred towards the *dēmos* on the part of me or my father or my ancestors. He will not be able to say that I participated in the oligarchy, because I came of age[26] after that date; or that my father did so, because he died in Sicily while holding public office well before the civil strife;[27] [22] or that my ancestors were subject to the tyrants, because they spent the entire time in rebellion against them. He cannot even claim that we obtained our

[22] I.e., those oligarchs who committed no crimes.

[23] "Citizenship" or "constitution" or "[process of] government."

[24] I.e., the amnesty, as at 26.16.

[25] The details make clear that this is Thrasybulus of Collytus rather than his more famous namesake Thrasybulus of Steiria (see the Introduction). One at least of the allegations in 26.23–24 is the subject of a less prejudiced account in Xenophon, who recounts the capture of an entire squadron of eight ships under Thrasybulus' command in the Hellespont in 387 (*Hellenica* 5.1.27). The allegation about the prisoners may refer to the aftermath of this battle. The alleged revolution in Boeotia cannot be identified for certain, but Thrasybulus is known to have had strong links with Thebes (Aesch. 3.138), the dominant Boeotian city.

[26] Lit. "passed the *dokimasia* as a man," referring to the judicial scrutiny faced by young men before they could become adult citizens.

[27] It is difficult to imagine a context for an Athenian holding public office in Sicily after the Athenian expedition of 415–413, which would imply that the speaker was orphaned as a young boy, but there could be advantages for an Athenian political family in having none of its members alive as adults in 411 and 404/3.

property in wartime and spent nothing on the city. Quite the reverse, our household was worth eighty talents in peacetime, and it was all spent during the war for the purpose of preserving the city. [23] Concerning Thrasybulus, however, I can say three things, each of such a scale as to be worthy of death. In the first place, he took bribes and overthrew the constitution in Boeotia and deprived us of this alliance. Secondly, he betrayed the ships and forced the city to consider its very survival. [24] And finally, by sykophancy[28] he obtained thirty minas from the prisoners of war (for whose loss he had been responsible), saying that he would not pay their ransom unless they provided him with this from their own property. Now that you know what kind of life each one of us leads, you must decide on that basis whom to trust about the *dokimasia* of Euandrus. In this way you will not be making a mistake.

---

[28] "Sykophancy" normally implies malicious prosecution, but here it suggests blackmail. Blackmail and malicious prosecution can of course be associated (by the threat of prosecuting if no payment is made), but no obvious connection is made here. The allegation that Thrasybulus had been "responsible for their loss" (lit. "whom he destroyed") is presumably intended to suggest that it was his bad generalship that had led to their capture.

27. AGAINST EPICRATES

INTRODUCTION

Lysias 27 is the first of three speeches described in the manuscript as an *epilogos,* which can denote either a peroration (implying that the first part of the speech has disappeared or was never written)[1] or else a supplementary speech (implying that the principal speech has already been delivered by somebody else).[2] Like its two successors, this is a prosecution speech in a political trial, and there are similarities also in the stridency of the tone adopted and the urge to find somebody to blame for policy failures. However, there is no indication that it derives from the same series of episodes as do Lysias 28 and 29, which belong to successive stages of the aftermath of a single military fiasco.

The legal setting of the speech is hard to determine, not least because there is an inconsistency over the way in which the hearers are addressed both as "men of Athens" (*andres Athēnaioi:* 27.1, 27.8), and as "gentlemen of the jury" (*andres dikastai:* 27.6, 27.9, 27.16). The former usage suggests that the speech was being made in front of the Assembly, presumably sitting as a judicial body to hear an *eisangelia* (impeachment); but the latter usage suggests any one of various public

[1] Possible parallels would be Lys. 18 (also described as an *epilogos*), of which the second word is "therefore," and Lys. 21 (not described as such), which opens by saying that the charges have been adequately refuted.

[2] Lys. 6 appears to be the speech of a supplementary prosecutor, as are also Lys. 14–15, even though none of these is described as an *epilogos* in the manuscript.

prosecutions that would have come before a dikastic court. From the text of the speech, we may infer that Epicrates is himself a politician of enough standing to have prosecuted other politicians in previous cases (27.1).

The impression is given that public funds are more than usually short (27.1–3), and the defendant and his friends are attacked for having been poor in peacetime but having made themselves rich at public expense as a result of a war that is apparently continuing (27.9–10). The most probable date for the speech would be some time during the Corinthian War (395–387 BC). The type of short-term crisis that is characteristic of policy failures during war might help explain why the speaker seems to think it worth his while to call for Epicrates' execution (27.16), ideally without trial (27.8–10).

27. PROSECUTION SPEECH AGAINST EPICRATES: *EPILOGOS* [1]

[1] Sufficient accusations have been made against Epicrates, men of Athens. You need to bear in mind that you have often heard these men,[2] when they want to ruin somebody unjustly, claiming that if you do not vote to convict the people they tell you to convict, your state pay will run short. [2] It is no less short today, with the effect that suffering and shame belong to you because of these men, whereas the benefits belong to them. They have found by experience that whenever they and their speeches appear responsible for your voting against justice, they can easily take money from those who are being wronged. [3] And yet what hope of safety can we have, when the survival and

[1] Either "peroration" or "supplementary speech" (see the Introduction). The full title in the manuscript reads: "Prosecution Speech against Epicrates and His Fellow Delegates, *Epilogos:* Thus Theodorus," and the first sentence reads: "Sufficient accusations have been made against Epicrates, men of Athens, and against his fellow-delegates." The rest of the speech, however, contains no reference to a delegation, and many editors suspect that Theodorus (presumably an ancient commentator) has introduced the delegates into the text after identifying Epicrates here with the leader of a delegation mentioned by Demosthenes (Dem. 19.276–277).

[2] I.e., Epicrates (and those like him) when prosecuting other people in previous trials.

nonsurvival of the city depends on money, and the defendants, who have been appointed by you as guardians, to punish those who commit offenses, nevertheless steal our money and accept bribes? This is not the first time they have been seen doing wrong, but they have been convicted of corruption previously as well. [4] The thing for which I have to criticize you is that you voted to convict Onomasas[3] but to acquit the defendant of the same offense, even though the same prosecutor was accusing all of them, and the same witnesses were testifying against them. The witnesses had not heard about it from other people but were themselves the ones who arranged the money and the bribes for the defendants. [5] And yet you all know that when you punish those who are not capable speakers, this will not set an example to prevent people wronging you, but when you punish those who are capable, then everybody will cease trying to commit offenses against you. [6] At the moment, it is safe for them to steal your property, because if they escape unnoticed, they will be able to enjoy it without fear; but if they are seen, then either they will buy their way out of danger with a share of the profits from their crimes or they will be rescued by their own influence when brought to trial. Today you must punish the defendants, gentlemen of the jury, and make an example to encourage the others to behave justly. [7] All those who manage the affairs of the city have come here, not to hear us, but to know what attitude you will have towards offenders. If therefore you vote to acquit these men, then it will not seem terrible to them that they have deceived you and are profiting from your property. If, however, you convict them and punish them with death, by the same vote you will punish the defendants and make the others better behaved in future than they now are. [8] In my opinion, men of Athens, even if you refused the defendants a trial, or declined to listen to them making their defense, and if you convicted them and sentenced them to the ultimate penalty, even so you would not be executing them without trial, but you would simply be giving them the appropriate punishment. It is not these men who are denied a trial—because you will be voting about them in full knowledge of their actions—but rather

[3] Presumably at a previous trial, but the name is unknown, and several editors think that the text is corrupt.

those who are slandered by their enemies and do not receive a full hearing on matters that you do not know about. The facts are what accuse these men, and we simply provide testimony against them. [9] I am not afraid that you will acquit them if you hear them. However, they would not in my opinion have paid an appropriate penalty if you wait to convict until after you have heard them.[4] How could this be the case, gentlemen of the jury, given that they do not even share the same interests as us? During the war, the defendants have used your property to go from poverty to riches, and you became poor on account of them. [10] The task of honorable leaders[5] is not to take away your property during your misfortunes but to give you their own property. We have reached the point where those who previously, in peacetime, were not able even to maintain themselves, are now contributing to your war taxes (*eisphorai*) and serving as choregoi[6] and building large houses. [11] And yet there was a time when you envied other people for using their ancestral property in this way. At the moment, however, the city is in such a state that you are not yet angry at what these men are stealing but are instead grateful for what you yourselves can get, as if you were receiving their money as pay rather than them stealing your property.[7] [12] What is most monstrous of all is that in private cases those who are wronged weep and receive pity, but in public cases the people who do the wrong receive pity, and you who are wronged are the ones who pity them. Now perhaps the defendants' friends and deme members will do what they have generally done in the past, which is to weep and to beg you to let them off. [13] My advice, however, is as follows: if they believe that these men are doing nothing wrong, they should demonstrate that the accusations are false and thus persuade you to acquit. But if they intend to plead in the belief that these men are guilty, it is clear that they are

---

[4] Lit. "if you convict them after hearing." The sequence of thought here is condensed, and the point of the following sentence is by no means clear.

[5] Lit. "of good demagogues." The word does not always have a pejorative tone.

[6] The *chorēgia* (cf. the Introduction to Lys. 21) was a form of liturgy or compulsory public sponsorship. Only the very rich undertook liturgies.

[7] I.e., the jurors see only the public benefits of the liturgies undertaken by the defendants, and do not notice that the resources came ultimately from public funds.

more friendly to wrongdoers than to you who are being wronged. Consequently they deserve to receive not reward (*charis*) but punishment, when you get them in your power. [14] You need to realize, moreover, that the same people have been pleading fervently with the prosecutors, in the belief that they would receive this reward more rapidly from us, because we are few, than from you—and that other people would more readily surrender your property corruptly than you yourselves would. [15] We refused to betray you, and we ask you to refuse too. Bear in mind that if we had made terms with the defendants, either because we had accepted bribes or for some other reason, you would have been exceedingly angry with us, and would have punished us whenever we came into your power, as is appropriate for criminals. And yet if you are angry with those who did not prosecute in a just manner, surely you must punish the criminals themselves. [16] You must vote now to convict Epicrates, gentlemen of the jury, and sentence him to the harshest penalties. Do not do as you used to do previously, when you voted to convict the criminals and then let them off unpunished at the sentencing (*timēsis*).[8] If you do this, you will incur the criminals' hatred rather than punish them, as if what concerned them was shame rather than punishment. You know full well that by your first vote you simply impose disgrace on those who do wrong, but it is with your sentence that you punish the criminals.

---

[8] In cases where the penalty was not fixed by statute, the conviction of the defendant in the first vote would be followed by a second vote to assess the penalty. The jury had to decide between two proposals, one from the prosecutor and one from the defendant (as most famously in the case of Socrates).

28–29. AGAINST ERGOCLES AND AGAINST PHILOCRATES

INTRODUCTION

Like Lysias 27, speeches 28 and 29 are both described in their manuscript titles as *epilogos* ("peroration" or "supplementary speech"), and they are both prosecution speeches in political trials. Unlike Lysias 27, however, the military background to this pair of speeches is well attested. They derive from successive prosecutions brought against former colleagues and associates of Thrasybulus of Steiria (the man who had led the democratic counterrevolution in 403), following Thrasybulus' final campaign and death in 390–389 BC.

Thrasybulus' naval expedition is an important episode in the Corinthian War (395–387 BC), because it achieved significant initial success (a point that predictably is not highlighted in the present speeches) but had disastrous consequences in the longer term. In his account of the expedition (*Hellenica* 4.8.25–34), Xenophon states that it was sent out to counter Spartan activity around Rhodes, which is just off the southwest coast of Asia Minor. Thrasybulus, however, decided to concentrate his initial activities on gaining direct control of the Northern Aegean grain route, and he succeeded in constructing an alliance with the Thracian king Seuthes (mentioned at Lys. 28.5), whose territory was a major source of grain, and in recovering control for the first time since the Peloponnesian War of the important cities of Byzantium (also mentioned at 28.5) and Chalcedon. He then proceeded southwards towards Rhodes, gaining control of the island of Lesbos. This success allowed him to win over various other cities, but money evidently ran short, because he resorted to a series of pillaging raids in the hope of exacting tribute from previous subject allies:[1] he never in fact reached Rhodes, and clearly such raids took him well out of his way, because he ended up dying in a skirmish at Aspendus, which is some two hundred miles east of Rhodes on the southern coast of Asia Minor.

Thrasybulus had clearly achieved some significant successes, but the costs of maintaining this level of military activity were perhaps higher than Athens could afford without the imperial revenues of the fifth century. Even more significant was the long-term impact of his expedition: despite his successes, or perhaps because of them, his activities aroused fears that the Athenians were trying to revive their fifth-century empire. Among other things, this encouraged the Great King of Persia to accept Spartan overtures (in 388), which led to his helping the Spartans to impose the Peace of Antalcidas in 387/6.[2]

The date of our two speeches cannot be precisely determined, but they clearly belong after the death of Thrasybulus (28.8) in the summer of 389 and the return of the remnants of his expedition (28.4) some time later. It would perhaps be easier to understand the speeches if sufficient time had passed for the initial hopes engendered by the expedition to have dissipated, and the disastrous diplomatic consequences to have begun to become clear. This would help account for the fate of Ergocles (evidently one of the generals who had been serving under Thrasybulus; cf. 28.12n). Since Lysias 28 is addressed apparently to the Assembly ("men of Athens," throughout), we can surmise that Ergocles is being impeached by *eisangelia,* presumably on charges of embezzlement and receiving bribes (28.3; cf. 29.2).

To a modern reader, the speaker's case would appear fairly weak, and it appears to rest largely on a perception that the expedition has been a disaster, though it is of course possible that he is simply supporting a more substantial case made in the main prosecution speech

---

[1] This is presumably the context in which the speaker claims that the defendants wronged the people of Halicarnassus (Lys. 28.12, 28.17), a city on the southeast coast of Asia Minor, some fifty miles north of Rhodes itself, though Xenophon makes no mention of it in connection with the expedition.

[2] Events leading up to the Peace of Antalcidas provide the background to Lys. 22, itself a prosecution concerned with the grain trade, and one in which the strident tone is reminiscent of Lys. 28–29.

against Ergocles. At any rate, Ergocles was convicted and executed, despite his having been one of Thrasybulus' associates in the democratic counterrevolution of 403: the possible use of such democratic credentials in Ergocles' defense is vigorously attacked at 28.12–14, although the speaker can afford to be patronizingly generous to the memory of Thrasybulus himself (28.8).

The evidence for Ergocles' fate is Lysias 29, a speech against his associate[3] Philocrates, whose property[4] has been denounced by *apographē* (writ of confiscation) on a charge of illegally withholding the confiscated property of the dead Ergocles. The case is heard by a dikastic court, and it has been suggested that some of the differences between this speech and Lysias 28 may reflect the different social composition of the audiences in the Assembly and in the lawcourt.[5]

The arguments against Philocrates are even more farfetched than those against Ergocles. They include most notably the assertion that the shortage of prosecutors is somehow an indication of the defendant's guilt (29.1), and also the incomplete alternatives at 29.5, which ignore the possibility that the defense might seek to prove that Ergocles had not had any money, as the defendant of Lysias 19 does in a similar situation.[6] However, we do not know the result of his case, and it would be dangerous either to assume acquittal because of the weakness of the arguments or to assume conviction because of the depth of popular feeling. The latter may have been dissipated by the execution of Ergocles, and Philocrates may have been less closely associated in the popular mind with the negative aspects of the expedition.

28. PROSECUTION SPEECH AGAINST ERGOCLES: *EPILOGOS*[1]

[1] The accusations are so many and so terrible, men of Athens, that in my view Ergocles would not be able to pay an adequate penalty to your democracy even by dying many deaths for each of the things

[3] On the position held by Philocrates, see 29.4n.

[4] See 29.8n.

[5] Thus R. K. Sinclair, "Lysias' Speeches and the Debate about Participation in Athenian Public Life," *Antichthon* 22 (1988): 54–66.

[6] For the parallels, see the Introduction to Lys. 19.

[1] *Epilogos* denotes either "peroration" or "supplementary speech"; see the Introduction.

he has done. It is clear that he has betrayed cities, has committed offenses against *proxenoi*[2] and against your citizens, and has gone from poverty to wealth at the expense of your property. [2] Why should he receive forgiveness, when you see that the once-large fleet these men commanded is now reduced to a few ships and is breaking up because of a lack of money, and that these men, who were poor and needy when they sailed out, have so rapidly acquired the largest property of any of the citizens? It is your task, men of Athens, to be angry at this. [3] What is more, it would be extraordinary if now, when you are yourselves so oppressed by war taxes (*eisphorai*), you were to forgive those who embezzle and who take bribes, whereas in the past, when your households were substantial and your public revenues were substantial also, you punished with death those who merely desired your property. [4] I think you would all agree that if Thrasybulus had proposed to you that he should sail out with brand-new triremes and bring them back to you in a decrepit condition, that you should take the risks while his own friends took the profits, and that he should impoverish you through war taxes, while making Ergocles and his other flatterers into the richest of the citizens—if he had proposed all this, not one of you would have allowed him to sail out with the ships, [5] particularly because as soon as you had voted that he should produce a written list of the money received from the cities, and that the officials who were with him should sail back and undergo an audit of their accounts (*euthunai*), Ergocles stated that you were once again engaging in sykophancy and hankering after the old *nomoi*.[3] He advised Thrasybulus to seize Byzantium, retain the ships, and marry the daughter of Seuthes,[4] [6] "so that you can cut short their sykophancy,"

---

[2] A *proxenos* was similar to a modern diplomatic consul, except that he took responsibility in his own city for the citizens of another city with which he had links. Among the instruments of Athenian imperial control in the fifth century had been the granting of this status to Athenian sympathizers among the subject allies, and there may be a hint here of attempts to renew this policy.

[3] The word *nomos* (pl. *nomoi*) could denote either (or possibly both) "laws," or in other words imperial tribute regulations imposed on the allies, or more broadly "customs," including habits of imperial control over Athenian imperial officials. "Sykophancy" is normally malicious prosecution, but here it may perhaps suggest a general attempt to deprive the rich of their money.

[4] For Byzantium and Seuthes, see the Introduction.

he said, "because you will make them fear for themselves, and stop them sitting and plotting against you and your friends." In this way, men of Athens, as soon as they had glutted themselves in their enjoyment of your property, they saw their own interests as separate from those of the city. [7] As soon as they become rich, they come to hate you, and they are no longer prepared to be ruled by you but to rule over you. Because they are afraid for the property they have stolen, they are ready to seize strongholds, to establish an oligarchy, and to do everything to ensure that every day you will be in the greatest dangers. They think that in this way you will cease paying attention to their crimes but will be afraid for yourselves and for the city and will do nothing about them. [8] There is no need to say more about Thrasybulus, men of Athens: he did well in ending his life as he did. It was not right for him to live after plotting such deeds, nor to be executed by you (since he was thought to have done you some good in the past), but to be removed from the city in this manner. [9] However, I see that because of the Assembly meeting the day before yesterday,[5] the others are no longer sparing any money but are purchasing their own lives from the orators, from their enemies, and from the Prytaneis,[6] and are corrupting many Athenians with money. So it is right, now you are punishing the defendant, to defend yourselves against such suspicions and to show the whole human race that there does not exist enough money to prevent you from punishing wrongdoers.[7] [10] Bear in mind, men of Athens, that it is not only Ergocles who is on trial but the entire city. Today you will demonstrate to your officials whether they should behave justly, or embezzle as much of your property as possible, while preparing an escape route, just as these men are now trying to do. You need to be fully aware of this, men of Athens: [11] if anybody betrays cities, or claims the right to embezzle money or to receive bribes, when your affairs are in such trouble, he is also handing over your walls and ships to the enemy, and establishing an oligarchy in place of a democracy. It is not right that you should be

---

[5] The precise function of this meeting is unclear, but it evidently paved the way for Ergocles' present trial.

[6] The executive committee of the Council.

[7] Evidently an effective argument, because this sentence is repeated almost verbatim at Lys. 29.13.

defeated by the defendants' preparations. Instead, you should set an example to all mankind that you will not rate either profit or pity or anything else at a higher value than the punishment of these men.

[12] I imagine, men of Athens, that Ergocles will not attempt to defend himself on the subject of Halicarnassus, his tenure of office,[8] and his own actions, but instead he will claim that he returned from exile from Phyle, that he is a democrat, and that he shared in your dangers. However, I do not take the same attitude towards all such people, men of Athens.[9] [13] As for those who shared in your dangers because they desired freedom and justice, and wanted to strengthen the laws, and hated wrongdoers, I do not regard them as bad citizens, and I do not claim that it would be unfair for their exile to be taken into account. But in the case of those who, after returning from exile, injure the People (*plēthos*) under a democracy, and enrich their own households at the expense of your property, you should much more readily be angry with them than with the Thirty. [14] At least the Thirty were elected with the specific aim of damaging you in whatever way they could, whereas you entrusted yourselves to these men so that they could make the city free and powerful. They have achieved none of this for you. Instead, their achievement has been to place you in the greatest danger, and it would therefore be much fairer for you to pity yourselves and your wives and children, not the defendants, because you are being mistreated by men like these. [15] Whenever we think we have finally achieved security, we are treated worse by your own officials than by the enemy. And yet you are all aware that you have no hope of security if your affairs are in disarray. So it is right that you should advise yourselves now to penalize these men with the utmost

---

[8] Evidently as general under Thrasybulus.

[9] For a possible context for these activities at Halicarnassus, see the Introduction at n. 1. The admission that Ergocles had been at Phyle rather than simply at Piraeus implies that he had been among the few to join the democratic counter-revolution of 403 at its outset, which would normally count strongly in his favor. The present invective is an interesting example of how to counter this point, by dividing the democratic heroes ("such people") into good ones and bad ones, so as to undermine the latter. This is the only example we have of this strategy, though a similar argument is used at Lys. 26.16–20 to distance former supporters of oligarchy from the protection of the amnesty.

severity and to demonstrate to the rest of the Greeks that you punish wrongdoers. If so, you will improve the quality of your officials. [16] That is what I advise you to do, but you need to recognize that if you accept my advice, you will be making good decisions about your own interests, but if you do not, you will render the rest of the citizens more corrupt. Moreover, men of Athens, if you acquit these men, they will feel grateful not towards you but rather towards the sums of money they have embezzled and disbursed. You will yourselves inherit their enmity, while they give thanks for their rescue to other people. [17] If you punish these men with the utmost severity, men of Athens, the people of Halicarnassus and the rest of those who were wronged by these men will believe that although they were ruined by them, nevertheless you yourselves have come to their assistance. If, however, you rescue the defendants, the allies will think that you take the same attitude as those who have betrayed them. You should therefore remember all these things[10] and repay your gratitude to your friends at the same time as you exact punishment from the wrongdoers.

29. PROSECUTION SPEECH AGAINST PHILOCRATES: *EPILOGOS*[1]

[1] In this trial, gentlemen of the jury, there has been a greater shortage of prosecutors than I expected. Many people made threats and claimed they would prosecute Philocrates, but none of them is visible today. That seems to me at least to be evidence second to none that the *apographē* (writ of confiscation) is truthful, because if he did not possess a great deal of Ergocles' money, he would not have been able to get rid of his prosecutors in this way. [2] I imagine you all realize, gentlemen of the jury, that the reason you voted to condemn Ergocles to death was because he corruptly administered the affairs of the city and built up a fortune of more than thirty talents. None of this money was found in the city. So where should we turn, and where should we seek the money? If it cannot be found in the hands of his

---

[10] Or "all these people."

[1] *Epilogos* denotes either "peroration" or "supplementary speech"; see the Introduction.

relations by marriage and those people whom he treated as his closest friends, it is hardly going to be discovered in the hands of his enemies. [3] Whom did Ergocles value more highly than Philocrates? To whom was he a closer friend? Did he not remove him from the ranks of your hoplites[2] and make him the *tamias*[3] in charge of his money, and finally appoint him as trierarch?[4] [4] It is remarkable that whereas those with property lament their service as trierarchs, this man, who had not previously possessed anything, at that time voluntarily undertook this liturgy. Ergocles did not appoint him trierarch in order that Philocrates would suffer loss, but so that he would benefit and would protect Ergocles' money, because Ergocles did not have anybody else in whom he could put more trust. [5] In my opinion, members of the jury, there are only two defenses available to Philocrates. He needs to prove either that other people possess Ergocles' money or that Ergocles was unjustly killed because he had neither embezzled any of your money nor accepted bribes. If he does not do either of these, you have already resolved to convict him, instead of being angry with those who steal from other people while showing forgiveness to those who are in possession of your own property.[5]

[6] Which Athenian does not know that in Ergocles' case three talents had been deposited as a pledge in the hands of the orators in case they were able to rescue him? But when they saw your anger as you longed for vengeance, they kept quiet and did not dare display themselves openly. At first this man[6] could not recover the money from them and said he would denounce them to the city. [7] But when he had recovered it, and had also gained control of the rest of

---

[2] Heavy-armed infantry.

[3] It is not clear whether *tamias* (treasurer or steward) denotes the steward of Ergocles' own property, or the treasurer of public property controlled by Ergocles in his capacity as general.

[4] The trierarchy was a form of liturgy (compulsory public sponsorship; cf. the Introduction to Lys. 21), and involved paying for the upkeep of a warship for a year and commanding it. It was an expensive responsibility as well as an honor. Registration of trierarchs was a responsibility of the generals.

[5] These are hardly comprehensive alternatives, and another possibility is suggested in the Introduction.

[6] I.e., Philocrates.

Ergocles' money, he reached such a level of audacity that he has produced witnesses who will testify for him that of all mankind he was particularly hated by Ergocles. But could you imagine him, members of the jury, being so insane that he voluntarily served as trierarch, when Thrasybulus was general, and Ergocles was on bad terms with himself?[7] How else could he have been more quickly ruined or more devastatingly humiliated?

[8] Enough has been said about these matters. I believe you should assist yourselves, and should punish those who do wrong much more readily than you pity those who possess the property of the city. Philocrates will not be losing any of his own property[8] but will be giving you back what is yours, and much more will be left over for him. [9] It would indeed be extraordinary, gentlemen of the jury, if in your anger at those unable to contribute their own property to war taxes (*eisphorai*), you were to confiscate their possessions on the grounds that they were criminals,[9] and were not to punish those who possess your property, but were instead to deprive yourselves of the money and have the defendants as particularly troublesome enemies. [10] As long as they know that they possess your property, they will never give up their hostility towards you, in the belief that only the city's misfortunes will provide a release from their difficulties.

[11] In my opinion, gentlemen of the jury, Philocrates should be on trial not simply for money but for his life. It would indeed be extraordinary if those who are accomplices when the property of private individuals is stolen were to be liable to the same penalties as the thieves, whereas the defendant, who connived with Ergocles when he was stealing the property of the city and when he received bribes over the conduct of your affairs, should not face the same punishment but should receive as a reward for his wickedness the property stolen by Ergocles. They deserve your anger, gentlemen of the jury. [12] When

---

[7] I.e., Philocrates. The possibilities for conflict in such a situation are illustrated by Dem. 50.48–52, where Apollodorus claims that as trierarch, he had been afraid that the general would arrest him for disobeying an allegedly illegal order.

[8] I.e., if he is convicted. The wording of this sentence may suggest that only part of Philocrates' property is under threat of confiscation, but it may be an attempt to imply that it is only what does not belong to him that is at issue.

[9] I.e., for nonpayment of tax.

Ergocles was convicted, these men went around the Assembly and said that five hundred from Piraeus had been bribed by them, and sixteen hundred from the town (*astu*).[10] They pretended that they had more confidence in the money than fear of their own crimes. [13] On that occasion you demonstrated to them—and today as well, if you are wise, you will make the point clear to all mankind—that there does not exist enough money[11] to prevent you from punishing those you catch committing crimes, and that you will grant no immunity to those who pillage and steal your property. That is what I advise you to do. [14] You all know that Ergocles sailed out not to win honor at your hands but to make money. Nobody else has that money, besides the defendant. If you are wise, you will take back what belongs to you.

---

[10] Following J. Roy (*Electronic Antiquity* 3.3 [December 1995]), I take this to denote those who now live in Piraeus and in the town, rather than (as was traditionally thought) the former democratic counterrevolutionaries and former supporters of the Thirty (which would be "five hundred of those from Piraeus," etc.). The vagueness of the conspiratorial plural ("these men") implies that the allegation of mass bribery may rest on little more than rumor, but the use of specific numbers is interesting, even if it merely reflects what was perceived as plausible.

[11] Cf. Lys. 28.9n.

30. AGAINST NICOMACHUS

INTRODUCTION

The end of the fifth century saw extensive revision of the laws of Athens. A commission of *anagrapheis*[1] was appointed to undertake this task after the overthrow of the first oligarchic revolution of 411 BC and served for six years; a second commission, appointed by the restored democracy following the oligarchy of 404/3, served for a further four years.[2] Nicomachus, who is the defendant in this case, is said to have served on both commissions (30.2, 30.4). He is not widely known outside this speech. A passing reference to him in Aristophanes' *Frogs* (1504–1514), dating from 406/5, simply identifies him as one of a group of politicians and of public officials who would be better dead. Nor do we know anything about the speaker, who is the prosecutor.

We know rather more about the process of legal revision, which is alluded to in various literary sources, including most notably a highly confusing account given by Andocides (And. 1.71–89). Moreover, there survive pieces of several inscriptions that were produced either by Nicomachus and his colleagues or at least by other related boards of officials. Most famous of these is the homicide law attributed to the seventh-century legislator Dracon, as reinscribed in 409/8.[3] More directly relevant to this speech, however, are the scattered fragments of

[1] *Anagrapheus* (pl. *anagrapheis*) denotes somebody who causes an official text to be written in a public place.

[2] Presumably therefore 410/09 to 405/4 for the first commission, and 403/2 to 400/399 for the second.

[3] Translated in Fornara 1983: no. 15.

a calendar of sacrifices, dating evidently from the period immediately after 403/2;[4] it is generally assumed that this is the product of Nicomachus' second term, which would help explain the heated discussion of proper and improper expenditure on public sacrifices at 30.17–22.

The date of the speech can be determined within a few months. The manuscript title describes the procedure as *euthunai,* which is the judicial examination of an official's accounts, and more generally of his conduct in office, at the end of his term. This would suggest a date for the speech shortly after the end of the calendar year, in mid-Summer 399. *Euthunai,* however, may be no more than a copyist's guess, and other evidence suggests *eisangelia* (impeachment).[5] This could be brought against a currently serving as well as a former official, so it is possible that the reference to "four years" at 30.4 is inclusive, that Nicomachus has not yet laid down his office, and that the case has been initiated by the anonymous prosecutor in the Spring or early Summer of 399.

The main problem with the speech is that it is extremely difficult to identify the charges against Nicomachus. We would expect to find these charges set out at the start of the speech, but there is very little here that is specific. To a modern reader, such vagueness appears weak, but we should not necessarily therefore conclude that Nicomachus will have been acquitted. As an expert in the technicalities of law, he may have been politically a marginal figure who was open to attack; and part of the background may be the politically charged atmosphere that appears to underlie Lysias 13 (a speech with striking similarities to this one, which may suggest that the two cases are close in time). Moreover, whatever the vagueness of the charges, the speaker certainly deploys his innuendoes with considerable sophistication. For instance, the allegation that Nicomachus "published some laws and erased others, while receiving payment on a daily basis" (30.2) is meant to sound

---

[4] A representative fragment is translated in Harding 1985: no. 9.

[5] The claim that Nicomachus has consistently refused to submit his accounts (30.5) might fall flat if that was what he was now doing. Moreover, a preliminary hearing before the Council is characteristic of *eisangelia,* and there may be an allusion to such a hearing at 30.7. (The present speech is addressed to a dikastic court [30.1], which would fit either process.) See further Todd, "Against *Nikomakhos*" (cited below), at pp. 104–106.

as if he took bribes for perverting the law code, but it need formally mean no more than that he had a post for which he received a daily stipend and that he was allowed some discretion over the texts he selected as authorities. Similarly, the complaint that he should have been able to complete his second term of office within thirty days (30.4) is clearly meant to recall the allegation that he had improperly extended his first term beyond the four months to which he had been appointed (30.2), but it is carefully not said that the thirty days was the period of the second appointment. Even the allegation that Nicomachus has failed to present his accounts (30.5) is inconclusive, because we have no evidence that an extraordinary official appointed without a fixed term of office was liable to do so during the course of his term.

For a general reading of the speech, with further discussion of many of the issues raised, see S. C. Todd, "Lysias *Against Nikomakhos:* The Fate of the Expert in Athenian Law," in L. Foxhall and A. D. E. Lewis, eds., *Greek Law in Its Political Setting: Justifications not Justice* (Oxford, 1996), 101–131.

30. PROSECUTION SPEECH AGAINST NICOMACHUS [1]

[1] It has on occasion happened, gentlemen of the jury, that men have been brought to trial, and although they were seen to be guilty, they nevertheless obtained forgiveness from you by making a show of their ancestors' merits and their own benefactions. But since you are prepared to accept it if defendants show that they have performed any service for the city, then I think you ought to listen also to the prosecutors, if they can show that the defendants are criminals of long standing. [2] Now to tell you that the father of Nicomachus was a public slave, to tell you how Nicomachus conducted himself as a young man, to tell you how old he was when he was presented to his phratry[2]—all this would be a major undertaking. But is there any-

[1] Reasons for rejecting the manuscript title ("Prosecution Speech against Nicomachus the Clerk at His *Euthunai*") are discussed in the Introduction.

[2] It is probable that every male Athenian belonged to a phratry, as well as to a deme: you became a member of your father's deme on coming of age but were normally presented to his phratry in infancy. The innuendo is that Nicomachus was not born a citizen but has squeezed himself late into his phratry.

body who does not know the damage he did to the city after he was appointed *anagrapheus*[3] of the laws? He had been instructed to publish the laws of Solon[4] within four months. Instead, he set himself up as lawgiver (*nomothetēs*) in Solon's place, he extended his term of office from four months to six years, and he received payment on a daily basis for publishing some laws and erasing others.[5] [3] We were reduced to such straits that we had laws rationed out to us at the hands of this man, and rival litigants presented contradictory laws in the lawcourts, both sides insisting that they had received them from Nicomachus. When the Archons imposed summary fines (*epibolai*) on him, and summoned him before a lawcourt, he still refused to surrender the laws. The city had been reduced to utter disaster[6] before he gave up his office and agreed to submit accounts (*euthunai*) for his conduct of office. [4] And in fact, gentlemen of the jury, since he paid no penalty for those deeds, he has now established a similar office again for himself. But in the first place, this is a man who held office as *anagrapheus* for four years, even though he could have relinquished his post within thirty days. Moreover, although the things he was to publish were strictly defined,[7] he put himself in authority over the whole of it, and although he has handled more public business than anybody else ever has, he alone among those who have held office did not submit his accounts. [5] Others give an account of their office every prytany,[8] but you, Nicomachus, have not seen fit to put your accounts in writing at any time during four years. You believe that

[3] For the term, see the Introduction at n. 1.

[4] By the time of this speech, the sixth-century reformer Solon had come to be regarded as the founding father of Athenian law, to the extent that "the laws of Solon" became a synonym for "the laws of Athens currently in force."

[5] For these charges, and for the dates, see the Introduction.

[6] Evidently a reference to the battle of Aegospotami in 405. Nicomachus presumably did undergo *euthunai* before the Thirty came to power, or Lysias would have said otherwise.

[7] Lit. "it was defined, out of which things he must publish." This presumably means "the sources from which he was to draw his information," but Lysias may want us to think it means "the areas of law in which he was to have competence."

[8] A prytany was the term of office (lasting 35–36 days) of one of the ten tribal contingents on the Council, who served successively as the Council's executive committee. See the Series Introduction.

you alone among citizens have the right to go on holding office for an extended period—without having to submit accounts, without having to obey the decrees, without having to take any notice of the laws. Instead, you published some things and erased others, and you reached such a pitch of arrogance (*hubris*) that you thought the property of the city belonged to you, who are yourself public property. [**6**] And so it is your duty, gentlemen of the jury, to punish Nicomachus, recalling what sort of people his ancestors were and the ingratitude he has displayed towards you by his illegal behavior. Since he has not paid the penalty for his crimes individually, you must exact satisfaction now for all of them collectively.

[**7**] It is possible, gentlemen of the jury, that he will attempt to slander me, since there is nothing he can say in his own defense. But I think you should trust what this man says about my affairs only if I am given an opportunity to defend myself and fail to demonstrate that he is lying. If he attempts to repeat what he said to the Council, that I was a member of the Four Hundred,[9] you should bear in mind that those who make such allegations will turn four hundred into more than a thousand. Indeed, those whose aim is to stir up slander make these defamatory comments about men who were still children or were out of the country at the time. [**8**] As for me, so far from membership of the Four Hundred, I was not even registered among the Five Thousand. This seems to me a terrible thing: if I were suing him over a private agreement, and had clearly demonstrated that he was in the wrong, not even my opponent would expect to be acquitted on the basis of a defense of this sort; but when he is on trial concerning the affairs of the city, he believes he should escape the penalty he owes you by bringing accusations against me.

[**9**] It is, in my opinion, even more astonishing that Nicomachus thinks he should be allowed to rake up grudges[10] unjustly against oth-

---

[9] The first oligarchy, who were in power for four months in the summer of 411 BC, came to office promising to create a body of five thousand citizens who would enjoy full political rights under their regime.

[10] The verb used is *mnēsikakein,* which is clearly an allusion to the most famous clause of the amnesty agreement of 403/2 ("it shall be unlawful for anybody to remember wrongs [*mnēsikakein*] against anybody": *Ath. Pol.* 39.6), where it evidently denotes use of events before the democratic restoration as the basis of a judicial charge, including presumably the following anecdote about Cleophon.

ers, when I shall prove that he has been plotting against the People. Please listen carefully. It is legitimate, gentlemen of the jury, for you to accept accusations of this kind against people like this, who now claim to be democrats but were at that time subverting the democracy. [10] For when your ships had been lost[11] and the revolution was being engineered, Cleophon[12] criticized the Council, saying that it was engaged in a conspiracy and was making decisions which were not in the best interests of the city. Satyrus[13] of the deme Cephisia, a member of the Council, persuaded them to imprison him and hand him over to a dikastic court. [11] The Council wanted to destroy Cleophon and were afraid that they would not be able to get him executed there. So they persuaded Nicomachus to produce a law which said that the Council should judge the case together with the *dikastai* (jurors). And this fellow, the greatest of criminals, was so blatantly part of the plot that he produced this law on the day the trial was held. [12] One could bring many accusations against Cleophon, gentlemen of the jury, but this much is conceded by everybody: those who were destroying the democracy wanted to remove him, more than any other citizen; and Satyrus and Chremon, who became members of the Thirty,[14] accused Cleophon not because they were angry on your behalf but so that after killing him they could make you suffer. [13] And they achieved this by the law that Nicomachus produced. Even those of you who believed that Cleophon was a bad citizen, gentlemen of the jury, should remember this: perhaps there were one or two criminals among those

---

[11] A euphemism for the battle of Aegospotami in 405 BC. The "revolution" is that of the Thirty, who came to power in summer 404.

[12] Cleophon was the leading "demagogue" or radical democratic leader in the final decade of the fifth century; cf. the parallel account of his execution in Lys. 13.12.

[13] Satyrus is known to have been one of the Eleven, the officials in charge of prisons and executions, under the Thirty in 404/3 (Xen., *Hellenica* 2.3.54). It is not inherently implausible that he was a member of the Council in 405/4, as stated here, but not everything said in this speech about Satyrus is necessarily reliable (see 30.12n).

[14] Xenophon's list of the original members of the Thirty (Xen., *Hellenica* 2.3.2) includes Chremon but not Satyrus, so what is said here about the latter is probably untrue (cf. 30.10n), though there remains the possibility that he was later chosen to fill a casual vacancy.

who died under the oligarchy, but you were nevertheless angry with the Thirty even on account of men like this, because the Thirty killed them not as criminals but for partisan ends. [14] And if he tries to defend himself against these charges, you should remember that he produced the law in question at a moment of crisis when the constitution was being overthrown, that he did this to curry favor with those who overthrew the democracy, and that he gave judicial authority to the same Council in which Satyrus and Chremon held the dominant power and under which Strombichides and Calliades and many other excellent citizens perished.[15]

[15] I would not have mentioned this, if I had not heard that he would try to save himself in defiance of justice by portraying himself as a democrat and that he would use his exile as an indication of his goodwill towards the People. But I could point out others who also conspired to overthrow the democracy, some of whom were killed, while others went into exile and lost their share in the *politeia.*[16] So it is not legitimate for him to have this reckoned to his credit. [16] This man has contributed his share to your exile, but your democracy was responsible for his return. It would be terrible if you were to feel grateful for what he suffered involuntarily, while failing to exact satisfaction for the crimes he committed deliberately.

[17] I gather he claims I have committed impiety by destroying the sacrifices.[17] If I had been the person who proposed the laws about the process of publishing (*anagraphē*), then I admit that Nicomachus

---

[15] Strombichides is highlighted at Lys. 13.13 (immediately after the parallel account of Cleophon's death; cf. 30.10n) as one of the generals and Taxiarchs (regimental commanders) and other citizens whom Agoratus is charged with having denounced to their deaths. Calliades cannot be firmly identified (the name is a common one) but may have been one of his colleagues.

[16] Nicomachus was presumably exiled under the Thirty, but the implication of 30.16 is that he was not active among the democratic counterrevolutionaries at Phyle or at Piraeus. *Politeia* in this passage may denote either "citizenship" or "constitution."

[17] *Thusiai:* what follows is clearly connected with the surviving fragments of the inscription recording the sacrificial calendar (for which see the Introduction), but many of the details are obscure.

would have been entitled to say things like this about me. But as it is, I believe that he should obey the established rules that we hold in common. When he claims that I am committing impiety by saying that we should perform the sacrifices from the ancestral and inscribed laws and decrees,[18] I am astonished at his failure to realize that he is accusing the city also—for this is what you have decreed. And if you, Nicomachus, think this is so terrible, then presumably you believe that those who used to sacrifice only from the ancestral laws were committing the greatest of crimes. [18] And yet, gentlemen of the jury, in matters of religious observance we need not learn from Nicomachus, but should look instead to those who have gone before us. Our ancestors, who celebrated their sacrifices from the ancestral laws, handed down to us the greatest and most blessed city in Greece, so it is fitting for us to perform the same sacrifices as they did, if for no other reason than the good fortune that has resulted from these rites. [19] How then can anybody display a greater sense of religious propriety than mine? I am claiming that our sacrifices should be, first, in the manner of our ancestors; secondly, in the best interests of the city; and thirdly, the ones that the democracy has decreed and that we are capable of funding from our revenues. You, on the other hand, Nicomachus, are doing the reverse of this. By publishing more than those that were commanded, you have caused our income to be spent on these, rendering it inadequate to pay for the traditional sacrifices. [20] For example, some of the rites written in the ancestral laws remained uncelebrated last year, to the value of three talents. One can hardly say that the city's income was insufficient, because if this man had not published sacrifices costing more than six talents, our revenues would have sufficed for the traditional sacrifices with three talents left over for the city. I will provide you with witnesses for the things that I have said.

---

[18] Lit. "the *kurbeis* and the *stēlai* according to the *sungraphai.*" *Sungraphai* here probably denotes a decree; *stēlai* (which is a textual emendation, though it is accepted by most editors) are "pillars" of stone with texts inscribed on them; none of our sources is sure what a *kurbis* was, but Dracon and Solon, lawgivers of the Archaic period, are both said to have inscribed their laws on "*axones* and *kurbeis,*" so the word presumably denotes some form of ancestral regulation.

[WITNESSES]

[21] I ask you therefore, gentlemen of the jury, to bear in mind that when we act according to the decrees (*sungraphai*), the traditional sacrifices are performed in full, but when we act according to the inscribed stones (*stēlai*) which this man has put up, many of the rites are suppressed. And in the middle of everything, this temple robber charges around, claiming that his activity as *anagrapheus* owes more to religious propriety than to penny-pinching. Moreover, he says that if his work does not please you, you should erase it. By this means he expects to persuade you that he has committed no crime, but this is the man who in two years has already spent twelve talents more than necessary, and has tried to defraud the city of six talents per year, [22] even though he could see that the city needed money, that the Spartans were making threats whenever we did not send them payments, that the Boeotians were resorting to raids because we were unable to repay two talents, and that the shipsheds and the city walls were in ruins.[19] He also knew that whenever the Council in a given year has enough money for its administration, it does no harm, but whenever it is reduced to desperation, it is forced to accept impeachments (*eisangeliai*), to confiscate the property of the citizens, and to allow itself to be persuaded by those of the orators whose advice is most corrupt. [23] So do not get angry with those who serve on the Council at any given time, gentlemen of the jury, but with those who have reduced the city to such poverty. Those who want to steal public property are paying careful attention to the result of Nicomachus' trial. If you acquit him, you will make them effectively immune from punishment. If, however, you convict him and sentence him to the ultimate penalty, by that single verdict you will punish the defendant and make the others more virtuous. [24] You realize, gentlemen of the jury, that it will be an example to the others, so that they will not dare

---

[19] We have no other evidence for the specific financial problems mentioned here, but the restored democracy is said to have paid back to the Spartans the money borrowed by the Thirty to pay for mercenaries (*Ath. Pol.* 40.3), and the democratic counterrevolutionaries are known to have received support for their coup from Thebes, the dominant city in Boeotia (e.g., Xen., *Hellenica* 2.4.2., though there is no explicit mention there of financial help).

to commit offenses against you, if you punish not those who are ineffective at speaking but instead those who are expert orators. And who in the city deserves to be punished more than Nicomachus? Who has done less good for the city or more evil against it? [**25**] He became *anagrapheus* of secular and religious matters,[20] and has offended equally in both. Remember that you have already executed many of the citizens for theft of public money, and yet the injuries that they did you were merely temporary, whereas these men have damaged the city for all time by receiving bribes for their publishing of the laws.

[**26**] Why would anybody wish to acquit my opponent? Perhaps because he has been brave in the face of the enemy and has been present in many battles by land and by sea? But while you were sailing out to face danger, he stayed at home and perverted the laws of Solon. Or because he has spent his resources and contributed to numerous war taxes (*eisphorai*)? But not only has he given you nothing of his own: he has taken much of your property. [**27**] Or perhaps on account of his ancestors? Admittedly some people have in the past been forgiven by you for that reason. But if this man deserves to be executed on his own account, then on account of his ancestors he ought to be sold into slavery. Or because if you acquit him now, he will repay this kindness in future? But this is a man who has no recollection even of the benefits he has already received from your hands. And yet from a slave he has become a citizen, from poverty he has risen to riches, and instead of a low-grade clerk (*hupogrammateus*), he is now a lawgiver (*nomothetēs*). [**28**] And you as well, gentlemen, deserve criticism on this point: whereas your ancestors chose as lawgivers Solon and Themistocles and Pericles,[21] because they believed that the laws would be of the same caliber as the legislators, you have chosen Teisamenus[22] the son of Mechanion, and Nicomachus, and other persons from subordinate clerical posts. Although you realize that public office is being

[20] Lit. "of *hosia* and of *hiera.*" This may (but need not) imply that Nicomachus' commission dealt with the former in 410–404, and the latter in 403–399.

[21] Solon (590s BC) is an obvious choice as the founding father of Athenian law. Themistocles (480s–470s) and Pericles (440s–429) are major political figures, but their importance as lawgivers (despite Pericles' citizenship law) is less obvious.

[22] Evidently the same as the proposer of the decree quoted at And. 1.83–84.

destroyed by men of this caliber, you still put your trust in them. [29] Worst of all, even though a man cannot legally serve twice as clerk under the same official,[23] you have allowed the same man to remain for an extended period in full control of matters of the greatest importance. And finally, you have selected Nicomachus as *anagrapheus* of our ancestral regulations, when by his ancestry he has no part in the city. [30] As a result, a man who deserves to be judged by the People can be seen conspiring to overthrow the People.[24] It is time for you to change the way things have been done. Stop continually putting up with ill-treatment from these men. Stop criticizing criminals in private, only to acquit them as soon as you have a chance to exact punishment.

[31] On this subject I have said enough. But I want to add a few words to you about those who are going to come and plead for him. Certain of his friends, and certain of those who hold power in the city, have been getting ready to beg him off. Some of them, I fancy, would do better to compose a defense for their own actions rather than choose to try and rescue these criminals. [32] In my opinion, gentlemen of the jury, it is a terrible thing that these men made no attempt to beg this single individual, who had suffered no wrong at the hands of the city, to stop committing offenses against you. Now, however, they are seeking to persuade you, who are many, and who have been wronged by this man, that there is no need to punish him. [33] You can see these men eagerly striving to rescue their friends. In the same way, you must punish your enemies, because you know that it is to these men above all that you will display your good character, if you exact punishment from criminals. Bear in mind that none of those who will be pleading for him has done as much good for the city as the damage he has done it—so you have more right to exact vengeance than these men have to offer help. [34] It is important for you to realize that these same men have made repeated approaches to the

---

[23] I.e., to continue as clerk under successive holders of the same office in successive years.

[24] *Dēmos* (the People of Athens) can denote both "the Assembly" and "the democracy."

prosecutors, but they have not won us over.[25] They have come into court with the aim of testing your verdict. They hope to deceive you, and for the future to gain immunity to do whatever they choose. [35] We, for our part, refused to yield despite their pleas. In the same way, we beg you not simply to hate the criminal before the trial, but to demand satisfaction in court from those who try to eradicate your process of lawgiving. It is in this way that all matters concerning the constitution will be administered within the law.

---

[25] We have only the speaker's word for the allegation that the defense have tried to buy him off.

31. AGAINST PHILON

INTRODUCTION

This is one of several speeches in Lysias that relate to the *dokimasia* of prospective officials: that is, the judicial scrutiny of a person's right to hold a public office to which he has been appointed.[1] Here the issue is membership of the Council of Five Hundred (as in Lys. 16), and the speaker is challenging the candidature of a man named Philon (31.1), who belongs to Acharnae, the largest of the Athenian demes (31.16n), but who cannot be otherwise identified. We know nothing about the speaker except that he is a member of the outgoing Council (31.1), before which the hearing takes place.

As is usual in the *dokimasia* speeches of Lysias, the allegations against the candidate focus on his behavior at the time of the Thirty, but this time there is an unusual twist. Philon is accused not of remaining in Athens as a supporter of the oligarchs, but of evading his moral responsibility to participate in the civil strife that accompanied the democratic counterrevolution, by having left Attica and gone to live in Oropus at the outbreak of the conflict (31.8–9).[2] This argument has elicited considerable discussion from scholars, because the speaker makes no reference to a law that is attributed to the sixth-century reformer Solon by later sources: "If anybody did not take up a position[3] alongside one of the two groups at a time when the city

---

[1] The procedure is discussed in the Introduction to Lys. 16; the other *dokimasia* speeches are Lys. 25, 26, and Fr. 9 (*Eryximachus*).

[2] Oropus was on the border between Attica and Boeotia. At this date it evidently had at least the formal status of an independent community, though at various times it was under Athenian or Theban control.

[3] Lit. "place his shield" (Gk. *hopla thesthai*).

was in a state of *stasis* (civil strife), he was to suffer *atimia* (loss of civil rights) and to have no share in the city" (*Ath. Pol.* 8.5). Not only is no such law mentioned in the speech, but the speaker explicitly counters the argument that there was no law banning what Philon had done by claiming that the reason no such law existed was that no legislator could have predicted that anybody would behave as badly as Philon (31.27–28). Earlier scholars tended to infer that the law attributed to Solon was unknown at the time of the speech, which would suggest either that a genuine law had become so obsolete as to have been forgotten, or more likely that the law had never existed but was a fourth-century invention after the time of Lysias. More recently, it has been suggested that the speaker's phrasing betrays knowledge of the law but that he is deliberately refusing to mention it, perhaps because it only covered people who were present at the outbreak of strife, whereas Philon had been at Oropus.[4] The view that the speech is deliberately alluding to the law has not won widespread acceptance, but it is now commonly though not universally conceded that the speech is compatible with the law's being genuine.[5]

The argument that Philon has evaded his moral responsibility is cleverly manipulated, because the speaker begins with the inclusive assumption—designed to win the sympathies of former oligarchs as well as former democrats among his audience—that what is culpable is neutrality, and that it would have been legitimate for Philon or anybody else to have joined either the oligarchs in the town or the democrats when they were at Phyle and at Piraeus (31.8), but he moves towards the assumption that what is culpable is Philon's failure to have joined the democratic side (31.9, 31.15). To this is added the prejudicial assertion (it is hardly an argument) that Philon operated as a bandit while based at Oropus (31.17–19), and the more specific allegation that he had failed to bury his mother after her death (31.20–23). The latter charge is important, because maltreatment of parents was something

---

[4] Thus J. A. Goldstein, "Solon's Law for an Activist Citizenry," *Historia* 21 (1972): 538–545. The linguistic parallels he suggests are the phrase "take up his position" (lit. "place his shield") at 31.14, and the verb "share" (e.g., 31.5, 31.10, 31.14), but the latter in particular is such a common metaphor as to be unremarkable.

[5] Carey 1989: 198–200, discusses the responses of various scholars to Goldstein's paper, while himself arguing that the law is genuine but obsolete.

that was explicitly investigated at the *dokimasia* of the Archons (*Ath. Pol.* 55.3) and probably therefore of other officials also. There may, however, have been good reasons for Philon's mother to entrust her burial to somebody else, if her son was abroad when she died.

The date of the speech is unclear, though it clearly belongs at least a year after the democratic restoration of 403/2, because there is already a democratic Council in office, of which the speaker is a member. We do not know the result.

There is a useful commentary by Carey 1989.

31. ACCUSATION AGAINST PHILON AT HIS *DOKIMASIA*

[1] I would never have expected Philon to reach such a level of audacity, members of the Council, that he would be willing to appear before you to face his *dokimasia.* However, since he is audacious not just in one respect but in many, and since I took an oath when I became a member of the Council that I would offer the best advice for the city, [2] and since moreover it is required by that oath to make known if one is aware that any of those selected by lot is not suitable to serve on the Council—for all these reasons I shall deliver the accusation against Philon here. I am not pursuing any private hatred, nor have I been stirred by speaking ability and the habit of addressing you. Instead, I put my confidence in the scale of his crimes, and in the oaths that I have sworn and intend to keep. [3] You will be aware that I have not had as much practice in exposing this man's nature as he has had in attempting to be a criminal. Nevertheless, if I should omit some argument from the accusation, he should not deserve to benefit on that account but should instead be rejected to the extent that my explanation is sufficient. [4] I would have spoken inadequately because of my ignorance of all he has done, but adequately because of his criminal nature. I ask those of you who are more skilled at speaking than I am to show that his crimes are even greater. Let them subsequently accuse Philon on the basis of what they know about any topic that I may omit, because you need to make your decision about what sort of man he is not simply on the basis of what is said by me.

[5] My contention is that it is not right for anybody else to offer advice in our affairs, other than those who in addition to being citizens are also enthusiastic about their citizenship. For these people, it makes

a great difference whether this city is prosperous or not, because they believe it is necessary for them to share in what is bad, just as they share in what is good. [6] As for those who are citizens by birth, but who take the view that every place in which they possess anything[1] is for them a fatherland, it is clear that such people would even discard the public good of the city and pursue their own private profit, because they regard not the city but their property as their fatherland. [7] I shall demonstrate that my opponent Philon has placed a higher value on his personal safety than on the public danger faced by the city, and that he regarded it as better that he should go through life without danger than that he should rescue the city by undergoing danger like the rest of the citizens.

[8] When the city suffered misfortune, members of the Council,—I shall mention this only to the extent that I am forced to do so[2]—this man, together with the majority of the citizens, was banished by herald from the town by the Thirty.[3] For a time, he lived in the countryside,[4] but when those from Phyle returned from exile to Piraeus, and not only those from the countryside but also those from abroad[5] rallied together, some of them to the town and others to Piraeus,[6] each bringing help to the fatherland to the extent that he was able, this man did the opposite of all the other citizens.[7] [9] He collected

[1] Or perhaps, "every place where they have any business." Lit. "every land in which they may possess necessities."

[2] The language of "misfortune" in Lysias is normally a euphemism for the crushing Athenian defeat at Aegospotami in 405, but here it seems to be broader, encompassing the siege of Athens in 405/4, and the surrender to Sparta, followed by the establishment of the oligarchy of the Thirty, in 404.

[3] Towards the end of their term of office, the Thirty restricted full citizen rights to three thousand of the wealthiest citizens and banished the rest from the town (*astu*).

[4] I.e., still in Attica, and therefore in Athenian sovereign territory.

[5] I.e., outside Attica.

[6] I.e., some to join the oligarchs in the town, and others the democratic counterrevolutionaries, who had initially occupied Phyle and then marched on Piraeus.

[7] The speaker implies here that it would have been morally legitimate for Philon to have supported the oligarchy. The contrast with 31.9 and 31.15 is explored in the Introduction.

together his property from here and went to live abroad. He paid the metic tax at Oropus, and lived there under a *prostatēs,*[8] preferring to be a metic with them rather than a citizen with us. He did not even change sides, as some of the citizens did when they saw that those from Phyle were succeeding in their efforts. He did not think it worth sharing in their success but preferred to come back to a task that had been accomplished rather than to join in the return from exile and accomplish something that would benefit the community (*politeia*) as a whole. He did not go to Piraeus, and at no time did he offer himself for your military service. [10] And yet if this man had the audacity to betray us when he saw us succeeding, what on earth would he have done if we had been unsuccessful? Those who, because of private misfortune, did not share in the dangers which then faced the city, deserve to be treated with a certain leniency, because nobody suffers misfortune voluntarily. [11] But those who did this deliberately deserve no forgiveness, since they acted like this not because of misfortune but with deliberation. There is an equitable custom established among all mankind, that when dealing with the same offenses, we should be most angry at those who are most able to avoid doing wrong, but should forgive those who are poor or physically weak, because of the presumption that they are committing crimes unwillingly. [12] Consequently this man deserves no forgiveness, because he was not physically incapable of enduring hardship, as you yourselves can see. Nor, as I shall demonstrate, did he lack the property to undertake liturgies. Imagine somebody who, to the extent that he was capable of assisting, was simply evil. Surely it is reasonable for such a man to be hated by all of you. [13] What is more, if you reject this man at his *dokimasia,* you will not incur the hatred of even a single citizen. He clearly betrayed not just one side but both. So it is not fitting that he should be treated as a friend of those who were in the town, because he did not deign to join them when they were in danger, or as a friend of those who captured Piraeus, because he was not willing to return with them from exile, even though he himself had also been made an exile.[9]

[8] Metics at Athens were required to register the name of a citizen as their *prostatēs* ("protector" or "guardian"). The implication is that the same was required of an Athenian living as a metic at Oropus. (On Oropus, see the Introduction.)

[9] The text here is very uncertain.

[14] If any group of citizens remain who shared in the same activities [10] as this man, and if ever they take control of the city—though I pray this may never happen—let him claim with them that he has a right to be a Council-member.

As to the facts that he lived at Oropus under a *prostatēs,* that he had acquired sufficient property, and that he did not take up his position [11] either at Piraeus or in the town, listen to the witnesses, so that you may be sure I am telling the truth in these matters first of all.

[WITNESSES]

[15] It remains for him to claim that he was physically incapable of bringing help to Piraeus because of some infirmity that afflicted him, but that out of his property he offered either to contribute money to your democracy or to provide weapons [12] for some of the members of his deme, as many other citizens did, because they were unable to undertake this duty in person. [16] To ensure that there is no opportunity for him to tell lies and deceive you, I shall now clarify these points as well, since it will not be possible for me later to come forward here and prove him guilty. Please call Diotimus of the deme Acharnae [13] for me, and those members of the deme who were elected with him to provide weapons from the money that had been contributed.

[TESTIMONY OF THOSE ELECTED WITH DIOTIMUS]

[17] This man did not consider how to assist the city in such a situation of crisis but plotted how to profit from your misfortunes. He made his base at Oropus, operating sometimes on his own and sometimes as the leader of other people for whom your misfortunes became

---

[10] "Activities" (Gk. *pragmata*), perhaps even "desired the same constitution."

[11] Lit. "place his shield": the same phrase as in the law quoted in the Introduction.

[12] The verb *hoplizō* suggests hoplite armor, which has implications for Philon's economic and social status. Soldiers were expected to supply their own armor, so broadly speaking the richest 5–10% of Athenians served in the cavalry, and the next 40–50% as hoplites (heavy infantry).

[13] Diotimus is otherwise unknown, but this passage implies that Philon also was a member of Acharnae, the largest Athenian deme, about eight miles north of the city.

their good fortune. [18] He traveled round the countryside, and whenever he met the oldest of the citizens, who had remained in their demes with little but the bare necessities, people who supported your democracy but were unable to assist it because of their age, he stripped them of their remaining property, thinking it more important that he himself should make a small profit than that he should do them no wrong. These people cannot all now accuse him, for the same reason that they were incapable of assisting the city at that time. [19] However, it is not right that my opponent should benefit twice from their weakness—that he should then have stolen their property and now be approved by you at his *dokimasia.* Even if only one of those whom he has wronged should appear, you should regard that as very important and should despise this man, who has dared to deprive those people of their remaining property when others pitied their poverty and chose to give them some of their own resources. Please call the witnesses for me.

[WITNESSES [14]]

[20] For my part, therefore, I do not see how you can view him in a different way from the view taken by those who are close to him. The point is so compelling that even if he had committed no other crime, he should rightly have failed his *dokimasia* for that reason alone. I shall pass over the things of which his mother accused him while she was alive, but judging from the arrangements she made at the end of her life, you can easily recognize his character from the way he treated her. [21] She did not trust this man enough to put herself in his hands when she died, but instead she entrusted herself to Antiphanes,[15] even though she was in no way related to him, and gave him three minas of silver for her burial, passing over this man, who was her own son. Clearly she knew full well that he would not perform the necessary rites even for the sake of his relationship with her. [22] And yet because a mother assesses what happens [16] on the basis more of goodwill than of close examination, she is naturally inclined

[14] Whether the speaker was able to produce more than one witness may perhaps be doubted, in view of the defensiveness of the preceding discussion.

[15] Otherwise unknown.

[16] Lit. "conducts a *dokimasia* of what happens."

to be very tolerant even when wronged by her own children and to regard it as a great thing when she receives the slightest support. If his mother expected this man to rob her even after her death, what ought you to think of him? [23] For if a man commits such crimes against his own relatives, what would he do to strangers? To show that this also is true, listen to the person[17] who received the money and buried her.

[TESTIMONY]

[24] What reason could you have to approve this man at his *dokimasia*? Because he has done nothing wrong? But he has committed the greatest crimes against his fatherland. Or because you think he will improve? Let him first improve his conduct towards the city and then claim he has a right to be a Council-member, after he has done some good to match the evil he has already committed. The more prudent course is to reward everyone afterwards for their actions, for it seems strange to me if he is never to be punished for offenses he has already committed but is now to be rewarded for the good he intends to do in the future. [25] Must he pass his *dokimasia* so that the citizens may become better when they see everybody being honored alike? But the danger is that even honorable men will cease behaving honorably, if they see criminals being honored in the same way as themselves, because they will conclude that the same people generally tend to honor those who are evil and forget those who are good. [26] You should bear in mind the following point as well: if anybody betrayed a fortress, or ship, or a military camp with some citizens in it, he would pay the severest penalties. This man, however, betrayed the entire city and is planning not simply to avoid punishment but also to receive honor.[18] Anybody who, like this man, has openly betrayed freedom, should properly be on trial, not for a seat on the Council, but facing slavery and the severest punishment.

---

[17] I.e., Antiphanes. Another possible reason for Philon's mother's action is discussed in the Introduction.

[18] There is an untranslatable pun here on *timōreomai* ("be punished") and *timaomai* ("receive honor," often in the sense of "public office"). Equally untranslatable is the pun in the following sentence on *bouleuō* ("to be a Council member") and *douleuō* ("to be a slave").

[27] I understand he claims that if not being present during that crisis had been a crime, there would be a law dealing with it explicitly, as there is for other offenses.[19] He expects you not to realize that no law has been written about this precisely because of the enormity of the offense. What public speaker would ever have predicted, what law-giver would have expected, that any citizen would commit so great a crime? [28] I really do not think that a law would have been passed making it a great crime if somebody were to desert the ranks when the city was not itself in danger but was in fact reducing its enemies to that state,[20] but that no law would have been passed dealing with the situation if somebody were to desert the city itself when the city was in danger. Indeed such a law would certainly have been passed, if anybody had believed that any of the citizens would commit such a crime. [29] Everybody would have reason to criticize you, if you rewarded the metics in a manner worthy of the city for having assisted the democracy beyond their duty,[21] but are not going to punish my opponent—at least with the type of *atimia*[22] that is available today, if not more severely—for having betrayed the city in contravention of his duty. [30] Bear in mind the reason why you honor those who behave well towards the city and dishonor those who are evil: both honor and dishonor have been conferred not for the sake of previous citizens but for future ones, so that they will deliberately want to become good and will try not to be bad in any respect. [31] Bear in mind also the following: what oaths do you think this man would respect, when he

---

[19] The relationship between the argument here and the Solonian law on neutrality during civil strife is discussed in the Introduction.

[20] I.e., desertion during time of war against another city (as contrasted with civil war).

[21] Whether and how to reward the metics who had assisted in the restoration of democracy was a contested question in the period after 403/2, but some at least of them (though probably not Lysias) appear eventually to have been granted citizenship.

[22] *Atimia* (lit. "dishonor") denotes "loss of civic rights," including the right to hold public office. Lysias may have in mind the fact that *atimia* had originally been a more severe punishment than it was by the time of the speech, but he probably means that rejection at the *dokimasia* would have the same result as *atimia* (i.e., disqualification from office), even though this would not formally be a judicial punishment.

has betrayed the ancestral gods by his actions? How would he give good advice about the *politeia* (constitution), when he did not wish even to liberate the fatherland? What secrets would he guard, when he did not think it his duty to obey public orders? This man did not even go to face danger at the very end. How can it be reasonable for him to be honored in this way ahead of those who completed the task?[23] It would be outrageous if you do not reject this one man at his *dokimasia,* when he regarded all our citizens as valueless. [32] I see certain people who are now preparing to assist him and to plead with you, because they have been unable to win me over.[24] But they did not plead with him to assist both you and the whole city in the past, when you faced danger and the greatest difficulties, when the *politeia* itself was the prize, and when there was a struggle not simply for membership in the Council but for freedom. Nor did they plead with him not to betray either his fatherland or the Council—which he now claims a right to join, even though he has no share in it, since it was other people who accomplished our success. [33] He is the only person, members of the Council, who would have no right to be angry if he does not achieve membership, for it is not you who dishonor him today, but he who deprived himself of honor in the past, when he was not willing to take his stand with you to fight for the city,[25] even though now he has eagerly come forward to have his name drawn by lot.

[34] Enough has been said, in my opinion, even though there are many things I have left out. I am confident that even without them you will yourselves make the decision that is best for the city. In judging those who are worthy to serve on the Council, you should not use any other evidence apart from yourselves—I mean what sort of people you yourselves were in your dealings with the city when you passed your *dokimasia.* This man's behavior is a revolutionary precedent, which is alien to the whole concept of democracy.

---

[23] This seems to be the general sense of this sentence, but the text is very uncertain.

[24] The implication is that they have used threats or (probably) bribes.

[25] Or "the Council," or "the constitution": a feminine noun is assumed but not expressed in the Greek.

32. AGAINST DIOGEITON

INTRODUCTION

Whereas speeches 1–31 derive from mediaeval manuscripts of Lysias' speeches, what we call Lysias 32–34 are the opening sections of three speeches that are quoted by the rhetorical theorist Dionysius of Halicarnassus in his essay *On Lysias* as examples of Lysias' style in three genres of oratory.[1] Since in each case the rest of the speech is lost, it would in many ways be more logical to class them among the surviving fragments, but the convention of including them as numbered items within the corpus is universal.[2]

Lysias 32 is by far the longest of the three, and consists of the introduction, the narrative, and part of the proof section of a speech. At issue is a private lawsuit dealing with guardianship, which has been brought before a dikastic court by an orphan[3] who has recently become an adult: his brother-in-law (speaking on the young man's behalf because of the

---

[1] Dionysius' essay is translated in full by S. Usher in the Loeb series (*Dionysius of Halicarnassus, Critical Essays,* Vol. 1 [1974]). It is not clear whether Dionysius' threefold division of oratory—into forensic speeches (delivered to a lawcourt), epideictic speeches (written for display) and deliberative speeches (delivered to, e.g., the Assembly)—would have been familiar to an early orator like Lysias, and Dionysius has notable difficulty in finding an example for the third of his genres.

[2] This translation includes also Dionysius' hypothesis (summary) of each speech, because hypotheses of incomplete speeches sometimes give information about the rest of the speech. In the case of Lys. 32, we possess also a hypothesis by Syrianus, and this is translated here as well.

[3] Greeks regarded as an "orphan" anybody whose father had died, even if (as here) the mother was still alive.

TABLE 32.1
The Family Tree (so far as it can be inferred from the speech)

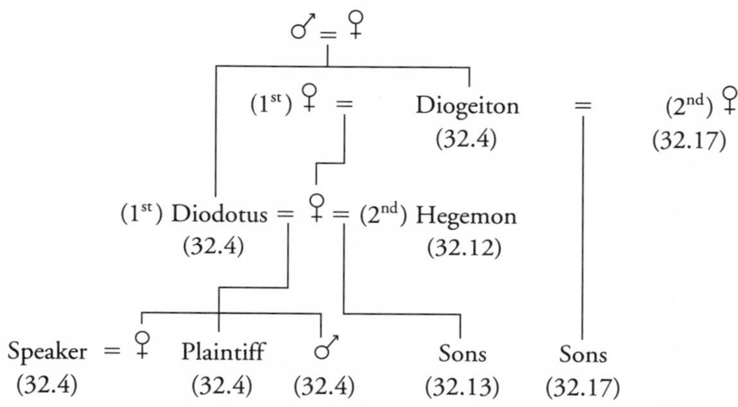

latter's inexperience) alleges that the plaintiff's property has been corruptly mismanaged by its former guardian. Relationships within this family are complicated (see the family tree above [Table 32.1]) because the original owner of the property, a man named Diodotus, had married the daughter of his brother Diogeiton.[4] Such uncle-niece marriages were common at Athens and served to keep property within the family. In this case, Diodotus had died in battle in 410/09 BC, after leaving his children and his allegedly substantial property in Diogeiton's care (see Table 32.2), but there had been virtually nothing left when the elder son came of age in the ninth year afterwards.[5]

One reason for suspecting that Diodotus may have miscalculated the extent to which his brother could be trusted as guardian (particu-

[4] Her name is not given, because it was regarded as improper to name a respectable woman during her lifetime in the public context of a lawcourt. See D. Schaps, "The Woman Least Mentioned: Etiquette and Women's Names," *Classical Quarterly* 27 (1977): 323–330.

[5] The eighth year after their mother's remarriage (32.9), itself apparently a year after her husband's death. Assuming inclusive counting by calendar years, this would bring us to 401/0. The date of the speech may be a year or two after this, if we allow for alleged delaying tactics by Diogeiton.

TABLE 32.2
The Value of Diodotus' Estate as Claimed by Those Involved

	Reference	*Athenian Currency*[1]	*Foreign Currency*
Diodotus' Assets			
Silver on deposit (*parakatathēkē*)	32.5, 32.13	5 talents (30,000 drachmas)	
Maritime loans (*nautika*)	32.6, 32.14	7 talents, 40 minas (46,000 drachmas)	
Loans on land (*engeios tokos*)	32.15	100 minas (10,000 drachmas)	
Owing from Chersonnese	32.6, 32.15[2]	2,000 drachmas	
Left with wife	32.6	20 minas (2,000 drachmas)	30 staters[3]
TOTAL		15 talents (90,000 drachmas)	30 staters
Liabilities, etc.			
Dowry promised to wife	32.6	1 talent (6,000 drachmas)[4]	
Dowry promised to daughter	32.6	1 talent (6,000 drachmas)	
Size of estate initially admitted by Diogeiton	32.9, 32.15	20 minas (2,000 drachmas)	30 staters
Size of estate eventually admitted by Diogeiton	32.28	7 talents, 40 minas (46,000 drachmas)	
Expenditure on children as claimed by Diogeiton	32.20	7 talents, 7,000 drachmas (49,000 drachmas)	

[1] See the table of monetary equivalents in the Series Introduction.

[2] It is possible that these two references are to separate investments (the Chersonnese is not mentioned at 32.15). If so, then an extra 2,000 drachmas must be added to Diodotus' total assets.

[3] From the city of Cyzicus on the Propontis (Sea of Marmara). The value of the Cyzicene stater was 28 drachmas in the mid-fourth century but may have fluctuated over time.

[4] The dowry which Diogeiton eventually paid, according to 32.8, was only 5,000 drachmas.

larly as guardian in charge of liquid assets, which were easier to hide from the heirs than was land) is that both Diogeiton and his daughter appear to have remarried, with both marriages producing sons. Diodotus' own children had therefore become marginal to both households, and the only relative they can find to take the initiative on their behalf is their sister's husband, who is hardly a central figure within the family (for details, see the family tree). Given the dates, however, there may have been good reason for the disappearance of Diodotus' property, because most of it appears to have been invested in ways that were extremely risky (maritime trade, etc.), and the period between his death and his son's majority saw the collapse of the Athenian maritime empire and all that went with it. It is striking that the speaker makes no attempt to counter this point: he may have done so in the lost portions of the speech, or he may have hoped to leave to his opponent the opprobrium of raising an unpopular subject.

After a brief introduction, the speech begins with a lucid statement of the background (32.4–10), followed by a memorable quoted diatribe against the defendant placed in the mouth of his own daughter (32.12–17). As a woman, she could not appear in court as a witness, so this was the only picture the jury would have of her, and it is used effectively to create the impression that Diogeiton's behavior has alienated his family and friends. Our text breaks off after a set of arguments about individual expenditures (32.19–29). Although calculations based on account books rarely have the capacity to enthrall an audience, these arguments are particularly effective. Small items are used to create pathos (as in the case of the lamb: 32.21), and larger ones to create a sense of systematic fraud (as with the maintenance claims in 32.28). Selected points are supported with evidence to create the impression that other allegations are justified: so for instance, the argument about the trierarchy in 32.26–27 is assumed to demonstrate that Diogeiton has been playing the same trick with the tomb and the lamb in 32.21. We do not of course know the result of the case, or the truth of the speaker's allegations, but artistically this is one of Lysias' most persuasive speeches.

The centrality of the household in this speech, and the role played by Diogeiton's daughter, are discussed in Todd 1993: 202–206. On the details of the speech, see Carey 1989.

32. PROSECUTION SPEECH AGAINST DIOGEITON

Syrianus' Hypothesis

Diodotus married the daughter of his brother Diogeiton and had children by her. Going on campaign during the Peloponnesian War, he left his brother as guardian of the children, and he died in battle at Ephesus. An anonymous Athenian married the daughter of Diodotus, who was also the niece of Diogeiton, and on behalf of the children he prosecuted Diogeiton for corrupt guardianship. It is for him that Lysias has written the speech *Against Diogeiton.*

Dionysius of Halicarnassus' Hypothesis[1]

Diodotus was one of the men who were called up during the Peloponnesian War to serve with Thrasyllus.[2] When he was about to set out for Asia, in the Archonship of Glaucippus (410/09), he made a will, because he had children who were minors. As their guardian, he appointed his own brother Diogeiton, who was the children's uncle and also their maternal grandfather. He himself died in battle at Ephesus. Diogeiton took over the management of the orphans' entire property. He is now claiming that out of a very large estate there is nothing left for them, and he is being prosecuted for corrupt guardianship by one of the young men, who has come of age.[3] The prosecution speech against him is delivered by the husband of Diogeiton's niece, who is the sister of the young men.

The Speech as Quoted by Dionysius

[1] If the differences between the parties in this dispute were not so great, gentlemen of the jury, I would not have allowed the plaintiffs to appear before you. In my opinion, it is highly shameful to disagree with family members, and I know that you have a low opinion not

---

[1] Dionysius, *Essay on Lysias* §21, in Usher's Loeb edition (*Dionysius of Halicarnassus, Critical Essays,* Vol. 1 [1974]).

[2] Cf. 32.7n.

[3] "Come of age" (here and at 32.9, 32.24) is used to translate the Greek phrase "pass his *dokimasia,*" which was the judicial scrutiny that young men had to undergo before becoming adult citizens.

only of those who have done wrong but also of those who cannot tolerate ill-treatment at the hands of their relatives. But the plaintiffs have been defrauded of a large amount of money, and have suffered many terrible things at the hands of those from whom this was least to be expected, and have come to me for help, because I am related to them by marriage. In view of all this, gentlemen of the jury, I had no choice but to speak on their behalf. [2] I am married to the plaintiffs' sister, the niece of Diogeiton. After many entreaties from both sides, I persuaded them to refer the matter to their friends for arbitration, because I thought it important that no outsider should know about their affairs. But Diogeiton refused to take the advice of any of his own friends about things that were clearly proved to be in his possession. Instead, he preferred to defend himself against a lawsuit, to bring counterproceedings alleging that there was no case to answer, and to risk the severest penalties,[4] rather than to do the right thing and reach a compromise with the indictment (*enklēma*) brought by the plaintiffs. [3] If therefore I can demonstrate that they have been treated more shamefully by their grandfather during his guardianship than anybody in this city has ever been treated even by those who are not relatives, then I ask you to bring justice to their assistance. If I cannot, then you may trust my opponent in every respect and treat us in the future as criminals. I shall try to tell you their story from the beginning.

[4] Diodotus and Diogeiton, gentlemen of the jury, were full brothers by the same father and mother. They divided their invisible property between them, but they held the visible property in common.[5] Diodotus made a lot of money from import trading (*emporia*), so Diogeiton persuaded him to marry his daughter, who was his only child, and they had two boys and a girl. [5] Some time later, Diodotus was called up to serve as a hoplite.[6] He summoned his wife (who was

---

[4] A considerable exaggeration, because this expression normally designates the death penalty.

[5] Visible property normally consisted of land and houses, and invisible property of cash and other liquid assets. (For the distinction, see also Fr. 3b and the Introduction to Fr. 7 at n. 8.) Here the division presumably occurred after their father's death.

[6] Hoplites were heavy-armed infantry.

his niece) and her father (who was his father-in-law and his brother and was also grandfather and uncle to the children); he thought that because of these relationships there was nobody who was more likely to behave justly towards his children. He gave him his will, and five talents of silver on deposit for safekeeping. [6] He drew attention to seven talents, forty minas that had been lent out on maritime loans,[7] and two thousand drachmas that were owed to him in the Chersonese.[8] He instructed Diogeiton that if anything should happen to him, he was to provide a one-talent dowry for his widow, and give her the contents of the bedroom, and a one-talent dowry for his daughter. He also left behind with his wife twenty minas and thirty Cyzicene staters. [7] After completing these transactions and leaving a duplicate copy at home, he went off with Thrasyllus to fight.[9] After his death at Ephesus, Diogeiton for a while concealed her husband's death from his daughter, and took possession of the sealed documents he had left behind, saying that he needed them to recover the maritime loans. [8] In due course, he told them about the death, and they performed the customary rites. They continued to live in Piraeus for a year, because all their supplies were there. When these began to give out, he sent the children to the town (*astu*) and gave their mother in marriage with a dowry of five thousand drachmas, which was one thousand less than her husband had provided for her. [9] In the eighth year after this, the elder of the two young men came of age. Diogeiton summoned him and told him that their father had left them twenty minas of silver and thirty staters. "As a result," he continued, "I have had to spend a lot of my own money on your upkeep. As long as I had enough, I did not mind, but now I too am hard up. Given that you have passed your *dokimasia* and become a man, from now on you

---

[7] The total value of these various holdings is very considerable. For the various amounts mentioned, and their drachma equivalents, see Table 32.2 in the Introduction. One further investment is mentioned at 32.15 (one hundred minas invested in loans on land), and editors suggest that mention of this has dropped out of the text here.

[8] Either the Thracian Chersonese (the Gallipoli peninsula) or the Tauric Chersonese (the Crimea).

[9] A hundred hoplites were among those reported killed during Thrasyllus' campaign at Ephesus in 409, which is described in Xen., *Hellenica* 1.2.5–13.

must find the means of living for yourself." [10] They were devastated to hear this and went weeping to their mother. Then they brought her to see me. They had been shamefully dispossessed and were reduced to a pitiable state by their sufferings. They wept and pleaded with me not to allow them to be deprived of their inheritance nor to be reduced to destitution by the outrageous treatment (*hubris*) they had received from those who were least expected to behave in this way, but to help them, both for their own and their sister's sake. [11] It would be a long story to recount all the lamentation that took place in my house at that time. In the end, their mother begged and pleaded with me to gather together her father and his friends. She said that even if she had not previously been accustomed to speak in front of men, nevertheless the scale of the disaster would compel her to tell us the whole story of their sufferings. [12] So I went and expressed my feelings to Hegemon, the husband of my opponent's daughter,[10] and talked with the rest of his friends, and persuaded him to undergo an investigation into the money. (Diogeiton at first resisted but was eventually forced into it by his friends.) When the meeting took place, the woman asked him how he had had the heart to treat the children in this way, "given that you are their father's brother, and my own father, and their uncle and grandfather.[11] [13] Even if you were not ashamed of any man, you ought," she said, "to have feared the gods. But you are the one who received five talents from the dead man when he sailed.[12] I am willing to swear an oath about this in whatever location this man may name, surrounding myself with the children and swearing destruction both on them and on those I have borne subsequently. And yet I am not so wretched, nor do I value money so

[10] "My opponent's daughter" is a rather roundabout way of describing somebody who was also the boys' mother, especially as she was herself the subject of 32.11. However, it serves to make it sound as if even Diogeiton's side of the family are appalled at his behavior.

[11] This serves to make the most out of what is in fact only two relationships, by expressing each one in several ways: their father's brother is necessarily also their uncle, and what makes him their grandfather is that he is their mother's father.

[12] Most of the items listed in 32.13–15 have already been mentioned at 32.5–6. See Table 32.2 in the Introduction.

highly, that I would depart this life after committing perjury in the name of my own children or would unjustly take away my father's property." [14] She then demonstrated that he had received seven talents and four thousand drachmas in maritime loans, and she produced documentation of this: during the process of dividing up the household, when he was leaving Collytus for the house of Phaedrus,[13] the boys came across an account book (*biblion*) that had been thrown away and brought it to her. [15] She showed that he had received one hundred minas lent out at interest on land,[14] and a further two thousand drachmas, and household furniture of considerable value. Moreover, they were receiving grain every year from the Chersonese. "And did you dare," she said, "when you had so much money, to say that the father of these boys left merely two thousand drachmas and thirty staters—the amount that was left with me and that I handed over after his death? [16] You thought it right to throw out of their own house those who were your daughter's sons, wearing only threadbare garments, without shoes, without attendants, without bedding, without clothing, without the household furniture their father left them, and without the sums on deposit which he placed in your hands. [17] You are at this moment bringing up my stepmother's children in prosperity, with plenty of money, and as far as that goes I do not blame you. But you are wronging my children, by throwing them out of the house in dishonor and by daring to display them in public as beggars rather than rich men. Such behavior shows that you do not fear the gods, that you are not ashamed of my knowing your guilt, and that you do not respect the memory of your brother. Instead, you rate us all as less important than money." [18] By now, gentlemen of the jury, she had recounted terrible things, and all of us who were present

---

[13] Collytus was one of five demes inside the city walls of Athens. Phaedrus may be Phaedrus of Myrrhinus (the interlocutor of Socrates in Plato's *Phaedrus,* for whom see also Lys. 19.15). This man had been exiled with confiscation of property for his part in the religious scandals of 415 BC, but we do not know when he returned to Athens. It is not clear whether this is a house he is renting or has just sold, or whether it is one that is famous as having been his in the past.

[14] I.e., lent in the form of a mortgage, with land as the security for the debt. (The contrast is with maritime loans, for which the security is the ship and/or its cargo, as at 32.6.)

had been reduced to such a state by this man's behavior and by the woman's speech—we saw the sufferings the boys had endured, we remembered the dead man and how he had left an unworthy guardian of his property, and we considered how hard it was to find somebody to trust with one's private affairs—we had been reduced to such a state, gentlemen of the jury, that none of those present was able to say anything. Instead, weeping just as much as the victims, we went away in silence.

First of all, then, let my witnesses come forward.

[WITNESSES]

[19] I ask you, gentlemen of the jury, to pay close attention to the statement of accounts, so that you may pity the young men because of the scale of what they have suffered, and may realize that my opponent deserves the anger of every citizen. For Diogeiton has reduced all mankind to such a level of distrust that both the living and the dead can rely on their closest friends no more than on their bitterest enemies. [20] After denying receipt of part of the money, and eventually acknowledging the rest of it, he has dared to claim that he received and spent seven talents of silver and seven thousand drachmas for two boys and their sister during a period of eight years. He has become so shameless that when he ran out of expenses to claim, he recorded the sum of five obols per day for food[15] for two little boys and their sister. Instead of a monthly or yearly figure for shoes or laundry or haircuts, he recorded as a lump sum over the whole period more than a talent of silver.

[21] On the tomb of their father, he spent no more than twenty-five minas out of the five thousand drachmas he claimed, but he charged half this sum to himself and the rest to their account.[16] And I think you deserve to hear another story as well. He claims, gentlemen of the jury, to have spent sixteen drachmas buying a lamb for the feast

[15] Lit. *opson* ("food other than bread"). The Athenian diet, like that of many preindustrial societies, was dominated by bread, to the extent that the word *opson* was used to denote anything eaten as an accompaniment to bread (i.e., cheese, onions, olives, etc.).

[16] Five thousand drachmas is fifty minas. The accounting fraud alleged here and in the following examples is discussed in the Introduction.

of the Dionysia, and of this sum he charged eight drachmas to the boys' account. We were particularly angry about this: it is in this way, gentlemen, that the small things in great crimes sometimes hurt the victims more than the large ones, because they make the wickedness of the perpetrators so terribly clear. [22] As for the other festivals and sacrifices, he charged to the boys an expenditure of more than four thousand drachmas, and there were all sorts of other things he reckoned up together as a lump sum. It was as if he had been left as guardian for the boys so that he could show them paper instead of money, so that he could make them paupers instead of rich men, and so that they could forget about the enemies (if any) that they had inherited, and should instead fight with their guardian for depriving them of their inheritance. [23] And yet if he had been prepared to behave honestly towards the boys, he could have followed the laws about orphans, which apply to guardians who are incapable of fulfilling their responsibility as well as to those who are capable. He could have rented out the property, thereby ridding himself of many responsibilities, or he could have purchased land and used the income to bring up the children. In either case, they would have been as rich as any Athenian. As it is, it seems to me that he never intended to convert the estate into visible property.[17] Instead, he wanted to keep their property for himself, because he believed that his own wickedness should inherit the dead man's wealth.

[24] The most shocking story of all, gentlemen of the jury, concerns his service as joint trierarch[18] with Alexis the son of Aristodicus. He claimed to have contributed forty-eight minas, but he then charged half of this sum to the boys—even though they were orphans, and the city has not only made them exempt throughout their childhood but has freed them from all liturgies for a year after they come of age. But this man, who is their grandfather, broke the law by charging half the cost of his own trierarchy to his daughter's children.

---

[17] See 32.4n.

[18] The trierarchy was a form of liturgy (compulsory public sponsorship imposed on rich Athenians), which involved paying for the upkeep of a warship for a year. Shared trierarchies are well known in the fourth century (cf., e.g., Dem. 50); sharing appears to have been introduced in the final years of the Peloponnesian War, to cope with financial strains among the Athenian elite.

[25] He also sent to the Adriatic[19] a merchant ship with cargo valued at two talents. When it was leaving, he told their mother that the risk was the boys' responsibility, but when it arrived safely and doubled in value, he claimed that the cargo was his own. But if he is going to claim that the losses are theirs, while keeping for himself that part of the property which arrives safely, then he will have no difficulty filling in the accounts to show what the money has been spent on. On the contrary, he will find it all too easy to enrich himself at other people's expense.

[26] It would be a tedious task, gentlemen of the jury, to go through the accounts for you item by item. After I had eventually extracted the documents from him, I took witnesses with me, and since Alexis is dead, I asked his brother Aristodicus whether he had the accounts of the trierarchy. He said that he did, and we went to his house and found that Diogeiton had contributed twenty-four minas to Alexis for the trierarchy. [27] This man claimed, however, to have spend forty-eight minas, so in fact he has charged to the boys the entire amount that he spent. But what do you think he has been doing in contexts where nobody else knew his guilty secrets and he had complete control?—given that this is a man who dared to deceive his own grandchildren and charge them forty-eight minas, in dealings that were conducted through other people and that were not difficult to trace.

Let my witnesses of this come forward.

[WITNESSES]

[28] You have heard the witnesses, gentlemen of the jury. However, I will base my calculations on the figure of seven talents, forty minas, which he eventually admitted having received. I will claim nothing in interest payments but will deduct all expenditures from the capital sum. I will allow one thousand drachmas per year (a sum that nobody in the city has ever claimed) for two boys and their sister and their *paidagōgos*[20] and their female slave. That is slightly less than three

[19] Notoriously dangerous for sailing; cf. Lys. Fr. 1 (*Aeschines*) §4.

[20] A *paidagōgos* was a male slave who performed the full-time functions of babysitter or child-minder for school-age boys.

drachmas per day, [**29**] and over eight years it comes to eight thousand drachmas. Even so, there remains a balance of six talents and twenty minas out of the original seven talents and forty minas.[21] He cannot show that he has been damaged by pirates, or has suffered losses, or has been paying off creditors. . . .

---

[21] The text is uncertain here, and this is one of a number of possible restorations.

33. OLYMPIC SPEECH

INTRODUCTION

This is the speech that Dionysius of Halicarnassus quotes as an example of Lysias' style in the genre of epideictic oratory (i.e., written for display). It is striking that he has selected this one ahead of the more famous Funeral Speech (Lys. 2), but he does not mention the latter and gives no explanation of his choice. One possible explanation is that he may have believed that speech 2 was not a genuine work of Lysias, but it is also possible that he regarded speech 33 as more likely to have been delivered by Lysias himself. Indeed, the circumstances of its delivery are independently attested by the historian Diodorus of Sicily.[1]

The Olympic Games, like other great Panhellenic festivals, were occasions at which prominent orators could show off their skills. An Olympic speech is attributed to the late-fifth-century Syracusan orator Gorgias, though this does not survive. Several speeches of Isocrates purport to have been delivered at other similar festivals (Isoc. 12, for instance, at the Panathenaea), though these are almost certainly pamphlets rather than real speeches. Diodorus claims that Lysias delivered his speech at the Olympic Games of 388, on the occasion when Dionysius tyrant of Syracuse in Sicily (no relation to the rhetorical theorist by whom the speech has been preserved) had sent to the games

[1] There is of course the possibility that Diodorus or his source has inferred the circumstances from the text of the speech. This seems unlikely, however, because Dionysius too insists that it is a real speech, whereas he is very hesitant about whether Lys. 34 was ever delivered.

a delegation of unparalleled magnificence, as a way of displaying his own wealth and power (Diodorus Siculus 14.109). Lysias' family had originally come to Athens from Syracuse,[2] so it may not be surprising that he reacted by denouncing Dionysius' delegation as evidence that the Greeks were being enslaved not simply by foreign rulers like the Great King of Persia but by a tyrant within a Greek city.

One puzzle about Diodorus' account is the date. In 388, the Corinthian War was still in progress between Athens, Corinth, Argos, and Thebes on the one hand, and Sparta and its allies on the other. We would expect the Olympic Games still to be taking place in time of war, but it would seem odd at such a time to describe the Spartans without qualification as the leaders of Greece (33.7), and the language about the Great King of Persia (at 33.5) might fit better a date after rather than before the Corinthian War was ended, on terms highly favorable to Persia and Sparta, by the Peace of Antalcidas in 387/6. Diodorus was not an original writer but constructed his work by summarizing earlier historians. His method of working means that he often places events in the wrong year, and one possible solution, accepted by many scholars, is to suppose that the speech belongs instead to the Olympic Games of 384.

33. OLYMPIC SPEECH

Dionysius of Halicarnassus' Hypothesis[1]

There exists a panegyric speech by Lysias, in which he seeks to persuade the Greeks, during a festival at Olympia, to remove the tyrant Dionysius from his position as ruler and set Sicily free, and to begin hostilities immediately, by tearing apart the tyrant's tent, which was adorned with gold and purple and much other wealth. Dionysius had sent *theōroi* (religious envoys) to the festival, bringing a sacrifice for the god, and an outrageously lavish residence had been provided for them in the sacred enclosure, in order that the tyrant would become even more admired throughout Greece. Taking this as his theme, Lysias begins the speech as follows:

[2] There was indeed a tradition that Lysias' father had left Syracuse as an exile at the time of a previous tyrant (Pseudo-Plutarch, *Lives of the Ten Orators* 835c).

[1] Dionysius, *Essay on Lysias* §29, in Usher's Loeb edition (*Dionysius of Halicarnassus, Critical Essays,* Vol. 1 [1974]).

The Speech as Quoted by Dionysius

[1] It is appropriate to commemorate Heracles for his many wonderful achievements, gentlemen, and in particular since he was the first to gather together this competition, because of his goodwill towards Greece. In those days, cities treated each other as strangers, [2] but after Heracles put an end to the tyrants and prevented their arrogance (*hubris*), he established a contest of physical strength, a competition of wealth, and a display of wisdom, in the most beautiful place in Greece, so that we should come together in the same place for the sake of all these things, to see some of them and to hear others. He believed that meeting here would be the beginning of friendship towards each other for the Greeks. [3] These were Heracles' instructions, but I have not come here to talk about trivialities or to fight about names.[2] In my view these are the tasks of those sophists[3] who are wholly useless, and who are desperate for a livelihood, whereas the task of an honorable man and of a worthy citizen is to give advice about great matters, when he sees that Greece is in such a disgraceful condition, that many parts of it are under the control of the barbarian[4] and that many cities have been destroyed by tyrants. [4] If this situation were caused by our weakness, we would have to accept our fate; but since civil strife (*stasis*) and mutual rivalry are the cause, it is surely right to put an end to the one and to forbid the other; for you know that rivalry is for people who are prospering, but prudence is best for those in the opposite condition. [5] We can see that the dangers are great and surround us on every side. You are aware that power[5] belongs to those who control the sea, that the Great King is the steward of money, that the bodies of the Greeks belong to those who have money to spend,[6] and that the Great King possesses many

[2] Complaints about the triviality of other genres of oratory are commonplace in the epideictic speeches of Isocrates, but these are usually phrased in terms of the pettiness of individual legal disputes (e.g., Isoc. 4.11, 12.11, 15.228).

[3] The term "sophists" was used to describe (and often to denigrate) intellectuals who made a living as teachers and rhetoricians.

[4] I.e., Artaxerxes, the Great King of Persia.

[5] *Archē,* perhaps "empire."

[6] An allegation that political leaders in the Greek cities have been accepting bribes, or a lament about the employment of Greek soldiers as mercenaries?

ships, as does the tyrant of Sicily. [6] We should therefore put aside our war against each other and cling to our security, having the same attitude as each other. We should be ashamed about what is past and afraid for what is going to happen. We should compete against our ancestors, who deprived the barbarians of their own property when they coveted the property of others, and who expelled the tyrants and established freedom for all.

[7] I am most surprised at the Spartans. I wonder what they have in mind when they look on as Greece is revolutionized,[7] given that they are the leaders of the Greeks (not unjustly, because of their innate merits and their knowledge of war). They alone live in homes that are unravaged and a city that is unwalled, they are united and undefeated, and have always followed the same customs. For these reasons there is hope that they have obtained an undying freedom, and that after being the saviors of Greece in previous dangers, they are taking precautions for the future also. [8] No opportunity will be better than the present one. We should not regard the disasters of those who have been ruined as alien to us but as our own concern, nor should we wait until the forces of both sides[8] come to attack us. Instead, we should restrain our opponents' arrogance (*hubris*) while it is still possible. [9] Who would not be angry to see how they have grown strong during our wars against each other? These events, which are not simply shameful but terrible, have given power over events to those who have committed great crimes, and the Greeks have exacted no punishment.

---

[7] This is a possible emendation for the implausible manuscript reading "burnt," but no suggestion has won widespread consent.

[8] Both our enemies, i.e., Artaxerxes of Persia and Dionysius of Syracuse.

34. PRESERVING THE ANCESTRAL CONSTITUTION

INTRODUCTION

This is the last of the three speeches quoted by Dionysius of Halicarnassus as examples of Lysias' style. Dionysius appears to have had considerable difficulty finding a deliberative speech (i.e., one that was delivered at an Assembly meeting) to match his examples of forensic and epideictic oratory (Lys. 32 and 33), because such speeches do not seem to have been composed, or at least circulated in writing, by the earlier Attic orators.[1] He betrays a certain unease by admitting that his chosen speech may be a pamphlet rather than a real speech that was actually delivered, though he seeks to recover the credibility of his enterprise by insisting that is "composed as if for a real debate."

Lysias 34 is an attack on a proposal by one Phormisius, immediately after the democratic restoration of 403/2, to restrict the number of citizens by introducing some form of property qualification. Lysias uses one of the most common political slogans of this period, the phrase *patrios politeia* (lit. "ancestral constitution"), to maintain that anything less than full democracy was a betrayal of the constitutional tradition of Athens. This is powerful rhetoric, but the slogan is noted for its adaptability: it is a striking feature of the political debates of the late fifth century that both sides—those who wished to impose a

[1] The first orator regularly to "publish" demegoric speeches is Demosthenes in the 350s and 340s, and such speeches form the bulk of Dem. 1–17. And. 3 is in form an Assembly speech dating from the 390s, but it deals with a debate in which Andocides was effectively on trial for his life, and anyway, it may be a pamphlet rather than a real speech.

property qualification, and those who wished to maintain the radical democracy—were equally keen to argue that their proposals matched the original intentions of the founding fathers of the Athenian *polis.*

Some aspects of Phormisius' proposal can be inferred from the speech itself as quoted by Dionysius. In particular, the speaker reports his opponents as using the phrase "what the Spartans command" (34.6), evidently to describe the proposal that is being debated. Most of what we are told about the proposal, however, comes from Dionysius' introduction, which presumably drew on those portions of the speech that we do not possess. There is a lot of important information here, but what he says should be used with caution. At least one of his statements is misleading, because he makes it sound as if the amnesty of 403/2 was an Athenian legislative enactment, rather than an agreement between two groups of Athenians[2] brokered by King Pausanias of Sparta. Moreover, we cannot determine the original context of some of the information he relates: the figure of five thousand landless Athenians who would have lost their civil rights under Phormisius' proposal is presumably drawn from Lysias, but without the relevant portions of the speech we do not know whether Lysias has invented this figure as a scare tactic (in which case it is presumably an exaggeration) or is quoting a figure put forward by Phormisius ("my opponent claims that it will only affect five thousand people," etc.). Nor do we know what is meant by "those who possessed land"—did this mean simply a house, or a house with a garden, or a farm of some minimum size?—and because the total size of the citizen body is unknown,[3] we do not know what proportion of citizens would have been affected.

The most important piece of information which Dionysius transmits, and which could not be inferred from the portion of the speech that he quotes, is the name of the proposer Phormisius. Phormisius is attested in several sources. *Ath. Pol.* 34.3 describes him as one of a number of minor political figures associated with Theramenes shortly

---

[2] The democratic counterrevolutionaries from Phyle and Piraeus and the former supporters of the oligarchs who had remained in the town.

[3] Modern estimates for the fourth century vary from about 20,000 to about 30,000 adult male citizens.

before the oligarchy of the Thirty, which serves to identify him as a politician, though some scholars doubt the link with Theramenes;[4] apart from that, Phormisius appears several times in Aristophanes.[5] Dionysius also makes clear, as is implied in the text of the speech (34.2), that Phormisius had himself been one of the democratic counterrevolutionaries alongside Thrasybulus in 403. It is at first sight surprising that such a recent opponent of oligarchy would propose restriction of the franchise: a proposal which clearly failed, as Dionysius implies, and as we know also from the fact that the franchise remained unrestricted until Macedonian abolition of the democracy in the 320s.

One possible explanation for Phormisius' proposal is to envisage a moderate "Theramenist" faction at Athens seeking to oppose excesses of all types, with Theramenes trying to restrain the Thirty and Phormisius seeking to moderate the democracy. However, the only evidence for such a grouping is the *Ath. Pol.,* which may not be a reliable source (cf. above). Perhaps a more satisfactory—if speculative—explanation can be inferred from what is said about Spartan support for the proposal. This cannot be accepted in the stark form in which Dionysius reports it, because although it is conceivable that Sparta would have made such a demand, it is inconceivable that Athens in 403 would have been in a position to resist it. On the other hand, we know that King Pausanias was put on trial when he returned to Sparta, evidently for imposing too soft a settlement at Athens, and that he was narrowly acquitted. If the Athenians knew about the prospect of his trial, or at least if some prominent Athenians had heard rumors of the prospect from their Spartan friends on Pausanias' staff, they might have thought it worth proposing some antidemocratic concession in advance, in order to reduce the risk of the Spartans convicting Pausanias, repudiating his settlement, and imposing harsher terms. The news of Pausanias' acquittal, on this hypothesis, would have removed

---

[4] *Ath. Pol.*'s picture of Theramenes is seriously misleading in at least one respect: it is nowhere admitted that Theramenes was a member of the Thirty.

[5] One passage (*Frogs* 965) contrasts him with Theramenes, in a way that may imply that the two were political opponents in 405; the other (*Assemblywomen* 97) shows that he was still worth mentioning in the late 390s, well after the failure of his proposal.

the impetus behind Phormisius' proposal, which would even allow for Lysias' speech to be a pamphlet circulated for rhetorical advantage after the proposal had collapsed.

The use of the slogan *patrios politeia* in Athenian constitutional debate is discussed by M. I. Finley, "The Ancestral Constitution," in Finley's book *The Use and Abuse of History* (London, 1986), 34–59. On Phormisius' proposal, and the broader context of Athenian debates over citizenship in this period, see J. K. Davies, "Athenian Citizenship: The Descent Group and the Alternatives," *Classical Journal* 73 (1978): 105–121.

34. CONCERNING THE PRESERVATION OF THE ANCESTRAL CONSTITUTION (*PATRIOS POLITEIA*) AT ATHENS

Dionysius of Halicarnassus' Hypothesis[1]

The *dēmos*[2] had returned from Piraeus, and had voted that there should be a reconciliation towards those in the town (*astu*), and that there should be no recriminations[3] for anything that had happened. There was a fear that after regaining its former power, the democracy[4] might arrogantly mistreat[5] those who were well off. Many speeches[6] on this subject were made; and Phormisius, one of those who had returned from exile together with the *dēmos*, put forward the proposal

[1] Dionysius, *Essay on Lysias* §32, in Usher's Loeb edition (*Dionysius of Halicarnassus, Critical Essays,* Vol. 1 [1974]).

[2] *Dēmos* can denote either the People of Athens (i.e., the Athenian state) or else, as here, the democracy together with those who support it (in contrast with the supporters of oligarchy).

[3] The reference is to the general amnesty of 403, between the democratic counterrevolutionaries ("those from Piraeus") and the former supporters of the Thirty ("those in the town"). The word "recriminations" here is used to translate the Greek verb *mnēsikakein,* "to remember wrongs," which is the core of the main clause of the amnesty text as quoted in *Ath. Pol.* 39.6.

[4] Or "the majority" (*plēthos*).

[5] Lit. "commit *hubris* against."

[6] Or "much discussion" (*logoi*).

that those who were in exile should return,[7] and that the *politeia* (voting rights) should not be granted to everybody but only to those who possessed land. The Spartans also wanted this to happen. If this proposal had been passed, approximately five thousand Athenians would have been deprived of their share in the community. To prevent this from happening, Lysias wrote the following speech for someone who was distinguished and politically active. Whether it was delivered on that occasion is unclear; at any rate, it is composed as if for a real debate.

The Speech as Quoted by Dionysius

[1] Just when we thought, men of Athens, that our recent disasters had left an adequate reminder to the city, such that not even our descendants would desire a different *politeia* (constitution), these men are now seeking to win over those who have suffered evil and have experienced both types of constitution, by means of the same proposals with which they have already deceived us twice before. [2] I am not surprised at my opponents, but I am surprised at you for listening to them, because you are either the most forgetful of all mankind, or else the most ready to suffer evil at the hands of men like this, who shared in the activities of those at Piraeus but shared in the attitudes of those from the town. What need was there for the exiles to return from exile, if you are going to enslave yourselves by means of an Assembly vote? [3] For my part, men of Athens, I have not been deprived of the citizenship either by my property or by my birth but am superior to the opposing speakers in both respects. However, I believe that the only hope of security for the city is that all Athenians should share in the *politeia,* because when we possessed the walls, the ships, money, and allies, we never considered driving out any Athenian. Instead,

[7] It is not entirely clear who these are, though the tense of *pheugontas* ought to imply not former exiles (i.e., the democratic counterrevolutionaries) but those in exile at the time of speaking (i.e., the remnants of the Thirty and their supporters).

we even created intermarriage (*epigamia*) with the Euboeans.[8] Are we now to take *epigamia* away even from our existing citizens? [4] Certainly not, if you take my advice. We will not, in addition to losing our walls, deprive ourselves of many hoplites and cavalry and archers.[9] If you hold on to these, you will be securely and democratically governed, you will become more powerful than your enemies, and you will be more helpful to your allies. You are aware that in the oligarchies that have arisen during our lifetime, it was not those who possessed land who controlled the city; instead, many of these were put to death, and many were expelled from the city. [5] It was the democracy that brought these men back from exile, and gave you back your city,[10] but did not itself have the boldness to share in it. As a result, if you take my advice, you will not (as far as you are able) deprive your benefactors of the *politeia,* nor will you regard speeches as more trustworthy than actions, or future promises as more trustworthy than past facts, especially when you remember those who fought for oligarchy, who are nominally making war on the democracy but in reality are coveting your property, and they will get possession of this, once they catch you without allies.

[6] Our situation is such that they ask what security there will be for the city if we do not do what the Spartans command. In my view, however, these men should say how the democracy will benefit if we do what they[11] recommend. Otherwise, it would be far better for us to die fighting than to vote to condemn ourselves publicly to death. [7] I believe that if I can win you over, the danger will be equal for both sides . . .[12] I see that the Argives and the Mantineans have the

---

[8] No other source refers to the grant of *epigamia* (i.e., the right for members of two communities to conduct valid marriages with each other) with the people of Euboea, which is a large island, and contained many separate cities.

[9] I.e., whereas the loss of the walls had been imposed as a condition of surrender in 405/4, to restrict the franchise would be unnecessarily to lose the service of these men.

[10] "City" (*polis*) is the most likely candidate for the feminine noun which is implied but not stated here. Other possibilities are "property" (*ousia*) or "constitution" (*politeia*).

[11] I.e., the Spartans.

[12] Editors suspect that some words have dropped out of the text here.

same attitude, and they inhabit their own land, with the Mantineans[13] sharing a border with the Spartans and the Argives living nearby, the Argives numbering no more than we do and the Mantineans not even three thousand. [8] The Spartans know that even if they repeatedly invade their land, those invaded will repeatedly take up arms and oppose them. So the Spartans consider it a poor risk, because they will not enslave them if they are victorious, whereas if they are defeated they themselves will lose their existing advantages. And the better the Spartans fare, the less they desire to risk. [9] We too, men of Athens, used to take this attitude when we ruled the Greeks, and we thought it was a good plan to look on while our land was being ravaged, and felt no need to fight for it. It was right for us to ignore small things and so to preserve many advantages. Now, however, when we have lost all those things in war, and our fatherland alone is left for us, we know that only this risk offers hope of security. [10] We must bear in mind that in the past we set up many trophies in foreign lands, when assisting other people who were being wronged; that we have behaved bravely on behalf of our fatherland and our own affairs; and that we have placed our trust in the gods and in the hope that once again justice will be on the side of those who are wronged. [11] It would be terrible, men of Athens, if while we were in exile we fought the Spartans in order to return from exile, but after returning we will go into exile in order not to fight. So is it not shameful that we have reached such a level of cowardice that whereas our ancestors faced danger for the freedom of others also, you do not dare fight a war, even for your own freedom? . . .

---

[13] This passage (34.7–8) makes extensive use of pronouns to denote the Argives, Mantineans, and Spartans. For clarity, I have in several places used nouns instead.

FRAGMENT 1. AGAINST AESCHINES THE SOCRATIC

INTRODUCTION

The Aeschines who forms the subject of this speech is not the later orator but a pupil[1] of Socrates (hence "the Socratic" in the title of the speech). Like Plato and Xenophon, he is known to have written a number of dialogues in which Socrates appears as a speaker, but none of them survive. He had a reputation as a spendthrift,[2] and the present speech concerns an action for debt, over money he has allegedly borrowed from the unnamed speaker and is refusing to repay. One odd feature of the case is that Aeschines appears to be the plaintiff (Fr. 1 §1), not the defendant as we might have expected a debtor to be, but not enough remains of the speech to resolve that problem.[3]

---

[1] Because Aeschines is described as a former pupil (Fr. 1, §2), the implication is that the speech belongs after Socrates' death in 399, but it cannot be more precisely dated.

[2] Socrates is reported to have advised him to borrow from himself by cutting down his expenditure on food (Diogenes Laertius 2.62), which implies gluttony as well as extravagance.

[3] The titles of two other Lysian speeches against Aeschines (probably but not certainly the same man) are known: one is a *Prosecution Speech against Aeschines, Concerning the Confiscation of the Property of Aristophanes* (the sole fragment is the name of a city in Cyprus, and together with the title, this suggests a connection with the events in Lys. 19); the other is entitled *Against Aeschines for Damage* (possibly a confused reference to our present speech, but the only fragment is inconclusive).

What does remain is one substantial fragment,[4] or more strictly perhaps a series of fragments, because it consists of three quotations, two of them discontinuous, interspersed once with a diatribe against perfumes, and more importantly with a paraphrase of what has been omitted between the second and third quotations. The context for this series of fragments is an extended attack on philosophers at the end of book 13 of Athenaeus' *Deipnosophistae* (for which cf. the Introduction to Lysias). It is delivered by Myrtilus, one of the guests at Athenaeus' imaginary dinner party, and directed against another of the guests, the Cynic philosopher Theodorus (nicknamed Cynulcus, "little Cynic"): Lysias' attack on Aeschines provides Myrtilus with plenty of ammunition. The tone of the fragments quoted by Myrtilus is unusual, because they contain several of the very few jokes in the Attic Orators. There is heavy sarcasm in the thought of people preferring to move house rather than continue as Aeschines' neighbors (§3) and in the procession of early-morning creditors being mistaken for a funeral (§4), while the quip about the number of Hermaeus' wife's teeth (§5) was appreciated by a later rhetorician (Demetrius, *On Style* §128). Perhaps the closest parallel to the tone of this fragment is in Lysias 24, and this may suggest that here too Lysias' technique was to seek to laugh the opponent's case out of court.

One of the striking features of this case is the different interest rates at which Aeschines has allegedly obtained his loans. Lysias claims that he had had a loan from a banker at the usurious level of 36 percent per year, which he had refinanced by borrowing from the speaker at half that rate (Fr. 1, §§1–2). The speech has proved something of a test case for the interpretation of Athenian economic history, in that two leading proponents of the subject take very different views of what is happening here. Cohen[5] sees Aeschines as an entrepreneur who had had to pay 36 percent because this was an unsecured high-

[4] In addition, Harpocration's *Lexicon to the Ten Orators* cites the speech as the source of three single words or phrases: "Aspasia" (Pericles' mistress, and the title of one of Aeschines' lost dialogues); "panic stricken"; and "unmarked (meaning 'unmortgaged') estate."

[5] E. E. Cohen, *Athenian Economy and Society: A Banking Perspective* (Princeton, 1992), 144, 213–214, and 216.

risk loan; for Millett,[6] on the other hand, Aeschines is a con-man who has to borrow at such a high rate only because he has already exhausted the nearer and cheaper possibilities of friends and neighbors as sources of credit. Part of the problem is that we do not know when the loans of §§3–5 took place in relation to the loans of §§1–2. For Cohen, they are additional financing, following Aeschines' success in negotiating the loan with the speaker, and are reported presumably as evidence of his terminal bankruptcy, whereas Millett sees them as subsequently discovered evidence of Aeschines' previous trickery.

FRAGMENT I. AGAINST AESCHINES THE SOCRATIC, FOR DEBT

Fragment 1[1]

There is nothing more unphilosophical than those who are called philosophers. Who would have expected Aeschines, the pupil of Socrates, to have behaved in the way that the orator Lysias describes in his speeches on agreements (sumbolaia)*? We respect Aeschines as a sensible and moderate man, on the basis of the dialogues handed down as his—unless of course they are compositions by the wise Socrates and were presented to Aeschines out of gratitude by Xanthippe, the wife of Socrates, after the latter's death, as Idomeneus'*[2] *supporters claim. Anyway, what Lysias says in the speech entitled* Against Aeschines the Socratic for Debt*—I shall recite it, even though what is said is lengthy, my dear philosophers, because of your considerable arrogance—this is how the orator begins:*

[§1] Gentlemen of the jury, I never thought Aeschines would dare to bring such a shameful case, and I do not think he could easily find one that was more full of sykophancy[3] than this. He owed money,

---

[6] P. C. Millett, *Lending and Borrowing in Ancient Athens* (Cambridge, 1991), 1–4, and 106–107.

[1] Lys. Fr. I.1 (Baiter and Sauppe), Fr. I.1 (Thalheim, Medda), Fr. XXXVIII (Gernet and Bizos), and Fr. IV (Albini). The context of the fragment is Athenaeus, 13.611d–612f (13.93–94 Kaibel), which is translated in full by C. B. Gulick in the Loeb series (*Athenaeus, The Deipnosophists,* Vol. 6 [1937]).

[2] Idomeneus of Lampsacus, third-century BC biographer.

[3] Malicious prosecution.

gentlemen of the jury, to Sosinomus the banker and Aristogeiton,[4] at a rate of three drachmas.[5] He came to me and begged me not to let him be deprived of his property because of the interest payments. [§2] "I am setting up," he said, "in the perfume business. I need funding (*aphormē*), and I will pay you nine obols per month as interest."[6]

This perfume business is indeed excellent as the goal of happiness for the philosopher, and the appropriate accompaniment for the philosophy of Socrates—given that Socrates rejected the use of perfume,[7] and Solon the lawgiver did not allow a male to supervise that type of business. That is why Pherecrates[8] also, in The Furnace *or* The Vigil, *says, "What must a man suffer, for him to sell perfumes, sitting loftily under an awning, having prepared a meeting place for young men to gossip throughout the day," and he goes on to say, "nobody has ever seen either a butcheress or even a fishmongeress." He means that matters of business should be appropriate to each sex. Immediately after this, the orator says as follows:*

I was won over when he said this, and I believed that my opponent—a former pupil of Socrates, who had himself spoken many fine words about justice and excellence—would never attempt or even dare to attempt things that only the most wicked and dishonest people try to do.

After this, Lysias again attacks him for the way in which he had borrowed. He had repaid neither the interest nor the original sum; he had become overdue in his payments and had been convicted by a verdict of a court after failing to attend; and a branded slave[9] of his had been seized as

---

[4] Aristogeiton cannot be identified, but Sosinomus is almost certainly the same as the Sosinomus who is later said to have had to give up all his property to his creditors when his bank failed (Dem. 36.20).

[5] Three drachmas per mina per month, i.e., 36% annually.

[6] Nine obols is one-and-a-half drachmas (again, per mina per month), i.e., 18% annually.

[7] Xen., *Symposium* 2.3.

[8] Athenian comic poet, contemporary of Aristophanes.

[9] This is the manuscript reading, but Millett 1991 (cited above): 242, suggests "mortgaged house" (*oikian* for *oiketēn*). This conjecture is supported by Lysias' use of the phrase "unmarked (i.e. 'unmortgaged') estate" elsewhere in this speech (cf. the Introduction at n. 4).

security. After making many other allegations against him, Lysias concludes as follows:

[§3] He has behaved like this, gentlemen of the jury, not merely towards me but towards everybody who has dealt with him. The retail traders living near him—people from whom he receives advances which he does not repay—have they not shut up their shops and are prosecuting him? Have not the neighbors suffered so badly at his hands that they are abandoning their own houses and renting other ones far away? [§4] As for the *eranos* contributions[10] that he has collected, he does not pay out the sums left over, but they are ruined when going round this peddler, as if going round a turning post.[11] So many people come to his house at dawn demanding what is owed to them that the passersby believe that the man has died, and they have come for a funeral. Those in Piraeus[12] are in such a state that they regard it as much safer to sail to the Adriatic than to make an agreement with him. [§5] For he thinks he has more right to whatever he can borrow than to the property his father left him. Has he not acquired the property of Hermaeus the perfume seller by seducing Hermaeus' wife, who was seventy years old? By pretending to be her lover, he managed to turn her husband and sons into beggars, while he himself rose from peddler to perfume seller. He made such erotic use of the young lady, enjoying the fruits of her youth—yet it was easier to count her teeth than the fingers of her hand. My witnesses will please come forward.

[WITNESSES[13]]

Such is the life of the sophist.

This, Cynulcus, is what Lysias says.

---

[10] *Eranos* loans (probably interest free) consist of contributions from friends and associates. The borrower was expected to repay them as soon as he could afford to.

[11] The text is obscure, but the metaphor seems to be of a pileup at the halfway stage of a chariot race.

[12] Maritime traders, or those who lend them money. The Adriatic was notoriously dangerous for sailing (cf. Lys. 32.25).

[13] Not in the manuscript, but supplied by editors in view of what precedes.

FRAGMENT 2. AGAINST TEISIS

INTRODUCTION

The shorter fragment here (Fr. 2.a) is preserved in an ancient rhetorical handbook. Litigants at Athens were expected to deliver their own speeches, and the employment of professional advocates was strongly discouraged, so those who spoke on behalf of other people were wise to explain their relationship to the case at the outset, in order to dispel suspicions of professionalism.[1] More important, however, is the second fragment (Fr. 2.b), an extended quotation from the start of the narrative, which presumably followed the speaker's opening remarks. It is quoted by Dionysius of Halicarnassus as the basis of a comparison with the narrative of Demosthenes' extant speech *Against Conon* (Dem. 54.3–9), which he also quotes.

Dionysius introduces his Lysias fragment as a "narrative of a type of *hubris.*" *Hubris* denotes a particularly humiliating form of assault, which was subject to a special public procedure, the *graphē hubreōs.* It is possible that the present case is a *graphē hubreōs,* but it is more likely to be an example of the regular private prosecution against assault, the *dikē aikeias.* This is suggested partly by the speaker's use of the word *dikē* at §1 (a *graphē* could be described as a *dikē,* but such usage would be abnormal) but also by the parallel with Demosthenes, where the speaker claims that although his treatment by the defendant had amounted to *hubris,* he had preferred the lower-profile and less risky option of a *dikē aikeias* (Dem. 54.1).

---

[1] Thus, e.g., Lys. 32.1–2, a family member supporting a very young plaintiff; and Lys. Fr. 3 (*Pherenicus*), §1 (evidently again from the start of the speech), a close friend with hereditary links to a foreign litigant.

None of the characters named in the speech is otherwise known, but a good deal can be inferred from the narrative. The *palaestra* or wrestling ground (§1) was a place where rich young men took exercise: the speaker (who is an unnamed friend of the plaintiff Archippus) is very happy to portray the defendant Teisis in such terms, because *hubris* was regarded as characteristic of rich young men, but Archippus' presence there implies that he was a member of the same social circle. Care is taken, however, to represent Archippus as the inoffensive victim of enticement (it is interesting to conjecture from this speech some of the arguments which might have been put forward by the prosecutors of Euphiletus in Lys. 1), and although the extant fragments do not tell us why Archippus has a friend arguing his case, one possible reason is that it would allow Lysias to take the line that he is so young and inexperienced that he needs somebody to speak for him. The speaker says little explicitly about himself, but he takes up a position as the advocate of responsible lawfulness by the use of the word "madness" to describe the defendant's actions (§3), whereas Teisis' friends are represented in a more hostile light: despite his reservations about Teisis' behavior, Antimachus has to be persuaded by bystanders to agree to the release of Archippus (§6), and Pytheas has been blinded to his responsibilities by his love for Teisis (§§1–2).

One of the striking features of this speech is the use of suggestive details. The speaker emphasizes that Teisis' second attack on Archippus took place when it was already day (§4), presumably because in Athenian eyes, as Demosthenes complains elsewhere (Dem. 21.73–74), assault is bad enough at night and when drunk, but gratuitous and therefore inexcusable during the day and when sober. There may similarly be a point behind the detail about the horse race (§3): Archippus' name literally means "horse ruler," and to whip such a person on such a day may be regarded as a peculiarly offensive insult. Finally, when Archippus' brothers take him to the market (§6), they are on one level doing this because it is an obvious place to arouse the sympathies of a crowd. But we are specifically told that this is the samples market (*deigma*), which seems to have been where samples of goods were laid out for selection for those who wanted to buy in bulk, which is perhaps also a way of suggesting that Archippus was himself a sample of the way that rich young aristocrats like Teisis treat supposedly ordinary people.

On violence at Athens, see N. R. E. Fisher, *Hybris: A Study in the Values of Honour and Shame in Ancient Greece* (Warminster, 1992) and Cohen 1995.

FRAGMENT 2. PROSECUTION SPEECH AGAINST TEISIS

Fragment 2.a[1]

If you speak on behalf of a friend, you need to explain that as well, as Lysias does when he says:

"The plaintiff Archippus is a close friend (*epitēdeios*) of mine, gentlemen of the jury."

Fragment 2.b[2]

It will not hinder the reader's understanding, and may indeed make it more pleasant, if I quote first a passage of Lysias which I think resembles that of Demosthenes. It involves a narrative of a type of hubris.[3]

[§1] The plaintiff Archippus, men of Athens, went to take exercise at the same *palaestra* (wrestling ground) as Teisis, the defendant in this trial.[4] A quarrel broke out, and they engaged in mutual mockery, taunts, hostility, and insults. Pytheas is the lover of the young man[5]—you will be told the whole truth—and had been left as his guardian by Teisis' father. [§2] When Teisis told him about the insults at the

---

[1] Lys. Fr. CXIX.231 (Baiter and Sauppe), Fr. CXIX.76 (Thalheim, Medda), Fr. XVII.1 (Gernet and Bizos), and Fr. VI.2 (Albini). The context of the fragment is Anonymus Seguerianus, *Art of Rhetoric* §7 (on proems).

[2] Lys. Fr. CXIX.232 (Baiter and Sauppe), Fr. CXIX.75 (Thalheim, Medda), Fr. XVII.2 (Gernet and Bizos), and Fr. VI.1 (Albini). The context of the fragment is Dionysius of Halicarnassus, *On Demosthenes* §11, which is translated in full in the Loeb series by S. Usher (*Dionysius of Halicarnassus, Critical Essays*, Vol. 1 [1974]).

[3] Aggravated assault; see the Introduction.

[4] *Dikē;* cf. the Introduction.

[5] For this translation of *meirakion* (here referring to Teisis), see the Introduction to Lys. 3.

palaestra, Pytheas wanted to please him and to appear powerful and cunning, so he told Teisis (we have inferred this from what happened, and have asked those who knew all about it) to make peace for the time being but to look for a way of catching Archippus alone somewhere. [§3] Teisis took this advice, made his peace with Archippus, paid attention to him, and pretended to treat him as a friend. He took his madness to such a degree, young as he was, that when it happened to be the day of the horse race at the Anakeia festival,[6] and he saw Archippus in my company walking past his door (they happened to be neighbors) he first of all asked him to dinner, and when Archippus declined, Teisis begged him to come to a party (*kōmos*), saying that he should come and have a drink with him.[7] [§4] So we arrived after dinner, when it was already dark. We knocked at the door, and they told us to come in. As soon as we were inside, they threw me out of the house but seized Archippus here and fastened him to a pillar. Taking a whip, Teisis[8] struck him repeated blows and then confined him in a room. Teisis was not satisfied with these offenses but was eager to copy the most criminal of the young men in the city. Moreover, he had recently taken control of his inheritance and was playing the part of a rich young man. So when day arrived, he ordered his slaves once again to tie Archippus to the pillar and whip him. [§5] While Archippus' body was by now in such a terrible state, Teisis sent for Antimachus,[9] and told him nothing of what had really occurred, but stated that he himself had happened to be having dinner, and that Archippus had arrived drunk, had knocked down the door, had entered, and had made abusive remarks about Teisis himself and Antimachus and the women. Antimachus was angry with them for committing terrible offenses, but nevertheless he summoned witnesses and asked Archippus

[6] The Anakeia was a festival of Castor and Pollux. For the possible significance of the horse race, see the Introduction.

[7] The text is uncertain here, but this is a plausible restoration.

[8] The manuscript says "somebody" (*tis*), but editors generally agree that it should be Teisis.

[9] Not previously mentioned, but evidently (from what follows) a friend of Teisis who could plausibly be represented as the sort of person that Archippus would threaten. For the allegation of intruding on a house containing citizen women, cf. Lys. 3.6.

how he had gained entry. Archippus replied that he had done this because Teisis and the members of his household had invited him to do so. [**§6**] Those who had entered the house[10] advised them to set him free as soon as possible, taking the view that what had happened was outrageous, so Antimachus and Teisis gave Archippus back to his brothers. Because he was not able to walk, the brothers carried him to the samples market (*deigma*) on a litter and showed him to many Athenians and also many foreigners (*xenoi*). He was in such a state that the people who saw him not only became angry at those who had done this, but also blamed the city for not immediately and publicly punishing people who had committed offenses of this type.

This is Lysias' narrative from the prosecution speech Against Teisis.

---

[10] Presumably the potential witnesses summoned by Antimachus.

FRAGMENT 3. FOR PHERENICUS

INTRODUCTION

This is one of three speeches[1] of which Dionysius of Halicarnassus quotes the prologue in his essay *On Isaeus,* comparing each one individually with the prologue of a lost speech by Isaeus, which he also quotes. In this case the comparison is with Isaeus, *On Behalf of Eumathes,* which belongs to a very different type of dispute. Whereas the *Pherenicus* of Lysias deals with a disputed inheritance, Isaeus' *Eumathes* is the defense of a freed slave whose liberty is being challenged by his former master. The point of comparison that interests Dionysius, however, is that in both cases the speaker is an Athenian citizen, who begins by justifying his decision to appear on behalf of a noncitizen litigant.[2] Dionysius' conclusion is that Isaeus does this in a much more elaborate and artificial way than does Lysias, which is striking because (although Dionysius does not mention this) Lysias' case is set at a much higher social level than that of the former slave Eumathes.

Underlying the *Pherenicus* are the affairs of a very prominent group of democratic exiles from Thebes, whose story is told in some detail by Plutarch (Plut., *Pelopidas* 5–6 and 8). In the year 382, a pro-Spartan group at Thebes encouraged Phoebidas, the Spartan commander at nearby Thespiae, treacherously to seize and garrison the Cadmeia (the citadel of Thebes) in time of peace. Among the Theban democratic leaders were Androcleides and Pherenicus, who both escaped into ex-

---

[1] The others are Fr. 5 (*Archebiades*) and Fr. 6 (*Sons of Hippocrates*).

[2] The need to justify yourself under such circumstances is discussed in the Introduction to Fr. 2 (*Teisis*).

ile at Athens, but the pro-Spartan leaders at Thebes contrived to have Androcleides assassinated there. It is this assassination that has given rise to the present litigation, the date of which must presumably be between 382 and 379, the year when the exiles recaptured Thebes.

It appears from the prologue as quoted by Dionysius (Fr. 3.a) that Androcleides has somehow left his property at Athens to his colleague Pherenicus. The legal basis of this bequest is not clear, but Fragment 3.b (from the *Suda,* a lexicon of the Byzantine period) may be relevant here. It is evidently taken from the proof section of the speech and focuses on the distinction between two classes of property: visible (i.e., land) and invisible (i.e., money or other movables). The fragment states that Androcleides' estate at Athens consisted entirely of invisible property, which is hardly surprising: as a metic (free noncitizen), he would not normally be able to own land at Athens. What is puzzling, however, is the implication that Pherenicus has been able to take possession without the need for a court verdict, which would normally have been required if he had been the beneficiary of a will.[3] This may suggest that Pherenicus is not strictly Androcleides' heir, but rather that Androcleides has handed over his personal property informally on his deathbed.

Such a reconstruction would have a loose but interesting parallel in Demosthenes' speech *Against Callippus* (Dem. 52.5, 8–11), where the property of a childless and heirless citizen of Heraclea was claimed as his own by Callippus as *proxenos* of the Heracleans at Athens (an Athenian citizen who was responsible for looking after their diplomatic interests). If we are to infer that a *proxenos* would have a residual claim in a situation where there was no clear heir, this would suggest that a plausible opponent in the present case might be whoever was currently the *proxenos* of the Thebans at Athens. Given that the post would presumably have been held by an Athenian appointee and ally of the pro-Spartan oligarchs who were currently in power at

[3] In principle, family law among metics at Athens was regulated in just the same way (though by the Polemarch rather than the Archon) as among citizens. Sons inherited automatically, but other heirs had to go through the judicial process of *epidikasia* (this seems to have applied as much to invisible as to visible property), at which rival claimants could dispute a claim.

Thebes and who had allegedly arranged Androcleides' assassination, this would have given the case a peculiar political frisson.

FRAGMENT 3. ON BEHALF OF PHERENICUS, CONCERNING THE ESTATE OF ANDROCLEIDES

Fragment 3.a[1]

There is also in Lysias a speech made by somebody on behalf of a xenos[2] *who is the defendant in a case over an inheritance. Callimachus*[3] *labels this speech* On Behalf of Pherenicus Concerning the Estate of Androcleides, *and it came to trial many years before the other one.*[4] *In it, the person delivering the speech about the* xenos *first of all describes the charge, just like somebody defending the freedom of a metic. This is the prologue to the speech:*

[§1] In my view, gentlemen of the jury, I must tell you first about the friendship (*philia*) between Pherenicus and myself, so that none of you will be surprised that I am now speaking on his behalf, even though I have never previously spoken for any of you. [§2] His father Cephisodotus, gentlemen of the jury, was my *xenos.* When we went into exile,[5] I—and any other Athenian who wished to do so—lived in Cephisodotus' house at Thebes. We received many private and public benefits from him, before returning from exile to our father-

---

[1] Lys. Fr. CXX.233 (Baiter and Sauppe), Fr. CXX.78 (Thalheim, Medda), Fr. XXIV.1 (Gernet and Bizos), and Fr. VIII.1 (Albini). The context of the fragment is Dionysius of Halicarnassus, *On Isaeus* §6, which is translated in full in the Loeb series by S. Usher (*Dionysius of Halicarnassus, Critical Essays,* Vol. 1 [1974]).

[2] *Xenos* can simply mean "foreigner" but may also denote a person with whom one has a hereditary link of ritualized friendship (such as the speaker's relationship to Cephisodotus at Fr. 3.a, §2).

[3] The poet Callimachus of Cyrene was librarian at Alexandria in the third century B.C. He compiled a catalogue of the library, but it does not survive.

[4] I.e., Isaeus' speech *On Behalf of Eumathes.*

[5] "We" clearly denotes the Athenian democrats in 404/3, thus conveniently stressing the speaker's own credentials.

land. [§3] When these men[6] experienced their own misfortune and arrived as exiles in Athens, I felt the greatest gratitude towards them, and received them in such a friendly fashion that none of my visitors—unless any of them happened to know already—realized which of us was the owner of the house. [§4] Pherenicus is aware, gentlemen of the jury, that many people are more skilled at speaking than I am, and more experienced in such cases. Nevertheless, he regards my friendship as the most reliable. So when he begs and entreats me to assist him in obtaining justice,[7] it seems to me shameful not to do all I can to prevent him being deprived of the property that he has been given by Androcleides.

Fragment 3.b[8]

Visible and invisible property. Lysias in the speech On Behalf of Pherenicus *says:*

If Androcleides had left behind land or other visible property, anybody who wished would have been allowed to claim that it had been given to himself, and that this man[9] is lying. Concerning silver and gold and invisible property, on the other hand, it is clear that whoever is found in possession is the person to whom Androcleides gave them.

---

[6] Presumably "Pherenicus and his political allies."

[7] There are some parallels here with the opening of Lys. 5, also delivered in support of a noncitizen.

[8] *Suda, s.v. ousia phanera kai aphanēs:* Lys. Fr. CXX.234 (Baiter and Sauppe), Fr. CXX.79 (Thalheim, Medda), Fr. XXIV.2 (Gernet and Bizos), and Fr. VIII.2 (Albini). For the distinction between visible and invisible property, see 32.4n and the Introduction to Fr. 7 at n. 8.

[9] I.e., Pherenicus, but the text is uncertain here, and some editors prefer "and that he (the alternative claimant) is not lying."

FRAGMENT 4. AGAINST CINESIAS

INTRODUCTION

None of the other names involved in this case can be securely identified, but the speaker's opponent Cinesias was a well-known poet, who specialized in the composition of dithyrambs (a form of choral poem, which was performed alongside tragedy and comedy at the annual drama festivals). No complete poems or substantial fragments survive, but Aristophanes makes fun of him repeatedly.[1] He appears as a character in a short scene in *Birds* (1387–1390), seeking admission to the new avian community, for which his primary qualification is his high-flown poetic style. Even more important for the present fragment is a passing reference in *Assemblywomen* (330) to a story that he had "defiled a shrine of Hecate" by urinating in or on it; unfortunately we are not told the context of this action, and whether it was a deliberate and public attempt to offend religious sentiments. Other comic poets are said to have made fun of his physique, and it is to this that he owes his inclusion in Athenaeus' *Deipnosophistae* (for which see the Introduction to Lysias). The subject of the quotations in Athenaeus' book 12 is pleasure and luxury, but the book concludes by way of contrast with a short excursus on poets who were tall and thin (550f–553a), among them Cinesias.

The title of the speech[2] as reported by Athenaeus refers to an "un-

[1] As does Lysias on one occasion (21.20), but there the issue is an allegation of cowardice.

[2] The lexicographer Harpocration (*s.v. Cinesias*) says that Lysias wrote two speeches against him, but nothing is known of the other speech.

constitutional proposal."[3] This implies that the case was a *graphē paranomōn,* which was fairly common at Athens, though the only other case in this volume is Fragment 10 (*Theozotides*). It was a high-profile public procedure and would be brought by a politically active citizen (in this case Cinesias) against the person responsible for having proposed an Assembly decree (in this case the defendant Phanias), alleging that his proposal had been unlawful.[4]

It is, however, striking that in the extant fragment nothing is said about Phanias or his proposal. Instead, the whole passage is devoted to an attack on Cinesias himself, not simply as a lawbreaker but in particular as somebody who has committed crimes of impiety.[5] He is attacked specifically for having deliberately offended popular religious feeling, both by establishing a sort of Hellfire Dining Club (in which he together with three others chose to dine together on an ill-omened day), and also by giving their club a name that seems to have been a parody of the type of name that would be used by a group of people associating for a religious purpose. This is interesting evidence for the existence of such religious associations and for the desire of at least some Athenians deliberately to shock their more orthodox contemporaries. As a statement of outraged orthodoxy, there are some interesting parallels between this fragment and the attack on Andocides in Lysias 6: in particular, the argument that the gods have deliberately allowed the offender to stay alive so that he can suffer a fuller punishment for his crimes (though here, because of Cinesias' illness, it is much more convincingly argued than the rather clumsy version put forward in Lys. 6.19–20).

---

[3] Titles attributed to lost speeches are not always reliable, but this one is supported by the statement in the fragment about Cinesias' posing as defender of the laws (Fr. 4, §1), which was a standard position for a prosecutor in such a case to take.

[4] After 403/2, the Assembly was confined to passing decrees (i.e., temporary and/or individual regulations), whereas the passing of laws (regulations of permanent and/or general relevance) required a special procedure in front of a panel of *nomothetae* (lawmakers).

[5] It is possible that the proposal that Cinesias was attacking had something to do with religion, but there is no direct evidence for this, and Lysias is quite capable of making irrelevant attacks.

FRAGMENT 4. AGAINST CINESIAS, ON BEHALF OF PHANIAS, CONCERNING AN ILLEGAL PROPOSAL

Fragment 4 [1]

The orator Lysias, in the speech entitled On Behalf of Phanias, Accused of Making an Unconstitutional Proposal, *states that Cinesias was unhealthy and in other respects dangerous; and that he abandoned his* technē,[2] *became a sykophant,*[3] *and grew rich on this basis. That this is the poet, rather than another Cinesias, is clear because Cinesias is publicly ridiculed in comedy for atheism, and the same thing is revealed in the speech. The orator speaks as follows:*

[§1] I am surprised you are not ashamed that Cinesias poses as the defender of the laws, because you all know that he has been the most impious lawbreaker of all mankind. Is not this the person who commits such crimes against the gods that other people[4] are ashamed even to mention them, [§2] whereas you hear the comic poets ridiculing him every year?[5] Did not Apollophanes and Mystalides and Lysitheus[6] regularly dine together with my opponent, arranging one of the days that it is impious to name, and giving themselves, in place of *noumēniastai* (devotees of the new moon), the name *kakodaimonistai* (devotees of the evil spirit), a name that was suitable for their own fates? Of course they had no intimation that they would bring about this end but were simply mocking the gods and your laws. [§3] In the event, each of them perished, as such men deserve. But this man, the one who is known by the greatest number of people, the

---

[1] Lys. Fr. LXXIII.143 (Baiter and Sauppe), Fr. LXXIII.53 (Thalheim, Medda), Fr. V (Gernet and Bizos), and Fr. IX (Albini). The context of the fragment is Athenaeus, 12.551d–552b (12.76 Kaibel), which is translated in full by C. B. Gulick in the Loeb series (*Athenaeus, The Deipnosophists,* Vol. 5 [1933]).

[2] A *technē* is a trade or craft-skill: presumably in this case his poetry.

[3] Malicious prosecutor.

[4] There appears to be a double standard for comedy and other discourse. Other people cannot mention them without shame, but the comedians can make fun of them.

[5] I.e., at the annual drama festivals.

[6] None of these can be reliably identified.

gods have reduced to such a state that his enemies want him to live rather than to die—as an example for others, so that they can see that for those who treat the gods with excessive arrogance (*hubris*), the gods do not pass on the punishment to their children[7] but horribly destroy the culprits themselves, subjecting them to disasters and illnesses that are greater and more terrible than those that afflict other people. [§4] To die or to fall ill in the normal course of events is common to us all, but to linger for such a long time in a condition like this, and to be unable to end one's life, despite being on the verge of dying every day—that is a fate fit only for those who have committed the same sort of crimes as my opponent.

This is what the orator says about Cinesias.

---

[7] For the idea (common in Greek religious thought) that the gods do pass on punishment in this way, see, e.g., Lys. 6.20.

FRAGMENT 5. AGAINST ARCHEBIADES

INTRODUCTION

The main fragment here is the opening of the prologue, one of three[1] quoted by Dionysius of Halicarnassus for comparison with a lost speech of Isaeus, in this case *Against the Deme Members.* As with Fragment 3 (*Pherenicus*), though to a lesser extent, the two speeches being compared here deal with different types of cases: Isaeus' client, according to Dionysius, is disputing possession of a piece of mortgaged land, whereas our speaker appears to be defending himself against an action for a debt allegedly incurred by his dead father. Nevertheless, Dionysius regards them as comparable because both seek by similar means to establish a similar persona. Dionysius' view is that Lysias succeeds in creating an original portrait of a young, ordinary, retiring citizen, of which Isaeus can only produce a rhetorical copy. Lysias may, however, have had the easier task, because his speaker is evidently a very young man able to plead inexperience, which does not seem to be true of Isaeus' client.

Of particular historical interest in this speech is the reference to the "law about arbitrators" at the end of the prologue. Fourth-century Athens knew two forms of arbitration, private and official. Private arbitration had existed since time immemorial, the principle being that if both litigants voluntarily agreed to refer their dispute to an arbitrator, they therefore bound themselves in advance to accept his verdict.

[1] The others are Fr. 3 (*Pherenicus*) and Fr. 6 (*Sons of Hippocrates*).

Official or public arbitration[2] was introduced around the time of the democratic restoration in 403/2, and was a system whereby the majority of *dikai* (private cases) were compulsorily referred to an arbitrator appointed by the city: each successful arbitration would help to reduce the burden of litigation on the courts, but litigants seem to have had the right to appeal to a lawcourt precisely because (unlike private arbitration) it was compulsory. It is not quite clear what is being referred to here. One possibility is a law regulating the effects of private arbitration,[3] but more probable is the law that introduced official arbitration.[4] If so, the implication would be that Archebiades had been trying to push ahead with litigation despite the speaker's requests for private arbitration, but that the introduction of official arbitration has intervened and has forced Archebiades to go through the arbitration process. If this is correct, Archebiades is presumably now appealing against an arbitrator's decision in the speaker's favor, and Lysias is presumably making the most of this.

The second fragment, from the Byzantine lexicon known as the *Suda,* most likely belongs to the proof section of the same speech.[5]

---

[2] I owe the term "official arbitration" (much clearer than the traditional "public arbitration") to A. C. Scafuro, *The Forensic Stage: Settling Disputes in Graeco-Roman New Comedy* (Cambridge, 1997). This is the best available treatment of the topic, though I remain unconvinced by her argument that official arbitration was binding (Scafuro 1997: 391) and that private arbitration was not (Scafuro 1997: 122–126).

[3] E.g., the one quoted at Dem. 21.94, if it is a genuine law.

[4] D. M. MacDowell, "The Chronology of Athenian Speeches and Legal Innovations in 401–398 BC," *Revue Internationale des Droits de l'Antiquité* 18 (1971): 267–273, argues that this law and the resulting case can be securely dated to 400/399. This dating, however, rests on a series of inferences, not all of which are in my opinion conclusive (cf. 17.3n), and my own view is that the law may be a few years earlier, though not before 403/2.

[5] There is some uncertainty, because the *Suda* quotes a sentence in which Archebiades' name appears (with the spelling "Archibiades"), but then ascribes it to another lost speech with a similar title (*Against Alcibiades*). The *Against Alcibiades,* however, seems to have been about the recovery of confiscated property, and the content of the quotation would fit the proof section of this speech much better, so it is most likely that it is the title which the *Suda* has misquoted.

FRAGMENT 5. AGAINST ARCHEBIADES

Fragment 5.a[1]

Each of the speeches[2] *depicts a private individual who is young, takes no part in public affairs, and has been forced to speak in court against his nature and inclination. In the speech* Against Archebiades, *Lysias does this in the following way:*

[§1] As soon as Archebiades filed this *dikē* (private prosecution) against me, gentlemen of the jury, I went to him, and explained that I was young and inexperienced in public affairs, and had no desire to appear in court. "So I beg you not to regard my youth as a godsend, but instead gather together my friends and yours, and explain how the debt originated. If they decide you are telling the truth, you will have no need for a trial but can take what belongs to you and go. [§2] However, justice requires that you leave nothing out but tell the whole story, because I am younger than the agreement (*sumbolaion*).[3] In this way we shall hear what we do not yet know, and reach a decision about your claim. Perhaps it may somehow become clear whether you are unjustly attacking my property or else seeking justly to recover what is your own." I issued this challenge (*proklēsis*), but he consistently refused to meet, or hold discussions about his indictment (*enklēma*), or hand over the matter to arbitration, until you passed the law about arbitrators.[4]

---

[1] Lys. Fr. XX.44 (Baiter and Sauppe), Fr. XX.16 (Thalheim, Medda), Fr. XXXVII.1 (Gernet and Bizos), and Fr. V.1 (Albini). The context of the fragment is Dionysius of Halicarnassus, *On Isaeus* §10, which is translated in full in the Loeb series by S. Usher (*Dionysius of Halicarnassus, Critical Essays,* Vol. 1, [1974]).

[2] Lysias *Against Archebiades* and Isaeus *Against the Deme Members;* see the Introduction.

[3] I.e., the agreement was made before the speaker was born, so it would be unfair for Archebiades to take advantage of this.

[4] This law is briefly discussed in the Introduction.

Fragment 5.b[5]

The word aisthanesthai *is used to mean "to be suspicious" rather than "to know for certain." Lysias in the speech* Against Alcibiades *says:*

"So I think that you suspect (*aisthanesthai*) this too, that Archibiades was not seeking to recover anything else but was in dispute about my property."

---

[5] Lys. Fr. XX.45 (Baiter and Sauppe), Fr. XX.16.a (Thalheim, Medda), Fr. XXXVII.2 (Gernet and Bizos), and Fr. V.2 (Albini). The context of the fragment is *Suda, s.v. aisthesthai kai aisthanesthai* (an extract from a longer entry). For the manuscript readings "Against Alcibiades" and "Archibiades," see the Introduction at n. 5.

FRAGMENT 6. AGAINST THE SONS OF HIPPOCRATES

INTRODUCTION

This is the shortest of three prologues of Lysias[1] quoted by Dionysius of Halicarnassus for comparison with a lost speech of Isaeus, in this case the *Against Hagnotheus,* of which he also quotes the prologue. Here the two speeches deal with very similar types of cases involving guardianship, and Dionysius draws attention particularly to Lysias' simplicity and refusal to use the elegant phrasing that he finds in Isaeus' prologue.

What can be inferred from the fragment is that Hippocrates has evidently died leaving orphaned sons and has made the speaker their guardian. It was normal at Athens to choose a close relative for this task, and Dionysius states that the boys were the speaker's brothers-in-law,[2] a detail he presumably picked up from a part of the speech that he does not quote. On reaching adulthood, the boys have prosecuted the speaker, alleging that he has corruptly mismanaged their estate. Hippocrates cannot be identified, and we do not know the names of the litigants. The main interest of the fragment, apart from what Dionysius makes of it, lies in the contrast with Lysias 32: it gives us some idea of the sort of things that could have been said in that case by the speaker's opponent Diogeiton.

---

[1] The other two are Frs. 3 (*Pherenicus*) and 5 (*Archebiades*).

[2] Cf. Lys. 32, where the guardian was simultaneously paternal uncle and maternal grandfather to the orphans.

FRAGMENT 6. AGAINST THE SONS OF HIPPOCRATES

Fragment 6[1]

Writing a speech for a man who has been accused of corrupt guardianship by the brothers of his own wife, Lysias uses the following prologue:

It is not enough of a responsibility for guardians, gentlemen of the jury, to be burdened by the work of their guardianship. Even when they preserve their friends' estates, many of them experience sykophancy[2] at the hands of the orphans. That is what has now happened to me as well. I was left as guardian of Hippocrates' wealth, gentlemen of the jury, and I administered his property correctly and justly. When they came of age,[3] I handed over to his sons all that had been left in my control as guardian—and now I am unjustly experiencing sykophancy at their hands.

---

[1] Lys. Fr. LXII.124 (Baiter and Sauppe), Fr. LXII.43 (Thalheim, Medda), Fr. XXII (Gernet and Bizos), and Fr. VII (Albini). The context of the fragment is Dionysius of Halicarnassus, *On Isaeus* §8, which is translated in full in the Loeb series by S. Usher (*Dionysius of Halicarnassus, Critical Essays,* Vol. 1 [1974]).

[2] Malicious prosecution.

[3] Lit. "after their *dokimasia,*" the judicial scrutiny that they had to pass before becoming adult citizens.

FRAGMENT 7. AGAINST HIPPOTHERSES

INTRODUCTION

P.Oxy. 1606,[1] published in 1919, is the most substantial and most important papyrus of Lysias to have been identified. It consists of a large number of fragments from a papyrus roll,[2] which when complete is likely to have contained several hundred columns (each of some 150 words of text) and to have included a number of speeches. The two of these speeches that are included in this volume appear together in the largest single fragment: this is a five-column spread, containing the final three columns of the *Hippotherses* (a speech that was previously known only from two brief citations in Harpocration's *Lexicon to the Ten Orators*[3]) together with the opening two columns of a previously unknown speech *Against Theomnestus* (Fr. 8, below).[4]

[1] B. P. Grenfell and A. S. Hunt, eds., *The Oxyrhynchus Papyri,* Vol. 13 (London, 1919), no. 1606.

[2] Originally some 200 fragments but reduced by various joins to about 120. These include a number of joins made by E. Lobel after the original publication of the papyrus, which have never been properly published, but which will be included in the new Oxford Classical Text to be published by C. Carey (forthcoming): use of these unpublished joins is indicated in the notes as appropriate.

[3] Harpocration, *s.v.* "Hieronymus" (an Athenian general probably in 395/4), and *s.v.* "invisible and visible property" (below, n. 8).

[4] Only those fragments which can be securely attributed to the *Hippotherses* or the *Theomnestus* are included in this volume; other fragments include the final column of a defense speech against somebody whose name appears to end with the letters "-lios" (there is a reference to somebody having sold a ship in Carthage, and the speaker denies having been his partner, but not enough remains to make any continuous sense).

The *Hippotherses,* like speech 12, is a case in which Lysias was personally involved as litigant. Both speeches stem from the arrest of Lysias and his brother Polemarchus during the oligarchy of the Thirty in 404/3, and both seem to have been used as evidence by ancient biographers (cf. the Introduction to Lysias). The circumstances underlying the two speeches, however, are very different. Speech 12 concerns an attempt by Lysias in person to pin criminal responsibility for Polemarchus' execution on Eratosthenes, the official who admitted arresting him. In the present speech, on the other hand, Lysias is being prosecuted by Hippotherses (otherwise unknown) in a dispute over property confiscated from Lysias by the Thirty. The speech was written for somebody else (whose name is not reported) to deliver on Lysias' behalf.[5]

The title as preserved in the papyrus mentions a slave girl as being somehow involved in the case, and there has been considerable controversy over her role. The most common view is that she is the object of litigation, or in other words that she is the item of property under dispute.[6] This hypothesis, however, leaves unanswered the question of why such a case is being undertaken for one slave girl, however highly valued. Athenian litigants normally maximize their claims, because Athenian law had no doctrine of precedent and therefore no concept of the test case (that is, claiming a single article as a way of testing the legal validity of parallel claims), and the fragments certainly give the impression that what is at issue is substantial litigation over substantial property.

One striking feature of this speech is the quotation of a previously unknown clause of the amnesty (for which see the Introduction to Lys. 12) which regulated the restoration of democracy in 403 BC. The

[5] Why Lysias did not deliver his own speech is unclear. It is possible that as a metic (free noncitizen), he could not appear in person, at least in certain categories of case, but this raises the problem of how he could appear against Eratosthenes (if he did; cf. the Introduction to Lys. 12).

[6] The alternative view is that Lysias is being prosecuted as owner for actions that she had undertaken on his behalf (presumably as his agent in an attempt to recover his property). This is possible (the preposition *huper* in the title can mean either "concerning" or "on behalf of"), but it is hard to imagine a legal context in which a slave girl could have acted as a business agent. See further Todd 1993: 234–235.

clause deals with disputed claims to confiscated property (Fr. 7.b, lines 38–43), and distinguishes between property that the Thirty had sold (unrecoverable) and property that was still in public hands (to be returned to its original owners). Lysias goes on to claim that the amnesty permits former owners of confiscated land to recover it,[7] which suggests that he is contrasting their rights to "sold" land with rights to "sold" movable property. This may supply a context for one of the two citations of this speech by the lexicographer Harpocration, who uses it to distinguish between "visible" and "invisible" property.[8] One of the many puzzles of the speech is why Lysias has unsuccessfully offered compensation for part of his property (Fr. 7.a, lines 13–17, evidently full compensation), but has apparently rejected the offer made (perhaps by Hippotherses) to return another part of his property for half its market value (Fr. 7.c, lines 76–86). A possible explanation that has been suggested is that the amnesty may also have distinguished between the rights of the initial purchaser of confiscated property and the presumably more secure rights of somebody to whom he then sold it.

The details are obscure, but it certainly appears that the amnesty was a more complicated document than might otherwise have been suspected, and the speech does show that dealing with disputed rights to confiscated property may have been a very complex matter. What is even more striking is the probable implication of the distinction drawn between Hippotherses' attitude towards the building and the destruction of the walls of Athens (Fr. 7.f, lines 193–197): whereas the "destruction" is clearly that carried out by the Spartans in 404, the "building" seems to refer to the reconstruction by Conon in 394, which implies that disputes of this kind continued for at least a decade after the democratic restoration. But it is necessary to be cautious here, because it is possible though less likely that this is a reference back to the original construction of the walls by Themistocles after 480.

The *Hippotherses* is the subject of one of the case-studies in Todd 1993: 232–236, though my views on some issues have been changed

[7] It is possible that they may have had to offer some level of compensation, but the text is not secure. See Fr. 7.b, line 47n.

[8] Harpocration glosses "invisible" property as "what is in money and stock and equipment," and "visible" property as "what is in land." (The distinction is not uncommon in the orators; cf. Lys. 32.4 and Fr. 3.b.)

as a result of Carey's work on the papyrus (see the Introduction to Lysias).

FRAGMENT 7. AGAINST HIPPOTHERSES, CONCERNING A SLAVE GIRL[1]

Fragment 7a[2]

[7] . . . ⟨Lysias⟩ escaped, but they[3] killed his brother ⟨without trial⟩ and seized his property. [10] While he was living in Piraeus,[4] Lysias believed that he should get back his property on his return from exile. Now that he is back, however, he cannot recover it, not even by paying [15] the price to those who purchased it. For Nicostratus is bringing a *dikē* (private prosecution), together with Xenoc⟨les⟩, the person who sold . . .[5]

Fragment 7.b[6]

[28] . . . having seized ⟨property worth?⟩ seventy talents, they ⟨sold it?⟩—property that for many days these men were not able to hide[7] or sell. So when [35] Lysias fled into exile with you, and returned

---

[1] The meaning of the preposition *huper* (here translated "concerning") is discussed in the Introduction at n. 6. Figures in square brackets for papyrus fragments denote line numbers in modern editions of the papyrus text, whereas angle brackets are used to indicate textual restorations that are probable rather than certain. The placing of Frs. 7.a–7.d is uncertain, but Frs. 7.e–7.g belong to consecutive columns at the end of the speech.

[2] *P.Oxy.* 1606, Fr. 1 = Lys. Fr. I.1 (Gernet and Bizos), Fr. I.1 (Albini), and Fr. LXI.43a (Medda).

[3] The Thirty.

[4] I.e., in the latter stages of the democratic counterrevolution against the Thirty in 404/3.

[5] No further continuous sense can be made of this fragment, but the words "shield(s)," "fifty," and "drachmas" can be read.

[6] *P.Oxy.* 1606, Fr. 2 = Lys. Fr. I.2 (Gernet and Bizos), Fr. I.2 (Albini), and Fr. LXI.43b (Medda).

[7] Lit. "make invisible," which probably means "turn into cash" (cf. Harpocration, as cited in the Introduction at n. 8). "These men" are either the Thirty or else the initial purchasers.

with your democracy—given that the amnesty (*sunthēkai*) orders that [40] the purchasers should possess the things which had been sold but that the returning exiles should recover what was unsold—this man,[8] having obtained neither land nor house, [45] which even the amnesty gave back to the returning exiles, . . . [9]

Fragment 7.c [10]

[76] . . . [11] After this, therefore, gentlemen of the jury, he[12] claimed a right to recover half the price from Lysias, by describing [80] his misfortunes—as if this man[13] had discovered a treasure during the period of the Thirty and not lost his property. When Lysias grew angry [85] and was annoyed at . . .

Fragment 7.d [14]

[113] . . . for it would be a terrible thing, gentlemen of the jury, [115] if you returned from exile because you were suffering wrong but are being deprived of your property as wrongdoers. And yet you would have every right to be angry at those who purchased [120] your

---

[8] Very obscure: "this man" is probably Lysias (as elsewhere in the speech), but it could denote Hippotherses, and it is not clear whether the point is that Lysias as a noncitizen had not previously owned such property for the Thirty to confiscate, or that Hippotherses had not obtained it under the Thirty, or that Lysias had not yet recovered it after the democratic restoration.

[9] The remains of the next line have been variously restored by editors to read either "provided that ⟨the returning exiles⟩ repaid" or "whereas of the slaves ⟨*sc.* he had obtained a few?⟩"

[10] *P.Oxy.* 1606, Fr. 4 = Lys. Fr. I.4 (Gernet and Bizos), Fr. I.4 (Albini), and Fr. LXI.43d (Medda).

[11] An additional fragment (placed here by Lobel and read by Carey but not in any published edition) yields the end of the preceding sentence: "but if anybody, paying no attention to the amnesty (*sunthēkai*), was in dispute with you, the one who ⟨one word missing⟩." The "you" is singular, but the addressee (and the point being made) is obscure.

[12] Presumably Hippotherses (unless he is the "you" in the previous note).

[13] Evidently Lysias.

[14] *P.Oxy.* 1606, Fr. 5 = Lys. Fr. I.5 (Gernet and Bizos), Fr. I.5 (Albini), and Fr. LXI.43e (Medda).

property during such misfortunes: for in the first place, the Thirty would not have sold it if purchasers had not existed, and secondly . . .

Fragment 7.e[15]

. . . We turn the matter over to you, now that you have heard what Lysias and Hippotherses did, to give whatever verdict about the affair you choose as to which of them behaves better towards your city. I beg you to listen, so that this man,[16] who has a good reputation, may be still more eager to maintain it for the future, and so that Hippotherses may hear the truth about himself and behave better in future. . . .[17] For while you were prosperous, Lysias was the richest of the metics, and when the disaster[18] took place, he remained here: he did not avoid even the smallest part of your misfortunes but was illegally deprived by the Thirty of his brother and of considerable wealth. After he left Athens as an exile, he sent three hundred mercenaries towards your return, and provided ⟨two hundred⟩[19] drachmas in money . . .[20]

Fragment 7.f[21]

. . . ⟨going to Thrasydaeus⟩ of Elis, who was his *xenos* (hereditary friend), Lysias persuaded him to supply two talents without deduction,[22] and he has not received any favor or reward in

[15] *P.Oxy.* 1606, Fr. 6, col. i = Lys. Fr. I.6.i (Gernet and Bizos), Fr. I.6.i (Albini), and Fr. LXI.43f (Medda).

[16] Evidently Lysias.

[17] Four lines of the papyrus (lines 149–152) are illegible here.

[18] Euphemism for the decisive Athenian defeat at Aegospotami in 405 BC.

[19] The figure of 200 here, and the name of Thrasydaeus at the start of the next column, are derived from Pseudo-Plutarch, *Lysias* 835f, which lists Lysias' benefactions towards the democratic exiles and evidently draws on this passage.

[20] Seven lines of text, or about thirty words, are lost at the bottom of this column, but otherwise Fr. 7.f follows immediately.

[21] *P.Oxy.* 1606, Fr. 6, col. ii = Lys. Fr. I.6.ii (Gernet and Bizos), Fr. I.6.ii (Albini), and Fr. LXI.43g (Medda).

[22] *Atelēs,* lit. "untaxed," a generally accepted amendment for the manuscript's "in taxes," *telēi.*

return for this. That was how he behaved while in exile. Since his return, he has never offended any of the Athenians, either by mentioning his own benefactions or by drawing attention to other people's offenses. But now something must be said about him, because he is defending this *dikē* (private prosecution) against the sort of man who under the Four Hundred[23] went into exile, made Decelea his base, and joined the enemy in attacking his fatherland. It was the enemies of the city[24] who brought him back from exile and made him your citizen, so I think it is clear to everybody that he now despises the walls[25] that have been built as much as he did the ones that were then destroyed, nor does he have equal hopes about your good fortunes and your misfortunes. Afterwards, as a full[26] citizen, even though he has shown no sign of repentance or of increased maturity, he is making malicious[27] attacks against the democracy after what he has done to you . . .[28]

Fragment 7.g[29]

. . . Lysias deserves to receive gratitude from the People, given that he has been a great benefactor. So I beg you, gentlemen of the jury, to acquit him, bearing this in mind as well as everything else that has been said. Otherwise who of all mankind will be more

[23] The first oligarchy, in 411 BC. When the regime collapsed, a number of the hard-line oligarchs joined the Spartan army, which was at that time occupying a fort at Decelea in Attica.

[24] I.e. the Spartans, following the Athenian surrender after Aegospotami.

[25] Lit. "he now thinks ⟨nothing⟩ of the walls . . ." This reading (which confirms the previously uncertain reference to the walls of Athens) is the product of an additional fragment, placed here by Lobel and read by Carey but not in any published edition. The implications for dating are discussed in the Introduction.

[26] The text is uncertain here.

[27] Lit. "sykophantic," i.e., those that are characteristic of a malicious prosecutor.

[28] Only traces remain of lines 208–215 at the bottom of this column (about thirty words), but otherwise Fr. 7.g follows immediately.

[29] *P.Oxy.* 1606, Fr. 6, col. iii = Lys. Fr. I.6.iii (Gernet and Bizos), Fr. I.6.iii (Albini), and Fr. LXI.43h (Medda).

unfortunate than he is, if they[30] are to take some of his property themselves by force, and you are to give them the rest? Or who will be more fortunate than these men, [230] if you are not simply going to forgive them for what was done in the past but are now going to approve whatever they demand on any issue they bring before you?

---

[30] Probably a conspiratorial plural. There is no evidence that anybody except Hippotherses is prosecuting.

FRAGMENT 8. AGAINST THEOMNESTUS

INTRODUCTION

This was found in the same papyrus[1] as the *Hippotherses* (Fr. 7). We have the two opening columns of the speech, together with one other substantial fragment. Although the extant portions of the papyrus do not report the title, the content would have suggested "⟨Prosecution Speech⟩ Against Theomnestus," except that Lysias 10, which is an entirely separate case, is also a prosecution speech against somebody called Theomnestus. It is conventional, and is probably least confusing, to refer to speech 10 by its number and to the present speech as *Against Theomnestus,* but we should bear in mind that the title of this fragment may instead have taken the form "On behalf of somebody," or "Concerning a debt," or whatever.

Theomnestus is a relatively common name, so there is no particular reason to identify the two defendants, though if they are the same man, it may be significant that the one in Lysias 10 has been involved in high-profile public litigation. The other person mentioned in the present speech is Theozotides, which is a much rarer name, and although this is clearly not the same speech as the fragmentary *Against Theozotides* (Fr. 10 in this volume), it is tempting to identify the two men. If so, it is again noticeable that the Theozotides of Fragment 10 is a high-profile politician. If either identification is correct, there may be a political subtext to the present speech.

The circumstances underlying the present litigation can only be

[1] B. P. Grenfell and A. S. Hunt, eds., *The Oxyrhynchus Papyri,* Vol. 13 (London, 1919), no. 1606.

inferred from the fragments, from which it appears that the speaker claims to have loaned the sum of thirty minas to Theomnestus, which the latter required in order to pay a debt arising out of a judgment incurred during his previous litigation against Theozotides (Fr. 8.a, lines 246–251). The alleged loan has apparently been made without witnesses, which to us seems surprising, though there is a parallel for a loan without witnesses in Isocrates 21 (admittedly in special circumstances under the rule of the Thirty).

FRAGMENT 8. PROSECUTION SPEECH AGAINST THEOMNESTUS

Fragment 8.a [1]

[**239**] It seems that Theomnestus has ⟨been deceitful?⟩ in almost every respect towards you through⟨out this dispute?⟩: [2] for ⟨he⟩ has arranged things in such a way that trustees are not only ⟨regarded as wicked?⟩ [**245**] but even ⟨lose?⟩ their property.[3] Since he was a close friend, I gave thirty minas to Theomnestus, because he had to pay this sum to Theozotides [4] [**250**] before the sun set, or else he would be in

---

[1] *P.Oxy.* 1606, Fr. 6, col. iv = Lys. Fr. XXXIX.6.iv (Gernet and Bizos), Fr. II.6.iv (Albini), and Fr. LVa.41a (Medda). Figures in square brackets for papyrus fragments denote line numbers in modern editions of the papyrus text, whereas angle brackets are used to indicate textual restorations that are probable rather than certain.

[2] The restoration of this opening sentence is conjectural, but is included because the spacing of the fragment makes clear that is the opening sentence of the speech: it is the top of column 4 of a fragment in which the first three columns contain the conclusion to the *Hippotherses.* It is a very abrupt opening, though Lys. 9 and 20 provide parallels for beginning a lawcourt speech without an address to the court.

[3] This is one restoration of the sentence, but others are possible, and would yield very different meanings, e.g.: "⟨I⟩ was in a position where ⟨I had⟩ trustees but still ⟨gave him⟩ the money," or "⟨he⟩ contrived things in such a way that not only were there trustees ⟨in control⟩, but ⟨they genuinely controlled⟩ the property."

[4] The manuscript says Theodotides, but cf. the Introduction to Fr. 10 (*Theozotides*).

default.[5] After giving the money, as was reasonable, without witnesses, I am now being deprived of it and am compelled to bring a *dikē* (private prosecution). Before this time, Theomnestus was a very close friend of mine. Now, however, he has been won over by my enemies, and is doing both this and whatever else he may dare against me. Before this quarrel between us broke out, I did not bother him, nor did I demand the money . . . [6]

Fragment 8.b [7]

. . . If he did not receive the money from me, then he must necessarily be claiming one of two things: either that somebody else gave it to him or else that he himself paid the entire sum to Theozotides. So if he is going to claim that he received it from somebody else, . . . [8] . . . that he was afraid to ask me, who knew about his difficulties, but thought it right to borrow from people who would denounce him to his enemies. And yet how is it reasonable that he would join in lending out my money to other people, and himself borrow from others? To show that he did not think it right to borrow from anybody else, I shall produce a significant piece of evidence for you: when he was producing a men's chorus at the

---

[5] *Huperēmeros,* the standard term for one who fails to discharge on time a payment imposed by court verdict.

[6] Of the remaining twenty-two lines of the column (about a hundred words), and the first eight lines of the following column (about thirty words), only a few scattered phrases are recoverable: "guardianship of the property having been established for him (or perhaps 'over him')" (lines 267–269); "when I gave to him without witnesses. Having given, and having made the request for repayment in front of a single witness, I thought it was superfluous . . ." (lines 271–277).

[7] *P.Oxy.* 1606, Fr. 6, col. v = Lys. Fr. XXXIX.6.v (Gernet and Bizos), Fr. II.6.v (Albini), and Fr. LVa.41b (Medda). This follows immediately after Fr. 8.a, though see previous note.

[8] Nothing can be made of the next eight lines (roughly thirty words of text), but tentative sense can be drawn from lines 312–315, on the basis of a smaller fragment placed here by Lobel and read by Carey (cf. the Introduction to Lys. Fr. 7 at n. 2): "it is ⟨preposterous⟩ that he would ⟨borrow⟩ the money at interest from other people, when it was possible ⟨for him to have it⟩ interest free."

Dionysia, he received ⟨two⟩ thousand drachmas from me and spent it as wages . . .[9]

Fragment 8.c[10]

That is what I have to say about the possibility of his claiming that he had received the money from somebody else. If however ⟨he says he repaid it?⟩ from ⟨his existing?⟩ money, then you must ask Theomnestus the following questions. How is it likely that ⟨being short?⟩[11] of silver, he would have been happy to face extreme danger, and would offer this much power to his enemies? And did he entrust himself so completely to fortune, even if he suddenly suffered something, to be compelled to suffer concerning his body and his life at the same time, having come to this situation, with the result that if the sun set with him being in default?[12] And who is so unwise that he makes arrangements for himself to be subject to his enemies? Or who is so mindless that . . .

---

[9] For the *chorēgia* (paying for a production, in this case by a dithyrambic chorus, at a festival) as a form of compulsory public sponsorship imposed on rich Athenians, see the Introduction to Lys. 21.

[10] *P.Oxy.* 1606, Frs. 7+45+73 = Lys. Fr. XXXIX.7 (Gernet and Bizos), Fr. II.7 (Albini), and Fr. LVa.41c (Medda). No continuous sense can be made of the first five lines, though there are references to being "afraid to request from me," and having done something "against me in the matter of the bull, given that I am a friend." Fr. 8.c must come after Frs. 8.a–10.b, but we do not know how many columns are missing.

[11] Lines 341–342 and 344–345 cannot be convincingly restored, and the words in angle brackets are merely suggestions intended to illustrate a possible train of thought.

[12] This is an attempt at a literal translation, which does not make much sense (the closing conditional has no main clause), and the first editors suggested that the text is probably corrupt.

FRAGMENT 9. FOR ERYXIMACHUS

INTRODUCTION

This papyrus is in two parts. The smaller but more legible fragment (*P.Lond.* 2852) was originally published by H. J. M. Milne in 1929; in 1938, C. H. Roberts identified the larger fragment (*P.Ryl.* 489) and published the whole.[1] Together, the two parts of the papyrus make up a single sheet from a codex (i.e., not part of a roll but a page from a book), each side of which contains two columns of text, making four consecutive columns in all. Of these, the first column-and-a-half holds the closing stages of one of the speeches that has been preserved in the medieval manuscripts (Lys. 1), but the remaining two-and-a-half columns contain a new speech, of which previously even the title was unknown: *On Behalf of Eryximachus, Who Had Remained in the Town.*

The phrase "remained in the town (*astu*)" fits a speech delivered in the first quarter of the fourth century, so that even if the papyrus had not contained the conclusion of another Lysias speech, we would have been inclined to have attributed the *Eryximachus* to Lysias. When alluding to the events of 404/3, Athenian orators typically refer to the democratic counterrevolutionaries as "those from Phyle" or "those from Piraeus," whereas "those from the town" or those who "remained in the town" are the former supporters of the oligarchy of the

---

[1] H. J. M. Milne, "A New Speech of Lysias," *Journal of Egyptian Archaeology* 15 (1929): 75–77; C. H. Roberts, ed., *Catalogue of the Greek Papyri in the John Rylands Library at Manchester,* Vol. 3 (Manchester, 1938), no. 489. For convenience, it is Roberts' rather than Milne's line numbers that are used in this volume.

Thirty.[2] Eryximachus, therefore, is defending himself against the allegation that he had supported the Thirty during the civil war. But it is difficult to imagine that having "remained in the town" could have been a prosecutable offense, partly because we have no other evidence for such a charge, but chiefly because its existence would have undermined the whole basis of the amnesty of 403/2 under which the democracy had been restored. On the other hand, there are a number of parallels between this fragment and Lysias 25, which is also a defense of those who had "remained in the town" (Lys. 25.1);[3] Lysias 25 is generally regarded as a speech for a *dokimasia* (the judicial scrutiny of a person's right to hold public office),[4] and the majority of scholars think that the *Eryximachus* too is a *dokimasia* speech.

The name Eryximachus is not common, and it is tempting to identify the speaker with Eryximachus son of Acumenus, the doctor, who appears as one of the guests in Plato's *Symposium.* Against this identification, however, it should be noted that Plato's Eryximachus was exiled after being implicated in the affair of the Herms in 415 and is not known to have returned to Athens before 404, whereas the speaker was present at the battle of Aegospotami in 405.

If the manuscript is correct at line 106, the speaker's claim to have "ransomed one of my trierarchs" at the end of the siege of Athens[5] must imply that he had held a position of command over a number of ships, and there is no known office to which this could refer except the generalship. There is certainly room for Eryximachus either to have been general at the time of the battle (we know the names of only six of the ten generals at this date) or to have been among those elected to fill vacancies afterwards. The former hypothesis would be particularly interesting, because there is evidence that at least one of the defeated generals, Adeimantus, was blamed and later accused of treason

[2] E.g., Lys. 12.92, 13.88–89 ("those from the town"), 18.19, 25.1, 25.18, 26.16 ("remained in the town").

[3] The attention devoted to the speaker's record finds a parallel also in Lys. 21, but that speech, unlike the *Eryximachus,* does allude to specific charges (Lys. 21.1).

[4] The *dokimasia,* and its peculiar prevalence in the corpus of Lysias, is discussed in the Introduction to Lys. 16.

[5] A trierarch was a wealthy citizen who had the task of funding and commanding a warship.

in connection with the defeat (Lys. 14.38, Dem. 19.191). On the other hand, it is odd that the speaker makes no attempt to respond to possible criticisms, for instance by emphasizing (as appropriate) either that he was elected only after the battle or that he had opposed the strategy of his colleagues but had been outvoted. It is tempting therefore to accept Körte's emendation of *emōn* at line 106 to *allōn,* which would mean "I ransomed one of the other trierarchs," implying that he had been not an incompetent commander but a heroic junior officer.

FRAGMENT 9. FOR ERYXIMACHUS, WHO HAD REMAINED IN THE TOWN (*ASTU*)[1]

Fragment 9.a[2]

[41] I very much wanted not to run the risks of a trial, gentlemen of the jury, either individually against any of the citizens [45] or publicly against the city itself. And if that proved impossible, I wanted at any rate to have a clear conscience on the basis that I am being brought to trial without having committed any crime. [50] ⟨You can easily⟩ be sure of this, gentlemen of the jury . . .

Fragment 9.b[3]

[58] . . . I will defend myself against my accusers. [60] For it is not because of the crimes of my opponents that I expect to win this case, but instead because of my own good character. [65] I have run many risks on your behalf in my own person, and I have willingly spent much of my family property on your behalf. I did this for two reasons: [70] so that for my part the city would be prosperous, and so that in case I were ever brought to court unjustly, I would be able to give a

---

[1] Figures in square brackets for papyrus fragments denote line numbers in modern editions of the papyrus text, whereas angle brackets are used to indicate textual restorations that are probable rather than certain.

[2] *P.Lond.* 2852 + *P.Ryl.* 489, col. 2 (for the first column-and-a-half of the papyrus, see the Introduction) = Lys. Fr. XLVa.35a (Medda). The title of the *Eryximachus* is at lines 38–40, so what follows is the opening of the speech.

[3] Lys. Fr. XLVa.35b (Medda) = col. 3 of the papyrus. About twenty lines (roughly 70 words) are missing or unreadable at the end of the preceding column and the start of this one, but otherwise Fr. 9.b follows Fr. 9.a.

confident account of my past actions. [75] So you can easily see, gentlemen of the jury, that if my opponents had been able to find any crime committed by me as an individual, [80] nobody would ⟨have blamed me for all the crimes of the Thirty⟩. . . .

Fragment 9.c[4]

[93] ⟨. . . I would expect⟩ to make matters clear on my behalf [95] if I were caught doing wrong, and to obtain mercy, if I were ⟨found?⟩ to be worthy of ⟨punishment?⟩.[5] I will defend myself before you on the basis of what I suffered at their hands:[6] [100] for it was after I had caused much damage to the enemy that I sailed home, and so I brought my own ship safely out of the battle;[7] [105] and after the battle was over, when the walls had already been destroyed, I ransomed one of my trierarchs.[8] And at the time of the Thirty, gentlemen of the jury, [110] nobody can prove that I served as a member of the Council, or that I held any public office; nor that I took revenge on any of my enemies (even though they[9] were making summary arrests); [115] nor that I obtained an arbitration against anybody or put anybody's name on the list of those with Lysander; nor that I was one of the Three Thousand. . . .[10]

---

[4] Lys. Fr. XLVa.35c (Medda) = col. 4 of the papyrus. About twenty-five lines (roughly 85 words) are missing or unreadable at the end of the preceding column and the start of this one, but otherwise Fr. 9.c follows Fr. 9.b.

[5] The sense seems to be that Eryximachus had performed great services to the state with the aim that if he had done wrong he would have expected favorable treatment, but lines 97–98 cannot be restored with certainty, and the words in angle brackets with question marks are intended simply to give a possible idea of what might have been said.

[6] Evidently the Spartans, because the context of what follows is the battle of Aegospotami.

[7] Cf. Lys. 21.9n.

[8] For a possible emendation here, see the Introduction.

[9] The Thirty, or possibly their supporters.

[10] The Thirty created a body of Three Thousand of their supporters, who were the only people allowed full citizen rights under the oligarchy. The "list of those with Lysander" (cf. Isoc. 18.16 and 21.2) seems to have been a catalogue of those called up for Spartan military service as required under the terms of Athens' surrender.

FRAGMENT 10. AGAINST THEOZOTIDES

INTRODUCTION

This was the first of the Lysias papyri to be published, in 1906.[1] It consists of twenty fragments from a papyrus roll, but most of these are small scraps. This volume includes only the three largest fragments, from which some continuous sense can be obtained. They all show traces of more than one column of text, but no complete column is preserved, so we cannot be certain precisely how much is missing, even between consecutive columns.[2] More importantly, we cannot be certain of the order in which the separate fragments of papyrus occurred within the speech, although for convenience the line numbers used by the first editors have been used in this volume.

The papyrus contains no title, but the name Theozotides appears repeatedly as the speaker's opponent (lines 28–29, 41, 73), and this makes almost inevitable an identification with the citation in the lexicographer Pollux of a prosecution speech *Against Theodotides* (a variant spelling of the same name).[3] The subject matter of the papyrus fragments suggests that this is a prosecution in a case of *graphē para-*

[1] B. P. Grenfell and A. S. Hunt, eds., *The Hibeh Papyri*, Vol. 1 (London, 1906), no. 14.

[2] Such as Frs. 10.c and 10.d. Although numbered separately for convenience in this volume, these are in fact consecutive columns of a single papyrus fragment.

[3] Pollux, *Onomastikon* 8.46 (a confused discussion of the legal procedure of *probolē*, for which cf. Lys. 13.65n). The spelling "Theozotides" is confirmed in Stroud's inscription (below), which is a contemporary text.

nomōn: that is, a public prosecution brought against Theozotides for having proposed a decree that was unlawful.[4]

What makes this papyrus particularly interesting is that we now have an inscription recording the text of the decree proposed by Theozotides which is under attack here.[5] This allows us to make more sense of the proposal, and also to infer the result of the trial, because it is virtually inconceivable that the text would have been inscribed if Theozotides had lost his case, since this would have automatically annulled the proposed decree. The stele (inscribed stone) containing the decree is intact, but only the top third of its face can be read. After the introduction (lines 1–4), which names Theozotides as proposer, there is a highly provocative reference to those orphaned—but only on the democratic side—in the civil war of 404/3 ("whoever of the Athenians who died a violent death under the oligarchy while helping the democracy," lines 4–6), and a proposal "[to grant] to [all] their sons an obol a day as maintenance, [just as] they pay to the orphans . . ." (lines 9–11), together with traces of further regulations to scrutinize their claims (line 15) and to arrange responsibility for payment (lines 17–19).

From the inscription, it appears that Theozotides' proposal was designed to extend already existing provisions for war orphans so as to cover also those orphaned in the civil war, but provocatively and explicitly to limit this to the sons of those killed on the democratic side. The care taken to scrutinize claims, and the fact that the seven names recorded on the side of the stele are reported with full formal details (name, father's name, deme), makes it plausible that maintenance was extended only to legitimate sons by blood, but Lysias' attack on the proposal for denying the rights of adoptive and illegitimate children (Frs. 10.a and 10.b) may be an attempt to raise the temperature by focusing on a side issue.

There is no sign in the inscription of a second proposal that is attributed to Theozotides in Fragment 10.c of the papyrus,[6] which

---

[4] For this procedure, see the Introduction to Lys. Fr. 4 (*Cinesias*).

[5] The bulk of the inscription is translated by Harding 1985: no. 8. For the full text, see the original publication by R. S. Stroud in *Hesperia* 40 (1971): 280–301.

[6] Though room could be made for it at the bottom of the stele.

raises the question of whether this really is part of the same decree or whether Lysias is referring to previous activity by Theozotides to stir up prejudice against him. The proposal in question is to alter the level of cavalry pay, but its interpretation rests on a textual problem. What is clear is that Theozotides has proposed that the pay (presumably daily pay during wartime) of the regular cavalry should be reduced to four obols from one drachma (six obols), and that the *hippotoxotai* or mounted archers (that is, archers who rode on horseback) should receive eight obols instead of two somethings (Fr. 10.c, line 79).

The majority of editors agree that the traces of letters which remain here can be restored to yield only the word "obols." This would imply a threefold increase in the pay of the mounted archers at the same time as a one-third cut in the pay of the regular cavalry.[7] Although such a proposal would have yielded a small net saving,[8] nevertheless the pay increase for the mounted archers[9] can only have been intended to insult the cavalry. The aim would presumably be an attempt to punish the cavalry for having been among the main supporters of the Thirty, which would fit the provocatively prodemocratic tone of the inscription.[10]

---

[7] Cavalry, 6 obols down to 4 obols; mounted archers, 2 obols up to 8 obols.

[8] There seem to have been five times as many cavalry as mounted archers, so the proposal would have taken the total pay for each group of five cavalry plus one mounted archer down from 32 to 28 obols.

[9] Mounted archers are generally thought to have been of lower status than the regular cavalry, though see 15.6n.

[10] W. T. Loomis, "Pay Differentials and Class Warfare in Lysias' *Against Theozotides:* Two Obols or Two Drachmas?," *Zeitschrift für Papyrologie und Epigraphik* 107 (1995): 230–236, proposes the alternative reading "drachmas." This would remove the political subtext and leave us with a simple financial measure, cutting the pay of both groups by one-third (cavalry, 6 obols down to 4 obols, and mounted archers, 12 obols down to 8 obols) in the period of financial difficulty following the Peloponnesian War. Against this interpretation, however, is that the reading "drachmas" was considered by the first editors, Grenfell and Hunt, but rejected on the grounds that it is not compatible with the traces of ink which remain.

FRAGMENT 10. PROSECUTION SPEECH AGAINST THEOZOTIDES FOR AN ILLEGAL PROPOSAL

Fragment 10.a [1]

[2] . . . both the illegitimate and the adopted children, which is neither lawful nor right. It seems to me that of the orphans, the city ⟨has much more of a duty towards?⟩ those who are illegitimate than those who are legitimate: legitimate sons were left ⟨to inherit their father's property?⟩, whereas those who are illegitimate . . .

Fragment 10.b [3]

[4] ⟨What is⟩ most terrible of all is that Theozotides is going to slander the most wonderful of the announcements contained in the laws, and is going to establish a lie. For at the Dionysia,[5] when the herald announces the orphans with the names of their fathers, adding that the fathers of these young men died in the war as brave men while fighting on behalf of the fatherland and that the city was bringing up their sons until adulthood, will he[6] then make a separate announcement concerning the adopted and illegitimate sons,

---

[1] *P.Hibeh.* 14, Fr. a, col. i (only traces remain of the second column) = Lys. Fr. LIX.42.a (Thalheim, 2d ed., Medda), Fr. VI.1 (Gernet and Bizos), and Fr. III.1 (Albini).

[2] Some editors restore lines 3–5 to read "by this law (*nomos*), you (Theozotides) are depriving of their payment those who most need it, . . ."

[3] *P.Hibeh.* 14, Fr. b, col. i (only traces remain of the second column) = Lys. Fr. LIX.42.b (Thalheim, 2d ed., Medda), Fr. VI.2 (Gernet and Bizos), and Fr. III.2 (Albini).

[4] Some editors restore lines 24–25 to read: "of the payment ⟨which?⟩ that man left to them."

[5] For this proclamation, see Aesch. 3.154. The Great Dionysia is best known as the leading Athenian drama festival, but this parade of war orphans on the verge of manhood suggests that the festival had a wider role as a celebration of democratic Athens.

[6] The manuscript says "you," but editors agree that the reference must be to the herald.

saying that on account of Theozotides the city has not brought them up?—or will he announce all ⟨the orphans⟩ alike, and so tell a lie by keeping silent about the upbringing of the adopted and illegitimate orphans? Will not this be arrogance (*hubris*) and a great slander against the city? When Cleomenes . . . [7] captured your Acropolis, gentlemen of the jury, . . .

Fragment 10.c [8]

. . . concerning war, Theozotides here puts forward the proposal that the cavalry should be paid at a rate of four obols instead of a drachma, whereas the *hippotoxotai* (mounted archers) should receive eight obols instead of two ⟨obols?⟩; [9] and when he introduced this proposal . . . [10] he won the debate in the Assembly. Through this also . . .

Fragment 10.d [11]

. . . or to cut the payment for the sake of the present and of the future. But I believe that to provide money does not mean depriving people of existing resources, but taking care that public funds increase above their present level, or at least do not decrease. There is no need to be afraid . . .

---

[7] There is an eight-letter space here, but the general sense is clear. The Spartan king Cleomenes occupied the Acropolis in 508 in an attempt to force the Athenians to acquiesce in the abolition of the new Council of Five Hundred, but a popular uprising forced him to withdraw (Herod. 5.72).

[8] *P.Hibeh.* 14, Fr. c, col. ii = Lys. Fr. LIX.42.c (Thalheim, 2d ed., Medda), Fr. VI.3.ii (Gernet and Bizos), and Fr. III.3.ii (Albini). Only traces remain of the first column of this fragment, but for the third column, see Fr. 10.d below.

[9] "Obols" here is a generally accepted restoration, but see the Introduction.

[10] There is a gap of five or six letters in the text here, followed by five more letters that are fragmentary and incomprehensible.

[11] *P.Hibeh.* 14, Fr. c, col. iii = Lys. Fr. LIX.42.c, contd. (Thalheim, 2d ed., Medda), Fr. VI.3.iii (Gernet and Bizos), and Fr. III.3.iii (Albini). The length of the column, and so the amount lost between Frs. 10.c and 10.d, is uncertain, but the order of these two columns is clear.

FRAGMENT 11. CONCERNING ANTIPHON'S DAUGHTER

INTRODUCTION

Only eleven fragments survive of this papyrus (*P.Rainer* 13),[1] none of them yielding more than twenty lines of continuous text. The papyrus seems to have contained a number of inheritance speeches,[2] but one of these is of some interest, because it relates to a case that is attested elsewhere. Pseudo-Plutarch's *Life of Antiphon* includes a rather confused attempt to distinguish between the orator and other people of the same name, including an Antiphon who was executed by the Thirty and whose daughter was the subject of a speech of Lysias, "for he had a daughter whom Callaeschrus claimed by *epidikasia*"[3] ([Plutarch], *Antiphon* 833a).

Not enough can be made of the fragments to permit a detailed reconstruction, but the speech does provide evidence both for a type of dispute that may have been exacerbated by the activities of the

[1] H. Oellacher, ed., *Mitteilungen aus der Papyrussamlung der Nationalbibliothek in Wien* (*Papyrus Erzherzog Rainer*), New Series, Vol. 1 (1932), no. 13.

[2] Antiphon is named in each of the three fragments included in this volume. None of the other fragments of this papyrus can be shown to belong to the *Antiphon's Daughter* case, and at least one certainly does not: enough survives of Fr. 5 of the papyrus (not included in this volume) to show that it deals with an entirely different inheritance dispute.

[3] *Epidikasia* is the process of applying to a court to marry an *epiklēros* (daughter without brothers, in whom her father's estate is vested) and to gain control of her property. Antiphon's execution by the Thirty is also mentioned in Theramenes' speech at Xen., *Hellenica* 2.3.40, which adds that he had supplied the city with two triremes out of his own resources during the war, giving an indication of his wealth.

Thirty, and also for the presence of inheritance speeches in the corpus of Lysias.

FRAGMENT 11. CONCERNING THE DAUGHTER OF ANTIPHON[1]

Fragment 11.a[2]

. . . after Antiphon had been acquitted,[3] ⟨somebody else⟩[4] received back the *arrhabōn* (pledge) from Pyronides, and prosecuted him[5] by *dikē bebaiōseōs,*[6] until . . .[7]

Fragment 11.b[8]

. . . they will ⟨do something⟩.[9] Epistratus, claiming that it was his own, so as to keep it safe for the daughter of Antiphon, retained the estate for more than five months, until the Thirty, realizing that it was no business of theirs,[10] summoned the People and compelled . . .[11]

---

[1] The order of the fragments is conjectural. Editors generally agree that Fr. 11.c belongs towards the end of the speech, but they do not agree about the relative placing of Frs. 11.a and 11.b. Figures in square brackets for papyrus fragments denote line numbers in modern editions of the papyrus text, whereas angle brackets are used to indicate textual restorations that are probable rather than certain.

[2] *P.Rainer* 1.13, Fr. 2, col. ii (only traces remain of the first column) = Lys. Fr. XI.8c (Medda).

[3] This seems to be the only possible meaning for *dikēn pepheugotos,* so it must refer to an earlier trial rather than his execution by the Thirty.

[4] The name is missing, but grammatically it cannot be Antiphon.

[5] Presumably Pyronides, or possibly Antiphon.

[6] A private prosecution seeking to force the opponent to guarantee something.

[7] It is possible but not certain (the evidence is a word beginning with the letters "AN . . . ") that the subject of the "until" clause is Antiphon.

[8] *P.Rainer* 1.13, Fr. 1, col. i = Lys. Fr. XI.8b (Medda). Only a few words ("the woman," "to do good") can be read in the second column of this fragment.

[9] Only the ending of the verb survives.

[10] It is unclear whether this means "of the Thirty" or "of Epistratus and his friends."

[11] Or (reading *klēron* for *dēmon*) "until the Thirty, realizing that the property was no business of theirs, summoned and compelled ⟨Epistratus⟩ . . ."

Fragment II.c[12]

Looking at what has been said, ⟨you?⟩ must realize that the inheritance is ⟨the property⟩ of Pyronides, if Antiphon appears to have behaved so badly towards the best of men[13] in the matter of those who are related to him. And indeed, how could . . .

---

[12] *P.Rainer* 1.13, Fr. 3, col. ii = Lys. Fr. XI.8d (Medda). Only a few words ("guard," "of him") can be read in the first column of this fragment.

[13] Lit. "has been the worst towards the best": presumably an ironic reference to the speaker's opponent. Another possible restoration would be "if anybody thinks that Antiphon has behaved extremely badly in the matter of those who are related to him."

INDEX